ECONOMIC REFORMS
IN
POLISH INDUSTRY

Economic Reforms in East European Industry:

General Editors

ALEC NOVE AND J. G. ZIELINSKI

Other volumes in this series

Iancu Spigler on RUMANIA (*already published*)

In preparation

Richard Portes on HUNGARY
Gert Leptin and Manfred Melzer on EAST GERMANY
Oldrich Kyn on CZECHOSLOVAKIA
Ljubo Sirc on YUGOSLAVIA
George Feiwel on BULGARIA

A comparative volume by G. Feiwel, A. Nove, R. Portes,
and J. G. Zielinski will conclude the series.

———————————————

Other books by J. G. Zielinski

(a) IN ENGLISH

Lectures on the Theory of Socialist Planning, Oxford University Press for the
Nigerian Institute of Social and Economic Research, Ibadan 1968 (available
also in Italian and Spanish).
Planning in East Europe—Industrial Management by the State, Bodley Head,
London, Sydney, Toronto, 1970 (together with Mr. M. Kaser) (available also
in Arabic and Spanish).

(b) IN POLISH

Labour Accounting Day in Soviet Collective Farms, Warsaw 1955.
Economic Calculation in a Socialist Economy, 3rd ed., Warsaw 1967.
Big Business. Problems of New Management Techniques, Warsaw 1962.
Outline of the Theory of the Socialist Economy—co-authorship in a collective
work, A. Wakar ed., Warsaw 1965.
The Theory of Socialist Trade—co-authorship in a collective work, A. Wakar
ed., Warsaw 1966.
The Political Economy of Socialism—co-authorship in a collective work,
M. Pohorille ed., Warsaw 1968.

INSTITUTE OF SOVIET AND EAST EUROPEAN STUDIES

University of Glasgow

ECONOMIC REFORMS IN POLISH INDUSTRY

JANUSZ G. ZIELINSKI

London
OXFORD UNIVERSITY PRESS
NEW YORK   TORONTO
1973

Oxford University Press, Ely House, London W1

GLASGOW NEW YORK TORONTO MELBOURNE WELLINGTON
CAPE TOWN IBADAN NAIROBI DAR ES SALAAM LUSAKA ADDIS ABABA
DELHI BOMBAY CALCUTTA MADRAS KARACHI LAHORE DACCA
KUALA LUMPUR SINGAPORE HONG KONG TOKYO

ISBN 0 19 215323 4

© *Oxford University Press 1973*

PRINTED IN GREAT BRITAIN
BY EBENEZER BAYLIS AND SON LIMITED
THE TRINITY PRESS, WORCESTER, AND LONDON

To the British people
whose hospitality has enabled
me to continue my work on
centrally planned economies

To those of my Polish
fellow-economists and sociologists who,
in spite of all difficulties, have retained
their personal and professional integrity

GENERAL INTRODUCTION TO THE SERIES

1. Problems

The present volume is a part of a series of monographs on economic reforms in East European industry. In addition to Poland the following countries will be covered: Bulgaria, Czechoslovakia, German Democratic Republic, Hungary, Rumania, and Yugoslavia. The series will also contain a separate volume devoted to comparative analysis of economic reforms in Eastern Europe as a whole.

In contrast to what we know of economic changes in the Soviet Union, our knowledge of economic reforms in Eastern Europe is very fragmentary, yet some of these countries have embarked on economic changes more far-reaching than the Soviet Union and/or have put forward proposals and started discussions of greater theoretical sophistication and practical potential than anything we can find in the Soviet Union itself. Also, taken as a whole, communist Eastern Europe represents substantial economic, political, and military potential whose importance within the Soviet Bloc is likely to grow. In sum, Eastern Europe represents a significant and interesting subject, on which we know too little. Taking a broad view, one can argue that there may be overconcentration on research on the Soviet Union, while research on East European countries is neglected.

As a result of this conviction, the Institute of Soviet and East European Studies in the University of Glasgow took the initiative in starting a comprehensive project on Economic Reforms in East Europe. The fact that owing to the political events of 1968 in Poland and then Czechoslovakia a substantial number of East European economists, with first-hand knowledge of their countries, had to seek refuge in the West influenced the timing of our undertaking. This was an opportunity created by most regrettable events, but which we could not miss.

2. Approach

There are two distinctive features of the research approach which we took. First of all, we decided that the study should be in two stages: we must start by preparing the country-study monographs and only afterwards move to our ultimate objective—the comparative analysis of reforms in Eastern Europe. Secondly, the requirements of the comparative volume dictated to us the need for a uniform approach to country-studies. As a result, all studies are being written according to a uniform and fairly detailed outline. This uniformity of approach and scope of coverage we considered so important that its acceptance was made a condition of participation in the project. Time will show if we succeeded in achieving our goal in real terms and how important it will be in determining the quality of the Comparative Volume.

At the same time, all country-studies are self-contained, and as a counterweight to the agreed uniformity of scope and structure the authors have been given unrestricted freedom to treat their subject in their own ways theoretically and methodologically. The latter, hope-fully, may enable us to compare the effectiveness not only of different economic reforms, but also of the ways of studying them.

3. Scope

Because of scarcity of time, space and expertise the scope of our research is confined to economic reforms in those industries which are or were centrally planned, i.e. all major and large-scale industry. Local industries were omitted, as were the other sectors of the economy, e.g. foreign trade or agriculture, save in so far as they affected industrial planning and management.

Even within the bounds so defined, the scope of the country-studies is so broad that some subjects have to be treated only briefly, probably too briefly for the liking of the experts on these specific subjects. To satisfy the latter each country would probably have to be covered by a whole series of monographs devoted to it. This being out of the question, we tried to be encyclopaedic rather than detailed.

Readers should appreciate that because of the space constraint practically any statement in country monographs is supported in fact by much more evidence than it was technically possible to present in the books themselves. For those who want to go more deeply into any particular topic, there are ample bibliographical references in each chapter.

4. Sources

The country-studies are based on three types of sources: extensive reading of books and journals of the countries concerned, some un-published documents of unclassified nature, such as internal instruc-tions of economic ministries, and, finally, on personal knowledge of the authors. Needless to say, the first type of source is in all cases of predominant importance but the significance of the last one is much more important than the simple count of references would indicate. Its real importance lies first of all in interpretation of published material and in the ability to distinguish between intentions, declara-tions, and legislation on the one hand, and what actually happens or is implemented on the other. These things are quite frequently confused. Moreover, personal knowledge of the country helps to get one's priorities right. Many reform measures which seem important on the surface are not so in fact, for a variety of reasons, and most frequently because other elements of existing economic working arrangements render them ineffective. Readers will find many examples of this phenomenon in the pages of country-studies.

5. Acknowledgements

The Institute's initiative to start the project, of which this book is a part, was supported by a grant from the Social Science Research Council, which is gratefully acknowledged. The readiness of Oxford University Press to publish the results of our research in the form of this series helped us greatly in persuading our colleagues and authors of individual country-studies to join the project. We want to express our heartfelt thanks for their collaboration and co-operation.

CO-EDITORS[1]
Alec Nove
Janusz G. Zielinski

[1] Alec Nove is responsible for editing the volumes on German Democratic Republic, Poland, and Rumania and J. G. Zielinski for editing those on Bulgaria Czechoslovakia, Hungary, and Yugoslavia.

TABLE OF CONTENTS

PART TWO:

THE MANAGEMENT OF PLAN IMPLEMENTATION

Conclusion: A Mixed Industrial System

Appendix A: Tables and References

LIST OF TABLES AND DIAGRAMS

PREFACE

'It has been the fate of Poland, more than of most
countries, that outsiders have been mainly concerned to
see in it a spectacular object lesson, hurrying on from
interest in the Poles themselves to find evidence for
general truths of wider application.'

(R. R. Palmer, *The Age of Democratic Revolution*,
Princeton, 1959)

'Everything inhuman is senseless and useless.'
(W. Grossman, *Vsë techet . . .*, Posev, 1970)

In writing this book I was guided by the two mottoes above.

First of all, in analysing Polish economic reforms I was searching 'for
general truths of wider applications', for something which would be at
least a semblance of a theory of the *functioning* of the command
economy as it exists in Poland and, in very similar forms, in the USSR
and most other East European countries. From 1956 till 1966, i.e. until
his untimely death, I had the privilege of working on these problems in
close cooperation and under the guidance of Professor Aleksy Wakar.
Afterwards, I continued this work in my Research Unit of Price and
Incentives Theory in the Central School of Planning and Statistics,
Warsaw.[1]

Our approach to the study of the Polish 'economic working arrangements'—if I may use Professor A. Bergson's expression [1]—changed in
1960 and from then on substantially differed from the trend prevailing
among Polish economists working on the same problems. Moreover,
our approach was frequently misinterpreted both in the East and in
the West.

---

[1] In accord with the policy of the Polish Ministry of Higher Education of breaking
up any schools of thought emerging in the social sciences I was transferred from
Professor Wakar's Department as early as 1963, had no access to his manuscripts
after his death, and was unable to take part in preparing them for publication. My
name was also deleted from the editorial committee preparing the book *in memoriam*
of Professor Wakar [5] and my contribution to it was not published.

From 1960 on Professor Wakar and I started to develop our theory of direct economic calculation (DEC) [*11; 15; 12; 16; 13; 7; 17; 9; 21*] and to devote most of our attention to the analysis of the 'logic', the inherent limitations, and the potential for improvement of the *centralized* system, rather than to advocating decentralization. This should not be interpreted as a change in our *theoretical* position as formulated in our works written between 1956 and 1960 [*6; 15*]. It was, rather, a change in *tactical* position. We reached the conclusion—unfortunately proved correct by further events—that far-reaching reforms of the 'guided-market' type would be politically unacceptable in the foreseeable future, at least in Poland.[1] There were, then, only two alternatives open to us. The first was to continue work on postulational models, as we had before 1960. This was tantamount to limiting our active participation in debates on economic policy issues, losing contact with applied economists, and resigning any hope of being able to offer constructive, however partial and 'third-best', suggestions for the improvement of the actual economic system. This we rejected. The second alternative was to analyse the *existing* economic mechanism and expose its inherent weaknesses,[2] but at the same time to search for and advocate any feasible improvements in its functioning. This we chose to do, and this change in our objectives is clearly visible in the writings of Professor Wakar and myself after 1961. It is gratifying to learn that

---

[1] Our last attempt before starting to work 'full time' on DEC was my effort to develop what I called 'The General Theory of Market-Type (Economic) Calculation', and to prove, by outlining the possible functioning of 'Shadow Markets' and contrasting it with Lange's model, that a market-type economic calculation may take different forms and is compatible with '. . . *a wider range of institutional arrangements than is commonly considered possible*, which means that part of the opposition against it—stemming from preferences for certain institutional arrangements considered desirable—is no longer valid' [*15* (1961), p. 70, italics in the original]. The Polish CPB was not interested. Not only Lange's model with its decentralized decision-making and quasi-competition, but even 'shadow' or simulated markets which required 'only' acceptance of the strictly defined 'rules of the game' were unacceptable. Then we turned our attention to developing the theory of DEC, whose fundamental difference with market or market-type economic calculation and its inherent limitations we already fully realized [see *15* (1961), pp. 83–91].

[2] After all, we have the honour of being among the most outspoken and severe critics of the traditional economic system, so much so that some of our 'colleagues' found it necessary (or useful) to denounce us as 'Mises' disciples': '. . . again and again the ability of a socialist economy to adopt economically rational methods of production is being questioned. (Describing the system of economic calculation existing in socialist countries as direct, A. Wakar and J. G. Zielinski assert that this type of calculation is unable to choose economically rational methods of production (see the article by these authors 'Direct Economic Calculation', *Ekonomista*, Vol. 1, 1961).) It is one of the most serious objections that can be raised against this system of production on theoretical grounds. It is hence worthwhile showing in what way a socialist economy can choose economically rational methods of production . . .' [*2*, p. 415].

at least some distinguished economists seem to favour such an approach nowadays [*3; 4; 14*].

This book represents, first of all, my present understanding of the functioning of the command economy and the mechanism of economic reforms. It goes beyond our previous attempts [*13; 7; 9; 17; 21*], which I found inadequate.[1]

Secondly, in this book an effort is made to combine the arguments for the superiority of the 'guided-market' model with the search for partial improvements of the existing 'traditional economic system'. This second objective is due to my present conviction that the modifications of the existing system which could lead to a lasting and real increase in efficiency also require such *extensive* changes that the present party apparatus is unlikely to implement them. If this is the case, one may as well press for the 'guided-market' model, which in my opinion has the potential for a much better economic performance than even a substantially improved (i.e. internally consistent and rationally operated) traditional economic system. However, any improvement, however small, of the existing system, should be urgently sought after, because for many millions of our fellow East Europeans it may bring an easier life *now*.

I have no illusions that I have fully succeeded in achieving my aims and I hope that soon my fellow economists will tell me where I have failed. Nevertheless, the book goes well beyond Poland *per se* and I hope it may be useful as supplementary reading in general courses on Soviet-type economies and comparative economic systems. Some of my colleagues may even find that such chapters as those on success indicators or incentive systems, for example, may be used as the main reading in the respective parts of the Soviet economics courses, since I believe Polish economic thinking here far exceeds anything one may find in Soviet economic literature.

The motto I borrowed from W. Grossman 'everything inhuman is senseless and useless' I interpret broadly. I have chosen it to stress that economic growth which *disregards* human welfare is self-defeating not only politically, ideologically, and socially but also economically. Moreover, I wanted to indicate that *senseless* is inhuman, since man is a *thinking* creature. The truth discovered by F. W. Taylor that—*ceteris paribus*—efficiency in digging a useless ditch is less than that in digging a useful ditch, applies equally to the 'economic working arrangements' as a whole. The lack of faith in the rationality, feasibility, or usefulness of the required plan targets, existing regulations, obligatory norms, etc., is

---

[1] For a more detailed critique see [*15*, (1967), pp. 144–51] and Ch. 4, fn. 1, pp. 143-4. This criticism followed from my articles on management mechanisms first published in 1966 [*18; 19; 20*]. For the last works of Professor Wakar, see [*8* and *10*] which were published posthumously.

in itself an important obstacle to efficient performance. If the body of the book succeeds in conveying this truth effectively to those concerned, and they are *not* confined to Eastern Europe but live in all countries of the world, I shall consider a substantial part of my task fulfilled.

J.G.Z.
Glasgow, Spring 1972

References to Preface

1. Bergson A.: *Planning and Productivity under Soviet Socialism*, New York-London, 1968.
2. Laski K.: *Zarys teorii reprodukcji socjalistycznej* (Outline of the Theory of Socialist Reproduction), Warsaw, 1965.
3. Leontief W.: 'Theoretical Assumptions and Non-observed Facts', *AER*, March 1971.
4. Phelps-Brown E. H.: 'The Underdevelopment of Economics', *EJ*, March 1972.
5. *Problemy teorii gospodarki socjalistycznej. Pamieci Profesora Dr Aleksego Wakara* (Problems of the Theory of a Socialist Economy. In Memoriam of Professor Aleksy Wakar), Warsaw, 1970.
6. Wakar A.: *Wybrane zagadnienia z ekonomii politycznej socjalizmu* (Selected Problems of the Political Economy of Socialism), Warsaw, 1957.
7. —— *Morfologia bodzcow ekonomicznych* (Morphology of Economic Incentives), Warsaw, 1963.
8. —— *Handel zagraniczny w gospodarce socjalistycznej* (Foreign Trade in a Socialist Economy), Warsaw, 1968.
9. —— ed.: *Zarys teorii gospodarki socjalistycznej* (An Outline of the Theory of a Socialist Economy), Warsaw, 1965.
10. —— ed.: *Teoria pieniadza w gospodarce socjalistycznej* (The Theory of Money in a Socialist Economy), Warsaw, 1968.
11. Wakar A. and Zielinski J. G.: 'The Direct Economic Calculation'. *E*, 1, 1961.
12. —— 'Incentive Systems and Prices'. *E*, 2, 1962.
13. —— 'Socialist Operational Price Systems'. *AER*, March 1963.
14. Worswick G. D. N.: 'Is Progress in Economic Science Possible?' *EJ*, March 1972.
15. Zielinski J. G.: *Rachunek ekonomiczny w socjalizmie* (Economic Calculation under Socialism), Warsaw, 1961, revised edn., 1967.
16. —— 'An Attempt to Construct a Realistic Theory of Socialist Economy'. *Ost-Okonomii* (presently *EP*), 2, 1962.
17. —— 'Economic Tools of Plan Fulfilment'. *EP*, 3, 1964.
18. —— 'The Enterprise as a Cybernetic System'. *ZG*, 21, 1966.
19. —— 'The Management Mechanism of a Socialist Industry'. *ZG*, 22, 1966.
20. —— 'Two Models of Management in Socialist Enterprises'. *ZG*, 23, 1966.
21. —— *Lectures on the Theory of Socialist Planning*, Ibadan-London, 1968.

ACKNOWLEDGEMENTS

My thanks are due to Professor Alec Nove of the University of Glasgow for his comments on the manuscript and especially for creating conditions which made concentration on research really possible.

Professors Abram Bergson and David Granick from Harvard and Wisconsin Universities respectively were kind enough to read Ch. 2. Professors Richard Portes from London University and Frederic L. Pryor of Swarthmore College kindly read most of the manuscript. They all offered valuable comments and suggestions, but the responsibility for any errors and weaknesses which remain rests exclusively with the author.

I am particularly grateful to Roger A. Clarke, my colleague and friend from the University of Glasgow, for editing the most unsatisfactory translation from Polish of Chs. 4–7.[1] Without his help this work would not only have been delayed but also the exposition would have suffered badly.

I wish to record my debt to Dr. Renato Mieli, Secretary General of *Centro Studi e Ricerche su Problemi Economico-Sociali* (CESES), Milan, and to the Acting Director of the Thomas Jefferson Center for Political Economy, University of Virginia, Professor John H. Moore. By inviting me yearly to lecture on different aspects of economic reforms at the post-graduate Summer Course sponsored jointly by CESES and the Thomas Jefferson Center of the University of Virginia, Dr. Mieli and Professor Moore provided me with the unique challenge of a systematic examination of the multiple aspects of the economic reform movement in Eastern Europe and the necessity constantly to re-think and revise my understanding of this complex process. Many parts of this book were first delivered and discussed at the CESES/Jefferson Center Summer Courses in 1968–70.

It is my pleasant duty to express my gratitude to the Editors of *Co-existence, Economics of Planning, Revue de l'Est. Soviet Studies,* and *Jahrbuch der Wirtschaft Osteuropas* for allowing me to use—in one form or another—some of the papers I have published in their Journals.

My heartfelt thanks are also due to Mrs. Christine Gills, Miss Elizabeth Hunter, and Miss Eleanor Robertson for their most efficient secretarial help and meticulous typing of the whole work.

University of Glasgow, Spring 1972   J.G.Z.

---

[1] Cf. M. Pohorille, ed., *Ekonomia polityczna socjalizmu* (Political Economy of Socialism), Warsaw, 1968, pp. 566–726, for Polish original.

A BRIEF STATISTICAL PROFILE[1]

Most data are for 1969 (1968, 1967, or 1966 or their average). First figure in bracket gives data for United Kingdom, second—for Italy. If data for Italy were lacking, the data for France were substituted preceded by *F*. We are told that the data for countries other than Poland are quoted after various Western sources, such as UN Statistical Yearbook, UN Monthly Bulletin of Statistics, OECD Manpower Statistics, etc. All data are, however, taken from the source indicated, and no effort could be undertaken to verify *their* accuracy. To obtain a meaningful picture some data given in absolute figures were recalculated into percentages by the author. For obvious reasons absolute data in value terms are not used. The comparative data for UK are quoted for convenience of British readers, for Italy—because to this country Poland was very frequently compared by Polish political and government leaders. During what can be called 'the optimistic period' of 'socialist construction' the Polish people were even promised that Poland 'will reach and overtake' Italy in the late 1950s.

Population: total 32·5m (55·5; 53·2), of which males 48·6 per cent (48·6; 48·8); below 19 years old 37·6 per cent (30·4; 32·3), above 65—8·2 per cent (12·6; 10·2); urban: 51·5 per cent (77·4; 38·1); density per km²: 104 persons (228; 177); life expectancy at birth (1965–6), men: 66·8 years (68·3 in 1963–5; 67·2 in 1960–2), women (for the same periods): 72·8 (74·4; 72·3); living permanently abroad: 10·3m (in the UK 145,000; in the USA 6·5m).

Area and land use: total area 312,700 km² (244,000; 301,200), of which agricultural land (*uzytki rolne*) 62·8 per cent (80·1; 67·6), of the latter, arable land and orchards 78 per cent (38; 75), meadows and pastures 22 per cent (62; 25).

Employment: gainfully employed in total population 50·7 per cent (47·3; 43·9), of which in industry 26·7 per cent (38·8; 30·1), construction 6·5 per cent (7·8; 10·3), transport 5·6 per cent (6·6; 5·2), agriculture and forestry 42·0 per cent (3·1; 23·3).

Structure of National Income (NNP, in Marxian sense, in Poland; GNP in UK and Italy) by sectors of origin: industry 49·1 per cent (40·0; 30·5), construction 9·3 per cent (6 8; 8·1), agriculture and forestry 21·0 per cent (3·1; 11·1), transport and communications 6·2 per cent (8·5; 7·3), trade 10·7 per cent (11·3; 12·1), other 3·7 per cent (30·3; 30·9). (The last item consists in Poland of 'other material output', in UK and Italy of the value of 'other material output and non-material services such as administration, armed forces, judiciary, etc.'.)

Investment: share (including stock changes) in National Income: 28·8 per cent (19·7; 20·7); structure: industry and construction 44·4 per cent (38·0; 27·4), agriculture and forestry 15·9 per cent (2·8; 8·7), transport and communications 11·9 per cent (9·8; 9·8), housing (*gospodarka mieszkaniowa*)

---

[1] Source: *Rocznik Statystyczny*, 1970, Part II. International comparisons. Warsaw, 1970, pp. 579–670.

14·1 per cent (20·0; 30·5). The data in this section are not fully comparable owing to differences in price systems and classifications of the national economies involved.

Consumption and Essential Services: per 1,000 of inhabitants: length of railway network 0·82 km (0·36; 0·31); number of passenger cars 12 (204; 155), of telephones—51 (231; 144), of radio sets—173 (318; 226), of television sets—105 (279; 154), of newspapers—199 (488; *F* 248), of new book titles—0·26 (0·57; *F* 0·38), of medical doctors 1·45 (1·06; *F* 1·18), of dentists—0·40 (0·23; *F* 0·39), of hospital beds 7·35 (8·88, 10·4), of university students 9·9 (6·4; 7·2). Housing conditions—number of persons per room 1·5 (0·6; 1·1). Food consumption in kg per person per year: flour 132 (73; 131), potatoes 139 (103; 44), meat 53 (74; 39), fats 18 (22; 18), milk 266 (219; 153), eggs 10 (16; 9), fish 6 (9; 6), sugar 39 (49; 26).

GLOSSARY OF MAIN POLITICAL EVENTS
1956–1971

(compiled by Dr. Zbigniew Pelczynski, Pembroke College, Oxford)

The Poznan Events

On 28 June 1956, after the prolonged failure of the authorities to deal with a relatively minor wage grievance, the workers of the largest Polish railway engine and carriage factory in Poznan struck and staged a peaceful protest march, which was joined by workers of other Poznan factories. The demonstration escalated into armed attacks on local party and security police headquarters, the prison and the radio jamming station; it was suppressed with much bloodshed by the army, and punished by massive arrests.

Following Moscow's lead the Polish government at first denounced the Poznan events as a 'provocation' inspired by 'imperialist circles'. Moscow firmly stuck to this line. But on 1 July the Polish official attitude abruptly changed. The Poznan troubles were blamed on the shortcomings of the industrial and political system and on the neglect of the standard of living. A number of the responsible officials were purged and the small number of workers eventually put on trial were treated remarkably leniently. This *volte-face* meant that after initial hesitation the majority of the Polish Politbureau decided to continue the policy of 'democratization' which the new Party leader Edward Ochab had promised before the events.

This was confirmed at the VIIth Plenary Session of the Central Committee of the Polish United Workers' Party (PUWP) held on 18–27 July. After arguments about responsibility for the Poznan events, the Central Committee approved a comprehensive programme of political and economic reforms. The programme was greeted with enthusiasm by the Party intelligentsia, and stimulated a lively discussion of the reforms in the press and public meetings. Its implementation, however, was obstructed by a minority of the Politbureau and a section of the Party elite, whose numerical weakness was compensated for by the knowledge of Soviet support. This Stalinist faction, known as the 'Natolin group' from the place of their meetings, advocated inflationary wage increases for the workers, together with stricter curbs on the press and tighter control over intellectuals in general, and mooted the desirability of an 'ethnic regulation of the cadres' (i.e. a purge of prominent Jewish Party members). They also demanded the realignment

of the Polish with the negative Soviet party line on 'democratization'. The split in the Party leadership, which affected the lower
echelons and paralysed the power apparatus, necessitated in the end
a reconstruction of the PUWP Politbureau.

The Polish October

On 19–21 October 1956 the VIIIth Plenary Session of the PUWP Central
Committee met to implement the changes in the Politbureau and to
reconfirm 'democratization'. To strengthen the Politbureau the re-
formists proposed the inclusion of Wladyslaw Gomulka. He was a
former General Secretary of the Party, purged in 1948 for 'rightist-
nationalist deviation', released in 1954 from arrest, and readmitted to
the Party shortly after the VIIth Central Committee Plenum together
with some of his purged associates. Gomulka accepted the programme
of the VIIth Plenum although he insisted on a stronger condemnation
of the methods and results of compulsory collectivization, and on action
to end the Soviet economic exploitation and political tutelage of
Poland. Warned by the 'Natolin group' that 'counter-revolution' was
breaking out in Poland, the Soviet leaders attempted to interfere with
the proceedings of the Central Committee session, but were persuaded
to return to Moscow and to recall to their bases the Soviet troops
surrounding Warsaw.

Gomulka then delivered a scathing critique of the Stalinist system in
Poland and was unanimously elected First Secretary of the PUWP
Central Committee. All members of the 'Natolin group' were excluded
from the new Politbureau. The July programme of reforms was re-
affirmed. Although far less radical in his proposals for the future than
his criticisms of the past, Gomulka was at first widely regarded as a
strong champion of 'democratization' and enjoyed immense national
prestige for his toughness in standing up to the Russians. His immediate task was the restoration of order and discipline in the
country, swept by a wave of spontaneous political activity and anti-
communist feeling, which at one point threatened the results of the
general election to the new *Sejm* (Polish Parliament) in January 1957.
Only Gomulka's personal appeal and the spectre of a possible Soviet
intervention, as had recently happened in Hungary, persuaded the
voters not to cross out communist candidates *en masse*. To calm the
population the new leadership had to make numerous concessions
(e.g. to the peasants, the Catholic Church, the higher education
institutions) and to accept such unpalatable phenomena as the break-up
of four-fifths of the collective farms and the self-liquidation of the
Communist Youth Movement.

Gomulka successfully re-negotiated Polish economic agreements with
the Soviet Union and secured the departure of Soviet civil and military

'advisers'. Relations between the two countries continued to be strained until October 1957, when Gomulka and his policies were fully accepted by the Soviet leadership (now with Khrushchev firmly at the head) and Poland became a loyal member of the 'socialist common-wealth'. The price of this reconciliation was Gomulka's acceptance of the strongly anti-revisionist line of the bloc. By the end of 1958 Gomulka had restored firm Party rule over the country and the authority of the central leadership within the Party. At the same time many of the reforms promised between July 1956 and January 1957 were also imple-mented. Gomulka proved to be very conservative in the economic sphere and ignored plans for a radical reform of the socialized economy prepared by the Economic Commission of the Council of Ministers. The cancelling of huge state debts to the workers and the emasculation of the workers' councils, spontaneously set up before the VIIIth Central Committee Plenum, lost Gomulka much working-class popularity, and the *rapprochement* with Khrushchev lost him the popularity of the country at large. At the IIIrd Congress of the PUWP (March 1959) Gomulka proclaimed the process of 'democratization' to be completed at the present stage of 'socialist construction', and called for an increased industrial effort to improve the country's economic position.

The March Events

The last years of Gomulka's leadership were marked by considerable tension between the Party, the Church, and the intellectuals (especially writers), and the growing activity of the security police which, under the slogan of combating 'ideological diversion', acquired influence in the press, radio and television, publishing, and other areas of social life. The Minister of the Interior responsible for security was General Mieczyslaw Moczar, a wartime communist partisan leader. Moczar also controlled the 'Union of Fighters for Freedom and Democracy', which gave him wide access to non-communist circles and helped him to promote a cult of wartime resistance and patriotism. His followers formed a faction known as the 'Partisans', which enjoyed much support in the Warsaw Party apparatus and the middle echelons of the PUWP in other parts of the country. Like the 'Natolin group' the 'Partisans' tended to be strongly anti-intelligentsia, anti-Jewish, anti-democratic, and anti-reformist. But the emphasis on the merits of anti-German resistance in Poland rather than on service in the Polish army in Russia cast a suspicion of anti-Soviet attitudes on Moczar and his group.

On 8 March 1968 the students of Warsaw University held an unauthorized rally within the university precincts to protest against the expulsion of some fellow-students for organizing a demonstration against the authorities' ban on a play for political reasons. The brutal break-up of the rally by an auxiliary police force led to widespread student demonstrations and sit-ins throughout Warsaw, which brought about police repression, arrests, and trials. As some of the student leaders were Jewish, the Warsaw Party committee accused them, their parents, and professors, and some formerly prominent Jewish Party members, of organizing a 'Zionist' plot to discredit the Polish government. A massive purge of 'Zionists' and 'revisionists' was mounted in Warsaw and spread to most other towns in Poland. Universities and other teaching and research institutions, editorial boards of newspapers and publishing houses, and certain government departments were particularly badly hit. Since the government issued exit visas to those prepared to emigrate to Israel and pressure was put on many purge victims to apply, the March events caused an exodus of the majority of Jews still left in Poland.

The December Events

In 1970, after two years of stagnant consumption, the Polish government announced a new method of wage and salary assessment from the beginning of 1971, a reform which was supposed to increase productivity but was widely believed to reduce workers' earnings. On 13 December 1970 the government ordered a sharp increase in the prices of many consumer goods. The following day the shipyard workers and dockers of Gdansk struck in protest and, joined by other workers, marched to the city centre. Inflamed by rumours of arrests the demonstrators burnt the provincial Party headquarters, wrecked other buildings, shops and vehicles, and clashed violently with the police. The riot spread to the neighbouring cities of Gdynia and Elblag and to another major Baltic harbour and shipbuilding centre, Szczecin, following everywhere a similar pattern. Order was restored at the end of the week, after heavy casualties, by a massive deployment of troops and tanks.

The events caused a crisis in the Party leadership. Gomulka, who opposed any concessions to the strikers, and his closest associates were ousted from the Politbureau, and a new Politbureau headed by Edward Gierek as First Secretary was elected by the PUWP Central Committee on 20 December. The change in the Party leadership and the consequential government changes were heartily welcomed by the country and did much to calm the workers. Nevertheless large scale strikes broke out again on 22 January (Szczecin) and 13 February (Lodz) and countless small strikes and work stoppages occurred all over Poland. The new Party leadership set out to conciliate the workers by discussing their grievances and proposing moderate concessions, but the persistent unrest forced them to restore the old prices, abandon the unpopular wage reform, and revise drastically the

1971–5 economic plan. The increase in the standard of living, rather than industrial expansion, became the chief priority of the new economic policy. A crucial factor in stabilizing the situation was large-scale economic aid from the Soviet Union, which clearly approved Gierek's policy of conciliation. A general political relaxation, of which the Church and the intellectuals were the main beneficiaries, accompanied the economic concessions. Private farmers became relieved of compulsory deliveries and benefited from other measures designed to stimulate agricultural production.

At the VIIIth Plenary Sessions of the PUWP Central Committee on 7 February 1971 the Gomulka group in the old Politbureau were officially censured for infringing the principle of collective leadership, losing contact with the masses, and making numerous policy mistakes. Gierek promised a thorough overhaul of the whole system, but no radical reforms of the political or economic *structure* (as opposed to *policy*) had been proposed at the time of the VIth Party Congress (6 December 1971). The congress produced further changes in the Politbureau and renovated the Central Committee, strengthening the influence of the new First Secretary and his close associates. Although the 'Partisans' were rewarded for their help in overthrowing Gomulka after the December events, their influence waned during 1971 and Moczar himself had to exchange a seat in the Politbureau for an honorific government post.

More detailed accounts of the events can be found in the following books or articles:

POZNAN AND OCTOBER 1956

Syrop K., *Spring in October*, London, 1957.

Lewis F., *The Polish Volcano*, London, 1959. (1958 US edition had the title *A Case History of Hope*)

Dokumenty: Poznan 1956–grudzien 1970 (Documents: Poznan 1956–December 1970), Paris, 1971.

MARCH 1968

Bethell N., *Gomulka, his Poland and his Communism*, London, 1969.

Dokumenty: Poznan 1956–grudzien 1970 (Documents: Poznan 1956–December 1970), Paris, 1971.

Dokumenty: Wydarzenia marcowe 1968 (Documents: March Events 1968), Paris, 1968.

DECEMBER 1970

Bromke A., 'Beyond the Gomulka era', *Foreign Affairs*, April 1971.

Johnson A. R., 'Polish perspectives, past and present', *Problems of Communism*, July–August 1971.

Wacowska E., ed., *Dokumenty: Rewolta szczecinska i jej znaczenie* (Documents: The Szczecin Revolt and its Significance), Paris, 1971.

Bromke A., ed., *Poland since 1970*, a special issue of *Canadian Slavonic Papers*, 1973.

ABBREVIATIONS USED[1]

CC—Central Committee (KC)
CM—Council of Ministers (RM)
COMECON—Council of Mutual Economic Assistance (RWPG)
CPB—Central Planning Board
CSO—Central Statistical Office (GUS)
CSSR—Czechoslovak Socialist Republic (CSRS)
CWS—Conference of Workers Self-Management (KSR)
EDP—Electronic Data Processing (EPD)
FS regulators—feeding system regulators
FYP—Five-year plan
GDR—German Democratic Republic (NRD)
HAO—Higher Administrative Organs
MIS—Managerial Information System (SIK)
MPS—Material Product System
PC—Planning Commission at the Council of Ministers
PAS—Polish Academy of Science (PAN)
PUWP—Polish United Workers Party (PZPR)
R and D—Research and Development
T-E plan—technico-economic plan (TPF)

ABBREVIATIONS OF JOURNALS' TITLES
(with brief characteristics of Polish journals)[2]

AER—American Economic Review
DU—Dziennik Ustaw (Parliament Official Gazette), official gazette for parliament's (*sejm*) bills and government decrees implementing them
EP—Economics of Planning
E—Ekonomista (Economist), monthly of the Polish Economic Association
EOP—Ekonomika i Organizacja Pracy (Economics and Organization of Labour), monthly of the Committee of Labour and Wages

[1] Commonly used Polish abbreviations are given in parentheses.
[2] Titles of periodicals referred to only once or twice are given in full where quoted. All Polish journals are published in Warsaw unless otherwise stated.

F—Finanse (Finance), monthly of the Ministry of Finance

GP—Gospodarka Planowa (Economics of Planning), monthly of the Planning Commission at the Council of Ministers

MP—Monitor Polski (Government Official Gazette), official gazette for government decrees and regulations

ND—Nowe Drogi (New Directions), monthly of the Central Committee of the Polish United Workers Party

PUG—Przeglad Ustawodawstwa Gospodarczego (Review of Economic Legislation), monthly, frequently describes and comments on *unpublished* bills and decrees

RE—Revue de l'Est

RPES—Ruch Prawniczy, Ekonomiczny i Socjologiczny (Legal, Economic and Sociological Review), quarterly of the University and Higher Economic School in Poznan

SS—Soviet Studies

WS—Wiadomosci Statystyczne (Statistical News), monthly of the Central Statistical Office

ZG—Zycie Gospodarcze (Economic Life), the only Polish economic weekly

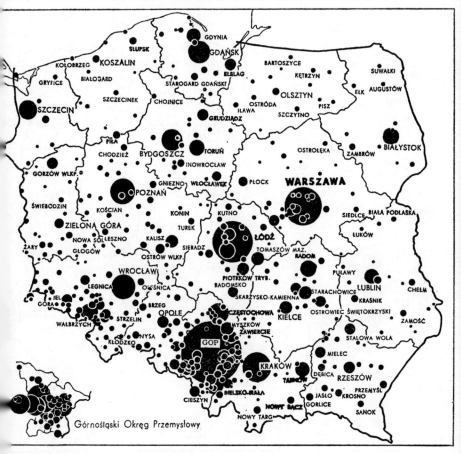

Górnośląski Okręg Przemysłowy

Map 1   Location of Main Industrial Centres in Poland

Source: Leszczycki, S., ed., *Zarys Geografii Ekonomicznej Polski* (An Outline of Polish Economic Geography), Warsaw, 1971, p. 24.

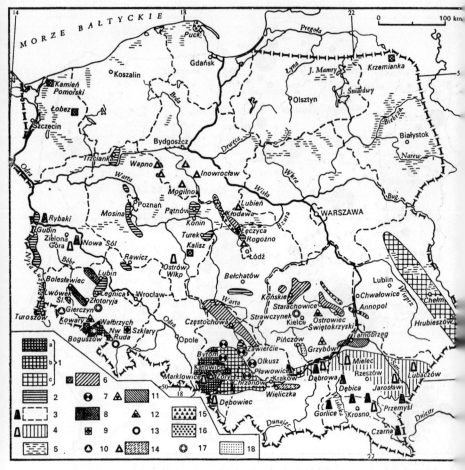

Map 2   Location of Mineral Resources in Poland

1. coal: (a) coking coal, (b) other types of coal, (c) coal deposits; 2. lignite;
3. crude oil; 4. natural gas; 5. peat; 6. iron ore; 7. zinc and lead ores; 8. copper
ore; 9. nickel ore; 10. tin ore; 11. sulfur ore; 12. pyrites; 13. bauxite; 14. rock
salt; 15. potassium and rock salt; 16. phosphorites; 17. barytes; 18. gypsum
and anhydride.

Source: as for Map 1.

INTRODUCTORY

INTRODUCTION

CHAPTER ONE

THE BEGINNING OF REFORMS

1.1 The Need for Reforms

The 'Polish October' of 1956 (see Glossary) started the process of economic reforms in Poland. In this section we want to examine the causes which made reforming the existing, traditional, Soviet-type economic system[1] an imperative economic and political requirement.

In general terms, economic reforms became necessary because previous socio-economic policies resulted in a very unsatisfactory economic performance, which had important and negative political and ideological consequences.

1.2.1 DISAPPOINTING ECONOMIC RESULTS

The unsatisfactory economic performance resulting from the application of Soviet-type planning and management showed itself in three basic spheres: growth, efficiency, and standard of living.

A *Growth*

The unsatisfactory growth performance—in spite of the continuing high rate of investment—was a freely admitted reason for economic reforms in some 'late-reformer' countries such as Czechoslovakia, whose rate of growth was first slowly and then drastically declining (see Table 1.1).[2]

In Poland, however, overall growth performance did not play a substantial role during the *first* wave of economic reforms in 1956–8. According to official statistics, Polish industrial production rose from

---

[1] The terms 'Soviet-type' and 'traditional' economic system will be treated as synonymous in the present work.

[2] All statistics are of East European origin and no effort has been made to verify their accuracy. Such an attempt lies beyond the scope of the present book and, moreover, East European reforms have been influenced by economic performance *as seen* by their leaders. It is true that many statistical (and qualitative) economic data of potentially negative political repercussion are not being released, but essentially there is only one set of macro-economic statistical data, and these reflect what East European leaders believe to be—by and large—the true picture of the situation.

Table 1.1: *Average Rate of Growth of National Income in Czechoslovakia*

1949–1953	1954–1960	1961–1965
9%	7%	2%

Source: K. Kouba, 'The New System of Economic Management in Czechoslovakia', *Mirowaja Ekonomika i Miezdunarodnyje Otnoszenija*, 2, 1966. Reprinted in Z. Lewandowicz, M. Misiak, eds.: *Reformy gospodarcze w krajach socjalistycznych* (Economic Reforms in Socialist Countries), Warsaw, 1967, p. 164.

Table 1.2: *Yearly Percentage Increases of Polish National Income (in 1961 prices)*

1950	15·1	1957	10·7	1964	6·7
1951	7·5	1958	5·5	1965	7·0
1952	6·2	1959	5·2	1966	7·1
1953	10·4	1960	4·3	1967	5·7
1954	10·5	1961	8·2	1968	9·0
1955	8·4	1962	2·1	1969	3·0
1956	7·0	1963	6·9		

Source: Rocznik Dochodu Narodowego 1965–1968 (Yearbook of National Income 1965–1968), Warsaw, 1969, pp. 12–13, and *Rocznik statystyczny 1970* (Statistical Yearbook 1970), Warsaw, 1970, p. 78.

100 in 1949 to 270 in 1955 [*11*, p. 46]. Even after deflating it to a more realistic 220–30 [*11*, pp. 48–9], this still left Poland among the fastest growing European countries.

Because of the big share of stagnating agriculture in total national output, the national income figures are much lower (if 1949 = 100, 1956 = 174 in 1956 prices [*20*, p. 124]), but still quite impressive.

Polish national income fluctuated substantially over the last twenty years (Table 1.2), but it did not show any such drastic decline as in Czechoslovakia. On the contrary, after declining in the late 1950s and early 1960s, it picked up again from 1963 on. If, however, we take the socialist countries as a whole, their growth position *vis-à-vis* their capitalist adversaries deteriorated markedly (Table 1.3). If for the period 1951–64 the socialist countries claimed that they were growing about 70 per cent quicker than the world economy as a whole and about 50 per cent quicker than the Common Market countries, for the period 1961–4 they had to admit that this superiority dropped to 21 and 17 per cent respectively, which represents a decline of 3·3 and 3 times respectively. Under those circumstances, the growth considerations—and all that this implies—must have been an important reason behind the economic reform efforts of the mid 1960s and their spread to all socialist countries. This is the more likely since most or all of national income growth in recent years has been swallowed by stock increases (Table 1.4). The first wave of Polish reforms (1956–8) was triggered, however, not

Table 1.3: Changes in National Income and Industrial Production in the World

	National Income			Industrial Production		
	1951–64	1956–64	1961–4	1951–64	1956–64	1961–4
	(average yearly growth in %)					
World as a whole[a]	5·0	4·7	5·1	6·7	6·4	6·8
Socialist countries[a]	8·4	7·4	6·2	10·8	9·4	8·2
Poland	7·1	6·3	6·0	9·7	8·4	8·5
All others except socialist countries	4·2	4·0	4·9	5·4	5·0	6·0
Developed countries	4·2	4·0	4·9	5·2	4·8	5·5
Underdeveloped countries	4·4	4·3	4·1	7·5	7·6	7·8
Western Europe	4·7	4·6	4·9	5·8	5·2	5·1
EEC	5·5	5·2	5·3	7·4	6·3	5·7
EFTA	3·4	3·4	4·0	3·5	3·3	3·8
North America	3·6	3·1	4·2	4·2	3·6	4·9
South America	4·8	4·6	4·1	5·7	5·8	5·1

[a] Without Asian socialist countries.

Source: Rocznik Statystyki Miedzynarodowej (Yearbook of International Statistics) Warsaw, 1965, s. XI, XV, XVIII; *Rocznik Dochodu Narodowego 1960–1965* (Yearbook of National Income 1960–1965), Warsaw, 1966, p. 10. Quoted after [*31*, p. 262]

Table 1.4: Share of Stock Increases in National Income[a]

Countries	1960	1961	1962	1963	1964
SOCIALIST:					
Bulgaria	13·0	8·2	11·4	11·5	11·8
Czechoslovakia	1·4	5·1	5·4	3·4	–
Hungary	6·8	9·4	10·0	10·1	9·8
Poland[b]	7·4	8·1	5·1	7·3	7·5
USSR	9·1	11·7	10·2	8·4	11·4
Yugoslavia	4·6	1·9	0·4	5·1	10·2
CAPITALIST:					
Austria	2·8	3·7	1·2	1·6	2·8
France	2·5	0·4	1·6	1·2	1·9
West Germany	3·2	2·0	1·1	0·7	1·4
USA	0·7	0·4	1·2	1·0	0·6
UK	2·3	1·2	0·3	0·7	1·7

[a] By stocks, working capital and reserves are meant.

[b] Data for 1963 and 1964 have been corrected according to *Rocznik Dochodu Narodowego 1965–1968*, Warsaw, 1969, p. 21. On the basis of the same source the data for Poland can also be extended as follows: 1965—8·3, 1966—8·3, 1967—6·2, 1968—6·9. Ibid., p. 21.

Source: Rocznik Dochodu Narodowego 1960–1965, Warsaw, 1966. *Wiestnik Statistiki SSSR*, 4, 1966. (Quoted after T. Cholinski, G. Michajlow, S. Milewski, *Gospodarka zapasami w krajach socjalistycznych* (The Management of Inventories in Socialist Countries), Warsaw, 1967, p. 81.)

2 *

by growth considerations—growth had been very rapid by any standards—but by gross inefficiencies of the system and the price paid for it in terms of complete failure to raise real wages.

B *Efficiency*

The basic data on 6-year plan performance are presented in Table 1.5.

Table 1.5: Basic Indices of the Polish 6-year plan 1950–1955
(1949 = 100)

	Plan for 1955	Fulfilment in 1955
National Income	212	175
Total Investment	240	262[a]
Gross Output of Industry	258	270
Gross Output of Agriculture	150	113
Employment	160	156
Real wages	140	104

[a] Recalculated by the author on the basis of data in A. Karpinski, *Socjalistyczna industrializacja Polski* (Socialist Industrialization of Poland), Warsaw, 1958, p. 69.

Source: K. Ryc, *Spozycie a wzrost gospodarczy Polski* (The Consumption and Economic Growth of Poland), Warsaw, 1968, pp. 60 and 61.

These data indicate that if investment and employment figures are close to those planned, the results in terms of national income and—especially —real wages, are much lower. Here only a few basic illustrations can be given of what this means in less aggregative terms.

At the expense of higher investment outlays than originally envisaged (actual investments reached 108·7 per cent of planned), only 62 per cent out of 210 main investment projects were completed, and out of the remaining 38 per cent, 67, i.e. 32 per cent, were not even started. The situation was actually worse than these figures suggest because the 6-year plan also envisaged construction of 630 smaller investment projects '. . . whose completion ratio was even lower than that of main investment projects' [*11*, pp. 69–70], e.g., out of 56 brickworks to be built in the 1950–5 period, only 5 were actually constructed [*11*, p. 88]. Nor does the 62 per cent completion figure take into account that in most investment projects completed during the 6-year plan, the planned level of output was not reached and the discrepancies were certainly not marginal. For example, in 'Nowa Huta' steel mill, the plan output for 1955 was 750,000 tons of steel, actual output 327,000 tons, i.e. 42 per cent. In 'Nowy Targ' shoe factory, plan output for 1955 was 1·2 million pairs of shoes, actual output 8 per cent of this target [*11*, pp. 93–4].

As all above comparisons are related to plan targets, one may wonder whether they nevertheless represent an acceptable economic performance in *absolute* terms. This, however, is not the case, as a number of comparative studies revealed. In respect of both construction periods and investment costs, Polish performance during the Stalinist period fell far below the performance level of not only capitalist countries but also her own performance during the 3-year plan 1946–9 or pre-war industrial achievements (Tables 1.6, 1.7). The labour productivity of new plants built during the 6-year plan also turned out to be lower than

Table 1.6: Selected Comparative Data on the Length of Construction Periods (in years)

	Poland 1950–5	Certain capitalist countries	Poland in 1946–9
Coal mine of 5,000 ton capacity per day[a]	13–15	8–10	—
Electric thermopower station of 200–300 MGW[b]	4–5	c. 2	—
Quality steel mill of medium size[c]	over 7	2–3	—
Canned meat factories, slaughter houses	3–4	—	0·75–1

[a] UK, West Germany.
[b] Western Europe.
[c] Western Europe (a similar steel mill, Stalowa Wola, was built in Poland before the Second World War in two years).

Source: A. Karpinski, op. cit., pp. 95–6.

Table 1.7: Construction Cost of Certain Comparable Investment Projects

	Construction costs in Poland (= 100%) in comparison to some foreign countries
	in %
Smelting coke plant[a]	120–150
Bloomery[a]	150–200
Iron ore mine[b]	170–250
Coal mine[c]	c. 150

[a] UK and USA.
[b] USA, W. Germany, France, Sweden (disregarding differences in quality of ore).
[c] Czechoslovakia.

Source: A. Karpinski, op. cit., p. 98.

in old plants in all branches except electricity generating and cement, where the impact of new technology on productivity is most pronounced (Table 1.8).

C Standard of Living

The failure of the 6-year plan was nowhere more evident than in the sphere of real wages. The planned target was 40 per cent increase, official statistics claimed 27 per cent, but even such a sympathetic economic historian of this period as A. Karpinski had to admit that 'no rise of real wages which would make itself felt has been achieved.

Table 1.8: *Differences in Labour Productivity in New and Old Polish Plants*

Labour productivity in 1955
measured by gross output per
man/year in constant prices
(thousand zlotys)

	Old plants	Plants built during 1950–5	1:2
	(1)	(2)	(3)
Electric thermopower stations	61·70	108·70	176
Coal mines	5·43	4·27	79
Iron ore mines	3·17	2·42	76
Steel mills	25·30	16·60	66
Artificial Fibres Industry	18·70	16·00	86
Cement plants	14·46	17·02	118
Brickworks	3·06	1·81	59
Paper mills	25·53	17·87	90
Breweries	30·62	15·24	50

Source: A. Karpinski, op. cit., p. 206.

and in comparison to 1950 real wages of certain groups of population actually declined' [*11*, p. 7]. A recent (1968) Polish study estimates the average increase of real wages during the whole 6-year plan at around 4 per cent [*31*, p. 118] and goes on to say that '. . . it means that most employees did not achieve any wage increases. Increases in wages were absorbed by changes in employment structure such as increased employment in branches of industry enjoying higher wages (steel mills, machine building, etc.), increases in the number of people with higher education, and higher earnings and similar changes' [*31*, p. 118].

1.1.2 POLITICAL CONSEQUENCES

An economic policy of this kind, together with the growing awareness that much of the sacrifice had been wasted in gross planning and economic blunders, added considerably to many other grievances of the Polish population. Together they resulted in widespread social unrest, starting with the Poznan riots in June 1956 (see Glossary) and culminating in country-wide political upheavals in October of the same year. At the same time anti-consumer bias and economic mistakes of the 6-year plan provided important ammunition and a sphere of attack in the intra-party struggle which inevitably develops (or rather intensifies) in all critical moments.

1.1.3 IDEOLOGICAL CONSEQUENCES

The ideological repercussions of the economic consequences of the Stalinist growth strategy and planning and management system were equally profound. First of all, they cast doubts on the economic capability of the system. In the ideological battle about the economic capability of a communist planned economy as compared to the present-day 'mixed' capitalist system, three basic stages may be distinguished. At the beginning, overall economic superiority was claimed for the former by Marxist scholars, both in allocative efficiency and growth and stability. This claim has never been supported by Western scholars, and permanent disequilibria on many producer and consumer goods markets forced most Marxist scholars, and many communist politicians as well, to admit the superiority of the market over central planning in the sphere of short-term adjustments. The second stage of the battle was fought over the 'growth versus choice' problem, to use Professor Peter Wiles's expression. Here many Western scholars—impressed by initially very high growth rates of communist countries—were willing to admit the superiority of planned over 'mixed' economies. When, even according to official East European statistics, the growth rates of socialist countries are decreasing—and are decreasing rather fast—and, on the other hand, '. . . capitalist rates of growth, contrarily to the socialist ones, are in general increasing' [2, p. 16], also the growth superiority of planned economies is being questioned, because 'if these trends are to continue socialist growth rates may in the near future come very close to the capitalist ones' [2, p. 19]. This, for obvious political reasons, cannot be explicitly admitted by East European economists,[1] but two phenomena are worth noticing: (1) superiority of market economies in more and more important fields, such as, say, national income–stock growth ratio, is being admitted (see Table 1.4); (2) the whole subject of economic 'catching up' and 'overtaking' capitalist countries conspicuously disappeared from official communist pronouncements after Khrushchev's fall.

The growth experience of socialist countries revealed also that they do not possess any distinct superiority as far as *stability* is concerned. Contrary to what many expected, the studies of socialist economic growth by a number of both Eastern and Western economists, such as A. Bajt of Yugoslavia [2], J. Goldmann of Czechoslovakia [9], or G. J. Staller of the US [35], indicated substantial fluctuations in growth rates of socialist countries. According to some authors, European socialist countries during the period 1950–68 showed even *higher* fluctuations than capitalist countries over the same period [2, p. 10].

---

[1] It may be interesting to notice that one of the Polish economists, Dr. S. Kurowski, defied this ban and bluntly stated that '. . . in the economic sphere socialism cannot win' [17, p. 385]. He based his thesis on two arguments: first, on the 'technological unity' of the modern world, by which he meant that socialism cannot develop or acquire technology superior to its capitalist rival, and second, that capitalism has introduced social changes on a scale sufficient for effective utilization and further development of modern technology. Kurowski's book immediately produced an uproar from Party circles and from dogmatists within the profession, and unpleasant consequences followed—the editorial staff of his publisher (PWN—Polish Scientific Publishers) was subject to purges and demotions.

At the consumer level the unsatisfactory economic performance of planned economies showed itself by a growing (during the early 1950s) and then, after initial considerable improvements, by a rather stable discrepancy between quantity, quality, and variety of consumer goods produced by the two systems. In the sphere of consumption growth even official figures claim only modest—if any—superiority over capitalist countries (Table 1.9), owing to '. . . a larger share of productive invest-

Table 1.9: *Average Yearly Increases of Consumption in Poland and some other Countries in 1951–1964* (in constant prices)

Country	Consumption		Consumption per capita	
	1951–64	1956–64	1951–64	1956–64
Austria	5·0	4·8	4·8	4·2
Czechoslovakia	5·1	4·5	4·1	3·7
France	4·7	4·7	3·6	3·5
Holland	4·2	4·4	2·9	3·0
Canada	4·5	3·9	2·1	1·5
GDR	—	4·6	—	5·1
West Germany	7·2	6·8	6·1	5·5
Norway	3·7	3·8	2·7	2·8
Poland	6·6	5·7	4·9	4·1
USA	3·7	3·3	2·2	1·9
Sweden	3·4	3·6	2·7	3·0
UK	2·5	2·6	1·9	1·9
Hungary	6·1	5·9	5·4	5·5
Italy	—	5·4	—	4·5

Sources: The source as in Table 1.3, pp. 48, 75–7 and 206–9 respectively. Quoted in [*31*, p. 277].

ment and stock increases in national income' [*31*, p. 278]. For example, for the period 1956–64, Polish statistics admit that consumption *per capita* was growing quicker in a number of European capitalist countries, such as West Germany, Italy, and Austria. Comparisons concerning *real wages*, where the record is very much worse (Table 1.10), are conspicuously absent. The Polish (and Czechoslovak) performance was particularly disappointing here. As a result, the gap in living standards is being closed only slowly, or even growing in some cases. On the other hand, the demonstration effects are in inverse relation to the ease of access of information, which increased in all socialist countries after Stalin's death. Under these conditions, the 'consumption gap' (particularly severe in the case of the socialist intelligentsia, whose real income in Poland in 1960 was still 25 per cent *lower* than in 1937 (Table 1.11)) could be exploited ideologically quite easily by Western propaganda. During the Malenkov era, the reduction of the gap between the living standards of communist and capitalist countries was briefly pronounced as one of the major tasks facing the government and the party

Table 1.10: Percentage Increases of Consumption and Real Wages In Polish Mid-Term Plans

	1947–9		1950–5		1956–60		1961–5		1966–70	
	Plan	Actual	Plan	Actual	Plan	Actual	Plan	Actual	Plan	Actual[c]
Personal consumption per capita	15[a]	30	50–60	35	30	24	22·5	18	18	—
Real wages	—	58[b]	40	4	30	29	22·5	8	10	—
Consumption of rural population	—	—	—	30	—	27	—	12	—	—

[a] 1938 = 100.
[b] 1946 = 100, op. cit., p. 32.
[c] No official data on 1966–70 plan fulfilment are available at present (March 1972). There are, however, numerous indications that both targets are drastically underfulfilled.[1]

Source: K. Ryc, *Spozycie a wzrost gospodarczy Polski* (The Consumption and Economic Growth of Poland), Warsaw, 1968, pp. 17, 25, 233, 234, 316.

Table 1.11: Index of Real Incomes of Polish Workers and Salaried Employees Outside Agriculture in 1960 (1937 = 100)

	Workers	Salaried Employees
Per employee	145	74
Per employee outside industry	129	

Source: M. Kalecki, *Z zagadnien gospodarczo-spolecznych Polski Ludowej* (On the Economic and Social Problems of People's Poland), Warsaw, 1964, p. 97.

[*21, 22*]. The military, and later space, economic requirements did not, however, allow such a drastic change of priorities as this statement implied and its author—and his most ardent follower Imre Nagy of Hungary (during his *first* premiership)—were soon ousted from power. But the problem remained and undoubtedly is an important factor behind efforts to improve the economic efficiency of East European economies.

Obviously political leaders of East European countries viewed the unsatisfactory performance of their economies with growing uneasiness, as they began to grasp more and more clearly the international and domestic implications. Before remedies could be suggested, however, the diagnosis had to be formulated, and to this problem we must now turn our attention.

[1] The full extent of this underfulfilment may not be known to us for quite a while. For example, official statistics claim that, during the 1950–5 plan, real wages increased by 27 per cent, and only from the mid 1960s was this figure allowed to be challenged in print (see *16*, p. 327 and *31*, pp. 104–19). See, however, our discussion in 2.1.1.

1.2 The Reasons for Failure

1.2.1 THE OFFICIAL EXPLANATION

When it became politically possible to admit that East European economic performance left something to be desired, the diagnosis was quickly formulated. From East Berlin to Bucharest, from Sofia to Prague, the existing mechanism of planning and management was singled out as the main cause of East European poor economic performance, and in almost identical terms: 'The existing system [of planning and management] became contradictory to the level of development of productive forces and productive relations' . . . said Todor Zivkov, 1st Secretary of Bulgarian Communist Party . . . 'This system no longer assures the necessary conditions for speedy technical progress, fuller development of workers' initiative and for managing the national economy on a completely scientific basis' [39, pp. 426–7].

'The contradiction emerged between the existing system of management of national economy and objective conditions,' writes the Hungarian economist György Varga. 'It hampers the rate of economic growth and the raising of the level of living standards' [37, pp. 335–6]. In Czechoslovakia, the diagnosis is exactly the same: 'With the increase of economic potential the society's needs have changed, and the existing system [of planning and management] ceased to conform to new requirements of economic development . . .' [15, pp. 163–4]. Similar quotations could be easily produced from other East European countries. The present official Polish position also limits the reasons for the continuing need of economic reforms to deficiencies of the existing management mechanism. It is interesting to notice, however, that during the first stage of Polish economic reforms in 1956–8, which was accompanied by substantial political liberalization, the reasons for the disappointing economic results of the 6-year plan were not confined to the management mechanism, but included at least four other elements of economic policy, namely: general growth strategy, planning process, agrarian policy, and policy towards small private business and artisans. Let us outline these problems very briefly.

1.2.2 THE COMPREHENSIVE PICTURE[1]

A *Growth Strategy*

The characteristic feature of Polish 6-year plan growth strategy was

---

[1] There is abundant evidence to document this section. Owing to the far-reaching liberalization following directly after the Polish October of 1956, the 6-year plan is the best documented and most thoroughly analysed period of Polish post-war economic history. This evidence is, however, so well known and uncontroversial that almost no direct support data or quotations are given in the text because of space limitation, but they can be easily found in the following publications: [5; 11; 24; and 33 passim; 27, pp. 437–848].

its lack of balance between investment and consumption, between Sector I (producing means of production) and Sector II (producing consumer goods), and among the different branches of the economy.

Generally speaking, the Polish 6-year plan was too taut. It assumed a too high rate of growth and favoured not only investment at the expense of consumption but also investment in heavy industry at the expense of investment in consumer goods industry.

As a result, there occurred: a drop in real wages and peasant income with accompanying disincentive effects; severe shortages of consumer goods and agricultural investment goods; decapitalization of the consumer goods industry; and a number of disequilibria within the priority heavy-industry sector and the economy as a whole.

All these were the result not only of planning mistakes and deficient planning techniques unable to cope with the consistency problem, but also of too ambitious, unrealizable plan targets.

B *The Planning Process*

The planning process is considered here as a technical tool for translating planning objectives formulated by growth strategy into an internally consistent programme.

The quality of planning depends on four main factors: scope of central planning; quality of information; available planning techniques (their ability to solve problems of consistency and optimality); planning objectives given and the ability of the planning apparatus to formulate alternative objectives for policy makers to consider.

The practical consequences of any initial planning mistakes depend on two factors. The first is the ability of the CPB[1] to notice and correct quickly and effectively the developing disequilibria; this ability depends on: (a) quality and speed of existing informational feedbacks; and (b) sufficient reserves within the socialist sector (including reserves in capacities and foreign exchange). Secondly, to rectify mistakes effectively the national economy should also be able to make spontaneous responses to disequilibria, changing supply–demand conditions (spontaneous = outside central planning framework). In a planned economy these can take the form of: (a) decentralized responses of socialist enterprises and/or industrial associations—for these to take place three conditions have to exist: authority to act; incentive to act; means to act—and (b) existence of non-socialist economic sectors, having the means to act (authority and incentives are assumed here to exist by definition).

Leaving aside the problem of planning objectives (mentioned briefly under growth strategy), we have to realize that most conditions of effective planning did not exist in the pre-1956 period. The scope of central planning was too broad, encompassing a large number of details which could not be handled properly at the CPB level. The

[1] See Appendix 1.1 (pp. 27–9) for a brief discussion of the CPB and related concepts.

mechanism of plan implementation was distorting the information flow from enterprise to CPB and—for a number of reasons—informational feed-backs were too slow. There were insufficient economic stabilizers: because of (a) too taut economic plan, inadequate reserves; (b) very limited enterprise authority sphere (see 4.10.); incentives tied to plan targets; extensive rationing of means of production; (c) practically speaking, non-socialist economic sectors did not exist (outside agriculture). Existing planning techniques were much too crude to be able to cope effectively with the immensely complex consistency problem, not to mention optimality.

C *Agrarian Policy*

The importance of agriculture during the period under discussion can be seen from the following figures: the share of agriculture in national income produced (in 1961 prices) was 28 per cent in 1955 and 1956, 19 per cent in 1965, and 13 per cent in 1969 [*30*, p. 76]. The collectivization of Polish agriculture never went beyond the very initial stages. At its peak in 1955 the share of collective farms in total agricultural output was 8 per cent, and the share of individual farmers over 81 per cent (the rest was produced by state farms) [*28*, p. 123]. Nevertheless, the agrarian policy of pre-1956 was one of the main reasons for the economic difficulties of this period.[1]

The main characteristic features of pre-1956 Polish agrarian policy were the following: (a) the collectivization drive; political and economic pressure to join collective farms; campaigns against 'kulaks' (bigger peasants employing hired labour), with inevitable disincentive effects not only for 'kulaks' themselves but also for the majority of peasantry enjoying middle incomes; (b) compulsory deliveries of main agricultural products (grain, meat, potatoes, milk) at low, state-fixed prices; during the pre-1956 period compulsory deliveries comprised a big share of peasants' marketable output; (c) insufficient supply of means of production for agriculture.

As a result there was a lack of incentives for peasants to develop production; a low rate of growth of agricultural output; decapitalization of fixed assets in agriculture; a weak, if any, response to market demand.

D *Policy towards Non-Socialist Economic Sectors (outside agriculture)*

One of the characteristic features of pre-1956 economic policy was a determined effort to eliminate all non-socialist economic sectors.

---

[1] We may note that the first important change in agrarian policy occurred in 1954/5 when the absolute level of compulsory deliveries per hectare was fixed and declared constant, irrespective of actual yield achieved. The incentive effect of this important policy change could not occur fully, however, because of the peasants' fear of compulsory collectivization.

After initial reforms of nationalization, the non-socialist economic sectors (outside agriculture) consisted of four types of economic activities: (a) private manufacturing and building enterprises employing up to fifty people; (b) private retail and wholesale enterprises; (c) private service sector: restaurants, barber shops, laundries, etc.; (d) all kinds of artisans.

In spite of Karl Marx's teaching that a precondition of successful nationalization is a high level of concentration of economic activity, during the first three years of the 6-year plan practically all forms of small private business enterprises were nationalized or taken over by so-called 'labour cooperatives', and even the artisan sector—quite important in less developed East European countries, including Poland —was severely curtailed by excessive taxation, licence revocation, cutting raw material supplies, etc.

The consequences of this policy were fourfold. First, there was no economic sector left which could respond directly to market demand. As a result, if central planners forgot to put into their plans pickled cucumbers, there were no pickled cucumbers on the market until the next season.[1] Second, the quantity and quality of consumers' goods and services markedly diminished as the 'carrying over' of these activities by the socialist sector could not be done smoothly and without considerable time lags. Third, the socialist sector was burdened with a number of economic activities that it could not handle profitably and effectively, which diminished the overall efficiency of the socialist sector directly and indirectly (by diverting effort and managerial personnel to marginal economic activities). Four, it was responsible for creation of pockets of local unemployment, especially in small towns and settlements [11, p. 118].

Generally speaking, experience shows that the possibilities for improving these different aspects of economic policy, which together were responsible for the disappointing results of the pre-reform period, vary greatly. The easiest is the re-establishment of the small private business and artisan sector, where the main problem is to remove the barriers imposed on non-socialist sectors and to allow the 'natural' market forces to operate. The most difficult is the improvement of the planning and management of the socialized sector, where a completely new *positive* policy of immense complexity must be formulated. In practice, reforms in any of these fields suffer frequently from inconsistencies and reversions to old, administrative practices, and/or the planners' excessive propensity to invest, regardless of absorptive capacities of their economies.

[1] This was an actual example given by Bronislaw Minc, then a high official at the Polish State Planning Commission (headed by his cousin Hilary Minc), in one of his post-1956 speeches. From then on, for a number of years pickled cucumbers became in Poland a symbol of over-centralized planning.

It may be politically convenient to limit the criticism of past (and present) economic policies to the management mechanism aspects only, but this implies that other causes, which in the past contributed to unsatisfactory economic performance, have been successfully eliminated. Unfortunately, this is not the case either in Poland or in other East European countries. In respect to Poland, we shall try to prove this thesis in our subsequent discussion.

1.3 Brief Periodization of Polish Economic Reforms

1.3.1 THE SCOPE OF FURTHER INQUIRY

Reforms, which started in 1956, included all five areas of economic policy discussed in previous sections. It would be impossible, however, to give here even the briefest outline of the steps undertaken on all these fronts, and to record the results achieved and the problems waiting for solution. As stated in the Introduction we shall concentrate on reforms in the socialist industrial sector only. These problems turned out to be the most intricate of all and their importance is witnessed by the share of industrial production in national income—50·6 per cent in 1965 and 56 per cent in 1970 (plan) [*31*, p. 213]. At the same time, Polish New Agrarian Policy is relatively well known [see e.g. *1, 10, 14, 34*] and the same is probably true about results achieved in re-establishing non-socialist economic activities in the many spheres of small business where the state form of ownership and/or management is not justified economically. The latter suffered substantial setbacks after the March 1968 events, but new Party leadership under E. Gierek is already trying to repair some of the damage done to private and artisan sectors during 1968–70.

1.3.2 PERIODIZATION OF POLISH ECONOMIC REFORMS

The history of Polish economic reforms is over fifteen years old already. Five periods—partially overlapping, whose terminal dates are sometimes difficult to ascertain precisely—can be distinguished here:

1956–8–9: the beginning of reforms; this period we shall label 'towards a grand design';

1959–64–5: intermediate period; it is stressed in the Polish literature that much has been done during these years in the sphere of economic reforms; it is true that a list of concrete steps undertaken would be quite substantial; we must remember, however, that these steps did not remove the basic principles of the traditional economic system and that during this period much of the initial impetus of reforms was dissipated and some reversions to old methods of planning and management occurred; if we forget these, then the need for the third stage cannot be understood;

1965–8: the start of the new wave of reforms; this period we shall call 'the period of gradual improvements';

1968–70: an abortive effort to reform; this period started with the Vth Congress of PUWP (November 1968) calling for 'a comprehensive and internally consistent system of planning and management'. It produced—as a result of numerous CC meetings and the flood of legislation which followed—an inconsistent, sketchy, and anti-consumer programme to be introduced from 1 January 1971 and which collapsed, together with the Gomulka leadership, after workers' protests in December 1970–April 1971. We shall call it 'abortive reform';

from 1971 on: the promise to reform; immediately after scrapping Gomulka's last reform blueprint, the new leadership officially announced that a new programme of 'improving and modernizing the system of planning and management' would be elaborated. As a study of the resolutions of the VIth Congress of PUWP (December 1971) reveals—the nine months' work of numerous subcommittees and working groups did not produce anything which could be called even a draft programme. The forthcoming period must therefore be called 'the uncertain future'.

Let me stress again that the above, tentative, periodization deals with Polish economic reforms within the socialist sector only. It does not necessarily apply to other spheres which were embraced by the reforms; particularly, it does not apply to the New Agrarian Policy.

A *Towards a Grand Design*

(1) Some characteristic features of this period are: the existence of an overall, master plan for reforms, however sketchy, incomplete, and imperfect; the belief that the transition to a New Economic System is possible within a relatively short period of three to four years; the far-reaching character of the reforms envisaged. However, it found Polish economists ill-prepared theoretically and with no practical experience of implementing reforms.

The general character of reforms proposed in this period was decidedly of the 'guided market model' or market-parametric type (see 4.9–4.11). It is worthwhile to notice that—in accord with this type of reform—the basic unit of plan executants was to be a relatively autonomous socialist *enterprise*. The creation of industrial associations at the end of 1958 may be considered as a first step—at this time disguised by misrepresentation of its true role—towards changing the reforms' character into the state-parametric type (see Chs. 3 and 4).

(2) Some economic and social factors slowing down the reform policy are:

the return of many pre-1956 leaders to prominent Party and Government posts;

the tendency of economic administration to do things 'the old way';
the lack of economic instruments to be used instead of administrative
orders;

inflationary pressure; this has been used as a main reason for tighten-
ing administrative controls again,[1] but is only partially convincing. In
1957 the NNP increased 10·7 per cent in constant prices (see Table 1.2).
At the same time, price increases were nowhere near danger point, e.g.,
prices of consumers' goods and services rose 5·2 per cent and of food
only 2·7 per cent [27, p. 821]. Moreover, a number of price changes
were not due to inflationary pressure but represented an attempt to use
price policy for influencing the consumption structure [27, p. 818]. The
movement of prices was also not uniformly upward. Prices of many
articles of mass consumption, such as flour, meat, and poultry, clothing,
shoes, and leather goods, etc., were actually slightly lower than in 1956
[27, p. 817];

the disequilibrating consequences of some of the instituted reforms;
here the most crucial resulted from broadening enterprises' authority
(see 4.10) without appropriate changes either in their 'rules of the game'
or in relative prices. These brought to light the disparity between supply
and demand in the producer goods sector and serious shortages and
stockpiling began to occur here also;

the stepping up of the rate of growth in 1959 and then in the 1961–5
plan.

B *The Intermediate Period*

Characteristic features are, in the first phase: slowing down the
reforms' policy both on theoretical and applied fronts; persistence of
numerous features of pre-1956 methods of planning and management;
gradual reversion to a number of old economic policies and instruments;
elimination of numerous secondary features of traditional economic
system or—in other words—reintroduction of those dozens of features
of market economy (from trade marks to after-season sales) which have
been wiped out during the first 'Sturm und Drang' Period. In the second
phase features are: growing manifestations that a number of old problems troubling the functioning of socialist sector persist in spite of all
the steps undertaken thus far; growing realization that there is a need
to remedy them by further changes in the management mechanism.

C *The Period of Gradual Improvements*

(1) The new wave of reforms was initiated by the IVth Congress of
PUWP in June 1964 and particularly by the IVth Plenary Meeting of
the CC of PUWP in July 1965 [13, passim].

---

[1] 'The deflationary measures necessary for avoiding the danger of inflation required that many intended economic changes, e.g. in the sphere of economic
mechanism, had to be curtailed or postponed' [27, p. 442.]

(2) The characteristic features of the new period are: (a) widespread belief that 'the solution of all these complex problems [of economic reforms] is not possible on the basis of a single theoretical approach' [25, p. 13]; (b) stress on partial remedies (however large these parts may be); (c) stress on improvements as a continuous process; not a relatively brief period of overhauling the system, but a long, gradual process of partial improvements; (d) stress on testing the principles of proposed changes on a limited scale by economic experimenting (this feature was already pronounced during the intermediate period).

(3) The aim of the reforms was the removal of long persisting, negative features of the pre-1956 mechanism of plan implementation and planning methods, which did survive—in one form or another, on the national economy or branch scale—after the first waves of reforms. More particularly, reforms were aimed at improving: (a) the systems of success indicators (see Ch. 5) and managerial incentives (see Ch. 6); (b) the methods of planning the volume and changes of the enterprise wage fund (see Ch. 6); (c) the financial system of enterprises and industrial associations (see Ch. 7); (d) the scope of enterprise authority (see 3.2 and 4.10); (e) the role of industrial associations (see Ch. 8); (f) lengthening to two years the time horizon of operational plans (see Ch. 2), etc.

(4) Most of these problems were on the agenda of the 1956–64 period but were not implemented successfully enough.

D Abortive Reform

(1) The March 1968 events (see Glossary), and the political turmoil which followed, did not seem—at the beginning—to have any lasting effects on the economic policies outlined above. The resolution of the Vth Congress of PUWP of November 1968 [36, pp. 15–22] did not depart in essence from the spirit and character of the 1966–7 reforms in spite of the fact that the congress found it necessary to propose many changes in concrete, partial solutions. It is true that the Vth Congress called for 'a comprehensive and *internally consistent* system of planning and management' [36, p. 16, italics added]. This, formally speaking, was in contrast with the eclectic approach thus far advocated by Party spokesmen [see section C above]. As this idea, however, was neither particularly stressed nor substantiated by the congress programme, no one, as far as I know, considered it as anything more than a new addition to Party slogans. Moreover, as it is always the case with such resolutions, it was impossible to predict how far-reaching are the changes in the offing, when they will begin, and what their actual character will be.

(2) In fact the reform evolved and collapsed within almost exactly two years. It started with the resolution of the IInd (April 1969) Plenary Meeting of the CC of PUWP [32], devoted to the problems of

new methods of constructing mid-term plans (see Ch. 2) and to problems of investment policy and ways and methods of increasing the
effectiveness of investment, and was followed by:

new principles for financing Research and Development (R and D)
(IVth CC Plenum, November 1969 [7]);
the draft of CM decree on new financial system of industry
(December 1969, see Ch. 7, ref. 40);
radical reform of the existing incentive system (Vth CC Plenum of
May 1970 [6]);
extensive reform of transfer price system for domestic goods to be
introduced by stages, starting 1 January 1971 [see 12];
reform of transfer prices for imported and exported goods consisting
of introducing so-called 'transaction prices' (ceny tranzakcyjne), defined
as a price paid or received in foreign currency multiplied by the
rate of exchange differentiated by three groups of countries: socialist,
capitalist, and developing [see 12];
final version of the new financial system of centrally planned industry
(November 1970, see Ch. 7, ref. 19);
reform of retail prices (13 December 1970) of which the main aspect
was the steep rise of foodstuff prices (on average +8 per cent [see 38,
p. 15]);
the beginning of unrest of Polish workers in coastal towns of Gdansk
(14 December 1970), Gdynia, and Szczecin;
downfall of Gomulka and his closest associates; E. Gierek becomes
First Secretary of PUWP (VIIth CC Plenum, 20 December 1970);
withdrawal of the 'new incentive system' (January 1971);
promise of a food price-freeze for the next two years, i.e. 1971–2
(January 1971);
abolition of the December 1970 retail price increases and the return
as from 1 March 1971 to the pre-December price level (15 February
1972);
change in the 'new financial system' to take into account the reversal
to the pre-1970 incentive system (February 1971, see [3] and Ch. 6);
severance of the connection between the foreign trade results calculated in transaction prices and the awards (bonuses) for the management and workers; for the purpose of the latter the sellers prices (ceny
fabryczne) are again used [see 3].

(3) The detailed analysis of the abortive reform 1969–70 in all its
dimensions—political, social, economic, and international—requires
separate study.[1] Its basic features, however, are already quite evident

---

[1] It so happened that at the time this book was being written the new reform's
blueprint was being elaborated in Poland (see above). My original intention was to
present extensive analysis of these systemic changes. As Gomulka's last reform
proved abortive and the new reforms are already being elaborated (see 1.3.2E)

and documented by voluminous critical literature published in Poland after the December 1970 events (see the basic Polish socio-economic periodicals for 1971 and—to a lesser extent—also for 1972).

The main feature of the 1969–70 reform blueprint was its deflationary and anti-consumer character. Moreover, this was also characteristic of the economic policies of this period.

Efforts to reduce the level of consumption were very extensive and included the reduction of nominal and real wages during the years 1969–70. Its purpose was twofold. First to ease existing inflationary pressure which—by the way—was not the result of rises in money wages but of the substantial underfulfilment of the planned output of consumers' goods and services (see 2.1.1). Secondly, the new incentive system, which was to be introduced on 1 January 1971, related, in percentage form, all potential pay increases for 1971–5 to the actual level of enterprise wage/bonus funds in 1970. To depress the so-called 'basis of comparison' (see 6.2.1) of pay increases for 1971–5 to the lowest possible level, Polish enterprises were subjected during late 1969 and particularly during 1970 to continuous and ruthless pressure and scrutiny to reveal all wage fund 'reserves'. This effort was so successful that according to numerous Polish articles published after the December 1970 events, it would take most enterprises about two years to achieve any increase in nominal wages above the 1969 level.

At the same time employment expansion was slowed down or halted by dismissing redundant workers, by forbidding the filling of existing vacancies, and even by stopping planned increases of employment, particularly in the social service sector, such as public health; housing expenditure was severely cut which resulted not only in failure to fulfil the FYP overall housing construction target but it also diminished the scope of necessary preparations for maintaining and expanding the housing programme in the next FYP. Substantial cuts occurred also in municipal, social, and public health spending, including investment expenditures. Moreover, the same tendency was also evident in the already approved FYP for 1971–5.

(4) The changes in *planning* methods were announced first (April 1969) and an effort was made to rely on them already in preparing the 1971–5 FYP (see Ch. 2). The changes in management mechanism were elaborated during the whole period 1969–70, with the latest change, concerning the new financial system of centrally planned industry, enacted on 9 November 1970, i.e. less than two months before coming into force [*sic*]. As a whole, these changes—from the point of view of

---

extensive coverage of the former is no longer necessary, particularly since as a whole it lacked originality (but not complexity, e.g. new investment regulations consist of over 84,000 words, new incentive regulations of over 55,000 words, etc.). The reader will find, however, that the 1969–70 regulations are taken briefly into account throughout the book.

their economic rationality—represented only a limited and half-hearted attempt to eliminate numerous defects of existing economic working arrangements. In this sense the changes were of the same *type* as the reform of 1966–7 and could bring only marginal—if any—improvements in the functioning of the Polish economy. The reasons why this *type* of reform is unlikely to be successful are discussed throughout this book and summarized in Ch. 9.

If the abortive reform blueprint of 1969–70 is worth study at all, it is decidedly for its *negative* features. One can say that the typical mistakes of all Polish reform efforts since the abandonment of 'The Grand Design' of 1957–8, were in this reform magnified to an extent which most certainly will make it a classic example of how *not* to reform.

Let me indicate briefly what I consider as basic mistakes of the 1969–70 reforms.

(i) *Unstable political situation.* The political precondition of successful economic reform is effective consolidation of power in the hands of *one* faction of the ruling communist party, i.e. thorough defeat of all opposing factions. This was achieved in Hungary, before Kadar started his extensive reforms, but was not the case either in Czechoslovakia in 1968 or in Poland in 1968–70. In Poland the takeover bid of the Moczar faction (March–November 1968) was successfully resisted at the Vth Congress of PUWP, but the faction itself was definitely not defeated.

The need of political consolidation for successful economic reform is twofold: firstly, it is a precondition for drawing a consistent reform blueprint. Without political consolidation reform proposals are, as a rule, lacking in both unity and clarity of purpose. Moreover, political compromises over the construction of the economic mechanism and/or its component parts usually result in grossly inconsistent solutions being adopted. They may be politically palatable to all factions concerned, but they do not work (see Ch. 9). The latest Polish reform blueprint was not an exception to this rule. It was both half-hearted in overall design and internally contradictory, in spite of the fact that consistency was a goal specifically proclaimed at the Vth Congress of PUWP.

The reform blueprint was moreover evolving in what seems to be a most haphazard manner. Not only was there no 'master plan' of the new system (see 9.2.2) but one had the impression that the very idea of comprehensive reform was born as a *result* of partial changes. This seems to be the only explanation of the illogical sequence of reform measures undertaken (investment—April 1969; draft of new financial system of industry—December 1969; incentive system—May 1970; final version of new financial system—November 1970) and total lack of coordination *between* them. It is more than obvious, for example, that the authors of the new financial system—and needless to say the participants of the debate about it—had no idea whatsoever that the existing incentive system (last reformed as late as 1966) was soon to be changed and replaced by a completely new one. As a result, the proposed new financial system became largely irrelevant even in the course of its being debated, and had to be elaborated all over again (this time, however, without a public debate).

Secondly, it would be naïve to expect that even the best designed economic reform could be implemented without serious problems arising. To overcome successfully the difficulties inevitably accompanying economic reform, there is a need for a special determination and sense of purpose on the part of party and government and at least a measure of popular support. For all these to achieve a really *united* leadership is a *conditio sine qua non*. Economic reform and intense intra-party struggle are simply incompatible and—for a wise leadership—too risky even to try. Gomulka embarked on economic reform ignoring the above truths.

(ii) *Strained economic conditions.* 'Never start changing an economic mechanism when in a difficult economic situation' should be a motto of all reformers. A rather obvious maxim and well understood by Hungarians [see *8*, pp. 11–39 and *passim*] and Bulgarians [see *19*, pp. 419–87]. The change of economic working arrangements (which cannot stop *working* when undergoing the overhaul) has numerous ill effects: the pace of growth may slow down temporarily, input–output relations may be disturbed, managers and workers put under extra stress, all the reform's opponents alerted and ready to exploit any sign of failure. Surely economic reform should not be either preceded or immediately followed by an extra squeeze of consumers. The first, however, was exactly what Gomulka's leadership did. Moreover, not only should reforms not be started under adverse economic conditions, but extra economic reserves in consumer goods, raw materials, components, and convertible foreign currencies should be built up beforehand to mitigate any difficulties which may (and will) arise during reform implementation. This was totally ignored also.

History has already provided the answer as to what the penalty is for disregarding political and economic constraints. Let us hope that before long historians will tell us *why* these constraints were disregarded. Pointing to simple ignorance rarely makes a convincing explanation. In our particular case—with Hungarians and Bulgarians quite aware of the constraints mentioned—the answer must go much further than Gomulka's and/or his close associates' personality traits.

E *The Uncertain Future*

One of the first steps of the new leadership headed by E. Gierek was the formation of two Party-Government Committees—one 'On the State of Education in Poland' chaired by Professor J. Szczepanski, Director of the Institute of Philosophy and Sociology of the Polish Academy of Science (PAN) and another 'On the Modernization of the

System of the Functioning of the Economy and the State' under the chairmanship of J. Szydlak, a Politbureau member and CC secretary.

In contrast to Professor Szczepanski's committee, almost nothing was published on the Szydlak committee, but with the help of various sources the following picture of its economic branch emerges. The committee consists of the five members' Presidium and the following economic subcommittees: (1) on wages, (2) on organization of industry, (3) on management mechanism and planning, (4) on finance, prices, and foreign trade, and (5) on material supplies system and wholesale and retail trade. Each subcommittee can create any number of groups of experts for consideration of problems which require particular scrutiny and is entitled to ask any government office to submit data and/or answer questions.

The disquieting aspect of the functioning of the economic branch of Szydlak's committee is a lack of proper terms of reference. The terms of reference they received—'the maintenance of the principles of central planning and socialism'—are so broad as to allow almost any interpretation. With members of the Presidium and chairmen of different subcommittees having quite divergent views,[1] the danger of lack of agreement on basic principles of economic reform and of lack of co-ordination between proposals put forward by individual subcommittees is very great indeed. This seems to be confirmed by the resolution of the VIth Congress of PUWP (December 1971).

The relevant section of the resolution entitled 'Improvement and Modernization of the Management System' is only three pages long (as compared with five pages devoted to the same subject in the resolution of the Vth Congress of PUWP) and its content gives rise to serious anxiety.

First of all it reveals complete lack of understanding of the need for a systematic approach to economic reform. There is no indication what are: (1) the basic assumptions of reforms, e.g. will the principle of yearly plan targets for enterprises be retained or not,[2] (2) how the internal

[1] The members of the Presidium are: J. Szydlak (Chairman); S. Kuzinski, Head of CC Department of Light Industry and Construction; K. Olszewski, CC member; J. Pajestka, CC member and Deputy Chairman of Planning Commission; F. Szlachcic, member of Politbureau and KC Secretary (the latter responsibility lies primarily in overseeing the subcommittees dealing with the reform of party and government). The secretary of the Presidium is J. Goscinski from the Main Centre for Improving Management Personnel (CODKK), Warsaw. The chairmen of sub-committees are: 1. A. Rajkiewicz, 2. A. Zaleski, 3. K. Porwit, 4. F. Siemiatkowski, 5. (?) Wojciechowski. My statement that the above have different views on economic matters is based on knowledge of published views of six and personal acquaintance with four of the above eleven persons.

[2] According to the unanimous opinion of about a dozen eminent Polish economists who were asked this question during 1971 and the spring of 1972, the principle of yearly plan targets for enterprises will be *retained* in the new, Gierek-sponsored, economic reform.

consistency of the economic reform blueprint is to be achieved, (3) how economic reform is to be implemented so as to minimize the cost of change, (4) what are the final goals of the reform, (5) how long a transition period is envisaged, and (6) what is the sequence of reform implementation (see Ch. 9 on all these problems). Moreover, what *is* in the resolution shows total confusion and inability to draw a proper lesson from past experience. To illustrate: 'Improvement of the system of functioning of the economy . . . should have a comprehensive character, in contrast to previously undertaken changes' [*26*, p. 159] but the section concludes: '. . . partial changes and improvements will gradually grow into comprehensive changes, which will make faster economic and social progress possible' [*26*, p. 161]. As we are trying to show throughout the book, this belief is in complete contradiction to Polish reform experience of the last fifteen years.

Secondly, the improvements proposed are of a very general and traditional character: (1) improvement of long-term (perspective) planning, (2) the FYP should be the main instrument of economic policy, (3) yearly plans should have a less bureaucratic character, etc. These postulates have been expressed in the past hundreds of times and it is difficult to see how repeating them once more can help in any way. There is, unfortunately, no explicit or implicit indication of *how* the new leadership is going to implement these changes, which all its predecessors failed to do.

Thirdly, the resolution states that 'For detailed elaboration of the general principles put forward by the Party–Government committee for solving problems in organizational, technical, economic, and social spheres and for the purpose of establishing standard solutions [*wzorce*] which later on could be applied to similar [economic] units—the government should start to implement partial solutions in 1972 in selected economic organizations' [*26*, p. 161].

If, as the result of nine months' work, Szydlak's committee was able to produce only the 'general principles' of the type indicated in the VIth Congress's resolution, the future of Polish economic reforms is not only uncertain, but grim.

1.4 Was the Traditional Economic System Beneficial at the First Stage of Industrialization?

Before we turn our attention to the detailed examination of Polish economic reforms, let us devote a few more pages to the traditional system.

East European critics of the traditional mechanism of planning and management maintain vigorously that the traditional system was, nevertheless, both necessary and beneficial at the first, initial stage of socialist industrialization and, accompanying it, social and economic transformation: 'The previous management system . . . conformed to objective needs of a certain stage of socio-economic and political development of the country'—maintains Todor Zivkov [*39*, p. 425]. '[Traditional] system of management . . . was in accord with then existing requirements and helped to achieve tasks which our State was facing,' writes Gy. Varga [*37*, p. 330]. The same was supposedly true in Czechoslovakia ('This type of management system conformed to the concrete situation of this period . . .' [*15*, p. 163]), in Poland (the traditional management mechanism 'was in a certain development phase efficient and effective' [*25*, p. 19]), and in other East European countries. But was it?

It seems that Oskar Lange was the first to argue the *necessity* of the traditional economic system. In his Belgrade lectures in November 1957, he maintained that 'the process of rapid industrialization requires such centralized disposal of resources for two reasons. First, it is necessary to concentrate all resources on certain objectives and avoid dissipation of resources on other objectives which would divert resources from the purpose of rapid industrialization . . . The second reason . . . is the lack and weakness of industrial cadres' [*18*, p. 101].

It is interesting to notice that Lange's thesis that the traditional system was 'necessary' was extended to make it also 'helpful' or even 'efficient and effective'. It may also be noted that while Lange's analysis puts the main stress on the fact that the conditions which made the traditional system necessary no longer exist, present defenders of the traditional system merely try to provide *ex post facto* justification of previous policies.

The original Lange thesis has been meanwhile generalized into the 'theory' of extensive and intensive stages of development and management mechanisms appropriate for them. It is argued that at the extensive stage, characterized by a very substantial increase of employment and capital investments, the centralized, administrative system of planning is both necessary and beneficial. Only at the intensive stage, when rational allocation and better utilization of existing resources become crucial, does the change to a more decentralized management mechanism, based on economic instruments rather than administrative orders, become—according to this theory—economically justified. The only proof, however, of this theory is the 'socio-economic achievements' of the Stalinist period [*25*, p. 9] and the disappointing results which the same system produced at a later stage. These arguments seem totally unconvincing.

First of all, the indisputable fact that the economic results of the traditional economic system were diminishing over time is no proof that the system was either adequate or necessary during the first period of its functioning. There are a number of reasons why the effectiveness of the traditional Soviet-type system diminished. Ever-growing complexity of the economy, the multiplication of priorities, and absorption of surplus labour are the most important ones among those listed by Professor Alec Nove [23, pp. 150–2]. The diminishing effectiveness of the traditional economic system cannot, however, logically be used to argue its initial effectiveness. Moreover, empirical evidence indicates a completely opposite thesis, namely, that during the initial period of the Stalinist economic policy in the early 1950s, substantial economic progress was achieved in spite (*not* because) of the existing management mechanism. The best proof of this is the tremendous waste which characterized this period of economic development not only in Poland but in all East European countries.

The high rate of growth in spite of all this waste is easily explained. With average investment during the 6-year plan maintained at one-third of national income (32·6 per cent to be exact [4, p. 47]), with an average yearly increase of employment at 9·2 per cent (during the 6-year plan, total employment increased from 4·4 million to 6·8 million persons i.e. 56 per cent [29, p. 44]), and with average annual real wage increases kept at 0·66 per cent, one can achieve a high rate of growth in spite of considerable waste.

Another point is also worth stressing. The high rate of growth produced by the traditional economic system should be put in proper perspective. Official statistics like to use pre-war Poland or the slow-growing Western countries, like the UK or USA, as a basis for comparisons. But the Polish rate of investment during the 6-year plan was over three times higher than in pre-war Poland and over two times higher than in Great Britain or the United States. Even if compared to the European Economic Community as a whole—the growth advantage is drastically reduced (see Table 1.3). Japan and West Germany—without the traditional economic system and its accompanying hardships—enjoyed much higher rates of growth *per capita* than Poland over the whole period 1950–65 (8·5, 6·1, and 5·4 [31, p. 266]). Only if seen in the light of the excessive rate of investment does the true picture emerge, namely of growth at all costs, with—as many Polish economists suspect— *negative* marginal efficiency of investment.

Secondly, there is no proof that the traditional economic system was necessary for *effective implementation of planners' preferences*—the other argument most frequently used. Some Western scholars argue that the traditional economic system was the *only one* capable of enforcing planners' preferences, and hence its built-in inefficiency was a necessary price for achieving what the planners wanted. In effect—they maintain—one cannot effectively criticize the traditional economic system, given the existing shape of the planners' preference function. This reasoning again does not meet the test of empirical evidence. (a) There is nothing further from the truth than the conviction that the centralized system is effective in implementing planners' preferences,

even in key sectors. The data on Polish 6-year plan fulfilment provide
ample illustration of this thesis. Even at the level of highest priority
individual *projects*—obviously easier to implement than sectoral targets—the traditional economic system shows an appalling record.
During the 6-year plan there was no project of higher priority than the
'Nowa Huta' steel mill. Nevertheless, as we have already pointed out,
it reached only 42 per cent of planned capacity on time. Such high
priority sectors as electric generating reached only 56 per cent of plan
target [*11*, p. 79], production of cement 74 per cent, of bricks 68 per cent
[*11*, pp. 164, 165], and such examples abound [*11*, *passim*].

(b) The need for reforms is a further proof that the traditional
economic system did not serve planners' preferences well.[1] One can go
even further and argue that even the present system—which is already
free from a number of excesses of the traditional economic system—is
still too centralized for effective implementation of planners' *economic*
preferences.[2] There are at least three indications of this: (1) continuing
wide divergences between planning objectives and performance;
(2) economic reforms in progress which demand—at least verbally—
more radical departures from the traditional economic system; (3) the
experience of the first years of the Hungarian 'guided market' model,
which with *indicative* planning only, achieved a better plan/performance
ratio than under the previous system.

(c) One is entitled to ask if these features of the traditional economic
system which made it possible to try to implement the most impracticable planners' dreams,[3] should be considered as virtues, even from the
planners' viewpoint? Would not planners' preferences be better served
if the system were equipped with—if not effective automatic correctors
—then at least an effective 'early warning system', both at the stage of
plan construction and its implementation?

[1] One can argue, of course, that planners' preferences changed, but there is hardly
evidence of much metamorphosis, at least in Poland. There is even no evidence of
the belated realization that pushing the investment rate beyond a certain ceiling
(in Poland about 21–23 per cent) produces a lower rather than higher rate of growth.
Planners' preferences are best revealed by studying what goals the Central Planning
Board is first willing to sacrifice when departure from original plan targets becomes
necessary. In Poland it is still the consumer goods sector, as it always was (see
Table 1.10, and our discussion in 2.1.1).

[2] It seems that there is a contradiction between planners' economic and political
preferences (the latter favouring the unchallenged role of the Party in economic life),
which could explain many inconsistencies and setbacks in economic reforms policy.

[3] The Polish 6-year plan abounds with examples of such staggeringly unrealizable
goals, e.g. it assumed a 250 per cent increase of industrial production, including a
50 per cent increase of cotton textiles, 220 per cent of pig iron, 200 per cent of petrol
products—all almost exclusively based on imported raw materials—with simultaneous 0·2 per cent *decrease* of imports of raw material and fuels. Inevitably raw
material and fuel imports actually rose 23 per cent, instead of declining 0·2 per cent,
producing probably one of the most drastic deviations between plan and performance
in the history of planning! (All figures from *11*, p. 137.)

Thirdly, the lack of industrial cadres at the beginning of industrialization does not really apply to such countries as Poland and Czechoslovakia. It is a historical fact that the best Polish plan—according to most observers—was the 3-year plan 1946–9. The Planning Commission of that period was also the best staffed. The scarcity of cadres was to a great extent artificially produced by purges, and it was later admitted that these purges were not justified by political necessity but were 'excesses connected with the personality cult'.

Fourthly, one should also add that the very fact that essentially the *same* management mechanism was applied both in highly developed East Germany and Czechoslovakia and agrarian and underdeveloped Bulgaria and Rumania, indicates that extra-economic factors were at work, rather than the objective requirements of that stage of economic development. Why such highly industrialized countries as Czechoslovakia or the German Democratic Republic had to go through the 'extensive stage of development' again has never been explained by the proponents of the theory under discussion.

It seems that a proper evaluation of the traditional economic system is important for theoretical, political, and economic reasons. Theoretical—as an element of our understanding of early industrialization policies of East Europe. Political—because the defence of the traditional economic system is a part of the broader policy of defending many past practices of the Stalinist period. Economic—to help us avoid many costly illusions about the effectiveness of certain economic policies. These illusions die hard within the bloc, as witnessed, for example, by the repetition of many mistakes of the 6-year plan only a few years later in the Polish 1961–5 plan and again in the 1966–70 plan. Proper analysis of the traditional economic system may also be important for the sake of developing countries, to help them to distinguish between the valuable experience of socialist countries and mistaken policies.

Our criticism of the traditional economic system is not intended to contradict the thesis that different economic policies might be necessary at different stages of the industrialization of a country. It is aimed at disproving the assertion that the appropriate policy in this case was a traditional, Soviet-type management mechanism.

APPENDIX 1.1

The Central Planning Board, Plan Executants, and Higher Administrative Organs

The planning and management of socialist industry is multi-levelled. In Polish practice and in the practice of most other East European countries the four-level administrative structure prevails (Diagram 1.1).

The present structure developed in most countries in the late 1950s or early 1960s from a three-level organizational hierarchy under which there were no

3

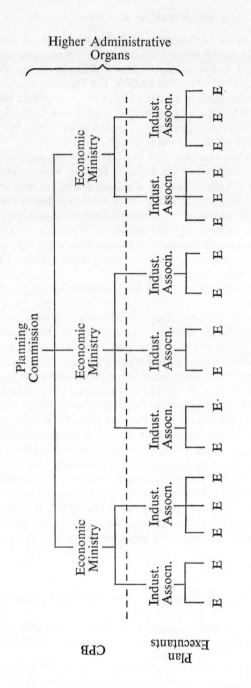

Higher Administrative Organs

Economic Ministry

Economic Ministry

Economic Ministry

Planning Commission

Indust. Assocn.

Indust. Assocn.

Indust. Assocn.

Indust. Assocn.

Indust. Assocn.

Indust. Assocn.

Indust. Assocn.

CPB

Plan Executants

E = enterprise

Diagram 1.1   Central Planning Board, Plan Executants, and Higher Administrative Organs

industrial associations but appropriate branch departments of economic ministries. In Poland the equivalent of the present-day, say, Industrial Association of Precision Industry, was previously the Department of Precision Industry in the Ministry of Heavy Industry. The change, however, had a deeper meaning than purely administrative convenience. The idea behind creating the industrial associations was to organize socialist corporations, not dissimilar to Western state corporations. It was an effort to change this intermediate level of industrial hierarchy from bureaucratic to business-like organization by, among others, applying to it the 'economic account-ability' principle and managerial bonuses based on performance of its subordinate enterprises. We shall return to this important subject at greater length in Ch. 8.

For the purpose of exposition and analysis we need also a division of the whole industrial hierarchy into two broad categories: the Central Planning Board (CPB) which formulates the basic planning goals and oversees their fulfilment, and plan executants whose main task is actual implementation of the plan. The latter does not necessarily mean the passive role of plan executants in plan formulation. Our discussion in Chs. 2–3 will indicate that this can and does vary at different times.

As the dividing criterion between the CPB and plan executants we shall take the *khozraschyot* or 'economic accountability' principle. Its application to current industrial organization in Poland means that industrial associations and enterprises are plan executants, whereas the Planning Commission and Economic Ministries form the economic—mainly executive—arm (part) of the CPB. The CPB in a narrow sense must be understood as the highest party (Politburo and Central Committee Secretariat) and government organs (Council of Ministers plus Chairmen of Committees and/or Commissions with cabinet minister rank). Such an interpretation of the CPB proper is in accord with Lenin's thesis that under the Soviet system the highest party and government organs conglomerate or 'blend'. In our further discussion we shall use the term CPB interchangeably in its narrow and broad sense. The explicit distinction between these two interpretations will be made only when it is not clear from the context.

In addition to the concepts of CPB and plan executants we shall need also the concept of 'higher administrative organs' (HAO). By the latter we mean the CPB *and* industrial associations, so it is a broader concept than that of the CPB. The need for this concept arises only when dealing with enterprises. For the enterprise both the CPB and industrial association represent higher administrative organs and, as the chain of command is not always strictly observed or even purposefully bypassed, the enterprise has to deal frequently with organs above industrial association level. For industrial associations the higher administrative organs are tantamount to the CPB, so here the need for an additional concept does not arise.

References to Chapter One

1. Adamowski Z., Lewandowski J.: *Rolnictwo Polskie w 25-leciu* (Polish Agri-culture during the last 25 years), Warsaw, 1970.
2. Bajt A.: 'Fluctuations in Growth Rates in Post-war Socialist Economies'. Mimeographed. N.d.

3. 'Changes in Financial System of Industry'. *F*, 3, 1971.
4. *Dochod narodowy Polski 1954–1955* (National Income of Poland 1954–1955). Warsaw, 1957.
5. Eighth Plenary Meeting of the Central Committee of PUWP, October 1956. *ND*, 10, 1956.
6. Fifth Plenary Meeting of the CC of PUWP, May 1970. *ND*, 6, 1970.
7. Fourth Plenary Meeting of the CC of PUWP, November 1969. *ND*, 12, 1969.
8. Friss I., ed.: *Reform of the Economic Mechanism in Hungary*. Budapest, 1971.
9. Goldmann J.: 'Fluctuations and Trends in the Rate of Economic Growth in some Socialist Countries'. *EP*, 4, 1964.
10. Herer W.: *Procesy wzrostu w rolnictwie* (The Growth Processes in Agriculture), Warsaw, 1970.
11. Karpinski A.: *Zagadnienia socjalistycznej industrializacji Polski* (Problems of Socialist Industrialization of Poland), Warsaw, 1958.
12. Karpiuk P.: 'The reform of transfer prices (the purpose, assumptions, and their implementation)'. *GP*, 11, 1970.
13. *Kierunki zmian w systemie planowania i zarzadzania gospodarka narodowa w latach 1966–1970. IV Plenum KC PZPR. 27–28 lipca 1965 r. Podstawowe dokumenty* (Directions of Changes in Planning and Management System of National Economy during 1966–1970. IVth Plenary Meeting of Central Committee of PUWP. 27–28 July 1965. Basic Documents), Warsaw, 1965.
14. Korbonski A.: *Politics of Socialist Agriculture in Poland, 1945–1960*, New York-London, 1965.
15. Kouba K.: 'The New System of Management of Czechoslovak Economy'. *Mirovaya Ekonomika i Mezhdunarodnye Otnosheniya*, 2, 1966. Reprinted in [*19*, pp. 162–84].
16. Kucharski M.: *Pieniadz, dochod, proporcje wzrostu* (Money, Income, and Growth), Warsaw, 1964.
17. Kurowski S.: *Historyczny proces wzrostu gospodarczego* (Historical Process of Economic Growth), Warsaw, 1963.
18. Lange O.: *Papers in Economics and Sociology, 1930–1960*, Warsaw, 1970.
19. Lewandowicz Z., Misiak M.: *Reformy gospodarcze w krajach socjalistycznych. Wybor tekstow* (Economic Reforms in Socialist Countries. Selected Readings), Warsaw, 1967.
20. Laski K.: *Zarys teorii reprodukcji socjalistycznej* (Outline of the Theory of Socialist Reproduction), Warsaw, 1965.
21. Malenkov G. M.: Speech at the Fifth Session of the Supreme Soviet of the USSR. Foreign Languages Publishing House, Moscow, 1953.
22. Mikojan A. I.: 'On Measures Leading to the Further Development of Retail Sales and to the Organizational Improvement of State, Co-operative, and Kolkhoz Trade'. *Pravda*, 25 October 1953.
23. Nove A.: *The Soviet Economy*, Allen and Unwin, London, 1961.
24. *O nowy program rolny. Przeglad wypowiedzi* (On the New Agrarian Programme. Collection of Articles), Warsaw, 1957.
25. Pajestka J., Secomski K.: *Doskonalenie planowania i funkcjonowania gospodarki w Polsce Ludowej* (Improvements in the Planning and Functioning of the Economy in People's Poland), Warsaw, 1968.
26. Resolution of the VIth Congress of PUWP. *ND*, 1, 1972.
27. *Rocznik Polityczny i Gospodarczy 1958* (Political and Economic Yearbook 1958), Warsaw, 1958.
28. *Rocznik Statystyczny 1957* (Statistical Yearbook 1957), Warsaw, 1957.
29. *Rocznik Statystyczny 1959* (Statistical Yearbook 1959), Warsaw, 1960.
30. *Rocznik Statystyczny 1970* (Statistical Yearbook 1970), Warsaw, 1970.
31. Ryc K.: *Spozycie a wzrost gospodarczy Polski* (The Consumption and Economic Growth of Poland), Warsaw, 1968.

32. Second Plenary meeting of the CC of PUWP, April 1969. *ND*, 5, 1969.
33. Seventh Plenary meeting of the CC of PUWP, July 1956. *ND*, 7–8, 1956.
34. Solecki M.: *Czynniki rozwoju produkcji rolnej* (The Factors of Growth of Agriculture Production), Warsaw, 1971.
35. Staller G. J.: 'Fluctuations in Economic Activity: Planned and Free Market Economies, 1950–1960'. *AER*, 4, Pt. 1, 1964.
36. *Uchwala V Zjazdu PZPR* (Resolution of the Vth Congress of the Polish United Workers' Party), Warsaw, 1968.
37. Varga G.: 'The Reform of Economic Mechanism'. *Kozgazdasagi Szemle*, 7–8, 1966 [in *19*, pp. 329–49].
38. Wacowska E., ed.: *Rewolta Szczecinska i jej znaczenie* (The Szczecin Revolt and Its Importance), Paris, 1971.
39. Ziwkow T.: 'New System of Management of National Economy', *Rabotniczesko Delo*, 29 April 1966 [in *19*, pp. 424–35].

PART ONE
THE THEORY AND PRACTICE OF ECONOMIC PLANNING

CHAPTER TWO

NATIONAL ECONOMIC PLANNING

2.1 Planning Priorities

2.1.1 PLANNERS' PREFERENCES EXAMINED

The actual plan targets are a result of three factors: production possibilities of the economy, consumers' preferences, and planners' preferences, the first two being the constraints from the planners' viewpoint. The importance of both these constraints is inversely proportional to the length of a plan's time horizon. While, say, in a yearly plan substantial changes in production and/or consumption structures obviously cannot be achieved—whatever the CPB's evaluation of these structures—during a long-term or to a lesser extent also during a medium-term plan, both can be significantly transformed.

The CPB's preferences which express the social and economic ideology—and prejudices—of the ruling political party cannot be unequivocally deciphered from studying actual plan objectives. As already indicated, plan targets are a compromise between the CPB's preferences and constraints and, moreover, most plan tasks, e.g. increased export or development of the chemical industry, are *de facto* means for achieving CPB ultimate goals such as economic independence, increased military might, higher living standards. Theoretically, the most clear-cut picture of CPB preferences should be obtained from studying the objectives of perspective (long-term) plans. Here its political, social, and economic preferences are least subjected to constraints and can be translated into a broad socio-economic programme. The *actual* priority scale of these preferences—their sincerity one is almost tempted to say—is, however, best revealed by studying the fulfilment pattern of the FYPs and the CPB's behaviour when confronted with economic difficulties. Such analysis indicates what goals the CPB is willing to sacrifice first when departure from original plan targets becomes necessary, in the course of plan fulfilment. It is equally important to study the planners' overall propensity to invest as reflected in the changes in relative plan 'tautness', of which the plan fulfilment ratio may be considered an approximate—however imperfect—measure.[1]

It is well known that during the Stalinist period Eastern European economic plans were excessively 'taut' and that CPB preferences were

[1] For a discussion of different aspects of plan tautness see 2.1.2, 3.2.3.D, and 6.1.2.

3*

strongly biased in favour of heavy industry and military objectives. When difficulties of plan fulfilment arose, the targets of the consumer goods sector were the first to be negatively affected. Were economic reforms accompanied by a *lasting* and significant change in the planners' propensity to invest and by more favourable treatment of consumers? In the case of Poland, no such radical and lasting change took place.[1]

A *Planners' Propensity to Invest*

(1) Poland has already completed her fifth mid-term plan. Leaving aside the 1947–9 'Reconstruction Plan' because of its special character, economically and politically (see below), these plans show a constant pattern of steeply falling *planned* growth rates of both consumption *per capita* (55, 30, 24, 18) and real wages (40, 30, 22·5, 10—all figures in percentages). During 1950–70 the real wage and consumption *per capita* targets approached fulfilment only once (in the 1956–60 plan, see Table 1.10). In two other plans the fulfilment of planned growth of real wages was 10 per cent and 35 per cent only. Serious underfulfilment of planned expansion of consumer goods in the 1965–70 FYP was expected already in 1967[2] and 1968 (see Table 2.1). Official statistics on *per capita* real

Table 2.1: Planned and Expected Increases of Producer and Consumer Goods Sectors in Poland, 1966–1970

Plan		Expected Fulfilment		
Producer goods	*Consumer goods*	*Producer goods*	*Consumer goods*	*Percentage deviation*
+ 47·7%	+ 36·5%	+ 55%	+ 33%	+ 11·5% −9%

Source: Pisarski G., 'Lessons of the Current 5-year Plan'. *ZG*, 41, 1968.

[1] This should *not* be considered as tantamount to saying that nowadays Polish consumers are not better off than in the pre-reform period. They are, and substantially so. But—as will be shown below—this is due not so much to changed growth priorities as to the substantial growth of the economy (the yearly average increase of Polish national income in constant 1965 prices was (in billion zlotys): 1956–60 21·4; 1961–5 27·5; 1965–70 35·9 (plan) [*15* (1968), p. 270]) and permanent overfulfilment of employment plans which kept consumption *per capita* growing at a much higher rate than real wages (see Table 1.10).

[2] How serious was the situation is well documented in [*20*]. The title of this article 'Investments in Light Industry—the State of Danger', is fully justified by figures quoted. 'Last year [i.e. in 1966] the investment plan of the Ministry of Light Industry was fulfilled only by 85·3 per cent. After the first half of this year, the percentage of fulfilled investment plan targets [of the FYP presumably] was below 30 and the lowest in the whole industrial sector . . . The Ministry of Construction already underfulfilled the investments for the Ministry of Light Industry (MLI) to the tune of 142 million zlotys, i.e. 16 per cent of the yearly target of construction work of the latter . . . Rather optimistic prognoses put the underfulfilment figure for 1967 at 150 millions . . . There are justified fears that the situation will get even worse because MLI investment quotas are growing in the course of the FYP (from 2·6 billion zlotys in 1966 to 3·2 billions in 1967 and to 4·4 billions annually in 1968–70).'

wage and consumption changes during 1965–70 have not yet been released [*11*, p. 210], but all available data indicate that these targets have not been met. Currently available estimates (March 1972) vary from zero growth of real wages (if changes in labour force composition are taken into account) [*11*, p. 210] to a substantial drop in real wages and an only marginal increase in *per capita* consumption [*12*; *13*].

(2) It is interesting to note the *political* circumstances which accompanied attainment of planned consumption targets. Consumption *per capita* targets have been overfulfilled only once in the history of Polish economic planning (increase of 30 per cent rather than 15 per cent was achieved, see Table 1.10). This happened during the 1947–9 'Reconstruction Plan', which was formulated and two-thirds implemented before the full consolidation of communist power in Poland.[1] The latter was achieved only in 1949 after the merger of the Polish Workers' (communist) and Socialist Parties. The second mid-term plan with a good record in meeting consumption targets, 1956–60, was formulated on the eve of the Polish October 1956 revolt and partly implemented during its immediate impact: out of the 29 per cent increase in real wages claimed for 1956–60, 20 per cent was gained during 1956–7, followed by an actual drop of 2 per cent in 1960 [*10*, p. 20].

(3) The real CPB preferences are also revealed by the fact that out of four mid-term plans thus far enacted in Poland by a fully communist controlled regime, three have been tightened up during the course of their implementation, increasing the original, approved plan figures: the targets of the 6-year plan 1950–5—already very ambitious indeed—were revised upward by the Vth Plenum of the PUWP Central Committee in July 1950; the 1956–60 plan was revised upward by the XIIth Plenum in October 1958; the 1961–5 plan was revised upward by the IInd (June 1959), Vth (June 1960), and XIIth (February 1963) Plena.

(4) It is also illuminating that periodic upward revisions have been carried out although the previous ones have—as a rule—led to breakdowns of the plans, accompanied by severe scaling down of investment projects, with very substantial losses involved—freezing some unfinished investments, under-utilization of others dependent on the former, stockpiling, etc. The record of *formal* plan downward revisions owing to excessive investments, is the following: the 6-year plan was revised downward by the IInd Congress of PUWP in March 1954 (upward revision—1950); the 1960–5 plan was scaled down by the XIVth Plenum in

[1] The authors of this plan—which turned out to be the most successful of all Polish economic plans—were all purged in 1949–50 after the so-called 'CUP Debate' (CUP stands for Central Planning Office; see [*14*, pp. 222–31; and *15*] for a one-sided but revealing presentation of the problems involved). The main architect of the Reconstruction Plan, Professor C. Bobrowski, then Chairman of CUP, had to seek refuge in France. He returned to Poland in 1956, only to be forced to leave again after the March 1968 events.

November 1963 (main upward revision—1960); the 1965–70 plan had to be revised substantially by the IInd, April 1969, Plenum.[1]

(5) Further insight into planners' preferences is given by the following two phenomena: (a) their reluctance to scale down the initial plan targets even if the plan's unfeasibility is pointed out to them in advance by almost unanimous expert opinion; (b) their refusal to take corrective measures when consumption targets are being systematically underfulfilled. Both of these phenomena are typical for the whole period 1950–69, but for the sake of brevity we shall illustrate them by analysing CPB behaviour in connection with the 1961–5 plan, which can be considered as an almost classic example of planners' 'revealed preferences'.

The basic plan targets approved by the IIIrd PUWP Congress (March 1959) were revised upward twice before the actual starting date.

The difficulties resulting from the drastic stepping up of the rate of investment in 1959–60 and from changing its structure towards heavy industry[2] were fresh in everybody's mind. The virtues of realistic planning were advocated by many Polish economists (see 2.2) to which a completely irrelevant answer had been given from Party circles: namely, that Poland has to plan a high rate of growth, because if she did not, the differences between economic development in the less and more advanced socialist countries, would grow rather than diminish. The very ambitious plan targets of Czechoslovakia were quoted in this discussion. A touch of irony was added to this debate by history, because shortly afterwards (in 1963) Czechoslovakia had a minus 2·2 per cent rate of growth in spite of maintaining the rate of investment in the 25 per cent range [2, p. 460, Table I].

When the Vth Plenum (June 1960) enacted a further increase of investment and instructed the Planning Commission to revise the FYP accordingly, professional opinion was practically unanimous that the Plan had become unfeasible. For the first time in its history, the Polish Planning Commission added to the revised version of the plan a statement to the effect that the plan was 'balanced' (i.e. made consistent) by assuming unusually high rates of improvement in labour productivity and in economies of raw materials not justified either by other plan parameters or by past experience.[3]

---

[1] Already in May 1968, a special decree of the Council of Ministers (CM) formulated a number of measures aimed at increased output of consumer goods. This, however, necessitated authorization of *additional* investment spending, hence, shortly thereafter the need for overall revision of the investment plan, undertaken by the IInd CC Plenum (April 1969).

[2] How drastic this change was can be seen from the following data: investment increases in socialist sectors jumped from 2·9 per cent in 1957 (previous year always = 100) to 8·5 per cent in 1958 and 16·4 per cent in 1959. On the other hand, the share of housing investment in total investment dropped from 20·4 per cent in 1959 to 8·8 per cent in 1960 (plan) and of municipal investments from 4·7 per cent to 4·0 per cent (plan) [19 (1960), pp. 417 and 418].

[3] Personal information.

Not only was this warning unheeded at the time, but a year later the IXth Plenum of PUWP, which in November 1961 was analysing the basic economic problems of 1962, decided to maintain the high rate of growth despite a number of warning signals already evident. Among these were: excessive costs of production, employment higher than planned, excessive stockpiling, diminished effectiveness of investment, and further deviation from planned proportions between the increase of consumer and producer goods in favour of the latter.

A year later, in November 1963, the XIVth Plenum announced the breakdown of the FYP, the need to revise its basic proportions, scaling-down of the investment effort, etc.

B *Absorptive Capacity as a Determinant of Investment Level*

The picture sketched already enables us to make a number of observations and tentative hypotheses.

(1) The interests of consumers are best taken care of when political pressure on planners is strong and—accordingly—their hold over the population weak. The wage/salary concessions and other pro-consumer measures granted after the events in Poland in October 1956 and in Czechoslovakia in spring 1968, testify to it. Immediately the pressure weakens—i.e. when the CPB considers the political situation under control—the rate of growth is raised again. The drastic nature of this increase (see p. 38, fn. 2) seems to support the hypothesis that the consumer-oriented policy of the previous period was forced on planners by political circumstances, rather than as a reflection of their own preferences. The short life of the consumer-oriented policy points in the same direction.[1]

(2) It is interesting to note that downward revisions of plans have a cyclical character and do *not* correspond to periods of political liberalization. The decision to revise the Polish 6-year plan downward and 'to raise substantially the standard of living of the working masses of our country' [16, p. 97] was announced by Hilary Minc in 1954. Neither the person nor the period could be described as 'liberal'. The same must be said about the *last* revision of the Polish mid-term plan in April 1969. The year 1963, when the third downward plan revision took place, was a politically undistinguished period in the de-liberalization trend leading from October 1956 to March 1968. Economically, however, these three years, 1956, 1963, 1968, had one basic thing in common: the technico-organizational ceiling of the economy's absorptive capacity to invest

---

[1] The breakdown of the 6-year plan produced an investment slowdown during 1954–7 [19 (1958), p. 459]. After the 1963–4 investment slowdown, the years 1965–7 brought about a threefold rise of the yearly incremental investment rate (previous year = 100): 1963 103; 1964 104; 1965 110; 1966 109; 1967 112 [19 (1968), p. 227].

had been reached.[1] These were critical years, when the investment programme collapsed after years of uncorrected distortions—structural (breakdown of inter-industry relationships, partly as a result of faster than planned growth of producer goods at the expense of consumer goods);[2] economic (drastic cost increases); and technical (longer than planned construction periods, unfulfilled capacity targets, etc.). Continuation became technically and organizationally impossible without fundamental revisions of existing plans, especially the investment plan.[3] To sum up, the record indicates that the Polish planners—except when under unusual pressure from the population—repeatedly go on pushing the rate of growth, structurally biased towards the producer goods sector, until they reach the technico-organizational ceiling of absorptive capacity and the plan actually collapses. Let us try to find out whether this is a deliberate policy on the part of the CPB.

C Is Constant Overinvestment a Deliberate CPB Policy?

The first question we have to analyse here is the possibility that the CPB simply lacks the necessary information—or gets it too late—to take

[1] See Professor Kalecki's concept of 'supply-determined industries' by which he meant those activities which have a certain ceiling for the long- and medium-run rate of growth for technical and organizational reasons, so that even a considerable increase in capital outlay will not help to raise their output at a higher rate. The technological and organizational factors which determine the ceilings of the rate of growth in supply-determined industries are varied: limited capacity of specialized construction-installation industries, the time necessary for adaptation of new technology, long construction periods, difficulties in recruiting manpower for certain industries (e.g. coal mining), etc. In Polish planning experience a number of such ceilings were encountered. In most branches of industry the capacity of specialized construction-installation firms is the main obstacle. If this capacity is exceeded and orders given to non-specialized firms, not only the costs of construction rise sharply, but also construction periods are prolonged. As a result, capacity does not increase in the required period, but instead more resources are tied up in unfinished investment. Constraints of this type determine the feasible output levels in individual supply-determined industries. For instance, in constructing the Polish perspective plan (1960–75, Kalecki's version) it was considered impossible to more than double the steel output within the FYP, in agriculture the assumption of more than 21 cetnars per hectare in 1975 was considered unrealistic, etc. (In 1958, i.e. at the time Professor Kalecki was presenting the first draft of his perspective plan (rejected later by Polish authorities), actual yields of 4 basic grains were 14·8 cetnars, in 1969 21·6). See [21, pp. 135–46] for a brief summary of Professor Kalecki's arguments and references to his original works on this subject.

[2] It may be noticed that in any given time period the technical possibilities of expanding the producer goods sector at the expense of the consumer goods sector are limited. This inherent rigidity of production apparatus is very fortunate from the consumers' viewpoint, because it acts as a technical (as contrasted with social or political) constraint on planners' propensity to invest. If costs are disregarded, however, this constraint can be considerably lifted in the short run, and further lifted in the long run by structural changes of the economy.

[3] It was of course economically very costly long before it became technically and organizationally impossible.

corrective action in time. This hypothesis is, however, not supported by facts. It is enough to study the evaluation of the Polish economic situation and policy, published yearly from 1958 in *The Political and Economic Yearbook* and written mainly by high government officials responsible for appropriate sectors or aspects of the Polish economy,[1] to see that the *warning* signals were known to the CPB and duly noted. Such facts as faster-than-planned growth of investment in general, and investment in the producer goods sector in particular, or the failure to reach the planned share of labour productivity in output growth, or excessive stocks and employment levels, or underfulfilment of investment and output in the consumer goods sector are there yearly recorded and fully documented.

Nor can the CPB claim that the general relationship between too taut planning and the actual rate of growth has not been repeatedly pointed out to it. Already in the late 1950s and early 1960s, the thesis that a too high *planned* rate of growth leads to a *de facto* rate of growth lower than a less ambitious but more feasible and hence consistent plan would produce was extensively discussed by Polish economists (see 2.2). These arguments, however, failed to convince the planners and did not have any appreciable impact on planning practice.

The second problem we have to examine is the possibility that the CPB is unable to correct this overinvestment which is taking place against its preferences because of the expansionist nature of the existing management mechanism. This hypothesis contains more than a grain of truth. The existing management mechanism is in fact an expansionist one and creates unplanned demand pressure far exceeding available resources. Much of the overinvestment is due to actions of plan executants unintended by the CPB but induced by the existing management mechanism. It would be naïve, however, to absolve the CPB from responsibility for overexpansionist policy on this ground. At least three arguments still point to the CPB as the main culprit:

(1) In many cases the *initial* plan targets themselves are too taut. One can argue that there is informational feedback between plan executants and the CPB; when the management mechanism induces plan executants to make excessive demands for resources this must be reflected in the plan itself. It is true that demands for resources from plan executants create pressure on the CPB, but not *irresistible* pressure. During the drafting of every mid- and short-term plan, the sum of investment requirements initially demanded by economic ministries and industrial associations considerably exceeds the ceiling acceptable to the CPB. As the CPB constantly slashes these requirements, there is no obvious theoretical or practical reason why it cannot push them further down, closer to equilibrium level. After all, the hard fact 'we simply cannot

[1] Such as K. Secomski, Vice Chairman of Planning Commission, J. Struminski, until 1969 Chairman of the State Price Commission, and others less prominent but equally well informed.

allocate more than we have' is difficult to dispute, especially if one can point to previous experience, showing clearly the disastrous results of excessively taut plans.

(2) The CPB is also not incapable of diminishing, if not preventing altogether, the consequences of *fait accompli* by plan executants of spending more than the planned amount of resources allocated. Pretty soon the degree of demand distortion built into the plan becomes known to the CPB in aggregate terms. For example, it is known that planned investment costs are on average 25–30 per cent lower than actual investment costs. This was known already in the early 1950s after the first few years of the 6-year plan. The fact that for over ten years the CPB did nothing to cushion in advance this effect of unplanned investment demand, which occurrence it had known beforehand, and then (in 1965) created an investment reserve of only 5 per cent is quite revealing as far as CPB preferences are concerned (see 2.2).

(3) We also cannot forget the substantial administrative power of the CPB in communist countries. When faced with growing investment costs and/or their unplanned structural changes, the CPB can take a number of corrective measures immediately it ascertains this fact and—under Polish conditions—this involves only a few months' time lag. Nobody can deny that the CPB is in possession of effective power to correct these distortions quickly. As will be shown in our later discussion on the management mechanism, the CPB is frequently completely unable to improve *qualitative* performance of the economy, i.e. increase its efficiency, but does possess the effective power to control its quantitative[1] and structural characteristics. With the power to issue direct orders supported by the rationing of the basic means of production and the monopoly of foreign trade and banking, nobody can argue that taking early corrective measures is beyond the CPB's range of action. The best proof of how great is the CPB's power when it wants to use it are the measures which it undertakes and implements after reaching crisis point. It is obvious that the same steps would be much more effective (and cheaper) if undertaken earlier. Why then, are corrective measures not undertaken as soon as information on plan deviations reaches the CPB? The implicit answer is given by the official interpretation of above-plan investment and of unplanned structural changes: as long as these occur at the expense of consumption it is either praised as the sign of dynamic growth (as in the early 1960s) or mildly blamed (as in the late 1960s). Only when very near, or at, the technical ceiling of absorptive capacity

---

[1] Constant overfulfilment of the employment plan does not contradict this thesis but only indicates (a) that rationing is only effective when *supply* (rather than demand) is controlled (this is the case with material means of production but *not* with the labour force) and (b) that the CPB is in fact quite prepared to employ more people for the same (or in fact always smaller than planned) amount of real purchasing power if it is necessary for meeting production targets. See also 2.1.1.D.

which threatens growth as such does the interpretation change, and criticism, then condemnation, then plan revision follow.[1]

D Reasons for the CPB's Growth Policy

In the previous section we considered whether CPB policy is deliberate. The available evidence indicates that it is. Why then does the CPB pursue such a policy?

An answer is, of course, speculative, but the information points in the following directions:

(1) The CPB treats personal consumption as a *cost* of growth rather than the ultimate goal of growth. There is abundant implicit proof of this thesis, because for obvious reasons the CPB cannot admit it openly. (a) Of five Polish mid-term plans, only two stated a rise in the standard of living as their main goal (the 1946–9 and 1956–60 plans). All the other plans openly stated that 'growth of productive forces' was their primary objective and standard of living second. (b) Planners have rejected growth alternatives which, by pushing further away certain so-called 'growth barriers', would produce higher rates of growth—but by expanding non-heavy industry sectors.[2] (c) Finally, there is the basic fact that '. . . plans of real-wage increases have never been fully achieved. Targets in this part of the plan (employment and wages) were not the basis for correcting production targets but, on the contrary, employment and wage policy was subordinated to fulfilment of production plans' [10, pp. 22–3].[3]

(2) The overinvestment policy may also be the result of a misguided effort of planners to forestall the declining growth rates of socialist countries *vis-à-vis* their capitalist adversaries (see our discussion in Ch. 1). The probable sequence of events may be described as follows: efficiency of the socialist economy declines and its growth rates fall; efforts to improve it by changes in the management mechanism fail; planners realize that they do not control effectively the qualitative aspects of the economy; they are unable to make it more efficient but as they still control its quantitative and structural aspects, they resort to excessive investment as a desperate effort to keep the growth rate at an acceptable level. The latter is important not only economically but politically too because when the growth rate of socialist countries was very high the CPB pronounced it the main criterion of the economic system's quality and performance.

The above interpretation has the merit of explaining the apparent

[1] See yearly evaluations of Polish economic policy in [19, 1958–68].
[2] See for example [5] and [6]. For a point of view which warns against relying too strongly on changes in the *structure* of production instead of in *methods* of production, see [8]. A brief summary of arguments presented in [8] may be found in [21, p. 27].
[3] *En passant* we may note that neither the figures quoted in 2.1.1.A nor the above statement can be found in the printed version of the author's paper [9, pp. 121–64].

lack of a CPB learning process: too taut plans are enacted despite previous failures. As evidenced by data already quoted, the plan targets in most respects show a strongly declining trend. Why is the economy still overstrained? The probable answer is that the overall performance of the Polish economy declines more quickly than planners' aspiration levels (or beliefs in the potential of the planned economy, which to a great extent determines their aspiration level). If this is the case, it would be psychologically understandable.

2.1.2 PLAN TAUTNESS AND SYSTEM REMODELLING

A *Formulation of the Problem*

The two-way relationship between growth strategy (especially plan tautness) and system remodelling was noticed early in Polish economic literature [*19* (1958), p. 422; *19* (1959), p. 416; *7*].[1] It has been argued that the feasibility of certain plan targets, e.g. increased share of labour productivity in output growth or lower ratio of stock increases in national income, cannot be assessed without knowing what changes in the management mechanism are going to be introduced. There was a general agreement that the Polish economy is capable of better qualitative performance than during the Stalinist period—hence the possibility of assuming improved performance in the plan [*4*]. The feasibility of achieving these more ambitious targets depends, however, on introducing a management mechanism which would *induce* this improved performance. On the other hand, (i) too taut an economic plan 'undermines the general principle of economic calculation'. The first result of a too taut plan is shortages, which directly endanger the fulfilment of certain plan targets. This leads to replacing economic calculation by the principle 'production regardless of costs' in order to avoid even greater losses as a result of the cumulative effect of shortages in an interrelated system. (ii) A too taut plan 'undermines the effectiveness of the incentive system' regardless of its type.[2] Where shortages prevail, enterprise results depend mainly on external factors: regularity and quality of supplies of raw materials, subcontracted components, frequency and duration of electric power cuts, etc. Under such conditions economic incentives must lose most of their effectiveness. (iii) Rationing of the means of production must follow too taut a plan sooner or later, in order to safeguard the CPB's priorities. The economic consequences of this rationing are a further weakening of economic calculation (many profitable choices are prohibited) and of many economic instruments, especially prices. Money also loses its feature as a universal means of exchange. (iv) Finally the negative impact of a sellers' market on quality of output and enter-

[1] High rates of growth *combined* with simultaneous structural changes create particularly difficult problems for economic policy (see especially [*1*]).
[2] Both quotations from [*7*].

prise product-mix policies (refusal to produce inconvenient output) should also be mentioned.

B General Evidence Presented

The history of Polish economic reforms is the best proof that these interrelations actually exist and are of overwhelming importance. Three types of evidence can be provided:

(1) Predictions of the following sequence of events which then come true: if appropriate changes in the economic mechanism are not implemented, this will lead to lack of the necessary changes in plan executants' behaviour, hence to lack of improved performance in sphere X, hence to underfulfilment of plan target X. Many such predictions have been made by Polish economists during the course of the economic reforms and most of them proved painfully true. Here are two illustrations:

(i) Professor W. Brus's prediction in 1959 [7]: The plan for 1961–5 assumes substantial improvements in inventory management (see Table 2.2). These improvements will not be achieved without substantial

Table 2.2: Planned and Actual Share of Total Investment; Net Investment and Stock Increases in National Income

(in percentage)

	1958[a] actual	1965[a] plan	1965[b] actual
Total investment	24·0	24·0	27·1
Net investment in fixed capital	15·5	18·5	18·8
Stocks	8·5	5·5	8·3

Sources: for ([a]) Brus, W.: 'Growth and Economic Model', ZG, 2, 1959 (in 1958 prices); for ([b]) Statistical Yearbook 1968, p. 74 (in 1961 prices).

changes in the overall management mechanism. These changes were *not* introduced and relative performance did not improve, as witnessed by column 3 in Table 2.2. It remained almost exactly the same as in 1958.

(ii) Professor Brus's prediction in 1959 [7]: The plan for 1961–5 assumes 80 per cent of industrial output growth from increased labour productivity. This is a very 'taut' target, and its achievement depends on far-reaching changes in management mechanism. These changes were not forthcoming, and neither were the economic results (Table 2.3).

Table 2.3: Share of Labour Productivity Increases in Growth of Gross Industrial Output (in percentage)

1961		1962		1963		1964		1965	
plan	actual	plan	actual	plan	actual	plan	actual	plan	actual
83	67	69	52	66	55	73	79	65·4	46·2

Source: Rocznik Polityczny i Gospodarczy (Political and Economic Yearbook) 1962, p. 207; 1963, p. 212; 1964, p. 232; 1965, p. 241; 1966, p. 352. (It is interesting to note that these data are not published in Polish Statistical Yearbooks).

(2) Another type of evidence is the CPB admission that the above-indicated two-way relationship between rate of growth and changes in management mechanism does exist. As early as 1957, Professor K. Secomski, Vice Chairman of the Planning Commission, stressed the impact of growth on system remodelling: '. . . Anti-inflationary measures required that many intended economic steps, e.g. changes in the [economic] model, had to be limited or postponed' [*19* (1958), p. 442].[1] A year later he stressed the influence of the economic system on growth: 'Transition to a new stage of more intensive development of the national economy must be preceded by a carefully controlled process of putting the national economy in order, by introducing changes in *methods of economic management*, and by taking into account the need for the new system of influencing all socio-economic phenomena by *economic means*' [*19* (1959), p. 416, italics in the original]. And as we indicated before, the transition to this 'more intensive development', i.e. more effective economic performance, was already assumed in the formulation of the Polish plan targets.

Because the warnings about feedbacks between growth and model were *directed* to the CPB, the planners' admission of their existence is of double importance. It constitutes additional evidence that such interrelationships exist, and evidence—moreover—by a 'hostile' witness and, secondly, it reveals the CPB's real commitment to economic reforms. If the CPB knows and admits that inflationary pressure makes system remodelling excessively difficult if not impossible, but nevertheless does step up the growth rate to the technico-organizational ceiling most of the time—this tells us a lot about planners' attitudes towards economic reforms.

(3) The third type of evidence at our disposal is provided by cases where certain changes in the economic system were introduced and then withdrawn under pressure of growth requirements. For the sake of brevity, only three such examples will be provided, but each from a

---

[1] At that time, inflationary pressure was the result of substantial increases in the purchasing power of the population rather than of high rates of investment. We should notice that the threat of inflation, used as justification for halting economic reforms, was grossly exaggerated. The overall price index of consumer goods and services in 1957 was 105·4 (1956 = 100) and of foodstuffs, on which, at that time, almost 50 per cent of personal income was spent, only 102·7 [*19* (1958), p. 821]. (The same figures for 1958 (1957 = 100) were 102·6 and 102·2 [*19* (1959), p. 720]). It is also characteristic that fear of inflation did not deter planners from drastic increases of investment rate the very next and the following year (see p. 38, fn. 2). In the light of the above, the thesis that reform measures were stopped as a result of the inflationary threat must be considered as a pretext rather than as truth. The present author gives much more weight to the changed *political* climate, witnessed, for example, by the return in 1959 of a number of pre-1956 political leaders, such as E. Szyr, J. Tokarski, T. Gede, and others, to high party and government posts, accompanied by simultaneous demotion of many supporters of reforms (J. Morawski, W. Bienkowski, S. Zolkiewski, and others).

different FYP to indicate that the problem could have been early identified by planners and that it is of lasting character.

C Three Examples

(1) Enterprise investments and taut planning (1956–60 plan)

An important part of an early (1956–8) Polish reform was to increase the share of so-called decentralized (i.e. enterprise) investments. The intention was that 'no ceiling should be imposed by higher authorities on decentralized investment, the volume of which should be determined by enterprises themselves' [19 (1959), p. 674]. Decentralized investment initially rose sharply as a result (see Table 2.4). A year later, however

Table 2.4: The Rise of Decentralized Investment in Early Period of Economic Reforms (in billion zlotys, 1957 prices)

	1957	1958	%
Centralized investment	48·5 (90)	43·8 (76)	90·3
Decentralized investment	5·4 (10)	14·2 (24)	262·9
	53·9 (100)	58 (100)	107·6

Source: as in Table 2.3, 1959, p. 675.

(when investment in the socialist sector increased 16·4 per cent over the previous year), we learn that 'the broad possibilities of . . . decentralized investment were widely used, exceeding original yearly plan prognoses . . . As a result . . . it was necessary *to limit* the total volume of these investments to assure equilibrium of the balances of construction materials and of the capacities of construction enterprises' [19 (1960), p. 419]. These limits have never been removed and in 1961–5 the share of enterprise investment in total investment in national economy was 7·1 per cent [18, p. 45].

(2) Export effectiveness and taut planning (1961–5 plan)

The analysis of Polish export effectiveness revealed a marginal group of exports of very low effectiveness. As a result, the permitted marginal rates of exchange for export transactions were lowered appropriately to eliminate these ineffective exports. The volume of planned export earnings was not lowered, however, even temporarily, to permit the expansion of exports of more profitable products. So, under the pressure of foreign exchange earnings requirements, the former marginal rate of exchange was soon reintroduced.[1] The effort to eliminate exports of low effectiveness failed, and meanwhile, Polish foreign trade lost a number

---

[1] Personal information.

of traditional customers (because of announced price increases), and it will not be easy to regain them.

(3) *Investment reserve fund and taut planning* (1966–70 plan)

According to official estimates of the Polish Investment Bank [*3*, p. 1], the planned investment costs are exceeded on average by 25–30 per cent. Because of the very taut investment plan, the investment reserve fund—introduced for the first time in the history of Polish planning in the FYP 1965–70—was only 5 per cent of planned investment outlays (40 billion zlotys of reserves for 800 billion zlotys of planned investment spending). It is not astonishing that this reserve fund was already spent by 1968 and cautious estimates talked of 900 billion zlotys as the minimum investment expenditure which would be required [*17*]. These estimates assumed that numerous investment projects—originally envisaged in the plan—would be cancelled, and completion of many already started would be postponed. Of course, this development caused serious imbalances in the plan, mostly in the form of not meeting investment and output plans in the consumer sector (see Table 2.1).

2.2 Planning Procedures and Techniques

The basic features of the Soviet-type planning, which was introduced and established in Poland in 1949–50, were not changed during the subsequent waves of Polish economic reforms 1956–70. This does not mean either that no effort was made to change them, or that a number of changes have not been implemented. It does mean, however, that the reforms were not sufficient to change the *basic* features of the traditional planning system. This section will try to prove this thesis.

2.2.1 THE UNIVERSAL CHARACTER OF PLANNING

One of the basic features of the traditional planning system is its *universal* character. By this two things are meant: first of all, there is a universal system of plans consisting of a separate plan for each unit of the national economy. If we take, as an example, the four-level planning hierarchy existing in most socialist countries, i.e. Planning Commission, economic ministries, industrial associations, and enterprises, there will exist, accordingly, a national economic plan, plans for every sector and branch of the economy, and for every enterprise. Secondly, the universal character of planning also means universal participation in the planning process. All units of the planning hierarchy take part in plan construction.

Under the system of universal planning, the process of constructing the plan for the national economy consists of three distinct steps:

(1) Macro-planning at the CPB level. On the basis of these calculations so-called planning guidelines are formulated for the lower units. (2) Lower units elaborate their plans according to received guidelines

and send them back to the CPB through the appropriate levels of the planning hierarchy. Each level supervises and aggregates the plans of subordinate units. (3) On the basis of the information received, the CPB formulates the final plan and sends it down as *directive* and—partially—*informative* plan indices (see 3.2.3).

The universal system of planning and its derivatives—the hierarchical structure of plans, their directive as opposed to indicative character and their detailed nature (the national economic plan is addressed to and derived from plans of individual enterprises)—still fully applies to today's Poland (and such countries as Bulgaria, GDR, and Rumania). Moreover, the planning guidelines emanating from higher administrative levels have remained very detailed indeed.[1] 'To inform the planning units about means at their disposal . . . each year the government issues "planning directives" pertaining to the next year . . . It should not be surmised that the planning units . . . can dispose of these means at will. The information about means at their disposal is usually supplemented by a list of specific planning tasks in the implementation of which those means should be applied . . . Because of . . . interdependencies, the government directives as they have been issued lately, *resemble a simplified and provisional draft plan* for the next year' [*32*, pp. 39–40, my italics].

Each subsequent 'wave' of Polish economic reforms—1956–8, 1965–8, 1969–70 (see 1.3.2)—included in its programme more or less ambitious tasks concerning diminishing the scope and the detailed nature of the national economic plan. The far-reaching postulates of the Economic Council[2] of 1957 [*24*]—to limit the central plan's directives to very few for industrial branches and to still less for individual enterprises[3]—

[1] In sharp contrast to this practice, recent economic reforms in Hungary (and the Czechoslovak reforms as originally envisaged) tend to limit planning to the first step described above, namely macro-planning at the central level. At the same time the guidelines issued by the CPB will be mostly in the form of general monetary and fiscal measures, with gradually decreasing use of *direct* and *specific* controls and restrictions.

[2] The Economic Council was created in 1957 as an advisory body to the Council of Ministers [*37*, pp. 96–7 lists its membership and functions]. It included many eminent Polish economists—together with several economic administrators—and for one or two years (1957–8) it was the main driving force behind Polish economic reform proposals. Its last document of major importance [*26*] was never approved by its own Plenary Meeting, not to say the government. The Economic Council formally existed until 1962, but there were no Plenary Meetings after 1958–9. Its Secretariat produced, however, a number of useful studies for a few more years.

[3] '(3) Branch industrial plans at the central level should determine: (a) value of commodity production, (b) volume of value added. In addition the central plan should consist of quantitative indices of basic raw materials and other inputs . . . (4) Determining branch indices of commodity production and value added does not mean that these indices are also needed at enterprise level. (5) Product-mix targets for enterprises should be determined only when they are really necessary, as in the case when output and basic input are centrally allocated' [*25*].

have never been implemented. In the mid 1960s—as the above quotation shows—national economic plan guidelines again 'resembled a simplified . . . draft plan' with scores of indices (see Ch. 3 for more detailed discussion of this problem).

The second wave of Polish reforms tried to combine the traditional planning system with enterprise initiative by putting forward the idea of so-called 'alternative plans'. Enterprises had to prepare their plans in accordance with official and detailed central guidelines but at the same time were asked and encouraged to prepare their own proposals in the form of 'alternative plans'. It has been officially admitted that this effort failed. In a recent interview, the Deputy Director of the Department of Plan Coordination of the Planning Commission gave the following reasons for this failure: '. . . Enterprises' proposals in the form of alternative plans had the character of additional activities independent from the "normal" planning process. We received them only when the outline of the whole plan should have been ready, and it was too late for any substantial revision . . . What was crucial, however, was the fact that enterprises' proposals frequently did not take into account the real possibilities of the national economy and were inconsistent with each other, and these prevented their broader use in plan construction' [30; see also 34].

The resolution of the IInd (April 1969) CC Plenum of PUWP [38, pp. 3–82] and the regulations and instructions which followed [36] made a new attempt to limit the scope of central guidelines and give enterprises more freedom in determining their own plans. It has been labelled as an effort to change the method of plan construction from the existing practice of the 'top to the bottom' into the 'bottom to the top' approach to plan building. This method was to apply to enterprises' plans for 1970 but especially to the next FYP 1971–5. 'What is new in this method of planning?'—asked rhetorically an editorial in *Zycie Gospodarcze*—'Participation of society in the preparation of multi-year plans was being stressed for years. That is true, but the actual method of plan construction did not fully allow for active social participation. Formerly the enterprise's staff was given practically ready draft plans, which were parts of an already "balanced" central plan. These drafts were as a rule very detailed and did not leave much room for alternative proposals. It was therefore a method of plan construction from top to the bottom . . . The new [method] introduced by the IInd Plenum consists of reversing this practice of plan construction into one "from the bottom to the top". Enterprises, industrial associations, and local councils [*rady narodowe*] will receive not ready-made draft plans, but the outline of the general development strategy of the new FYP in the form of initial guidelines of a more general character than was the case previously. Only after discussion and on the basis of plan proposals submitted by lower levels will the central authorities formulate the final and internally consistent version of the national economic plan' [27]. The new guidelines consist (formally) of only five directive indices: value of gross output, export tasks, increase in labour productivity, volume of output of selected priority products, and upper limit of investment outlays [30]. 'All other indices given enterprises by the industrial association must be considered as supplementary, as economic justification of obligatory indices and only as information which may help enterprises in their search for improved performance' [30].

This new method of plan construction is closely connected with an effort to improve economic efficiency by specialization. It has been admitted that Poland as a whole—and most Polish enterprises also—produces too broad a range of goods and that both economies of scale and the utilization of highly efficient techniques require specialization.[1] Specialization cannot be achieved by universal application of the ratchet principle (see 3.2.3.D). The CPB wants to classify products, industrial branches, and enterprises into three categories, according to their envisaged rate of expansion: I singled out for speedy development; II for modest development; III stagnant (or retrogressive) [34]. But how should the proper directions of specialization be chosen? To find the answer to this question an effort is being made to solicit the help of enterprises themselves, and the new method of plan construction is to play a major role here.

The success of this latest reform of Polish planning depends, obviously, on two premises being met: (a) that enterprises *can* produce meaningful plan proposals on the basis of a limited number of central indices; (b) that enterprises are *willing* to search for and reveal possibilities of improved economic performance.

Any serious student of Soviet-type economies can, *a priori*, answer negatively both these questions on the basis of existing knowledge about the functioning of centrally planned economies. But it is unnecessary to rely here on purely theoretical arguments. In spite of the short time which has elapsed since the reform was introduced, there is already substantial empirical evidence that the reform—as originally conceived —is encountering fundamental difficulties.

The inadequacy of the *informational* basis of the current planning reform has two basic aspects. First of all, enterprises do not have enough information to guide them in their search for an optimal plan variant. The director of one of the big Polish enterprises put it bluntly: 'Let us take such a basic problem as specialization. We are producing 5,000 specifications. Say that we have stopped producing specification M-3, because from our viewpoint its production is uneconomic. After

---

[1] '... many of our enterprises lack a clearly determined production profile, which would reflect a well thought out, long-run specialization ... It leads to high production costs, low economic effectiveness, and low quality of output' [31]. See also [34].

elaborating the plan and submitting it to the industrial association, we might well learn that what we eliminated from our product-mix is most needed . . . And what then? Rejection of our plan?' [24].

Another aspect of the informational dilemma, of which enterprise directors are well aware, is the consequence of existing price distortions for the results of their efficiency calculations, which they now have to produce to substantiate their plan proposals.

The instruction on the elaboration of the FYP 1971–5, issued by the Planning Commission in June 1969, requires that plan proposals of every enterprise contain calculations showing, among others: '(1) productivity of fixed capital, calculated by dividing gross output or gross value added by value of fixed capital; (2) productivity of investments, calculated by dividing increase of gross output or gross value added by value of completed productive investments; (3) productivity of labour, calculated by dividing gross output or gross value added by total number of employees (without apprentices)' [33].

If the results of these calculations based on existing prices are going to be taken seriously as a basis for decisions, the consequences may be simply disastrous. For example, according to a recent decree of the Council of Ministers [22], all investments are to be classified into five groups arranged in the descending order of effectiveness with more productive investments given priority. If this criterion were applied to, say, the Polish television industry it could well lead to expansion of the Warsaw Television Factory, which mainly assembles television sets and whose investments are in group 1, but with a simultaneous halt to the expansion of its subcontractors, because their investments all belong to much lower (3–4) productivity groups [33].

The second basic weakness of current planning reform consists of (implicit) unrealistic assumptions on enterprise *behaviour*. The fact that the CPB finally decided to ask enterprises what and how to produce does not by itself assure that enterprises will be *willing* to give economically optimal answers (within their information and knowledge constraints). Since the planning reform as such did not change any of the factors which had been creating substantial and *conscious* information distortions by plan executants, there was no reason to expect any improvement in this respect. On the contrary, there was ground for expecting *bigger* information distortions as a result of more latitude being granted to enterprises. And this is what actually happened.

Addressing top economic officials at the meeting devoted to the evaluation of the implementation of the IInd Plenum's resolutions, B. Jaszczuk, at that time (1969) Member of the Politburo, CC Secretary, and Chairman of the newly created CC Economic Commission, stressed how grave the situation was: 'Information and signals coming from enterprises and industrial associations indicate that *there are serious reasons for anxiety* . . . The strong tendency towards achieving a substantial part of the growth of production by increased employment, towards lowering labour productivity is still present. In four industrial ministries: engineering, heavy, light, and chemical, the sum of enterprises' employment plans for 1970 exceeded their employment guidelines by 63,000 . . . Plans submitted by economic ministries are a little better . . . but still exceed their total employment limits by 33,000. Acceptance of these plans would result in a 3·7 per cent increase of labour productivity. Such a low productivity rise was last recorded in 1966 . . . Acceptance of these proposals would be tantamount to going back four years' [*31*, italics in the original].

There is an interesting feedback between informational and behavioural aspects of the current planning reform. Obviously enough, substantial informational improvements could be achieved if industrial associations actively participated in planning at the enterprise level. This was postulated as one of the basic principles of new planning methods [*34*], and then urgently reiterated during the process of actual plan elaboration [*28*]. In practice, however, it turned out that a number of industrial associations was purposely withholding information from their member enterprises [*23*].[1] This practice was condemned, but the reasons for its existence were not examined. The secrecy on the part of industrial associations is, undoubtedly, designed to minimize information distortions from their enterprises. As will be discussed later (see Chs. 3.1 and 8), industrial associations are entitled to fix plan tasks of their enterprises above the level required to meet their own plan targets and to allocate less of rationed inputs than their own limits would permit. Needless to say, industrial associations do not want their enterprises to know to what extent the sum of plan targets demanded from them exceeds the industrial associations' own plan tasks, as making it known would encourage enterprises to increase pressure to have their targets lowered. The same reasoning applies to the level of industrial associations' reserves of wage fund or rationed material inputs and even to plan tasks of their different member-enterprises, as the access to any of this information would strengthen the bargaining power of individual enterprises.

The *new* method of planning which aims to build the national economic plan on the basis of enterprises' proposals and which envisages substantial flexibility of initial plan guidelines (e.g. enterprises are being encouraged to go beyond their initial investment limits if they

[1] 'At the Board meeting of a certain association, each enterprise director got his five directive indices separately, for his own information only. Those directors who, for obvious reasons, wanted to know something about the targets of their colleagues, could learn nothing (except privately). At such meetings enterprise directors could also not get any information on what are the association's investment reserve . . . or . . . wage fund' [*29*]. (On industrial associations' Boards of Directors see Ch. 8, refs. [*9*] and [*12*].)

can show the high efficiency of their investment proposals [*34*]), requires the maximum disclosure of information to enterprises. The *old* enterprise behaviour, of which industrial associations are only too painfully aware, induces the latter to use secrecy as one of the weapons to counteract enterprise pressure for high input–low output plan targets.

The latest Polish reform effort also brought sharply into focus the *psychological* consequences of repeated and partial reforms. The interviews with a number of enterprise directors carried by the Polish economic weekly *Zycie Gospodarcze* revealed that in many enterprises the preparation of plans has a purely formal character. Why so? 'Because people are tired of discussing the same problems over and over again . . . Because enterprise directors themselves . . . do not clearly see how our economy may be modernized more quickly through the fuller use of the enterprises' own initiative, in spite of the fact that they have always advocated the latter' [*39*]. This attitude is not astonishing if one recalls that Poland started her economic reforms in 1956–7. There is even no need to go so far back to find explanations of the attitudes just quoted: the previous major Polish reform dates from 1966–7 and was still in the process of implementation when the new changes were announced.

The lack of faith in the new reform effort is strengthened by the *partial* character of the present reform. At present only planning methods are being changed. The new system of plan implementation was to be introduced later, from 1 January 1971, the first year of the new FYP (see 1.3.2.D). As aptly noted by *Zycie Gospodarcze*, 'The present situation is rather complicated and difficult, because we are constructing the future FYP according to new methods but fulfilling our current planning tasks under the old system. Not everybody bears in mind that fulfilment of the new plan will be carried on under new conditions, within the framework of the new comprehensive system of planning and management' [*29*].

One cannot realistically expect that the *promise* of a new system of plan implementation—of which the basic features were very vague at the time of the planning methods reform (1969), and the final shape of which was not known to anybody—will affect the present behaviour of plan executants in the sphere of plan construction. Such change can be expected only *after* a few years of the actual functioning of the new system, when enterprises become really convinced that the ratchet principle is no longer being used. Meanwhile, however, the existence of the *old* system of plan *implementation* undermines the belief that the new system of plan *construction* will be in fact introduced: ' "How can we succeed in implementing the ideas of the IInd Plenum concerning enterprise initiative in mid-term planning, if our current activities are under everyday interference from higher authorities?" (director of a big engineering plant).

' "We do not notice the slightest relaxation of central *dirigisme* even in minor matters, so it is futile to put forward our own proposals once again" (director of a precision engineering factory).

' "In spite of the fact that we, as an exporting enterprise, have no formal employment limit, our industrial association has been pressing us for weeks to cut two posts from our administrative staff of about a hundred, because it wants to improve its appropriate plan indicator. Under such conditions, how can one take seriously the talk about our discretion in more serious matters?" (director of a machine-tool factory)' [*39*].

The higher authorities reacted to the situation described above by (a) use of administrative sanctions and (b) massive rejections of enterprise plan proposals.

B. Jaszczuk, in the key speech already quoted, made it quite clear that submitting too low plans will result in administrative sanctions against their authors, be they at enterprise, industrial association, or ministerial level. 'Conflicting opinions . . . are welcome and useful . . . At the moment, however, when the plan proposal has been formally submitted to higher authorities it represents the stand which the management of the enterprise, industrial association, or economic ministry has taken, and this stand can and should be examined. If, as a result of criticism, such a plan has been revised upward, this fact does not absolve from responsibility the authors of the plan, who violated the government guidelines. In such cases—and this is being stressed by a circular letter of CC Secretariat—workers' self-management (KSR) and Party organs have not only a right but also a duty to examine the attitude of enterprise management' [*31*].[1] The first dismissals of enterprise management which submitted too low plan proposals have been reported already by the Polish press [*23*]. Unfortunately, plan proposals submitted under the threat of administrative sanctions give rather small hope not only of their 'optimality' but even feasibility, especially if they pertain to the relatively distant future, as is the case with medium-term plans.

Simultaneously with the first dismissals for submitting too low plan proposals, a massive rejection of enterprise plans occurred—a complete *novum* in Polish planning practice. What happened in the Association of Electronic Industry 'Unitra' may serve as a good illustration: out of 44 enterprises constituting the association, plans of 11, i.e. of 25 per

---

[1] This approach resembles the procedure used by Polish censorship. There exists a 'gentlemen's agreement' between censors and editors that if an article submitted for censorship is in *typescript*, its rejection remains 'off the record'. Rejection of an article submitted in galley proofs is, however, a different matter: this fact is not only recorded, but also the rejected article is reprinted in restricted numbers for circulation among a selected audience of high Party officials. This practice gives rise to an interesting editorial strategy which, however, is well outside the scope of our present inquiry. (Personal knowledge.)

cent, have been completely rejected [23]. At the same time the 'Unitra' case reveals the extent of disparity between government guidelines and enterprise proposals. This is summarized in Table 2.5.

Table 2.5: *The Disparities between 1970 Plan Guidelines and Enterprise Proposals*
(Association of Electronic Industry 'Unitra')

Selected plan indices	Unit of measurement	Plan guidelines	Enterprise proposals
Average increase of labour productivity	%	11·5	7·4
Share of labour productivity increase in output growth	%	79·0	47·0
Total increase of employment	'000s	3·6	6·7

Source: Table constructed on the basis of data in Dudzinski W.: 'When an Industrial Association Says No!', *ZG*, 38, 1969.

The phenomenon of massive rejection of plans endangers the original deadline for plan preparation. The time allowed to enterprises for preparing their plan proposals for 1970 and 1971–5 was six months—May–October 1969—much too short a period to do the job properly according to the practically unanimous opinion of enterprise directors [39]. Now, when a substantial proportion of enterprises have to elaborate their plans anew, meeting this deadline seems out of the question.

The most puzzling aspect of current Polish planning reform is the complete lack of adequate preparation. Fundamental reforms of the guided-market type in most cases require for their implementation—and frequently even for their formulation—a favourable political situation. The latter may be shortlived, and hence haste in their introduction may be considered justified, in spite of negative repercussions resulting from efforts to implement policy measures which are neither fully elaborated nor internally consistent. There is, however, no obvious political or social reason why economic reforms which aim for the improvement rather than the radical change of the existing economic system could not be prepared thoroughly and without undue haste, as was, for example, the case with the GDR reforms which started in 1963. Unfortunately, there is no ground for believing that the political situation in Poland—or in the whole of Eastern Europe for that matter—is such that it gives a last chance to partial rather than radical reformers, so they have to rush. And there is a good chance that piecemeal reforms will dominate the scene for quite some time yet.

2.2.2 THE DOMINANT ROLE OF YEARLY PLANS

Four basic types of plans have developed in the planning practice of socialist countries. They are: long-term plans of fifteen to twenty years' duration (frequently called 'perspective plans'); medium-range plans, usually five years long; short-term plans of yearly (two-yearly) duration; and so-called operative plans, quarterly and monthly (at enterprise level also for shorter periods, usually ten days) [44, p. 7]. Judging by their names they differ only in respect to length of time covered, but in fact there are a number of other, important differences.[1]

(1) While medium- and short-term plans are enacted by parliaments and represent, at least theoretically, binding directives to be followed by the CPB and all plan executants, the perspective plans present a desired development path of the economy in the long run and have no binding power on anybody. The main function of the latter is to facilitate better medium-term planning by giving it a frame of reference with a longer time-horizon. Because of this, plan-fulfilment data refer only to yearly and medium-term plans, but never to perspective plans.

(2) The two aspects of the universal character of planning—mentioned above—apply to yearly and FYPs only, but not to the perspective plan. Perspective plans are mainly the result of the work of specialized organs (not of the whole planning apparatus from the enterprise up) and are usually drawn only for the national economy as a whole.[2]

During the whole period of Polish economic reforms, repeated efforts have been made not only to diminish the *scope* of the national economic plan, discussed in a previous section, but also to increase the relative role of mid-term plans at the CPB level and of yearly (two-yearly) plans at lower levels at the expense of short-term and operative plans, respectively. Unfortunately, these efforts have not succeeded.

Leaving aside the 1957–8 period, when most reform measures, including proposals concerning the scope and character of planning, rarely passed the stage of good intentions, let us concentrate on the 1965–6 reform programme. Here we have not merely a *formal* reform programme; it was proposed not by an advisory body such as the Economic Council (which formulated the outline of the 1957–8 reforms) but by the Plenum of the ruling PUW Party and then translated into a concrete action programme by numerous government decrees. Moreover, it is especially interesting that official propaganda claims that it was successfully implemented [40, pp. 98–9].[3]

The essence of the IVth Plenum resolution (July 1965) in the sphere which concerns us here is the following: to introduce *continuity* of

[1] These differences are due, however, to different time horizons of the respective plans.

[2] Recently in some countries, e.g. Poland, perspective plans for industrial associations (separate branches of the economy) and FYPs for enterprises are also being elaborated. See Ch. 3.

[3] The official character of [1] is indicated by the fact that it is published in the *Library for Teachers' Self-improvement* in 80,000 copies.

planning by proper coordination of perspective, mid- and short-term plans. The purpose was twofold: (a) to eliminate the impact of terminal planning on growth fluctuations and (b) to improve the quality of planning by better coordination of plans with different time horizons [44, pp. 7–12]. This was to be achieved by: (a) maintaining permanently the twenty-year time horizon of the perspective plan by constantly bringing it up to date, after completion of every FYP; (b) simultaneously with the formal FYP, the basic outline of the next two years was to be elaborated, to 'smooth' out the transition from one FYP period to the other; (c) simultaneously with the yearly plan the guidelines for the next year were to be prepared and passed to all subordinate units; only two groups of indicators of these guidelines for the next planning year were to be of obligatory character, namely targets in research and development and technical progress and in investment and construction [44, p. 11; 40, p. 97]. The next year's indicators as a whole were to replace the yearly issuance of guidelines for the next year's formal plan construction. 'This will make possible the elimination of the stage of guideline preparation for next year's plan and the use of the time saved in this way for . . . improving the quality of economic analysis in the process of plan building. It will enable enterprises and industrial associations to start their plan preparation earlier and hence contribute to their better quality' [44, p. 11].

These were the improvements to be introduced for the 1966–70 plan. Let us see what has been achieved, using the latest available data.

Only in the sphere of the perspective plan—which as we have already indicated, is a non-operative document produced by staff rather than the line of the planning hierarchy—was the promise formally fulfilled. Poland, thus far, has had three perspective plans: for 1960–75, produced under Professor M. Kalecki's guidance in 1957; for 1965–80, elaborated in 1964; and for 1970–85 in 1969 [41, pp. 405–6; 40, p. 102]. The quality of these plans is unknown, because they have neither been published nor made available to anybody except a very narrow circle.[1]

If we now turn to mid-term plans, not only did their extension in the form of the extra two-year guidelines not materialize in practice, but even the five-year time horizon turned out to be too long for effective planning. In this respect there is no visible improvement over the last twenty years or so. 'Experience indicates that in practice the time horizon of our planning does not exceed three to four years' [40, p. 102], and the author then indicates that *none* of the mid-term plans survived without fundamental revision in the second half of its implementation (see 2.1.1.A for details).

---

[1] On Professor Kalecki's plan we have, however, two of his articles. The first, published in 1958, describes briefly the Polish plan for 1961–75. The second, published in 1963, presents the method he used in constructing a perspective plan. For a summary of these two articles and detailed references, see [50, Appendix 1].

There is also no improvement in the length of the time horizon of short-term planning. Here the official point of view is that '. . . from 1964–5 substantial stability in the process of plan construction and its improvement has been achieved' [40, p. 98]. To prove his thesis, the author points out a number of changes supposedly introduced into the planning and management mechanism during the 1965–8 period. The points referring to changes in planning—which concern us at this moment—are the following: (a) introduction of two-year planning and (b) introduction of two-year financial norms [40, pp. 98–9]. Unfortunately none of these changes took place.

We shall analyse points (a) and (b) together. This is justified because changes of financial norms are tantamount to changes in plan directives (of course the opposite statement is not necessarily true).

The advantages of introducing stable financial norms have long been recognized by East European economists and planners. By extending the enterprise time horizon, they were to create the basis for policy decisions going beyond the short-term manœuvres to which, under yearly fixed financial norms, the enterprise is forced to limit itself. Moreover, stability of financial obligation is a necessary precondition for effective functioning of economic incentives based on profit or profitability success indicators (see below and 6.4 and 7.2) and for broadening the scope of enterprise decisions, including a certain measure of self-financing, which is also being advocated [49]. Because of these advantages, the long-term financial norms were always high on the list of reform measures.

The last effort to introduce a minimum of financial stability for Polish enterprises was made in 1966 when the principle of fixing financial norms for two years was introduced [42]. It proved, however, abortive, as had numerous previous attempts. In practice, most financial norms not only do not remain unchanged for two years, but are in fact changed several times a year, and this practice is almost universal throughout Polish industry.

Let us take, for example, the obligatory index of profitability. The findings of a special commission for studying the functioning of the financial system of Polish industrial enterprises, created in January 1968 by the CC of PUWP, revealed that in 1967 in all enterprises of the industrial association of Iron and Steel, the planned profitability was changed one to four times, averaging 2·6 changes per enterprise per year; and in 60 per cent of all enterprises, the last change was introduced on 20 December 1967 [45]. The industrial association quoted was by no means an exception. The same study found that in 1967 the obligatory index of profitability was changed in 100 per cent of metallurgical plants studied, in 98 per cent of light industry enterprises, in 95 per cent of machine building and chemical enterprises, and in 61 per cent of enterprises of the food industry. Another key financial norm—

4

the share of profit going to the enterprise development fund—was changed during the same year in 80–100 per cent of enterprises, depending on the industrial associations studied [46].

The reason why all efforts to introduce long-term financial norms proved unsuccessful lies in the fact that they cannot be combined with the practice of yearly planning targets. Because the reliability of planning tasks is very low (e.g. it has been found out that only 15–40 per cent of products planned are in fact produced by Polish cotton factories [47, p. 331]), and this applies not only to the product-mix target but also to material supplies, investment completion dates, etc. (see 3.2.2.C and E), the necessary changes and/or departures from plan targets cause great fluctuations in enterprise financial results. It turned out, for example, that in 1967, out of 533 enterprises representing 25 industrial associations, only 18 per cent fulfilled their profit target in the 95–110 per cent range. 284 enterprises were in the 50–95 per cent range and the rest in the minus 50 per cent to plus 600 per cent range [45]. Under such circumstances, long-term financial norms are clearly impossible. For the sake of stabilizing the enterprises' financial position and safeguarding the functioning of economic incentives, the variable financial norms must be used as a 'shock absorber' of planning changes.

Here we come across another serious drawback of yearly planning tasks. As the experience of all socialist countries shows, frequent changes in planning targets are inherent in administrative planning. Frequent changes of planning tasks, however, carry serious consequences.

First of all, they completely undermine the functioning of incentive systems connected with a profitability index and with the existence of a development fund dependent on volume of profit achieved. If the profitability target or share of profit going to the development fund are adjusted according to actual performance and subject to bargaining at any time, then the link between profit maximization and managerial bonus maximization—the latter constituting the real goal of the socialist enterprise—is broken, and profit maximization *sensu stricto* is replaced by bargaining behaviour aimed at favourable plan changes. Secondly, the time horizon of enterprise decisions is further shortened artificially. Instead of being of yearly duration—which is already much too short—the enterprise time horizon shrinks to the few months actually elapsing between plan revisions. Thirdly, it introduces an element of *institutional uncertainty*, as the enterprise management realizes that at any moment their losses or achievements[1] may be nullified or rectified by decisions

---

[1] In most cases the revision of plan targets during the year consists of lowering the original tasks. Discussing the 'sources' which enable Polish industrial associations to lower plan tasks for their member-enterprises, T. Kierczynski lists: (1) downward revision of plan targets of industrial associations themselves; (2) industrial associations' 'reserves', consisting of allocating plan tasks higher than necessary for meeting their own plan targets; and (3) 'increasing tasks of those few enterprises which were on the way to substantial plan overfulfilment' [45].

of higher authorities. It hardly needs stressing that this uncertainty is not conducive to economic behaviour. Fourthly, frequent plan changes not only destroy incentives for improving the quality of the plan but also undermine the very belief that planning itself is a useful exercise. This conviction is strengthened by the fact that most plan changes introduced during the year are not followed by proper adjustment in related plan indices. These adjustments would require in practice re-working the whole technico-economic plan during the year, which, for practical reasons, is not usually possible.[1]

As is well known, all short-term planning suffers from the inherent contradiction between the time required for its proper preparation and data availability, which improves the shorter the time span between the actual completion of the current plan and the start of preparatory work on the next. This is obvious because the time span referred to above must be covered by 'expected plan fulfilment' data, which frequently are off the mark (see 9.1.1). How tight the schedule is may be illustrated by quoting the official Polish timetable of yearly plan construction: the CPB's guidelines for economic ministries and District Councils—end of May; the economic ministries' plans, including allocation of planned tasks between industrial associations—end of August; national economic plan ready for approval by the Council of Ministers—20 October; industrial associations receive their guidelines also on 20 October and have to elaborate plan indices for their subordinate enterprises within three weeks, before 10 November; enterprises must finish constructing their technico-economic plans within one month (10 November–15 December); the remaining two weeks of December may then be used for introducing changes resulting from the Council of Ministers' decisions and the Act of Parliament approving the plan [43, pp. 275–6].

The only change which the reforms introduced was in stage one of this timetable of plan construction which now reads: industrial associations' plan proposals (based on guidelines received with the last year's plan tasks) must be submitted before 30 June [40, p. 97]. This change, which

---

[1] A Polish university textbook on the financial system of industrial enterprises describes the results of frequent plan changes in the following manner: '(1) the functioning of incentives becomes problematic . . . The change of plan targets by their adjustment to actual performance serves as justification of many irregularities which are the enterprise's fault, and it has a strong disincentive effect; (2) the practice of plan changes makes impossible, practically speaking, the functioning of incentives for taut planning; (3) there are no incentives for improving planning techniques . . . plan indices are frequently changed in a haphazard manner (e.g. the wage plan is changed but the cost plan is not, etc.), so the enterprise during the year has no internally consistent (balanced) plan at all; as a result, the yearly plan becomes less and less a management instrument and serves mainly as a formal document justifying payment of bonuses; (4) the planning work at enterprise and industrial association level goes on the whole year round; the employees are at the same time convinced that the usefulness of their work is minimal . . .' [47, p. 332].

could be important, proved in practice of illusory rather than real significance. Because even the yearly plan targets showed such instability, the initial guidelines for the next year required a lot of additional information before they could be used for preparing proposals for next year's plan. This additional information could not be supplied by the Planning Commission and economic ministries earlier than the regular (pre-reform) yearly guidelines had been supplied previously. Moreover, the deadlines for further stages of plan construction (given above) remained practically the same. As a result, the anticipated relaxation of the over-tight schedule of yearly plan preparation did not materialize, and the timetable is frequently violated. In consequence '. . . enterprise economic activity in the first quarter of the year, and sometimes even longer, is [frequently] based on temporary tasks provisionally approved for this period . . . This diminishes the reality of the plan, because temporary tasks for the first quarter of the year are not always identical with final tasks given to enterprises at a later date' [4, pp. 274 and 276].

As will be shown in 3.2 the counterpart of the dominant role of the yearly plan at macro-level is the dominant role of quarterly and monthly plans at enterprise level.

In drastic contrast to Polish practice, as well as the practice of other 'cautious reformers', were the radical reforms in Czechoslovakia of the pre-invasion period and in Hungary, which abolished—in principle— the yearly planning targets and elevated the medium-term plans representing government economic policy, intended economic and fiscal measures, to decisive importance. This represents a *basic* departure from the traditional economic system which—as will be seen later— is of profound consequence for the effectiveness of economic reforms not only of planning but also of the management mechanism.

2.2.3 THE METHOD OF PLAN CONSTRUCTION

As we have already indicated, the method of plan construction depends on the length of the time horizon. Because it is the yearly plan which is most intimately connected with industrial management, our further discussion will be limited to this plan alone. The prevailing method of constructing the *short-term* plan is still the process of successive approximation achieved by administrative procedure. We shall call this the *administrative iterative process*. The use of this method, which is well known and does not need describing here,[1] means that both its basic techniques and inherent limitations still apply to present-day Polish planning.

A *Material Balances*

The main tool of Polish planning remains material balances. Within

[1] See e.g. [76, pp. 15–23] for a brief description in English.

the present system of material balances the following basic categories may be distinguished: (1) According to the scope of a given balance there are so-called economic, users', national, and regional material balances. (2) According to the type of input, universal (e.g. coal), specific (e.g. wool), and spare parts, material balances are distinguished. (3) According to time horizon, long-term, yearly, and quarterly material balances are found in Polish planning practice. (4) Finally, balances of machines and equipment and balances of sub-contracting products are also prepared [56, p. 492].

At present, the majority of material balances are the so-called economic balances, which are prepared for inputs *not* centrally rationed (see Table 2.6).

For centrally rationed inputs, so-called users' balances are elaborated. The main difference between economic and users' balances is that the demand side of the latter specifies in detail the main non-market users of a given product. These balances form the basis for elaborating supply plans of rationed and use-controlled[1] goods. The number of such goods has diminished substantially in the late 1950s and early 1960s in most East European countries. The available data are given in Tables 2.6

Table 2.6: Number of Centrally Rationed Inputs and Material Balances in Poland

Year	Number of centrally rationed inputs	Number of material balances
1955	1,575	2,000–3,000[a]
1957	1,088	—
1958	455	—
1960	325	—
1963	400	—
1964	416	1,600
1965	463	—
1966–1970	c. 400–450	—[b]

[a] See source in Table 2.7, p. 52; at the period of maximum development of material balancing; year 1955 refers to the number of rationed inputs only.

[b] Lack of data. The figure 1,200–1,500 seems a reasonable approximation for FYP 1966–70.

Source: Ekonomika przemyslu (The Economics of Industry), Warsaw, 1966, pp. 503–4 and p. 253.

[1] In Poland and some other Eastern European countries there are two types of centrally allocated inputs: rationed and use-controlled. The rationed goods can be bought only by buyers who have been formally entitled by the appropriate authorities to buy a given good up to a strictly specified limit. The use-controlled inputs can be distributed exclusively by especially authorized suppliers, who also have the right to control the use of these inputs by their customers. It means that use-controlled inputs cannot be used for purposes other than those specified by appropriate regulations. Violating these regulations is usually considered a criminal offence, for example, in Poland the penalty for violating the use-control regulations is up to three years imprisonment. See [69, pp. 31–62; and 58, pp. 198–204].

Table 2.7: Number of Material Balances and Centrally Rationed
Inputs in some Eastern European Countries and USSR

Country	Year	No. of material balances	No. of rationed inputs
Bulgaria	1965	1,060	1,060
	1966	1,060	164
Czechoslovakia	1966	2,000–3,000[a]	76
GDR	1966	6,000	c. 4,500
Hungary	1966	2,000–3,000[a]	c. 300–400
USSR	1966	20,000[b]	20,000

[a] At the period of maximum development of material balancing; year 1966 refers to the number of rationed inputs only.

[b] This figure includes industrial inputs only. The total number of centrally balanced and rationed items is much higher, e.g. in the 1960s the USSR Ministry of Health itself rationed about 10,000 items.

Source: T. Cholinski, G. Michajlow, S. Milewski, Gospodarka zapasami w krajach socjalistycznych (Management of Stocks in Socialist Countries), Warsaw, 1967, pp. 43–54. The book is based mainly on over 50 papers delivered at the IVth International Conference on the Economics of Material Allocation (Warsaw, November 1965) by Bulgarian, Czechoslovak, GDR, Hungarian, Polish, and Soviet experts. The papers themselves are not easily available.

and 2.7. A proper interpretation of these data is, however, essential. First of all, as can be seen from the tables, the number of rationed and use-controlled goods is, in most East European countries, diminishing at a quicker rate than the number of material balances for planning purposes. As long as the principle of detailed planning and of yearly directive indices is adhered to, there is a need for a large number of material balances, if feasible and consistent plan targets are aimed at. It is worth quoting here an opinion of one of the Polish experts in industrial planning: 'The development tendencies of central rationing and material balancing are different ... During the period when excessive rationing was being eliminated there was also a tendency towards lessening the scope of [material] balances. But the proper development is different. If we want to diminish rationing, the scope and precision of balancing should be extended. For in practice only through balances can the demand for non-rationed goods be determined' [56, p. 504, italics in the original. See also 52, pp. 43–54]. Needless to say, it is true only for the traditional economic system.

Secondly, preparation of most material balances in Poland is no longer the exclusive task of the CPB but of economic ministries, industrial associations, and supply organizations, and the number of material balances which have to be approved by the CM and the Planning Commission (PC) has diminished considerably. For example, at present in Poland, the CM approves material balances of thirteen inputs particularly important and in short supply (among others they include coal types 31–8, coking coal, aluminium, zinc, copper, lead, steel pipes, bloomery products, cement, timber, meat, and food grains). The Chairman of the PC approves approximately 80 material balances, while the rest are approved by the appropriate economic ministries or authorized directors of industrial associations [54]. 'At the same time the total number of material balances increased considerably. However, owing to decentralization and the rights given in this sphere to supply organization, it is difficult to know what is the total number of material balances constructed at present [in Poland]' [52, pp. 48–9].

Thirdly, the number of material balances and/or rationed goods can be meaningfully compared over time or between countries only if their level of aggregation is constant and/or known. For example, in Poland in 1969, the commodity group 'Iron and Steel' consisted of 75 rationed sub-groups and 20 balanced (but not rationed) sub-groups [59, pp. 43–9]; the commodity group 'Raw Hides' consisted of 17 rationed sub-groups; and 'Treated Hides' of 18 rationed sub-groups [59, pp. 288–95]. These could be extended at any moment by the Chairman of the PC or diminished by the appropriate economic minister. Whether the level of aggregation at which the number of rationed goods (or material balances) is reported is kept constant in Poland and how it compares to other socialist countries, the present author has not been able to find out.

B 'Synthetic' Financial Plans

Material balances cannot assure consistency of even the 'material production sphere' (in the Marxian sense) of the economy [76, pp. 15–23]. A national economic plan requires, however, for its consistency that the supply of material production and 'non-material services' (in the Marxian sense) equals the demand of intermediate and final *buyers*. This requires coordination not only within and between the flows of 'material' and 'non-material' goods and services—which I shall call 'real flows'—but also between these 'real' flows and appropriate financial flows.

In Polish planning practice coordination of 'real' and financial flows is the task of two so-called *synthetic* financial plans: (a) the balance of money incomes and expenditure of the population which, for the sake of brevity, will be referred to in the following discussion as the household balance, and (b) the financial plan of the state [57, p. 171; 70, pp. 196–7]. In contrast to *operative* financial plans which form a part of the total plan of every economic unit—from the enterprise to the national economy as a whole—the synthetic financial plans are of a purely analytical character.

The essential function of the household balance is to assess, as precisely as possible, the purchasing power of the population and to assure its equilibrium with the amount of consumer goods and services available. Table 2.8 shows such a balance with data for 1964 and 1965.

Table 2.8: Balance of Money Incomes and Expenditures of Population (in million zlotys)

Income (1)	1964 plan (2)	1965 draft plan (3)	Expenditure (4)	1964 plan (5)	1965 draft plan (6)
1. Remuneration covered by wage-bill	92,567·5	101,200·0	1. Purchase of goods	120,040·0	128,950·0
1a. Reserve of wage-bill for overfulfilment of industrial production plan	—	500·0	1a. Purchase of goods from off-plan supplies from industry		500·0
2. Remuneration not covered by wage-bill	4,754·0	4,750·0	2. Purchase of services	10,706·5	12,440·0
of which: factory fund	1,900·0	1,800·0	3. Taxes and charges	14,496·0	14,262·0
3. Business trips allowance	1,135·0	1,210·0	(a) personal income tax	7,015·0	7,000·0
			(b) land tax	2,930·5	2,893·0
4. Social benefits	13,831·0	14,877·0	(c) turnover and income tax	1,340·0	1,322·5
			(d) other taxes and charges	3,210·5	3,046·5
5. Income of population from sale of agricultural products	30,135·0	30,830·0	4. Payment of credits	7,719·5	8,367·5
			(a) for circulating capital	3,789·0	4,060·0
6. Income of non-socialized sector from sales of goods and services to socialized sector	4,350·0	4,490·0	(b) investment credit	830·5	907·5
			(c) for instalment purchases	3,100·0	3,400·0
7. Credits:	8,646·0	10,185·0	5. Personal and material insurance charges	1,928·0	2,014·5
(a) for circulating capital	4,050·0	4,475·0	6. Fees for social organizations	2,290·0	2,375·0
(b) for investment	1,596·0	2,010·0	7. Other expenditures of population	1,686·0	1,733·5
(c) for instalment purchases	3,000·0	3,700·0	8. Total expenditures	158,866·0	170,692·5
8. Payments of personal and material insurance compensations	1,388·0	1,499·0	9. Changes in the volume of money holdings	3,250·0	4,750·0
9. Income from sale of non-agricultural goods	1,410·0	1,600·0			
10. Other incomes	2,849·5	3,256·5			
11. Total incomes	161,026·0	174,392·5			
12. Balance reserve	1,050·0	1,050·0			
Total (11 + 12)	162,116·0	175,442·5	Total (8 + 9)	162,116·0	175,442·5

Source: Wolski M.: Index Tables for Construction of Economic Plans. Central School of Planning and Statistics. Advanced Course of National Economic Planning. Teaching Materials Vol. 26, Warsaw, 1968. Mimeographed. In English, p. 128.

In Poland, the household balance includes incomes and expenditures of existing private sectors. The balance strives for a certain excess of planned expenditures of the population over their planned incomes, as an extra precaution. In Poland this reserve is set at about the 1 per cent level [57, p. 184].

Polish economists are not satisfied with the present methods of constructing the household balance. For example, they complain that both sides of the balance consist of estimated figures (past performance corrected by a number of factors, such as planned increase of output, changes in the level of stocks, export–import ratio of consumer goods, etc.), rather than figures arrived at by adding up the relevant parts of other plans. This is the result of the difficulty of aggregating the existing data according to the requirements of the balance.[1]

The objective of the state financial plan, illustrated in Table 2.9, is to assure the financial equilibrium of the state by coordinating material and financial planning on the one hand, and different financial plans on the other.

Again, Polish economists are not satisfied—and justly so—either with the state financial plan in its present form or with its role in the planning process. For example, Professor Z. Fedorowicz indicates that the plan in its present form: (a) does not help in coordinating physical and financial planning because, among other weaknesses the plan neither distinguishes between demands for capital and consumer goods nor takes either of them fully into account; (b) fails in its function as a device for coordinating different financial plans. Even its relation to the household balance—the other synthetic plan—is obscure and difficult to ascertain. Some items occur in both plans (e.g. increase of the population's money holdings), others overlap partially, etc.; (c) is too aggregative for coordination purposes. For example, financial outlays for increases of stocks and reserves constitute one item in the plan, but in practice are controlled by three different financial plans: state budget, credit plan, and enterprise financial plans. The practice, however, is better than the form of the financial plan implies. In the course of elaborating the state financial plan, a number of useful supplementary tables are calculated, which have operational significance. The rather discouraging state of synthetic financial plans may be due to the fact that their legal role is rather unclear (the state budget is approved by parliament, but synthetic financial plans are not), as is their organizational place (in contrast to operational financial plans, synthetic financial plans have no clear-cut place in the administrative hierarchy) [57, pp. 186–90]. This may be the reason why the financial plan in matrix form, long proposed by Polish experts on fiscal and

---

[1] For a comprehensive discussion on household balances see [53; 60, pp. 102–37; 63; 77, pp. 103–202].

4*

Table 2.9: Financial Balance of the State (in million zlotys)

Revenue	1964 plan	1965 draft plan
I. Financial accumulation of enterprises	69,896,5	75,217,0
II. Depreciation	23,244,5	25,300,0
III. Revenue of state budget	32,490,0	33,455,0
1. Income from national economy	2,410,0	2,300,0
2. Payment from social and cultural units and establishments	1,107,0	1,180,0
3. Taxes and charges paid by the non-socialized sector	5,143,5	4,970,5
4. Taxes and charges paid by population	8,836,0	8,687,0
5. Miscellaneous revenue	1,478,0	1,550,0
6. Social insurance	13,515,0	14,767,5
IV. Public services	377,0	431,5
1. Payments from the socialized sector	63,5	78,5
2. Payments from the non-socialized sector	308,5	347,5
3. Payments from population	5,0	5,5
V. Revenue of financial institutions	3,060,0	3,635,0
VI. Increase of money issue and savings	3,250,0	4,750,0
VII. Payment of credits by the non-socialized sector and population	7,747,0	8,331,5
VIII. Miscellaneous revenue	2,669,5	2,455,0
Total revenue	**143,328,0**	**150,105,0**

Expenditure	1964 plan	1965 draft plan
I. Current expenditure	53,589,5	58,476,5
1. Current budget expenditure	43,598,5	47,284,5
(a) national economy	6,158,5	6,720,5
(b) social and cultural services	18,901,0	21,041,0
(c) social insurance	13,486,5	14,523,0
(d) public administration and administration of justice	3,816,5	3,948,5
(e) internal transfers	541,0	666,0
(f) estimate of price and wage changes		—
(g) non-distributed expenditures	295,0	126,5
(h) expenditure from budget surplus	400,0	250,0
2. Appropriations for public services	311,0	392,0
3. Factory Fund and Cooperative Funds	2,630,0	2,625,0
4. Credits granted to non-socialized economy and population	7,050,0	8,175,0
(a) credits for circulating capital	4,050,0	4,475,0
(b) credit sales transactions	3,000,0	3,700,0
II. Accumulation expenditure	71,785,5	77,584,0
1. Investment appropriations	58,238,0	58,327,0
(a) investments in socialized sector	56,802,0	56,457,0
(b) credits for non-socialized sector and population	1,436,0	1,910,0
2. Outlays on major repairs and other outlays	10,417,5	11,200,5
(a) major repairs	10,092,5	10,848,5
(b) mining damages	325,0	352,0
3. Increase in stocks	2,825,0	7,975,0
(a) industry	3,215,5	4,405,0
(b) market stocks	1,668,5	1,300,0
(c) other stocks	1,279,0	2,052,0
4. Expenditure of state farms for increase in stocks	305,0	260,5
III. Other expenditures	10,832,0	11,408,5
IV. Reserves	1,050,0	2,300,0
Total expenditures	**137,257,0**	**149,769,0**

Table 2.10: National Income (in billion zlotys)

Contents	1964 plan	1965 draft plan
I. Domestic national income	226·2	235·2
II. National income created	229·6	237·8
III. National income distributed	230·8	234·7
1. Consumption (total)	174·2	179·0
2. Accumulation	55·2	52·8
(a) net investment	40·7	40·6
(b) increase in stocks and reserves	14·5	12·2
2. Commodity reserves	+1·4	+2·8

Source: As for Table 2.8, p. 66.

monetary matters,[1] is still at the experimental and study stage in spite of its unquestioned superiority as a coordinating and analytical tool,

Some authors [*60*, pp. 16–62; *62*, pp. 35–6; *74*, pp. 121–30; *77*, pp. 7–103] who prefer to use a broader category, synthetic balances of the national economy (rather than synthetic financial plans), include here also the balance of national income created and distributed. This balance, illustrated in Table 2.10, is an official part of the national economic plan but in a very aggregated and primitive form [*62*, p. 35; *74*, p. 130].

C *The Material Product System*

It is important to notice that Polish planning is still hindered by the use of the Material Product System, based on the Marxian theory of productive and non-productive labour, whereas all non-communist countries use the System of National Accounts.[2] A number of Polish

[1] See especially [*70; 71; 72; 73*] for a detailed examination of the development and application of the 'balances of material–financial flows'. [*70*] presents two such balances with a different level of aggregation for the real Polish data for 1962. Many of these data are not available anywhere else. The smaller of these balances is reproduced in Table 2.11. [*72*] gives the most comprehensive critique of existing synthetic plans as well as other 'summary financial balances' (*bilanse sumaryczne*), i.e. state budget, credit plan, and balance of foreign transactions. It also argues convincingly the superiority of the material–financial flows approach over current practice. The author of these articles, Professor J. Wierzbicki from the Research Institute of the Ministry of Finance, is at present the main expert and exponent of material–financial balances, which are also supported by almost all Polish financial experts, but ignored thus far by planners.

[2] For a comparative analysis of the Material Product System and the System of National Accounts see [*68*]. The continued use of the MPS illustrates to what extent subservience to an obsolete doctrine can be harmful. Without referring to this subservience it is impossible to explain, for example, why among Polish synthetic plans there is no 'balance of production and distribution of "non-material" services'. Lack of such balance is, according to most Polish financial experts, '. . . one of the main reasons for the internal inconsistency of national economic plans in respect of the redistribution of national income' [*72*, p. 2]. The MPS also unduly complicates

Table 2.11: Synthetic Table of Material–Financial Flows in Poland

Receipts (incomes) \ Outgoings (expenditures)	Number of line	Material production (costs)	Foreign transactions[a]	Non-material services not included in the state budget	State budget (expenditures)
Number of column	0	I	II	III	IV
Material production (receipts)	I	583·8	88·1	9·7	27·9
Foreign transactions[a]	II	60·0	0·7	1·0	49·7
Non-material services	III	15·8	1·5	2·8	5·3
State budget (receipts)	IV	148·2	52·3	7·9	3·1
Households (wages and incomes from non-socialized sector)	V	235·8	4·8	18·4	55·2
Funds for financing accumulation (incomes)	VI	7·9	0·1	1·0	78·5
Other funds (incomes)	VII	65·2	0·0	12·2	15·1
Increase of bank debits (means of payments)	VIII	—	2·0	2·2	7·5
Errors, omissions, and changes in the amounts due	IX	1·6	0·1	0·1	0·
Total	I–IX	1,118·3	149·6	55·3	242·

[a] In current zlotys (not deviza-zlotys as usually reported in the official statistics). The table was prepared in the Research Institute of the Ministry of Finance and is described in detail in [20, pp. 204–14] except *how* the deviza-zlotys were recalculated into current zlotys. It only says that it '. . . required tiresome calculations' [*sic*] [70, p. 205].

Source: [70, pp. 206–7].

economists—including high government officials[1]—suggest expansion of the Material Product System by adding to the sphere of 'material production' two others: (a) the sphere of so-called 'commercial services', i.e. services which are produced by khozraschyot enterprises and then sold to the population, and (b) the sphere of 'other non-material services', which would include general social services such as national defence, judiciary, and general state administration. The latter sphere would be treated as costs of the functioning of the national

[1] Professor P. Sulmicki, who conceived the balance of material and money flow, described in [70] and who directed their elaboration for 1958–61 (see [70, p. 197, fn.]), is Director of the Research Unit of the Polish National Bank, and Professor L. Zienkowski is Deputy Director of the Research Unit of Central Statistical Office.

the compilation of GNP and NNP statistics. The dividing line between 'material' and 'non-material' spheres frequently cuts through an enterprise where the accounting ignores this division and hence requires 'arbitrary estimations' [72, p. 3]. The use of the MPS is also largely responsible for the fact that '. . . the existing system of economic records and statistics is not adequate for the requirements of comprehensive macro-economic analysis and synthetic [comprehensive] planning' [72, p. 10].

1962 (in milliard zlotys)

useholds enditures)	Funds for financing accumulation (expenditures)	Other funds (expenditures)	Increase of bank credits	Errors, omissions, and changes in the amounts outstanding	Total
V	VI	VII	VIII	IX	I–IX
270·7	130·9	1·7	—	5·5	1,118·5
10·9	26·2	—	0·1	1·0	149·6
20·9	—	8·6	0·6	−0·2	55·3
20·7	0·8	4·7	4·7	—	242·4
2·1	5·6	6·3	0·6	4·1	332·9
0·5	—	62·1	13·6	3·4	167·1
1·5	—	—	—	—	94·0
5·6	0·0	2·5	—	—	19·8
—	3·6	8·1	0·2	—	13·8
32·9	167·1	94·0	19·8	13·8	—

economy [*78*, pp. 56–9; *60*, pp. 16–62]. These proposals differ in details, but all aim towards a more comprehensive and pragmatically useful picture of the national economy;[1] they are still at the research and postulational stage [*78*, p. 56].

D *Effectiveness Calculations*

The main role of material balances and synthetic financial plans is to achieve plan consistency. In addition, limited attempts at partial optimization are also being made by Polish planners. Calculation of economic effectiveness takes—at present—the following main forms: (a) 'comparative analysis and minimization of costs in the case of possible alternative use of existing productive capacities to assure a given volume of production; (b) the account of economic effectiveness

---

[1] 'The balance of the national economy constructed until now can be described as a specific type of branch statistics. It was confined to a narrowly defined balance of national product and income' [*78*, p. 53]. See Table 2.10 for an illustration of this statement.

of investments in considering patterns of replacement, modernization, and various ways of increasing productive capacities;... (c) the account of the so-called current effectiveness of foreign trade, calculated on the basis of existing productive capacities; and (d) the account of the so-called investment effectiveness of foreign trade envisaging different lines of transformation of productive capacities [for export purposes or import substitution production]' [65, pp. 11–12].[1]

The effectiveness calculations and consistency calculations are closely interdependent. Consistency calculations (or so-called balancing accounts in Polish planning parlance) are based on input coefficients, which—whenever possible—should be checked by appropriate effectiveness calculations. This is rarely the case, however, as will be proved in detail in the course of our further discussion.

2.2.4 THE ROLE OF MATHEMATICAL TECHNIQUES AND ELECTRONIC DATA PROCESSING

Socialist countries started working quite late on the application of mathematical techniques to their planning problems. As can be seen from Table 2.12 this delay—in comparison to capitalist countries—is of about ten years in the field of input–output tables. It is even greater in the field of econometric models. In the latter 'the interest in these problems [of econometric models] is only emerging in socialist countries, and any broader experience is still lacking' [94, p. 17].

A *Input–Output Tables*[2]

The state of statistical work on input–output tables in socialist countries in 1970 is given in Table 2.13. Possibilities of using input–output tables in the work of a number of COMECON commissions gave rise to the standardization of efforts in this sphere. During 1966–7, the Permanent Statistical Commission of COMECON elaborated proposals for uniform principles for the construction of statistical input–output tables of COMECON countries. It was also decided to accept a common starting date of 1968 or 1969 for elaborating standardized input–output tables. The experience of communist countries in the sphere of construction and application of input–output tables was compared and analysed at two COMECON conferences devoted to these problems: in 1961 in Budapest and in 1965 in East Berlin [88; 101; 102]. At the same time, the COMECON Economic Commission started to coordinate efforts in input–output application

---

[1] For a detailed discussion of Polish theoretical achievements and practical experience in effectiveness calculations, consult [55; 67; and 75]. These works contain also extensive bibliographical references.

[2] For this whole section see [103, pp. 200–20].

Table 2.12: Elaborated and Intended Input–Output Tables in Europe and the US

Countries	Starting year	No. of tables elaborated	Years for which tables have been prepared	Tables being elaborated	Intended tables	Intended frequency of tables' elaboration
UK	1949	4	1935, 1948, 1954, 1960	1963	.	.
Austria	1963	—		1961	—	every 3–4 years
Belgium	1956	2	1953–9	1965	.	every 3–4 years
Bulgaria	1960	2	1960, 1963	1968	.	every 2–3 years
Czechoslovakia	1958	5	1956–9, 1962	1967	.	
Denmark	1948	14	1930–9, 1947, 1949, 1953, 1958	.	.	
Finland	1958	2	1956, 1959	.	1964	every 5 years
France	1951	3	1956, 1959, 1962	1965	.	
Greece	1963	2	1954, 1960	.	.	every 4–5 years
Spain	1954	3	1954, 1958, 1962	.	.	every 4 years
Holland	1948	20	1938, 1947–61	1965	every year	every 2 years
Yugoslavia	1955	5	1955, 1958, 1960, 1962, 1964	1966	.	every 2 years
Norway	1947, 1952	16	1947–62	every year	every year	every year
GDR	1957	4	1959–62	1968	every year	every year
West Germany	1962	2	1960, 1962	1965	.	
Poland	1957	7	1956–62	1967	.	every 1–2 years small tables
						every 4–5 years big tables
Portugal	1961	1	1959	.	.	.
Sweden	1957	1	1957	.	.	.
Switzerland	1963	—	—	.	1968	
USA	1936	5	1919, 1929, 1939, 1947, 1958	1965	.	every 5 years
Hungary	1955	8	1957, 1959, 1960, 1965	.	.	every 2–3 years
Italy	1951	2	1950, 1959	1965	.	every 5–10 years
USSR	1924, 1960	2	1923–4, 1959	1966	.	every 3 years

Source: Szybisz B.: Wstep do statystyki przeplywow miedzygaleziowych (Introduction to Statistical Input–Output Tables), Warsaw, 1969, pp. 202–3.

Table 2.13: Statistical Input–Output Tables in Socialist Countries of Eastern Europe and USSR*

No.	Country	Period for which table was elaborated	Units of measurement	Size of the table (no. of separate branches of production)	Prices used	Methods of import calculation (table's variants) A, B, C[1]	Classification unit	Existence of non-balanced sums	Were inverse matrix coefficients calculated?
0		1	2	3	4	5	6	7	8
1.	Bulgaria	1960	monetary	68 × 68	2. Transfer prices	A, B, C	enterprise	Yes	Yes
		1963							
2.	Czecho-slovakia	1956	monetary	10 × 10	1. Final users' prices	·	enterprise	Yes	Yes
		1957	monetary	10 × 10		·			
		1958	monetary	10 × 10	2. Transfer prices	·			
		1959	monetary	10 × 10		B			
		1962	monetary	10 × 10		·			
		1967[2]	monetary	96 × 96					
3.	Poland	1956	monetary	27 × 27	1. Final users' prices	A, B, C	enterprise, commodity (supplementary variant)	Yes	Yes
		1957	monetary	27 × 27		A, B, C			
		1958	monetary	7 × 7	2. Transfer prices	A, B, C			
		1959	monetary	7 × 7		A, B, C			
		1960	monetary	7 × 7		A, B, C			
		1961	monetary	7 × 7		A, B, C			
		1962	monetary	144 × 144					
		1967[2]	monetary	89 × 89					
4.	Hungary	1957	monetary	38 × 38	2. Transfer prices	A, B, C	enterprise	No	Yes
		1959	monetary	95 × 95		A, B, C			
		1961	monetary	54 × 54					
		1960–64	monetary	13 × 13		A, B			
		1965	monetary	95 × 95					
5.	GDR	1959	monetary	28 × 31[3]	1. Final users' prices	B	enterprise	Yes	Yes
		1960	monetary	28 × 31		B			
		1961	monetary	28 × 31		B			
		1962	monetary	28 × 31		B			
		1968[2]	monetary	·					
6.	USSR	1959	monetary	83 × 83	1. Final users' prices	B	enterprise	No	Yes
		1966[2]	physical	157 × 157					

Table 2.13—continued

[1] A: table in which flows of material goods from domestic production and from imports are presented jointly.

B: table in which flows of imported goods are presented separately (in special line).

C: table in which each line presents separately flows of domestic and imported goods.

[2] Table in process of elaboration (1969).

[3] In GDR input-output tables the number of lines and columns is different. First figure refers to number of columns, second refers to number of lines.

* The following supplementary tables have been prepared:

In Bulgaria

1. Industrial commodity production according to product groups
2. Division of agriculture output according to groups of producers and of users
3. National income according to constituent parts
4. Employment and man hours spent in branches of material production
5. Capital goods in branches of material production
6. Norms for working capital in industry

In Czechoslovakia

None

In Poland

1. Rectangular input-output tables

2. Input-Output tables according to different socio-economic sectors
3. Investment and capital repairs matrices
4. Matrix of working capital stock changes
5. Tables characterizing structure of fixed and working capital
6. Labour inputs in physical units

In Hungary

1. Tables on the structure of imports
2. Tables on stock changes
3. Table on wholesale turnover
4. Input coefficients of selected raw materials in individual branches
5. Table on the size of turnover tax

In GDR

1. Partial material supplies balances
2. Balance of financial relationships in national economy
3. Balance of manpower utilization

In USSR

1. Balance of agriculture output
2. Household consumption
3. Social consumption
4. Table of labour inputs

Source: As for Table 2.12, Szybisz B., pp. 204-7.

to planning practice. This was discussed at two conferences in Moscow in 1966 and 1967 [*103*, p. 209].

In Poland, the Central Statistical Office (CSO) started to work on input–output tables in 1957. Thus far input–output tables for the 1956–62 period have been elaborated. At present the CSO is working on the period 1962–7, with 1967 singled out for more detailed (89 × 89) analysis. Such detailed tables will be elaborated only every four or five years. They require special information, which '... in many cases cannot be found in existing statistical reporting, but requires examination of primary sources, extra calculations, and, frequently, estimates. The technique of automatic data processing can, for this purpose, be used only on a very limited scale' [*103*, p. 219]. It is hoped that changes in standard statistical requirements and progress in data processing will facilitate construction of future input–output tables.

The purpose of detailed input–output tables is to create the basis for: (a) the statistical and economic analysis of the structure of economic growth and its long term changes; (b) the improvement of both statistical and planning balances; (c) the introduction of econometric methods and, particularly, of inter-industry analysis to economic planning.

The main purpose of highly aggregated, yearly input–output tables is to assure continuity of analysis and to provide planners with current information on changing structural growth relations [*103*, p. 220].

B *Econometric Models*

If the significance of input–output analysis for planning purposes is already universally admitted—and frequently even exaggerated—in communist countries, the usefulness of econometric models must be still argued. The world literature on econometric models is very extensive, but econometric models describing communist economies are very few indeed.[1] Why should this be the case? Trying to answer this question, the eminent Polish econometrician Professor Z. Pawlowski suggests that '... for too long econometric models have been considered merely as a tool for studying capitalist cycles, instead of a general method for quantitative analysis of economic growth. The second reason lies, probably, in the descriptive character of econometric models ... The fascination with optimizing techniques became so overwhelming that analytical tools presenting "only" the *status quo* have been neglected' [*94*, pp. 38–9].

The present author fully agrees with Pawlowski's argument that—from the viewpoint of planning needs—input–output and econometric models are complementary, and that a strong case can be made for their usefulness as planners' analytical tools, see [*94*, pp. 39–46].

[1] Except for the three Polish works [*79; 86; 94*], only the Hungarians published a small econometric model [*84*].

However, owing to lack of official support, Polish econometric models are few (see p. 76, fn. 1). The biggest one [94]—consisting of seventeen endogenous variables—brought a number of interesting results, among others, strong arguments against the thesis that 'changes in economic policies in subsequent FYPs . . . result in such substantial structural changes that a statistically computed model cannot reflect them' [94, p. 166]. This proved untrue, because most equations showed good or very good approximation to empirical data. It is hoped that further and more extensive work on econometric models will be carried on in Poland and other socialist countries, with greater official understanding of their usefulness.

C Electronic Data Processing (EDP) for Central Planning

At present (1972) all CPBs of socialist countries have their own Computer Centres. The oldest and, by far, the biggest is the Central Computing Centre of Gosplan in the USSR, created about ten years ago, employing over 700 people and equipped with four electronic computers.[1] A few years later, a Department of Electronic Computing was created in the GDR State Planning Commission and a similar unit—in the Czechoslovak CPB (equipped with IBM 7040). In Poland, a Computing Centre in the Planning Commission was organized in 1967-8 on the basis of the Russian built 'Minsk' computer. The Polish experience is far too short for any valid generalization to be made, but the experience of the USSR, GDR, and Czechoslovakia enabled Polish experts to formulate a number of interesting observations (see especially [82]):

(1) The first stage of EDP application to central planning is invariably limited to *partial* problems. As a rule its relation to the main planning process remains loose and frequently, especially in the case of mathematical models, is paralleled by traditional planning methods. At this stage two basic problems are encountered: first, an informational barrier—existing data are rarely adequate in form and content for EDP application, even to partial problems; secondly, what partial problems to choose? The proper answer to the latter should not only lead to concentrating on problems of the immediate biggest pay-off—in terms of improving the quality of planning—but should also facilitate the transition to the second stage of EDP application, i.e. constructing more complex systems.

(2) The socialist countries most advanced in the application of EDP to planning problems are already moving towards these more integrated systems. At this stage the question of the main role of EDP in central planning—encountered already in connection with solving partial

[1] There are also Computer Centres at some Republican Gosplans, e.g. in Ukraine, Bielorussia, Estonia, and Latvia, and plans to organize such centres in a number of other republics [82, p. 30].

problems—becomes particularly acute. Should the EDP at CPB level be used mainly for changing *technical*[1] or *methodological* aspects of planning? There is no uniform answer to this question within socialist countries.

The first approach is followed by the Gosplan Central Computing Centre, which works on the computerization of all central planning calculations. 'It must be stressed that, in spite of the fact that the system is intended to cover all planning computations carried in Gosplan, the system does not interfere with [planning] methodology . . . but limits itself to technical and organizational aspects, such as uniformity of planning forms, reorganization of their flow, assuring that necessary data are available on time, etc. The system as such does not predetermine either the need or the form of the economic-mathematical models which may be used' [*82*, p. 32].

In contrast to this approach, the Czechoslovak project—elaborated in 1967—aimed at far-reaching changes in planning *methodology*. It was based, from the very start, '. . . on the assumption that planning practice will make extensive use of a number of econometric and mathematical models . . . The Czechoslovak project rejected the idea of building the system [of computerized planning calculations] on the basis of a detailed description and analysis of existing methods of planning, because the traditional organization and methodology of planning was never stable enough[2] . . . [The Czechoslovak] project was, however, formulated only in general terms and never left the stage of initial discussions' [*82*, p. 32].

To conclude, '. . . in spite of the few years of partial experimentation, the ideas of more comprehensive solutions [of computerized central planning] are still at the very initial stage' [*82*, p. 32]. This fully applies to the present situation in Poland. With planning methodology basically unchanged, the Computing Centre of the Planning Commission is used mainly for processing a large number of planning data.

D *The Present and the Future*

In Poland, there is a practically unanimous view among planners and mathematical economists that mathematical techniques have, and will have in the foreseeable future, only a limited and supplementary role in central planning. This was unequivocally stated in 1967 at a Polish Academy of Science conference on methods of improving the planning and management of the national economy. '. . . Both our preparation

---

[1] By technical aspects of planning, its organizational, informational, and computing sides are meant.

[2] Similarly, in Poland 'the principles of drawing up the national economic plan have not so far been regulated by any Parliament Act. The Planning Commission submits a plan the composition of which is based on practical experience and theoretical discussions' [*89*, pp. 31–2].

and our informational basis prevent any significant use of optimizing techniques in FYP construction for 1970–5 . . . I personally doubt if even in plan building for 1976–80, these methods will play a role of real importance' [83, p. 376].[1] The prospects for improving plan *consistency* through the use of input–output techniques—a much less ambitious task than plan optimization—are only slightly better. Thus far in Poland mainly statistical, i.e. *ex post*, rather than planning, i.e. *ex ante*, input–output tables have been constructed [96, p. 236] and many difficult problems must be solved before input–output tables will have any operational planning value [see 92; 96; 105, pp. 21–3]. The impact of *ex post* input–output tables, even a relatively big one such as the Polish 1962 table, 142 × 142, has thus far been disappointingly small.[2]

The reasons for this state of affairs are numerous. The planners themselves point to the following: (1) lack of proper, trustworthy information which can be fed into available models [93; 100; 81]; (2) if one thinks of optimizing models on the scale of the national economic plan, there are neither such models of any practical value nor EDP equipment powerful enough to do the calculations which would be necessary [80]; (3) planning calculations based on big aggregates do not always lead to optimal solutions which have practical value. 'Experience indicates that conclusions from [aggregate] models cannot be considered as fully valid' [93, p. 384]. 'Even if solving [the aggregate] model produces better results than the results obtained by traditional planning calculations, we cannot be sure that the former solution is practically feasible, because it is based on aggregated or average data [parameters, limits, etc.]' [98, p. 414]. Frequently '. . . it is difficult to understand what is the impact [on results obtained] of the model's simplified assumptions, and these assumptions are multiple' [93, p. 384].

The present author would add to the above enunciation—which could be easily extended—one extra argument, but of a different nature. The many and profound difficulties of using modern mathematical techniques and EDP for central planning are multiplied in socialist countries by the very broad scope of central planning and its directive character. If one wants to disaggregate the calculations done at macro-level to individual enterprises—as the present planning practice requires—there are no technical possibilities available, either now or in the foreseeable future [96; 105, pp. 21–3].

[1] Planning practice has already proved W. Herer's prognosis for 1971–5 to be true. Instead of using optimizing techniques—an unfeasible proposal—the CPB appealed to enterprises for help in constructing the 1971–5 plan. As we have indicated in 2.2.1, the response has been deeply disappointing thus far.

[2] 'A few years have already elapsed since the input–output table for 1962 was elaborated, but until now it has not been used for tracing the impact of individual planning decisions on the national economy as a whole' [83, p. 376].

There seems to exist a paradoxical relation between the scope of central planning and the appropriate planning techniques. The broader the scope of central planning (and hence the more difficult its tasks), the more primitive the planning techniques it must employ. This sounds paradoxical, to say the least, but it is nevertheless true. The reason is obvious: sophisticated planning techniques are unable at present to cope with a quantitative task of the dimension of the yearly national plan. A task of this dimension can only be approached by an administrative iterative process, with sophisticated quantitative techniques playing only a very supplementary role. So the scope of central planning predetermines the planning techniques that can be used, and the latter predetermines the quality of quantitative calculations (the possibility or impossibility of reaching fully consistent solutions). This paradox explains why less comprehensive national economic plans can make fuller use of more advanced planning techniques, a fact admitted even by some Polish economists.[1] It also indicates that one of the most effective steps towards broader use of mathematical models in *central* planning would be to reduce its task to feasible dimensions, namely macro-planning only. This also means that the effective introduction of mathematical models into central planning is complementary to market-type economic reforms and not their substitute, a problem to which we shall return briefly later.

Because of the existing political climate, the proposals for more effective use of mathematical models in Polish planning do not mention its intimate relation with institutional, market-type reforms, but are limited to purely technical aspects. In addition to improving the informational basis of planning, the proposals include: (1) extensive development of partial optimization, especially at branch level [*83*; *98*; *99*; *100*]; (2) initially interrelating these sub-optimizations into a consistent whole through input–output techniques [*80*; *98*; *99*]; (3) working on multi-level planning, taking as a starting point the Danzig–Wolfe and Kornai–Liptak decomposition algorithms, in the hope that further development of multi-level planning may one day enable us to decompose certain problems of the national economy into a number of sub-problems, the solution of which will lead to overall macro-partial optima. Needless to say, this stage still lies far in the future [*80*, p. 403; *91*].

E *Polarization of Views*

In Poland there is currently an interesting polarization of views on the present and future role of mathematical techniques in central planning. The 'optimists' are theoretical economists, mainly of the dogmatic

---

[1] 'In some capitalist countries economic planning is developing and—we have to say this quite frankly—the planning methods applied there are more scientific than those used in socialist countries' [*104*, p. 391].

variety [as e.g. *90*; *104*]. The present author suspects that this sudden enthusiasm for mathematical solutions on the part of these economists should be seen as a technique for delaying reform of the traditional economic system through *institutional* changes. Moreover, this attitude is in accord with a strong similar trend in the Soviet Union. In contrast, the 'pessimist' ranks consist of planners, mathematical economists, and general economists of 'reformist' variety. The first two groups—as our previous discussion indicated—are too familiar with the problems involved to have any illusions that the 'mathematical solution' to central planning problems is in sight. Pro-reform economists willingly agree that there is a need to press for institutional reforms *now*. Moreover, I believe that even if the 'mathematical solution' were practically possible—which cannot be expected in the foreseeable future—it would leave unsolved the problem of motivation, and hence of improvements and innovations. It would not be a satisfactory solution if improvements in technical coefficients and changes in national product-mix lag behind other countries because of lack of innovations. As experience of the traditional economic system shows (see 7.6), the rate of technical progress is slow under the administrative system. The present author does not see any reason why it should be any better under an administrative system based on mathematical models rather than the institutional iterative process. I agree that potential initial savings are very great indeed. But even the best mathematical models invent neither new technologies nor new products, and these problems are crucial for *dynamic* efficiency in the longer run. For this reason, development of mathematical models for central planning should be considered as complementary to institutional economic reforms, but never as their substitute.

References to Chapter Two

2.1
  1. Beksiak J.: *Wzrost gospodarczy i niepodzielnosc inwestycji* (Economic Growth and Indivisibility of Investments), Warsaw, 1965.
  2. Bernasek M.: 'The Czechoslovak Economic Recession, 1962–5', *SS*, 4, 1969.
  3. Bienias T.: 'Investors' Sins', *Przeglad Techniczny*, 4, 1969.
  4. Bobrowski C.: 'The First Stage of Discussion', *ZG*, 1, 1959.
  5. —— 'The Housing Alternative', *ZG*, 2, 1964.
  6. —— 'The Service Sector Alternative', *ZG*, 7, 1964.
  7. Brus W.: 'Growth and Economic Model', *ZG*, 2, 1959.
  8. Kalecki M.: 'Remarks on the Economic Plan for 1966–70', *ZG*, 15, 1964.
  9. *Kierunki usprawnien metod planowania i zarzadzania gospodarka narodowa* (On Methods for the Improvement of Planning and Management of the National Economy), Warsaw, 1968.
 10 Krencik W.: 'Dynamics of Growth and Changes in the Structure of Employment and Wages'. Paper delivered at the Conference on Methods of Improving 5-year Planning organized by Institute of Economics, Polish Academy of Science, Warsaw, March 1967. Mimeographed.

11. Krencik W. 'The Goals and Means of the Strategy of Intensive Development', *GP*, 4, 1971.
12. Mieczkowski B.: 'Recent Discussions on Consumption Planning in Poland', *SS*, 4, 1971.
13. —— 'Estimates of Real Wage Changes in the 1960s', *Kultura* (Paris), 12, 1971.
14. Minc B.: *Wstep do nauki planowania gospodarki narodowej* (Introduction to the Study of National Economic Planning), Vol. 1, Warsaw, 1950.
15. Minc H.: 'Towards Proper Planning Methods in Poland', *ND*, 8, 1948.
16. —— 'Basic Economic Tasks of the Two Last Years (1954–5) of the Six-Year Plan', *ND*, 3, 1954.
17. Pisarski G.: 'Experience of the Current Five Year Plan', *ZG*, 41, 1968.
18. Plocica A.: *Inwestycje w Polsce. Zarys systemu i polityki.* (Investment in Poland. The Outline of System and Policy). Warsaw, 1967.
19. *Rocznik polityczny i gospodarczy* (Political and Economic Yearbook), Warsaw. Published from 1958 on.
20. Wisniewska B.: 'Investments in Light Industry—the State of Danger', *ZG*, 37, 1967.
21. Zielinski J. G.: *On the Theory of Socialist Planning*, O.U.P., Ibadan, 1968.

2.2.1

22. Decree 103 of the CM (of June 1969) concerning methods of the evaluation and classification of new industrial investments in 1971–5, *MP*, 24, 1969.
23. Dudzinski W.: 'When an Industrial Association says No!', *ZG*, 38, 1969.
24. Dzieciolowski J.: 'What is and what is not necessary?', *ZG*, 28, 1969.
25. Economic Council: 'Theses Concerning Certain Changes of the Economic Model', *ZG*, 22, 1957.
26. —— 'Theses Concerning the Principles of Price Fixing', *ZG*, 51–2, 1957.
27. Editorial: 'The Second Plenum', *ZG*, 15, 1969.
28. ——'The Industrial Association in the Planning Process', *ZG*, 28, 1969.
29. —— 'New Methods—Old Resistance', *ZG*, 30, 1969.
30. 'How to Plan the Five-Year Plan in a New Way?'. Interview with T. Gradowski, Deputy Director of Department of Plan Coordination, Planning Commission, *ZG*, 25, 1969.
31. Jaszczuk B.: 'Conditions and Requirements of Social Planning', *ZG*, 38, 1969.
32. Malicki M.: 'Polish Planning Techniques', in [*35*].
33. Misiak M.: 'Productivity', *ZG*, 41, 1969.
34. Pajestka J.: 'Methods of Five-Year Plan Elaboration', *ZG*, 20, 1969.
35. *Planning in Poland.* Central School of Planning and Statistics, Advanced Course in National Economic Planning. Teaching Materials vol. 17, Warsaw, 1964. Mimeographed. (After the March 1968 events, all teaching materials of the Advanced Course have been withdrawn from circulation. They are now being reviewed to find out if they contain 'revisionist ideas'.)
36. *Przepisy o planowaniu i inwestycjach* (Regulations on Planning and Investments). Council of Ministers Publication, Warsaw, 1969.
37. *Rocznik polityczny i gospodarczy 1958* (Political and Economic Yearbook 1958), Warsaw, 1958.
38. Second Plenary Meeting of the Central Committee of PUWP, 3–4 April 1969, *ND*, 5, 1969.
39. Szyndler-Glowacki W.: 'Resistance Must be Overcome', *ZG*, 29, 1969.

2.2.2

40. Bodnar A.: *Problemy polityki gospodarczej PRL* (Problems of the Economic Policy of the Polish People's Republic), Warsaw, 1969.
41. Buch W.: Discussion. In [*48*, pp. 405–8].

42. Decree 276 of the CM, 28 October 1965, concerning the financial rules of centrally planned industrial associations and their member-enterprises, *MP*, 61, 1965.
43. *Ekonomika przemyslu* (Economics of Industry), Warsaw, 1966.
44. Gradowski T.: *O planowaniu gospodarczym* (On Economic Planning), Warsaw, 1965.
45. Kierczyński T.: 'The Functioning of the Profitability Index', *ZG*, 42, 1968.
46. —— 'The Functioning of the System of Financing and Crediting the Stocks', *ZG*, 43, 1968.
47. —— Wojciechowska U.: *Finanse przedsiebiorstw socjalistycznych* (Finances of Socialist Enterprises), Warsaw, 1967.
48. *Kierunki usprawnien metod planowania i zarzadzania gospodarka narodowa* (On Methods for the Improvement of the Planning and Management of National Economy), Warsaw, 1968.
49. Szyrocki J.: *Samofinansowanie przedsiebiorstw* (Enterprise Self-financing), Warsaw, 1967.
50. Zielinski J. G.: *Lectures on the Theory of Socialist Planning*, Ibadan, 1968.

2.2.3
51. *Bilanse gospodarki narodowej* (Balances of the National Economy), Warsaw, 1968.
52. Cholinski T., Michajlow G., Milewski S.: *Gospodarka zapasami w krajach socjalistycznych* (Management of Stocks in Socialist Countries), Warsaw, 1967
53. Czarkowski J., Oyrzanowski B.: *Bilans pienieznych dochodow i wydatkow ludnosci* (The Balance of Money Incomes and Expenditures of the Population), Warsaw, 1957.
54. Decree 204 of the CM, 30 July 1965, changing the bill on material balances and central allocations, MP, 48, 1965.
55. *Efektywnosc handlu zagranicznego* (The Effectiveness of Foreign Trade), Warsaw, 1969.
56. *Ekonomika przemyslu* (The Economics of Industry), Warsaw, 1966.
57. Fedorowicz Z.: *Finanse w gospodarce socjalistycznej* (Finance in a Socialist Economy), Warsaw, 1968.
58. Gadomski K., ed.: *Podstawowe zagadnienia zbytu w przemysle* (Basic Problems of Material Supply in Industry), Warsaw, 1964.
59. *Informator zaopatrzeniowca* (Handbook for Material Supplies Officers), Warsaw, 1969.
60. Kucharski M.: *Bilanse syntetyczne gospodarki narodowej* (The Synthetic Balances of the National Economy), Warsaw, 1967.
61. Lesz M., ed.: *Ekonometria a praktyka planowania* (Econometrics and Planning Practice), Warsaw, 1965.
62. Malicki M.: 'Polish Planning Practice', in [*64*].
63. Mortimer-Szymczak H.: *Terenowe bilanse pienieznych dochodow i wydatkow ludnosci* (Regional Balances of Population Money Incomes and Expenditures), Warsaw, 1964.
64. *Planning in Poland*. Central School of Planning and Statistics. Advance Course of National Economic Planning. Teaching Materials Vol. 17. Warsaw, 1964. Mimeographed. In English.
65. Porwit K.: 'Problems of Balancing and Effectiveness Accounts in Planning', in [*64*].
66. —— 'Balancing Methods in Central Planning', in [*64*].
67. Rakowski M., ed.: *Efektywnosc inwestycji* (Efficiency of Investments), Warsaw, 1961.
68. Stone R.: 'Comparisons of SNA and MPS Systems', in [*51*, pp. 283–307].

84   THE THEORY AND PRACTICE OF ECONOMIC PLANNING

69. Tarka Z.: *Zasady obrotu srodkami produkcji* (Principles of Distribution of Means of Production), Warsaw, 1963.
70. Wierzbicki J.: 'The Balance of Material and Money Flows for 1962', in [*61*, pp. 196–231].
71. —— 'A New Method of Synthetic Plan Coordination', *ZG*, 46, 1967.
72. —— 'Problems of Synthetic Coordination of Economic Plan', *Finanse*, 7, 1968.
73. —— 'Distribution of Incomes in the System of Economic Plans', *Gospodarka Planowa*, 3, 1969.
74. Wolski M.: *Index Tables for Construction of Economic Plans.* Central School of Planning and Statistics. Advanced Course of National Economic Planning. Teaching Materials Vol. 26. Warsaw, 1968. Mimeographed. In English.
75. *Wybor ekonomiczny w projektowaniu inwestycji* (Economic Choice in Preparing Investment Projects), Warsaw, 1969.
76. Zielinski J. G.: *On the Theory of Socialist Planning*, O.U.P., Ibadan, 1968.
77. Zienkowski L.: *Zagadnienia podzialu dochodu narodowego* (Problems of National Income Distribution), Warsaw, 1965.
78. —— 'The Present and Future of National Economy Balances', in [*51*, pp. 53–65].

2.2.4
79. Barczak A., Ciepielewska B., Jakubczyk T., Pawlowski Z.: 'An Attempt to Construct Simple Econometric Growth Equations (based on the Polish Economy)', *E*, 3, 1964.
80. Bilinski L.: 'Discussion', in [*85*, pp. 402–4].
81. Buch W.: 'Discussion', in [*85*, pp. 405–8].
82. Eysymontt J.: 'Problems of Comprehensive Automatic Information Processing in Central Planning', *GP*, 11, 1968.
83. Herer W.: 'Discussion', in [*85*, pp. 372–6].
84. Kenessey Z.: *A Magyar Népgazdaság. M-1 Statisztikai Makromodelle*, (The Hungarian National Economy. M-1 Statistical Macro-Model), Budapest, 1965.
85. *Kierunki usprawnien metod planowania i zarzadzania gospodarka narodowa* (On Methods for Improving the Planning and Management of the National Economy), Warsaw, 1968.
86. Kruszczynski S.: 'The Quantification of Growth Factors in the Gross Output of Socialist Industry in Wielkopolska in 1945–65', *Przeglad Statystyczny*, 1966.
87. Lesz M., ed.: *Ekonometria a praktyka planowania* (Econometrics and Planning Practice), Warsaw, 1965.
88. Lukacs O., Cukor Gy., Havas P., Roman Z., eds.: 'Input–Output Tables— Their Compilation and Use'. Scientific Conference on Statistical Problems (Branch A), Budapest, 1962.
89. Malicki M.: 'Polish Planning Practice', in [*95*].
90. Minc B.: 'Methods of Improving Five-Year Planning', in [*85*, pp. 7–28].
91. Nykowski I.: *O planowaniu wieloszczeblowym* (On Multilevel Planning), Warsaw, 1968.
92. Pajestka J.: 'The Utilization of Input–Output Tables for Balancing the Plan and for Structural Analysis', *E*, 6, 1964.
93. —— 'Discussion', in [*85*, pp. 382–5].
94. Pawlowski Z., ed.: *Model ekonometryczny gospodarki Polski Ludowej* (Econometric Model of the Polish Economy), Warsaw, 1968.
95. *Planning in Poland.* Central School of Planning and Statistics. Advance Course of National Economic Planning. Teaching Materials Vol. 17. Warsaw, 1964. Mimeographed. In English.
96. Porwit K.: 'The Application of the Input–Output Method in Planning and Economic Analysis', in [*87*, pp. 232–80]. Translated into English in [*97*, pp. 41–86].

97. —— *Planning in Poland*. Central School of Planning and Statistics. Advanced Course in National Economic Planning. Teaching Materials Vol. 18. Warsaw, 1967. Mimeographed. In English.
98. —— 'Discussion', in [*85*, pp. 413–14].
99. —— Draft Programme for Introducing Optimizing Methods into Central Planning, *GP*, 5, 1969.
100. Rakowski M.: 'Discussion', in [*85*, pp. 386–9].
101. Szybisz B.: 'The International Statistical Conference in Budapest', *WS*, 5, 1961.
102. —— 'The International Seminar in Berlin Devoted to Optimization Models and Input–Output Tables', *WS*, 4, 1965.
103. —— *Wstep do statystyki przeplywow miedzygaleziowych* (Introduction to Statistical Input–Output Tables), Warsaw, 1969.
104. Wyrozembski Z.: 'Discussion', in [*85*, pp. 390–4].
105. Zielinski J. G.: *On the Theory of Socialist Planning*, O.U.P., Ibadan, 1968.

CHAPTER THREE

PLANNING AT BRANCH AND ENTERPRISE
LEVELS

3.1 Planning at Branch Level

3.1.1 THE SYSTEM OF BRANCH PLANS AND THEIR INTERRELATIONS

For planning, management, and statistical purposes, Eastern
European industry is divided into branches and sub-branches. In Poland,
for example, industry is divided into 21 branches and over 100 sub-
branches. All the most important enterprises of a given sub-branch are,
as a rule, subordinated to a particular industrial association. In Poland,
as in most Eastern European countries, horizontal integration is the
predominant form of industrial organization.

The sub-branch level is subjected to a complex set of plans and
programmes. In addition to 'normal' perspective, FYPs, and short-
term plans (see 2.2.2), from 1964 it has had to elaborate two extra
planning documents, the so-called 'programme of organizational and
technical reconstruction' [7] and 'general investments requirements' [6].

According to an instruction of the Chairman of the State Committee
of Science and Technology, the reconstruction programme should
formulate '. . . basic directions for the technical, organizational, and
economic development of branches, sub-branches, and regions of the
national economy . . . in principle without substantial investment
outlays, material or financial' [19]. General investment requirements—
which have been issued three months before the decree on reconstruction and obviously without any prior coordination—have practically
the same purpose, but are free from investment constraint. As a result
of this proliferation of plans, programmes, and requirements, the
elucidation of their mutual relationships and their connections with the
appropriate *national* plans become a matter of some urgency and
substantial practical importance.

It is now a unanimous opinion of Polish planning experts [e.g. *20*,
pp. 29–30; *38*, p. 315] that general investment requirements constitute
a part of the reconstruction programme. The reconstruction programme
should not, however, be considered as identical with the branch
perspective plan [*13*, pp. 3–4; *14*, p. 140–1; *20*, p. 31]. The former (a) is
not based on binding plan directives, (b) frequently goes beyond branch
administrative boundaries and (c) its time horizon may or may not

coincide with the time period envisaged in the perspective plan [*14*, pp. 140–1]. At the same time, the reconstruction programme is—or should be—intimately connected with industrial associations' perspective plan and FYP. There should be a feedback between them—the perspective plan utilizing the postulates of the reconstruction programmes and being used itself as an indication of CPB preferences and of needs and constraints imposed by the requirements and possibilities of other branches [*20*, p. 31]. On the other hand '. . . from the overall reconstruction programme the first five years are singled out for implementation [and elaborated in more detail], which is a way of interlocking reconstruction programmes [which in themselves have no binding power, because they represent analytical and postulational rather than operative documents] with the developing possibilities of the national economy' [*38*, p. 311].

The interrelationships between *perspective* planning at industrial association and national levels can be described in the following way [*17*, pp. 203–4]: (1) The preliminary indices of sub-branch development are given in the first guideline of the national perspective plan. On this basis (2) a more detailed long-term plan of a given industry is elaborated by the industrial association. At this stage the initial comparison between the branch potential and the demands of the national economy is undertaken. For this purpose a number of balances are drawn, including the capacity balance, investment balance, the balances of basic inputs and sub-contracting, etc. This is then carried one step downwards into (3) elaboration of perspective plans of basic enterprises, which will be the main executants of the development plan. When this stage is completed, the results are analysed again at national economy level (4), when new guidelines of the perspective plan are elaborated. These guidelines are then sent to all economic ministries and industrial associations and serve as a basis for final elaboration of perspective plans at sub-branch and branch level.

3.1.2 THE SIGNIFICANCE OF BRANCH PROGRAMMING AND ITS PRESENT STATE OF DEVELOPMENT

A *The Significance of Branch Programming*

Radical improvement of branch programming is now generally considered the key to overall improvement of the quality of the whole system of plans. On this question there is full agreement between planning experts [*14*, pp. 12–13; *36*, pp. 6–7] and the CPB [*6*; *7*; *19*].

Let us first examine the importance of branch programming for long- and mid-term planning. Experience seems to indicate that sensible long- and mid-term plans for the national economy as a whole can be built only on the basis of properly constructed branch programmes

[*36*, p. 6]. This is, first of all, due to the fact that the present level of concentration and specialization of production makes programming at enterprise level insufficient. At the same time the planning techniques available make direct programming of the national economy unfeasible. 'This means that the search for consistency and optimality must be undertaken at the level above the enterprise, but below the national economy as a whole. The branch [sub-branch] of production represents such a level in our [Polish] conditions' [*17*, p. 207].

Secondly, the organizational and management structure of the Polish economy—and most other East European countries as well—is based on branch organizations (called industrial associations in Poland) as the main planning and management units, having substantial authority over member-enterprises. This creates potentially favourable conditions for effective planning at the branch level.

Last but not least, the industrial association seems to be the most likely level to be equipped in the near future with electronic computers and to be able to put them to reasonably effective use [*42*, p. 12; see 3.1.4 below].

B *The Present State of Branch Programming*

In the mid 1960s the dissatisfaction with the existing quality and role of long- and mid-term planning became widespread and came into the open in numerous publications. To the dismay and shock of many, it turned out that 'the speedy development of the economy during three consecutive 5-year plans . . . lacked the conscious tendency to influence properly the structure and technical and organizational level of branches and sub-branches as a whole. Many branches . . . have been reconstructed and developed without substantial structural changes (e.g. light industry). At the same time . . . the narrow viewpoint of ministries and industrial associations frequently resulted in many distortions in the technical and organizational structure [of the economy]' [*14*, p. 12]. The economic consequences of this type of 'planned' development were very serious indeed. 'The existing situation . . . diminishes results achieved by branches, increases the costs of economic development, and slows down the growth rate' [*14*, pp. 12–13].

The lack of proper branch programmes has been singled out as the main reason for the low quality of long- and mid-term planning. 'Practical experience indicates that [because of the lack of proper branch programmes] the national economy incurs very substantial losses and that the lack of branch programmes is a main reason why the rate of growth is lower than it could be' [*36*, p. 7]. Where branch programmes existed, coordination between branch and national planning was lacking. 'Perspective plans for the national economy elaborated thus far were disappointing and of little use for mid-term programming because the former lacked a proper economic justification. Perspective plans were not intimately related to branch programmes and did not represent the logical result of the latter' [*36*, pp. 6–7].

This criticism was not only shared by the CPB but was officially inspired as a part of the campaign to improve branch programmes. This campaign was launched after the 1964 decrees on branch programming [*6*; *7*; *19*]—referred to in 3.1.1—were published and the work on branch reconstruction programmes was in full swing.

The results of the 1964–8 efforts to improve the quality of branch programmes were, however, rather disappointing. 'What is the present state of branch programming?' asks a group of Polish planning experts in the introduction to a recent book on this subject, and answers the question as follows: 'First of all, nobody knows how to elaborate these programmes from the viewpoint of the calculus of economic effectiveness. The 1964 decrees on branch reconstruction and general investment requirements did not contain clear indications in this respect. As a result, in practice programmes of branch reconstruction and general investment requirements have been elaborated according to the viewpoints of individual branches and in a way which the programmes' authors have considered proper. Most programmes lack an economic justification of their underlying assumptions and feasible variants as well as an analysis of partial problems ... There are also no convincing arguments that they represent optimal solutions. If these programmes are not based on even simplified optimizing calculations ... their value will remain negligible' [*36*, p. 9; see also *14*, pp. 92–8 ('The Faults Most Frequently Encountered in Branch Reconstruction Programmes') and pp. 143–4].

An example or two may help to illustrate more vividly the seriousness of the situation. A preliminary calculation (undertaken in 1968 by the Ministry of Heavy Industry) of how much it would cost to modernize the Polish machine-building industry—a branch which has always enjoyed a position of special priority—to bring it to a level comparable to its Western European counterparts produced the figure of over 800 billion zlotys, which is equal to the investment expenditure envisaged in the FYP 1966–70 for the national economy as a whole.[1]

In a recent interview for the Warsaw economic weekly *Zycie Gospodarcze*, Professor J. Tymowski, the head of the Department of Machine-building Technology in Warsaw Polytechnic,[2] stated that '... the backwardness of [Polish] technology is alarming. I am even of the opinion that the gap between Poland and the countries most advanced technologically is, recently, not narrowing but widening.'

---

[1] Personal information.

[2] There are no technical-engineering studies at Polish universities which consist exclusively of theoretical, natural, and social science and humanities departments. Polish polytechnics are equivalent to technical and engineering departments of British universities. Warsaw Polytechnic is the best in the country.

'Z.G.: What do you mean by "recently"? In relation to the 1950s?'
'J.T.: No, in relation to the *period between the wars*!' [*45*, my italics].

The planning reform 1969–70 represents the most recent effort to improve branch programming. As we have mentioned in 2.2.1, it increased the enterprises' and industrial associations' authority in formulating plan proposals, introduced the requirement of substantiating plan figures by economic effectiveness calculations, and announced that the era of selective development accompanied by much higher economic indicators is being irrevocably entered. Industrial associations and branch programming were to play an important role in achieving these goals. Unfortunately, they failed to meet this expectation.

The Computing Centre of Polish Planning Commission (see 2.2.4.C) has twice analysed—in August 1969 and in February 1970—the plan proposals of 118 industrial associations producing (for 1968) 84·3 per cent of gross output, employing 78 per cent of the labour force and commanding 91 per cent of the capital stock of industry as a whole [see *29*; *32*; and also *21* and *28*]. The results of these analyses are presented in Table 3.1 and give rise to the following basic criticisms of the branch programmes submitted:

(1) Lack of selectivity (see line 8 of Table 3.1; all figures in brackets given below refer to appropriate lines in Table 3.1). One can hardly speak of 'selective development' if almost two-thirds of enterprises are singled out for speedy development and only 12 per cent as the ones for which expansion is not envisaged.

(2) Adherence to extensive methods of development, shown not only by excessive investment and employment demands (5 and 6) but also by the required shift of investment spending to the beginning of the plan period (7). This last requirement was described as leading to '. . . most serious endangering of plan equilibrium, dispersal of investment resources, and—in fact—to delaying the policy of intensive development of the national economy' [29].

(3) Admission that there will be no substantial improvement in output quality, implicit in much lower exports to capitalist than socialist countries (10).

(4) Finally, industrial associations' plan proposals as a whole have been labelled completely 'unrealistic' because there are neither investment funds to the amount required nor any possibility of paying for the envisaged imports from capitalist countries.

One can sympathize with the planners' exasperation when faced with such plan proposals—especially after both carrot and stick have been used. But, as we have already pointed out in 2.2.1, there was no justification for expecting a *willingness* on the part of plan executants to submit taut plans. Moreover, the standards of branch programming

Table 3.1: Selected Indices of Plan Proposals for 1971–1975 submitted by 118 Industrial Associations

No.	Unit of measure-ment	CPB's guide-lines	First version August 1969	Corrected version February 1970
1. Increase of gross value of output	%		56·0	60·0
2. Increase of value added	%		56·0	69·0
3. Average yearly increase of labour productivity	%	5–6[a]	7 (gross) 6·8 (net)	7·4 (gross) 7·7 (net)
4. Average yearly increase of fixed capital per worker			5·7	5·6
5. Increase of total investment outlays	%	38–40		55
6. Increase of total employment	'000	450		500
7. Average level of investment outlays during first 3 and last 2 years of 1971–5 plan (average level for the whole 5 years = 100)	%		96:105	106:94
8. Share of enterprises classified to groups I, II, III in total value of fixed capital[b]	%		63:25:12	
9. Relative increase of import from socialist (= 100) and capitalist countries	%			100:102
10. Relative increase of export to socialist (= 100) and capitalist countries	%			100:70

[a] Plan for 1966–8 was 4·6 per cent, fulfilment 4·2.

[b] These groups refer to different anticipated rates of expansion. See p. 51.

Sources: Compiled on the basis of data contained in Misiak M.: 'Industrial Association Proposals', *ZG*, 11, 1970, and Plichcinski E.: 'Economic Relations in the 1971–5 Plan Proposals of Industrial Associations', *GP*, 11, 1969.

is still such that even without the motivational stumbling block, one could not realistically expect high quality branch programmes.

Polish planning experts, according to the latest available study of the development of branch programming, painted the following—bleak but realistic—picture (all references to [*36*]):

branch programming represents a much more complex problem than choosing optimal investment projects (p. 7);

elaboration of optimal branch programmes is not yet solved (p. 13) and there is not a single comprehensive branch programme available in Poland (pp. 8–9);

possibilities of elaborating such branch plans in the near future do not exist, because numerous partial problems must be solved first (p. 14);

the practical way out is to work on *partial* optimization of branch programmes;

the path towards better national economic plans can be divided into three basic stages: (1) partial intra-branch optimization with several variants assuming different levels of output, investment requirements, etc.; (2) intra-branch coordination and partial optimization; (3) revised intra-branch partial optimization on the basis of more precise data derived from stage two (p. 15);

Polish branch programming is entering at present stage one only (p. 17).

3.1.3 SHORT-TERM AND OPERATIVE PLANNING AT BRANCH LEVEL

The basic function of industrial associations is at present *operative* planning and management (the latter will be discussed in Ch. 8). In spite of the fact that the enterprise is considered a basic unit of economic organization in all East Europe, in Poland and such countries as Bulgaria, GDR, and Rumania, industrial associations are in fact granted very broad powers and play a decisive role in the process of industrial planning. In Poland, the industrial association '. . . has the right to determine production plans (and even production timetables) of the final products of all its member enterprises. In the case of extensive intra-branch sub-contracting, the association is entitled to prescribe the use of part, or even of all, of the productive capacity of its enterprises. This is tantamount to the determination of enterprises' production plans, inclusive of delivery dates of their final products, by the industrial association. The right of member enterprises to independent product-mix planning (within the predetermined production specialization and subject to agreements from buyers) and to fixing the time pattern of their output is confined exclusively to these final products, which are not subject to centralized distribution and are not included within association programming' [*34*, pp. 22–3]. This in Poland in the mid 1960s amounts to 20–40 per cent of enterprise output, depending on the branch of industry [*10*, p. 253].[1]

Needless to say, for the purpose of effective short-term and operative planning industrial associations must be granted very extensive rights over their subordinate enterprises. These rights include the power to fix all kinds of technological norms, including unit material and labour inputs and even the right to transfer machinery and equipment within the sub-branch without compensation, and raw materials and other elements of working capital with proper compensation [*8*, para. 2].

---

[1] The degree of detail of product-mix plans at ministerial and industrial association levels is determined by the 'Instruction for Elaborating the Project of the National Economic Plan' issued yearly by the Planning Commission of the Council of Ministers. Industrial associations are free to issue more detailed plan indices to their member-enterprises.

In their short-term planning, industrial associations themselves are bound by directives of the national economic plan—handed to them by economic ministries—which they have to implement. In current practice the basic directive plan indices imposed on the industrial association usually include most or all of the following: the volume and product-mix of basic products both in physical and value terms, the wage fund limit and—in most cases—also the overall employment limit and limits for basic categories of employees, the limits of rationed inputs, the limits of centralized investment funds, the limits of foreign exchange funds for imports, subdivided by basic markets: (1) convertible currencies, (2) socialist countries (except Yugoslavia which is in group 1), and (3) other, the volume of export earnings, a set of financial targets including the volume of profit to be paid to the state budget.

These plan indices are substantiated by a number of informative indices such as the cost reduction target, input norms for basic raw materials, labour productivity, capacity utilization targets, etc. These indices are invoked by higher authorities if during plan implementation some extra demands for inputs are advanced by industrial associations, demands not justified by overfulfilling production targets. Needless to say, the first worry of the industrial association is allocation of production tasks within its subordinate enterprises in such a way that all plan indices are met. Obviously, hard bargaining goes on during the whole process of plan preparation, with the industrial association usually siding with its enterprises against higher authorities. When the plan tasks for the industrial association are finally approved, then the situation changes and the industrial association and its enterprises view each other as opponents: the industrial association trying to allocate planning tasks as it seems best and necessary, while enterprises use all possible tricks to get the least demanding planning tasks. The reasons for this lie mainly in the management mechanism and will be discussed in Chs. 4 to 6.

How does the industrial association allocate its planning tasks among subordinate enterprises and what criteria and techniques does it use in the process? Polish authors agree unanimously that the present techniques of short-term and operative intra-branch planning are far from ideal. '. . . Thus far in industrial planning usually only one plan variant is elaborated, and it is a non-optimal variant and internally inconsistent [unbalanced]. This is the author's impression after analysing present planning methods as applied in a few dozen industrial enterprises and several industrial associations.'[1] 'The current method [of branch planning] consists of elaborating some initial plan variant and correct-

---

[1] The author of this statement, Dr. Radzikowski, was in 1960–4 on the staff of both the Centre of Information Processing of the Ministry of Heavy Industry and of the Institute of the Organization of Machine-Building Industry in Warsaw.

ing it as a result of discussion within the association. Because of the amount of labour involved and lack of time the consequences of these corrections are taken into account in an approximate and partial manner. After several approximations [i.e. after several corrections of the first variant], planning at the association level results in construction of enterprise plans. These plans fulfil the condition of meeting the plan tasks of the association as a whole . . .[1] There is, however, no certainty that the chosen variant of allocating tasks and resources is really optimal, that it leads to plan fulfilment with the minimum resource use, and that tasks have been allocated to enterprises best suited for their fulfilment' [10, p. 280].

The amount of calculation involved in operative planning on its present scale deserves some illustration. According to the author quoted, 'full and detailed calculation of five to six plan variants of inputs and outputs for industry as a whole would require more than a year' [10, p. 266] . . . with present manpower and calculating techniques presumably. 'In the Laboratory of Mathematical Methods at the Centre for Information Processing [of the Polish Ministry of Heavy Industry] it was calculated that elaboration of a yearly, optimal, internally consistent, multi-variant technico-economic plan for a medium size industrial enterprise would require over twelve years work by a single planner equipped with an electric calculating machine, if the method of constructing and comparing subsequent plan variants were used. Planning at branch [association] level using this method would certainly require an even longer period' [34, p. 63n.].

3.1.4 CURRENT EFFORTS TO IMPROVE THE QUALITY OF BRANCH PROGRAMMING

The present low quality of branch planning has given strong impetus to widespread efforts aiming at its improvement. These efforts can be broadly divided into three categories:

(1) Construction of a set of data which could be used for formalized and uniform presentation of an industrial branch at a certain moment

---

[1] As Professor B. Blass of Poland has rightly pointed out, the obligatory character of socialist planning has a different meaning in the process of plan *construction* and in the process of plan *fulfilment*. Industrial associations and enterprises *must* submit plans in accord with the goals given to them by higher authorities. No other plan would be accepted. This Professor Blass calls the 'directly obligatory character' of plan construction. In the process of plan fulfilment industrial associations and enterprises *should* fulfil the planned tasks and are stimulated to do this by a system of bonuses and sanctions [3]. The 'directly obligatory character' of planned directives does not prevent industrial associations (and enterprises for that matter) from asking for their revision during the process of plan implementation, from asking more than once, and with good results. For example, in 1967 the Polish industrial association of Iron and Steel applied three times to the Ministry of Heavy Industry for the lowering of its planned profit target, and succeeded in lowering it from the original figure of 6·18 to 5·97, to 5·20, and finally to 5·02. See [87] and p. 108, fn. 1.

't'. Every effort at branch programming must start with a description of the *status quo* of a given branch. At present, however, '. . . there is a lack of uniformity in the content and the form of branch description concerning such basic problems as definitions of certain magnitudes, aggregation methods of output, input and stocks and of algorithms showing interrelationships between different variables' [*31*, p. 5]. Such 'balance models of industrial branches'—as they have been called— when completed can be used for (a) checking the internal consistency of branch programming, (b) comparing different development alternatives, (c) formulating existing constraints, (d) reaching long-run decisions concerning national specialization, international cooperation, location, direction of investments, directions of R and D, etc. [*31*, pp. 6–7]. At the same time the standardization of the contents and way of presenting 'different composite elements of the matrix and [the standardization of] methods of aggregation of data should diminish the amount of work and shorten the time required for preparing branch programmes' [*31*, p. 2]. Similar work is being carried out in other East European countries, such as the Soviet Union and Czechoslovakia [see e.g. *33* and *39*].

(2) Partial optimization of branch programming, for alternative volumes and structures of output, by using an appropriately adapted and extended version of the current official methodology for calculating the investment effectiveness of individual projects [*36*; on Polish methods for evaluating the economic effectiveness of individual projects compare *15*; *18*; *35*; *43*; *44*]. Authors of this approach try to show that such adaptation is possible and rational and that '. . . applying even simple methods, the methodology and practice of optimizing branch programmes can be significantly improved' [*36*, pp. 16–17]. Moreover, they are of the opinion that at present, rigorous optimization of branch programmes is impossible; within the realm of practical possibility '. . . is not optimization *sensu stricto*, but a search for directions which can lead to [partial] optimization of branch programmes' [*36*, p. 17].

An important element of all efforts to improve branch programming is extensive work on estimating numerous parameters which must be available for the purpose of programming. The analysis of technico-economic coefficients consists of two stages: stage one is the gathering of information about the actual level of inputs of raw materials, labour, machine-time, etc., per unit of output. Stage two consists of studying the changes in these coefficients as a result of technical progress, raw material substitution, and non-investment factors such as higher average skills, etc. One may notice that for the sake of *perspective* programming another set of coefficients is needed, presenting mainly the relationship between investment and operating costs and size of plant and chosen method of production. 'At present elaboration of such a system of coefficients is still in its initial stage. Available technico-economic information about enterprises and different branches of industry are as yet unsatisfactory and a number of data are still not elaborated in a proper form' [*20*, p. 115].

(3) The present low quality of branch planning and the impossibility of any radical improvement within the existing framework, has given a strong impetus to efforts towards applying mathematical techniques (mainly of linear programming type) to problems of industrial programming at the industrial association level. If at the level of the national economy as a whole, the use of mathematical optimizing techniques (and to a lesser extent even consistency techniques) is still beyond the reach of practical applicability, at branch level the prospects are more promising, especially in industries of more homogeneous output and for partial problems. For example, application of linear programming techniques in the Polish paper industry revealed capacity reserves of over 3 per cent; calculations concerning grinders' utilization suggested the possibility of increasing production of over 100,000 tons per year; a model for the rational use of electric power stations indicated reserves between 3–5 per cent, etc. [*14*, pp. 142–3n.]. One has to remember, however, that mathematical programming at branch level is an extremely complex task, even from a purely technical viewpoint. Even such a relatively simple problem as the above-mentioned optimal utilization of grinders required a mathematical model of 100 equations and 270 variables [*23*, p. 44]. When we move to the incomparably more complex task of even partial optimization of branch programming, as, for example, an industrial sub-branch of machine-building type, it requires '. . . finding the maximum function of a few hundred [or thousand] variables subject to a few hundred [or thousand] constraints' [*34*, p. 63]. For tasks of this magnitude, we hardly have adequate computers (except very few at the Central Statistical Office, Planning Commission, etc., see below).[1]

The calculating aspects of mathematical programming are, however, its easiest part. A Polish textbook on industrial economics noted correctly that 'the analysis of [technical and economic] coefficients constitutes at least 90 per cent of planning work based on new methods [of mathematical programming], and mathematical calculations constitute no more than the remainder' [*10*, p. 288].

The most important stumbling block in introducing mathematical branch programming is, however, the fact that it requires '. . . new methods of branch planning and management' [*26*, p. 334]. Needless to say, it is an extremely complex task which must be solved in stages, and it can yield substantial results only in branches whose dependence on the rest of the economy—which is not optimized—is relatively

---

[1] 'Our not too good computers can solve models consisting of 100 equations and 250 variables within approximately 3 hours' [*23*, p. 56].

limited. The same is true about intra-enterprise optimization. Otherwise, external disturbances, e.g. in the form of irregularity of supplies, easily cancel intra-branch or intra-enterprise potential economies. Another interesting by-product of branch optimization efforts was the realization '. . . that basic faults of the existing system of planning and management cannot be eliminated even if an unlimited increase of employment and capital is assumed' [26, p. 334].[1] The inherent limitation of extensive methods of development can hardly be described in more concise and damaging terms.

Efforts to apply mathematical techniques to industrial programming placed great emphasis on the problem of criterion functions. One cannot use mathematical programming before knowing precisely what one wants to maximize. If under the administrative iterative process even such vague notions as 'fulfilment and overfulfilment of plan targets' or 'maximum satisfaction of users' needs', etc., could be used without causing an actual breakdown of the planning process, they are definitely not sufficient for mathematical programming.

For optimization at the branch level, most Polish authors suggest minimum use of resources (for planned volume of output) for most *manufacturing* industries, and maximum productivity (or maximum capacity utilization) for *extractive* industries and those manufacturing industries whose products are in short supply (so that a rise in their unit cost is justified economically) [see *34*, pp. 50–3; and *10*, p. 280]. For these criteria they claim the virtues of '. . . simplicity and measurability at the association level. They do not contain elements which lie outside the association's sphere of influence' [*34*, p. 53].

The above-mentioned criteria can take different concrete forms. For example, the criterion of minimum resource use can take the form of minimization of cost of production, or raw material inputs, or employment, or wage fund, or machine time, etc. According to the Polish author quoted: 'Association management must decide what specific criterion must be taken as the basic, most important one in given technico-economic conditions. The chosen criterion will then be used in optimizing calculations' [*34*, p. 58]. For example, it may be decided that the association's plan should aim at minimum cost of production, under four constraints: meeting the planned volume of commodity production, wage fund limitation, foreign exchange limitation (subdivided by foreign markets), and limitation of centralized investment funds. Such models were being elaborated in the years 1960–6 for the Polish machine-building industry. At the same time, work has been done on models with vector-valued objective functions, i.e. the maxi-

---

[1] For a very interesting and detailed description of the problems involved and the approach used in introducing—in two consecutive stages—a 'comprehensive macroeconomic automatic management system' in the Polish metallurgical industry, see [*25*, pp. 295–301; and *26*, pp. 333–7].

mand is a vector of 'goals' (usually main plan targets). These models do not maximize any single goal in the vector maximand, but look for an 'efficient solution'. By 'efficient solution' is meant that solution 'X' chosen is such that the value of any goal (component of the maximand) cannot be improved by any other solution, except at the expense of some other goal in the maximand. These models have the great practical virtue of meeting the CPB's demands. Plan targets require good performance in a number of respects (costs, employment, etc.), without specifying at the same time the trade-offs between them.[1] This is not to say that many of these 'goals' could not be set as constraints.

Efforts to improve branch programming are intimately connected with plans of introducing and developing EDP and the so-called MIS (Managerial Information System).[2] Alternative plans of development of EDP and MIS are now hotly debated in Poland [42; 4; 5; 11]. These debates have revealed both substantial areas of disagreement among experts and the unsatisfactory state of the present situation and of plans for the near future.

First of all, there is disagreement concerning the level at which 'computerization' should start. Some single out the enterprise (as e.g. Chairman of Commission for Management Organization, Minister T. Kochanowicz, or Dr. M. Greniewski from the Main Centre for Improving Managerial Personnel: see [11], others the industrial association [41]. There seem to be good reasons in favour of the latter approach. (a) It is in accord with the key role of the industrial association in planning and management, a role which is being strengthened, especially

---

[1] Needless to say there was a lively and interesting debate on theoretical and mathematical aspects of multi-goal functions (see [22; 24; 12; 27; 30; 26; 1; 2, pp. 36–42] which represent most important contributions to this debate in chronological order). As could only be expected, none of the proposed solutions was found completely satisfactory—including Lange's suggestions in [22, Ch. 4], which are convincingly criticized in [30]. The final conclusion of the debate was exactly the same as reached before in the West [37, Ch. 7.4], but everybody benefited in the process. This conclusion has been summarized most recently in [1, p. 729]: 'The only way to overcome the difficulties connected in choosing an optimum solution in case of multiple goals is to try to find a proper meta-criterion ... Mathematical programming cannot help us in choosing efficient programmes if we do not have a more general criterion function, which could be used as meta-criterion' [1, pp. 728–9].

[2] MIS may be briefly defined as a link between EDP and the management (at any level). Its basic purpose is to see that information necessary for the solution of a particular problem or sets of problems is quickly and efficiently supplied. MIS may serve, for example, the following requirements of increasing complexity: (1) transaction management, (2) operational, (3) tactical, (4) strategic, (5) political, or (6) social management. Each subsequent goal requires a bigger and more sophisticated EDP system and MIS helps to define and meet these requirements efficiently. Transaction management, for example handling of invoices or work cards, requires no integration of sub-systems. Operation management, say management of inventories, already requires partial integration of sub-systems, etc. For lucid presentation of MIS of different complexity, cf. [42, passim].

from 1966 onwards. (b) It takes into account the existing number of computers and their possible increase in the near future. If computers were to be installed at enterprise level, only one industrial association out of approximately 130 could currently be fully 'computerized' and only three or four at the end of 1975. If, however, the branch level were chosen for computerization, about 15 per cent of all industrial associations could be at present equipped with computers, and 45–60 per cent at the end of the 1971–5 plan [*41*, p. 12]. Moreover, installing computers at the industrial association level does not mean that enterprise data could not be automatically processed. They will be, but within the branch information processing system. One has also to remember that the sum of enterprise EDP and MIS is not tantamount to a branch information system, so that the problem of developing them for industrial associations would remain unsolved even after completing computerization at the enterprise level.

Secondly, there is the problem of aiming at integrated or partial systems. Again, in spite of the inclination of many experts towards integrated systems, economic considerations indicate that with few exceptions (such as, for example, the Planning Commission), partial systems must predominate for quite some time yet. They are simply about ten times cheaper than integrated systems, according to Polish estimates (see Table 3.2).

Table 3.2: The Cost of EDP Equipment as a Percentage of Yearly Volume of Sales[a] *(Selected Users, Poland)*

Models of data processing	Average cost of EDP equipment as % of yearly value of commodity production[a]
Transactions' Processing	2·8
Integrated System of EDP	37·0
Managerial Information System (MIS)	4·4
Integrated MIS	47·0

[a] Use of 'volume of sales' as a synonym of 'commodity production' occurs in the original.

Source: Targowski A.: 'Costs of Using EDP', *Maszyny Matematyczne*, 2, 1969.

Thirdly, the proper type of computer to be used as a basis for EDP and MIS must be chosen. It has been already decided that the basic computer for the Polish information system will be home-produced [*11*]. But what computer should be produced? Existing proposals are receiving strong criticism. 'We are planning to produce medium-size computers, which are too expensive for micro-economic calculations and too small for macro-calculations' (Professor W. Turski from the Polish Academy of Science in [*11*]). 'The proposed solutions [concerning the

5*

type of computer to be built] are non-economic, short-sighted and based on obsolete logical concepts' (J. Karpinski from Warsaw University in [*11*]). Needless to say, the choice of proper hardware (and software) cannot be properly made before the basic problem of the type of EDP and MIS Poland wants to build is agreed. It is to be hoped that the present discussion of this problem will produce a consensus and proper recommendations before investment decisions already taken in the Polish computer industry [*11*] will make it irrelevant.

3.2 Planning at Enterprise Level

3.2.1 INDUSTRIAL ENTERPRISES AND THEIR PLANS

A Types of Industrial Enterprise

As a result of the evolution of industrial organizations in the last twenty years, the following basic forms of industrial enterprises exist in Poland.

(1) Enterprises which have only one factory under their control (the so-called *przedsiebiorstwa jednozakladowe*) are still a dominant form of Polish industrial enterprise. They gained almost total predominance as a result of the Decree of Economic Committee of the CM of 12 May 1950 [*60*]. At that time, the choice of the one-factory firm as a basic form of socialist enterprise was part of an effort to establish effective central control over enterprises and to eliminate any intermediary levels between individual factories and newly expanded central economic administration. Paradoxically enough during the first period of decentralization, the one-factory firm remained the dominant form, but for entirely different reasons. This form of enterprise organization was considered essential for the proper functioning of newly established workers' self-management (see [*46*], and [*73*, p. 167]).[1]

(2) Enterprises which have more than one factory under their control (the so-called *przedsiebiorstwa wielozakladowe*) were almost eliminated by the Decree of 12 May 1950 [*60*], mentioned above. They started developing again after 1960, which marked the beginning of the new

---

[1] The problems of 'workers' councils' (1956), later administratively 'integrated' into the 'conference of workers' self-management'—CWS—(1958), lie outside the scope of this book for two quite different reasons. First, because, unfortunately but not surprisingly, CWS play a very limited role in planning and plan implementation in the enterprise. One would be almost justified in saying 'none at all' if not for the fact that the CWS are used by enterprise management as a 'rubber stamp', especially for their more far-reaching deviations from plan targets. Secondly, it is the field of study of industrial sociology rather than of economics and is very extensively and thoroughly covered by Polish sociological literature. Industrial sociology is—again unsurprisingly—the most developed branch of Polish sociology. It is fortunate to have such a distinguished leader as Professor Jan Szczepanski. For an illuminating discussion and extensive references to Polish writings on workers' self-management, see [*81*; *96*; *107*].

tendency towards creating bigger economic units. This period, however, also brought forward a number of completely new forms of industrial enterprises.

(3) The first of these new forms was the so-called 'leading enterprise' (*przedsiebiorstwo wiodace*) created at the beginning of 1960 [47]. These enterprises—which could be established by the appropriate economic minister—had rights analogous to those of industrial associations over enterprises subordinated to them (the number of the latter being usually much smaller than in the case of industrial associations). 'Leading enterprises' do not create, however, separate organizations for the purpose of supervision and coordination of member-enterprises. These tasks are carried out by the management of the 'leading enterprise' which, therefore, has double responsibility—towards its own enterprise and towards its member-enterprises.

(4) A few months later—on 17 November 1960—the Decree 308 of the CM [57] established two new forms of industrial enterprises. The so-called 'patron enterprises' (*przedsiebiorstwa patronackie*) have been granted no administrative authority over cooperating enterprises. Their role is limited to initiating voluntary collaboration, coordination of development and investment programmes, and joint service organizations. In addition they should be ready to provide organizational and technical assistance to cooperating enterprises. This form developed to a significant degree only in a very few industrial branches [73, pp. 168–9].

(5) The other new form of industrial organization established by the same Decree 308, are so-called 'principal enterprises' (*przedsiebiorstwa prowadzace*). Very similar to 'leading enterprises', 'principal enterprises' fulfil the functions of an industrial association in relation to their member-enterprises, but—in full analogy to 'leading enterprises'—have no right to create a separate management apparatus for this purpose. The form of 'principal enterprise' did not gain any widespread application. Its establishment only a few months after the creation of 'leading enterprises' seems to indicate very poor coordination of legislative activities.

(6) Finally, on 23 October 1969, Decree 193 of the CM [59] created so-called industrial *kombinaty* [singular *kombinat*]. There is neither an English equivalent of the word *kombinat*—the term was introduced into the Polish language only recently from Russian—nor any general agreement in the legal and/or economic literature of the USSR and East European countries as to what *kombinat* precisely means [99, pt. I, pp. 1–2]. In the form created by the quoted Decree a *kombinat* may be either practically identical to an industrial association (when it is subordinated directly to the economic ministry) or close to it—when it is subordinated to an industrial association. In both cases it fulfils the functions and has the administrative authority of an industrial association in relation to its member-enterprises. It may or may not have a

separate management to fulfil its functions. If it has not—then one of
the *kombinat* enterprises is singled out as a 'leading enterprise'.[1]

As can be seen from the above brief description, there is at present in
Poland a whole range of industrial organizations, most of which
represent different degrees of departure from the two basic forms—
enterprise and industrial association. At the expense of over-simplifica-
tion, the planning (and for that matter—the management mechanism)
of the enterprises discussed under (1), (2), and (4) can be considered as
of enterprises proper, while industrial organizations described under
(3), (5), and (6) are sufficiently similar to industrial associations that
their planning (and management) problems closely resemble (even if on
a smaller scale) those of the latter. This classification will enable us to
confine our discussion of planning (and management) to branch and
enterprise levels only as they are sufficiently representative of the problems encountered by the whole range of industrial organizations.

B *Types of Enterprise Plans*

The evolution of planning in Poland shows a pronounced tendency
to reproduce in enterprises those plans which previously were being
elaborated only at branch and/or national level. Until the late 1950s, the
short-term and operative plans were the *only* plans elaborated in
Polish enterprises. Medium-term planning was introduced in 1959. Its
aim was to prepare an FYP, 1961–5, for all enterprises. More important
enterprises are also required to prepare long-term perspective plans and
more recently (1966) 'big' enterprises should in addition elaborate a
'programme of organizational and technical reconstruction' [*49*, pp.
208–10] (see 3.1.1 and [*98*]). The purpose of the latter was to introduce
partial checks on the feasibility and economic effectiveness of branch
programmes [*49*, p. 208].

Efforts to introduce at enterprise level plans with a longer time
horizon were, however, operationally unsuccessful from the very start.
For example, one of the leading Polish university textbooks on industrial economics, comments on enterprise FYPs in the following manner:
'. . . from the very beginning they were not comprehensive programmes.

---

[1] There is already a growing literature on *kombinaty* [*48*; *50*; *70*; *77*; *79*; *80*; *99*;
102; *112*]. Particularly useful is [*99*], which, first, compares it in detail to the 'principal
enterprise' and then to *kombinaty* in the USSR and GDR (in Part 2). B. Glinski in
[*73*, pp. 170–1] describes briefly the experience of early Polish *kombinaty*, created
in 1959–60 in the leather industry. They did not last long, because the dominant
tendency was to curtail the economic independence of *kombinat* member-enterprises,
and—this accomplished—*kombinaty* became in fact simply enterprises which have
more than one factory under their control. Similar to the previous Polish practice,
according to the recent Decree 193, the *kombinat* members automatically cease to
be legal entities (as is the case with plants controlled by an enterprise) but supposedly
the *kombinat* is nevertheless intended as 'a special form of association' rather than
simply as an enterprise controlling many factories [*99*, pt. 1, p. 4].

Moreover, a substantial part of their assumptions quickly lost their validity and hence in most branches of industry the role of [enterprise] FYPs is, thus far, small' [72, p. 26]. To an even greater extent this applies to enterprise perspective plans and reconstruction programmes, as they reach much further into the future. These results are hardly astonishing, because as we have discussed in 2.2.2, even at national level, an effective plan horizon does not exceed three to four years, at the utmost.

C The Dominant Role of Operative Plans

If at national level short-term plans are still of predominant importance in spite of all the efforts to the contrary (see 2.2.2,) at the enterprise level, quarterly and monthly plans constitute the real operative action programmes, rather than a yearly (two-yearly) plan. This was the almost unanimous answer of Polish industrial managers to an Economic Council questionnaire in 1959 [62; 20].[1] It remains equally true today: 'The empirical analysis indicated that quarterly plans come closest to real plans of action. They are, as a rule, elaborated before the planning period they cover, do not change during implementation, and are based on a relatively sound basis . . . It is true that quarterly plans are not immune from changes during their time span. It is, however, much less frequent than is the case of a yearly plan. The latter, as a rule is not only fixed with much delay, but also subject to frequent changes afterwards [105, p. 62].

3.2.2 THE METHOD OF PLAN CONSTRUCTION

A Two Stages of Plan Elaboration

The formal method of plan construction and—more important—the actual role of enterprise management in plan construction alters and fluctuates with the recurrent waves of centralization and decentralization. As we have pointed out in 2.2.1, until the 1969 reform of planning, enterprises were given draft plans which were practically ready and their role was confined to the disaggregation of them into detailed, so-called technico-economic (T-E) plans.[2] The 1969 planning reform led to what is now called 'the two stages method of plan construction' at enterprise

---

[1] The Economic Council questionnaire was sent in 1959 to 467 industrial enterprises of which 361, i.e. 77·3 per cent answered. Returned questionnaires covered almost 10 per cent of all Polish state industrial enterprises employing over 25 per cent of the total industrial labour force (see [62] and [65]).

[2] Enterprise plans are still frequently called TPF plans, from the first letters of their former Polish name—*plany techniczno-przemyslowo-finansowe* (technical-industrial-financial plans). The official name was changed, however, into T-E plans a few years ago, see [67, Ch. 13].

level [89, p. 203; 86, p. 264]. The first stage consists of enterprise management preparing the preliminary plan. It is still based on guidelines from the industrial association, but of a much more general character than was previously the case (formally, they should now consist of no more than five directive indices, see 2.2.1). During stage two, elaboration of the final plan, incorporating industrial association revisions and *desiderata*, takes place. The two versions—as a rule—vary considerably, but industrial association decisions are binding for member-enterprises and the final plan *must* conform to industrial association instructions [89, pp. 204–5]. 'It should be noted that there is a well established procedure of arriving at the set of planned directives. Before passing to the enterprise the final documents representing the set of yearly directives ... the enterprise concerned is consulted. After reaching the enterprise, plan directives have yet to be approved by the Conference of Workers' Self-management (see p. 100, fn. 1). Adoption of such a procedure was probably intended to stress the importance of these directives' [74, p. 25].

The following characteristic features of the present method of plan construction are particularly worth noting:

(1) The lack of optimality calculations (see also 3.2.4). 'During the preparation of yearly and 5-yearly plans, the majority of economic organizations do not pay any attention to plan optimization. This applies to industrial associations, which determine the guidelines and directives for enterprises, and also to enterprises themselves. Production planning consists mainly of better or worse allocation of tasks and eventually of "balancing" production plan with production capacities, taking into account the size of subcontracting' [78, p. 18].

(2) The lack of alternative plan variants. 'As a rule only one plan variant is elaborated ...' [78, p. 31]. Among other reasons, this is due to the very high labour inputs required for plan construction according to the present method (see 3.1.3).

(3) The very limited range of choice left to the enterprise. Even at the first stage of planning, the enterprise has '... only a very small range of freedom in suggesting the quantity and structure of final output. This limited degree of programming freedom is further curtailed by two extra barriers against expansion: chronic lack of subcontracted components ... and lack of capacity reserves' [86, p. 264].

B *Informational Aspects of Enterprise Planning*[1]

According to Decree 426 of the CM (December, 1960) [58] the enterprise elaborates its T-E plan on the basis of the following sources of information: (1) relevant part of its FYP, (2) coefficients correcting the

---

[1] Informational aspects of plan implementation are discussed in Ch. 5.

enterprise long-term plan and received from higher authorities, (3) yearly plan directives, (4) agreements with buyers and suppliers, (5) the enterprise's own estimates (see also [*106*, p. 71; *89*, p. 203]). The Decree of the CM seems to suggest that long-term plan and coefficients correcting it are the most important sources of information for the construction of the enterprise's yearly plan. 'It is commonly known, however, that in practice neither enterprise long-term plans nor coefficients correcting it play any significant role in yearly planning at enterprise level[1] . . . In preparing projects of their yearly plans, enterprises rely mainly on plan directives received from higher authorities and on recent data on plan fulfilment' [*84*, p. 203]. With this information in hand, the actual plan is elaborated according to labour, technological, and input coefficients, approved by higher authorities (see 3.2.3.D).

It is well known that the quality of most of the above-mentioned information is very low for a number of reasons, of which one of the most important is the conscious information distortion induced by the existing management mechanism. The extent of these distortions is, however, rarely fully recognized. In a recent article in *Zycie Gospodarcze* [*83*] an author with fourteen years of planning experience provided a shocking insight into this problem:

(1) Information distortion starts at the planning stage. 'Out of about 100 basic data and technico-economic coefficients being prepared by my division—the true ones are few, such as: surface of workshops (coefficients calculated on the basis of this data are of no real consequence), in some months—volume of output, level of employment in some categories of employees. The rest are false. We report, for example, six pieces of machinery less than we actually have. This improves our coefficient of capacity utilization . . . The division knows true labour coefficients but does not report them . . . Instead, products, output of which is diminishing, have been "assigned" a lower labour coefficient and products on the increase a higher labour coefficient than the actual one. Data prepared in such a way and compared with planned output expansion then determine required investments, employment, etc.'

(2) Falsification of plan fulfilment data. 'The division—as a rule—does not meet its planned orders. For the sake of safeguarding bonuses the appropriate office reports a higher percentage of orders fulfilment

[1] 'Research carried out in 48 enterprises in Lower Silesia indicated that product-mix in 1966–8 differed fundamentally from FYP targets in 43 enterprises. Big differences occurred also in volume of output in 44, level of costs in 46, and volume of investment outlays in 45 enterprises. . . . In addition, higher authorities, as a rule, do not inform enterprises about changes in their long-term plans, confining themselves to fixing yearly plan directives' [*84*, p. 204]. The enterprises studied represented eight centrally planned (as opposed to territorially planned) industrial associations [*84*, p. 200].

than is actually the case. Because the volume of defective output is twice as high as allowed in the plan the division decides what percentage of output disqualified by quality control to "assign" to a given month . . . Some defective output, which quality control originally classified as "totally useless", is reclassified as "possible to repair". These are then treated as "unfinished products" and inflate the stock of the latter sometimes for years.'

(3) Falsification of data as a universal phenomenon. 'The situation is not better—and is frequently worse—in other divisions and enterprises. I am convinced of this on the basis of many conversations with employees of different organizational levels and units.'

(4) Falsification of data as necessity. '. . . Most valued are rascals who do not reveal the possibilities of their organizations. Managers who act otherwise risk material losses, reprimands, and dismissals. The mechanism of "natural selection" already eliminated—or will eliminate sooner or later—those managers who are "unadjusted".'[1]

(5) Moral consequences of information distortion. 'What is going to happen to the character of the young generation, if from the very beginning of their working career in the enterprise, they are being taught and morally forced to cheat at the expense of the whole society?' (all quotations from [83]).

Another important, but rarely mentioned, source of information deficiency results from the lack of coordination between the legally required timetable of plan construction (see 2.2.2) and actual availability of certain types of information essential for realistic planning. Let us illustrate this widespread phenomenon with two examples, one for producer, another for consumer, goods industries.

'In electro-engineering enterprises the period of plan elaboration coincides with the period of signing contracts [with customers]. As a result, the impact of the latter on the project of the plan is relatively small . . .' [89, p. 204].

In enterprises of the garment industry the data necessary for determining the volume and structure of output are lacking during the period of plan construction. The enterprise signs contracts with trade organizations during national trade fairs, which are being held twice a year in Poznan. In March the contracts for deliveries during the second half of the year are signed. They are signed in September for the first half of the next year. Elaborating its assortment plan in June, the enterprise cannot determine precisely the product-mix which it will contract in September . . . As a result, the plan is far from perfect. Experience indicates that the assortment plan is already invalid in the second stage of plan construction' [89, p. 204] (see 3.2.2.A).

---

[1] How closely it resembles Marx's pronouncement in the first volume of *Das Kapital* that capitalists *must* strive for profit maximization or face bankruptcy!

This poor quality of information is one of the basic reasons for the low reliability of enterprise plans, which is discussed under sub-section E.

C Formal and Actual Plan Elasticity

As we have already mentioned in 2.2.2, the enterprise's yearly plan is subjected to frequent changes. These changes take three basic forms (1) formal changes of the enterprise's yearly plan, (2) differences between quarterly operative plans (handed to the enterprise by the industrial association) and the original quarterly part of the yearly plan, and (3) operative orders from the industrial association introducing changes not envisaged in the yearly plan. In some branches of the Polish consumer goods industry, yearly plans have an informative character and only quarterly and monthly plans represent binding operational directives [106, p. 71].

In elaborating its T-E plan the enterprise is legally forbidden to change any of its obligatory plan indices. Polish regulations envisage only two exceptions to this rule: (1) the enterprise can increase its plan targets if this can be achieved within allocated raw materials and employment limits and if there is an assured demand for extra output; (2) the enterprise can refuse to fulfil the planned product-mix if it can prove that there is no demand for planned output [6]. Both prerogatives are rarely used, however. The first—because owing to existing 'rules of the game' 'it is not in the enterprise's interest to overfulfil its plan tasks. This we shall discuss at length in Ch. 6. The second—because (a) enterprises do not anticipate lack of demand at the moment of plan elaboration, (b) are afraid of a reduced employment quota, or (c) of shutting down some of their shops or divisions.[1]

Depending on the *form* of plan change, the change is or is not reflected in T-E plan. 'Current changes in the volume and structure of output are not introduced into the plan ... The situation is different when changes are of planned character, i.e. introduced by the formal order of a superior organization. The latter are incorporated into the plan.' In either case plan changes '. . . are not followed by appropriate adjustments in technico-economic coefficients' [78, p. 33]. This is prevented by the frequency of plan changes and the time required for tracing the impact of a given plan change on a complex set of interrelated magnitudes (see section D).

The quantitative dimension of plan changes on a national scale was presented in 2.2.2 and need not be repeated here. Regional studies over a longer time span (1967 and 1968) fully confirm this picture [84, pp.

---

[1] Out of 361 enterprises which answered the Economic Council's questionnaire [65], 107 had difficulties in selling some of their *centrally* determined output. Asked why they did not refuse to produce goods for which there was no demand—which they are legally entitled to do—63 gave reason (a), 13 gave (b), and 7 gave (c). Quoted after [73, p. 299].

209–10]. According to official findings [87],[1] the basic reasons of frequent plan changes are the following:

(1) The impossibility of predicting realistically the enterprise product-mix more than a year ahead. And with profitability of different assortments varying widely, the actual product-mix is a decisive factor in determining enterprise profitability. This difficulty was particularly acute in most branches of light industry, in steel mills (for bloomery products), in the machine-building industry and in some branches of the chemical and food industry.

(2) The unreliability of raw material supplies, changes in investments deadlines, and the difficulties of achieving planned parameters of new investments on time. All these led to input and cost changes undermining plan profit targets. Such difficulties were particularly frequent in enterprises using imported raw materials and in the chemical industry.

(3) Carelessness of both the higher authorities and enterprises themselves in fixing the profit target at a realistic level. This was a universal phenomenon because of the contradiction between the profit target and other obligatory plan indices (e.g. product-mix plan) and the strong belief—based on past experience—that the profit plan will in any case be changed during the year to conform to actual performance.

The harmful consequences of frequent plan changes are discussed in 2.2.2.

D The Structure of Enterprise Plans

The basic structure of enterprise plans has not changed materially in the last twenty years. As long as the principle of detailed yearly planning remains intact, the T-E plan is almost immune to current reforms, which simply change, diminish, or add to its numerous indicators. The T-E plan in its present form, remains a document of great volume and complexity and a product of countless hours of work not only of the Planning Division, which exists in every Polish enterprise, but of practically all enterprise organizational units and employees. It consists of several basic sub-plans dealing with production, technical development, maintenance, supplies, employment and wages, costs, finance and investment. Its more detailed structure is given in Appendix 3.1.

The characteristic feature of the T-E plan is the priority of its production targets. 'Very frequently enterprise financial plans are elaborated when all other parts of the T-E plan have been already decided. The balances of revenue and expenditure represent a financial summary of other parts of enterprise plan, elaborated earlier. . . Under these con-

[1] Professor T. Kierczynski's article is based on the findings of a special commission created in January 1968 by the CC of PUWP to study the functioning of the financial system of Polish industrial enterprises. The rest of the commission's findings are reported in his second paper [88].

ditions enterprise financial planning has a purely technical character and does not constitute "planning" *sensu stricto* . . . [Moreover] the determination of the financial results of production targets cannot presently be used as a basis for requesting changes in physical targets' [*84*, p. 197].

Secondly, some basic sub-plans of the T-E plan are elaborated in a form which is completely useless for enterprise management. Let us take as an example the plan for material-technical supplies. It is elaborated for rationed inputs only and moreover with the level of aggregation at which they appear on the yearly list of centrally allocated supplies. Of course what the enterprise requires—and in fact elaborates for its own purpose—is a purchasing plan, which covers all its inputs—rationed or not—and disaggregated to the level of individual specification. Concerning the latter, there is a particularly big gap between the supply plan, which the enterprise must legally prepare and the purchasing plan which is operationally necessary. For example, the supply plan under the heading 'metal sheets for general use' has only one sub-group (steel sheets class 2–4). This one group alone consists of 2,500 specifications. As a result, the supply plan '. . . is absolutely useless for the enterprise which elaborates it' [*111*, p. 11].

Similar criticism can be raised against many other elements of the T-E plan (see for example our discussion on product-mix planning in 3.2.2.B). The most fundamental weakness of T-E plans is, however, their very low reliability, which is discussed below.

E *The Low Reliability of Enterprise Plans*

Any discussion of planning at the enterprise level would be incomplete if we did not ask what is the plan's operational usefulness and to what extent does the actual course of events depart from the plan prepared with such painstaking effort and detail? All available data— some of which we quoted already in Chs. 1 and 2—indicate that reliability of macro-planning in Poland is small. This fully applies to operational planning at the enterprise level also. The extent of this phenomenon is boldly stated in a concluding volume of the semi-official 'Library for Economic Cadres in Industry': 'It is an exception rather than a rule when an enterprise works according to its plan' [*78*, p. 33]. This statement can be well illustrated by a recent Polish study giving detailed data of the planned tasks and actual performance of four light-industry enterprises for five consecutive years 1957–61. Recognizing the crucial role of *quarterly* plans, these are taken as a basis of comparison. Out of the wealth of data we reproduce below only figures concerning the product-mix plan, profit plan, and raw material supply plan (Table 3.3).

The very substantial deviations even from quarterly plans—when the time horizon is so short that most of the uncertain factors normally do

Table 3.3: Percentage Deviations from

| Period | ZPO | | | | SZOb | | | |
	Profit	Assort-ment*	Supplies c	Supplies w	Profit	Assort-ment	Supplies hh	Supplies sh
1957								
I	42·1	5·5	23·0	20·7	†	0·1	9·8	6·5
II	13·1	3·4	−0·3	9·6	244·3	6·6	0·6	−8·8
III	0·2	0·1	−1·8	−0·3	10·7	0·8	−9·8	−25·6
IV	102·0	0·9	12·4	−18·9	237·5	0·2	0·0	−3·9
1958								
I	44·4	0·8	14·9	12·0	†	0·4	−10·0	14·1
II	17·3	0·3	7·7	12·6	43·1	0·5	−5·1	4·4
III	−15·5	2·9	19·1	−8·7	118·6	0·0	−7·9	−6·2
IV	30·9	1·8	12·5	−42·6	81·6	4·4	−15·5	−7·8
1959								
I	31·3	3·3	−2·8	17·8	86·4	0·3	−13·1	−8·8
II	64·1	1·5	−33·4	−7·3	75·6	0·7	8·8	1·4
III	30·8	3·6	−4·2	−40·9	75·7	0·5	−16·7	−13·8
IV	172·5	1·9	5·1	19·3	−34·8	0·2	−10·8	−16·2
1960								
I	24·4	7·8	4·0	24·2	30·3	3·5	6·0	11·0
II	23·7	9·2	5·4	9·2	57·2	0·8	−6·7	−3·2
III	−9·3	15·3	−15·4	−10·6	16·9	0·7	16·2	16·0
IV	−13·3	10·7	5·5	−4·7	100·0	1·2	−20·0	−7·1
1961								
I	−16·1	3·8	−50·8	22·9	−1·6	0·3	−10·9	10·5
II	59·2	13·4	−6·1	−4·1	56·6	2·0	7·1	8·7
III	35·5	14·5	−27·1	−31·3	113·2	4·4	1·4	−7·9
IV	−9·3	10·0	2·5	7·2	−4·6	7·7	−9·2	−10·1

ZPO—Zaklady Przemyslu Odziezowego im. 1 Maja (Clothing Factory called 'The First of May').
SZOb—Slaskie Zaklady Obuwnicze w Otmecie (Silesian Shoe Factory in Otmet).
c—cotton cloth, w—woollen cloth, hh—hard hides, sh—soft hides
* All indices negative.

not enter the picture—best witness the fact that centralized planning does not lead to effective control over the economic process not only at macro- but also at micro-level. Most enterprises in a market economy can show a much better record than that quoted above. This can be an important argument for decentralized reforms. It can be shown that a wider reliance on market forces, instead of producing 'chaos', can in fact remove the institutional uncertainty and unreliability, which are produced by an over-centralized management mechanism.[1]

[1] It is difficult to distinguish with any precision when the worsening of plan indices is due to the failure of enterprise management and when to factors outside its sphere of influence. Such a study was nevertheless undertaken by the Polish National Bank in regard to excessive stocks. It turned out that in 70 per cent of cases studied, excessive stocks were not the fault of enterprise management [*68*, p. 525n.]. See also the irregularity of input supplies presented in Table 3.3. Fuller discussion of the economic consequences of a faulty management mechanism is given in Chs. 4–7.

Quarterly Plans in Four Polish Enterprises

Period	ZPB Profit	Assortment	Supplies f	Supplies y	ZPBII Profit	Assortment	Supplies f	Supplies y
1957								
I	†	21·5	−37·5	19·6	†	17·4		
II	a	1·9	7·9	−6·5	19·6	20·4		
III	a	10·1	−9·7	19·4	−12·9	15·4		
IV	a	2·3	8·7	25·2	6·4	0·9		
1958								
I	65·5	2·0	−11·7	3·7	†	10·9		
II	57·6	2·4	12·3	−29·2	31·8	23·8		
III	−53·6	3·7	−2·9	−4·3	7·5	2·4		
IV	49·1	1·4	5·7	−30·8	23·6	†		
1959								
I	23·8	0·3	17·9	−16·6	8·7	3·0	21·0	−6·1
II	b	1·0	−22·6	−26·9	6·0	3·0	−17·2	−27·6
III	57·9	3·9	−12·0	−31·7	17·1	3·8	−5·9	−4·2
IV	−77·4	3·7	−62·9	−24·7	−1·9	6·0	−36·1	−22·9
1960								
I	15·1	1·6	−17·0	−32·7	19·6	†	−19·9	−37·1
II	27·0	1·2	−14·3	−28·9	22·6	†	6·2	5·6
III	2·8	3·7	5·7	−33·9	23·8	1·2	−1·9	−17·8
IV	−73·5	5·5	2·7	−12·4	−11·8	8·5	12·4	−42·1
1961								
I	−1·8	16·7	1·4	−31·2	−0·8	10·0	6·1	−9·3
II	13·7	4·0	5·9	−33·8	3·3	14·2	2·0	31·8
III	9·3	7·1	2·4	−12·4	−20·6	11·2	21·6	−2·5
IV	−67·7	18·9	10·2	−31·5	−13·7	15·8	8·7	−16·7

ZPB—*Zaklady Przemyslu Bawelnianego im. 22 Lipca* (Cotton Textile Factory called 'The Twenty-Second of July').
ZPB II—*Zaklady Przemyslu Bawelnianego im. II Armii Wojska Polskiego* (Cotton Textile Factory called 'The Second Polish Army').
f—fibre,   y—yarn   †—data not available
a—profit achieved instead of planned loss
b—loss incurred instead of planned profit.
Source: Samecki W.: *Ryzyko i niepewnosc w dzialalnosci przedsiebiorstwa przemyslowego* (Risk and Uncertainty in the Functioning of the Industrial Enterprise), Warsaw, 1967, pp. 65, 102, 124–6, 128.

F *The Postulate of Branch/Enterprise Differentiation of Planning Methodology*

As one of the important measures for improving the planning and management system, the resolution of the Vth Congress of PUWP (November 1968) endorsed the idea of branch/enterprise differentiation of the planning and management system [*109*, pp. 15 and 21]. This idea is not new in Polish economic literature. It was advocated before the Vth Congress decisions [e.g. *90*] and has been warmly supported afterwards [e.g. *89*]. It is argued that 'because economic units are different, planning cannot be uniform, schematic, but must take into account these differences, and in particular (1) specific features of a given industrial branch, (2) specific organizational forms of enterprises' [90, p. 68].

'It is generally agreed that the wide differences in technical and production conditions do not always allow the application of uniform financial and economic solutions' [89, p. 207]. It is important to note that these arguments are valid only within their implicit assumption that detailed yearly planning will be retained. Only under conditions of detailed planning must the branch/organizational differences be taken into account if we want to avoid a 'schematic approach'. If, however, the concept of a detailed yearly plan is abandoned—as in Hungary— then the possibility of using 'uniform financial and economic solutions' increases enormously. Experience seems to indicate unequivocally that the only promising approach is the latter. Efforts to improve the efficiency of detailed planning and management by 'adjusting' it to specific branch/organizational requirements, are palliatives of which the results are bound to be disappointing.

3.2.3 PLAN INDICES

A *The Concept of 'Plan Directives'*

All reform measures undertaken in Poland in the last fifteen years did not change the role of the so-called plan directives (tasks, targets or indices)[1] which remained the 'basic tool for managing the national economy' [74, p. 23]. From 1950 till the present day, plan targets are the basic information carriers used by the CPB to direct plan executants not only in what to produce, but also how to produce.

In spite of the crucial role of plan directives in the functioning of a planned economy, there is astonishingly little theoretical and/or empirical research on this subject. A clear legal definition of plan directives is also lacking.

The CM determines yearly in the national economic plan which planning tasks, and resources for their implementation, should be passed to enterprises as plan directives [58; see also 82, p. 41; and 84, p. 205]. These are being expanded and supplemented by economic ministries and industrial associations and reach enterprises as so-called 'basic plan directives for the year X' [74, p. 24]. We shall call them a 'set of yearly directives'.

In practice all planning tasks enumerated in the set of yearly directives are considered as *obligatory* [74, p. 29]. However, formally and/or

---

[1] All these expressions we shall treat as synonyms. This is in accord with actual planning terminology and enables us to consider all plan directives irrespective of the form—quantitative or descriptive—in which they are formulated (produce X tons of Z or modernize the design of product Y).

terminologically speaking, they are quite heterogeneous and their legal character is far from clear.

First of all, within the set of yearly directives, which is *obligatory*, some sub-sets (e.g. concerning production or technical progress) are called 'obligatory tasks' (*zadania dyrektywne*), and others simply 'plan tasks' (*zadania planowe*) e.g. wage fund and employment or 'plan indices' (*wskazniki planowe*) e.g. financial norms.

Secondly, there is formal—at least—differentiation of individual indices within the sub-sets of yearly directives; for example, in spite of the fact that the whole production plan is called 'obligatory', only some of its targets are marked as such. The contrary is true about the wage and employment, investment and financial plans. As a whole, they are not called 'obligatory' but some of their indices are. To increase confusion, all these plans are parts of a yearly set of directives, and the whole set is obligatory in character. 'All these indicate how imprecise is in practice the notion of obligatory indices' [*74*, p. 30].

In the Polish literature, there is no universally accepted definition of obligatory plan target. There is a tendency, however, which the present author shares, to consider as an obligatory target only plan tasks of which under- or non-fulfilment unequivocally invokes sanctions [*69*, p. 24; *74*, p. 30; *110*, p. 271].[1] There are two types of sanctions at the CPB's disposal: administrative and economic. Because experience indicates that administrative sanctions are rarely used in practice, even when their use is legally prescribed,[2] we are left with the following definition: obligatory targets are indices fulfilment of which entitles enterprise employees to economic reward or invokes economic sanction. This definition is, however, broader than a formal definition of planning tasks and requires certain additional comments.

Formally speaking, plan tasks are only those targets which the enterprise receives according to the procedure of plan construction and its approval as described in 3.2.2.A. In addition, however, Polish enterprises receive so-called 'bonus tasks' (*zadania premiowe*) [see Ch. 5 and the literature quoted therein]. 'Bonus tasks are communicated to enterprises by a different procedure than the set of yearly planning

---

[1] 'Obligatory targets without sanctions may exist only when deviation from obligatory targets is impossible by its very nature. Centrally allocated inputs or machines may serve as an example. Enterprises . . . cannot violate this directive without the agreement and collaboration of the organ which administers central allocation. As a result such obligatory targets do not require sanctions' [*69*, p. 24].

[2] 'There are no detailed and generally accepted rules which would prescribe what [administrative] sanctions (admonition, reprimand, dismissal) will be invoked for violating plan targets. Theoretically speaking, they can be invoked but in practice—as is generally known—they are not used' [*74*, p. 30]. The author quoted also points out that approval of changes of plan targets during the planning period is, in a sense, tantamount to non-application of sanctions. This is, however, a separate problem, which requires special investigation.

targets. They are fixed by the industrial association and sent to the enterprise without its participation or approval ... Most of the bonus tasks represent new targets and indices, which are not to be found in the yearly set of plan directives' [74, p. 25]. Because, however, their under- or non-fulfilment is connected—*nomen omen*—with definite economic sanctions, they constitute obligatory tasks according to our definition, and—much more important—are treated as such by enterprise management. In our further discussion, we shall consider bonus tasks as a form of plan target.

B *Plan Directives versus Economic Parameters*

It is the author's opinion that one of the fundamental weaknesses of Polish economic reforms was the fact that from the very beginning the reformers confined their demands to *diminishing* the scope of plan directives instead of asking—as did the Hungarian reformers a decade later—for their complete elimination.

The famous (infamous?) Decree 704 of the CM of 10 November 1956 concerning the broadening of the authority of state industrial enterprises [51] limited severely the number of plan directives, retaining however, the principle of their use. The same position—unfortunately and astonishingly—was taken by the Economic Council in its 'Theses Concerning Certain Directions of Change in Economic Model' [64]. The Economic Council limited itself to demanding that 'The application of incentives should be systematically broadened in scope and plan directives should become less detailed' ... and that '... directives ... should not interfere with the enterprise's economic accountability'. Is it possible that the authors of the 'Theses' did not realize that their position is logically and practically untenable or was it one of those 'compromises'—enforced by a dogmatic majority of the Economic Council[1]—which is a thinly veiled defeat? Because a defeat it was undoubtedly.

It should be theoretically clear that, firstly, plan directives, as a rule, clash with 'incentives'. The very need for plan directives is mostly due to the fact that existing economic parameters do not induce plan executants to observe CPB preferences. If they did—plan directives would not be needed. Secondly, initial plan directives do not eliminate the contradiction between the economic interest of plan executants and CPB preferences, but merely try to enforce the latter at the expense of the former. As a result, a new set of plan directives must be issued to protect the initial ones and/or to safeguard the other spheres of conflict which develop between plan executants' behaviour and planners' preferences. To a substantial degree these new conflicts are produced by the first set of plan directives. Plan executants trying to meet the initial set of plan

[1] On the personal composition of the Economic Council see [103, p. 96; 104, p. 121].

directives at the minimum cost to themselves (in the form of bonus losses) undertake numerous actions, some of which will be contrary to planners' preferences. New plan directives are imposed to prevent this and soon the point is reached when plan executants' behaviour is essentially controlled by administrative orders, and economic parameters are reduced to the role of a residual force. At this stage the aim of economic parameters is in fact limited to strengthening plan directives but, usually, they also push plan executants off the course determined by administrative orders. This conflict gives rise to unrealistic dreams of devising 'neutral prices', 'neutral production indices', etc., which we shall discuss in Chs. 5, 6, and 7.

The Polish practice confirms only too well what could be theoretically predicted. First of all, within two years of the date of issue of the 704 Decree, the number of plan directives binding enterprises has been increased on four occasions—on 30 May 1957, 13 October 1958, and twice on 26 November 1958 [52; 54; 55; 56]. Secondly, already in 1958 it was observed that '. . . practice differs from the legal position—the actual number of plan directives is much greater than prescribed legally' [75, p. 14]. If we take the number of plan directives required by 704 Decree as 100 per cent, it has been raised by the above-mentioned four decrees to 237 per cent and in practice to 363 per cent (calculated on the basis of data available in [75, *passim*]). Thirdly, from 1960 to the present (1972), numerous efforts have been undertaken to diminish the number of plan directives binding enterprises and all to no avail (as will be proved in the next sub-section). To list only the most important of these efforts, in 1960 the right of the industrial association to increase the number of plan directives for its member-enterprises has been curtailed [58]. In 1963 the special Party–Governmental Commission established to suggest proper changes in methods of planning and management postulated a substantial reduction in the number of plan directives [97]. The same postulate was also repeated in the resolution of the IVth Plenum of the CC of PUWP in July 1965 [113] and again in both Theses [108] and resolutions of the Vth Congress of PUWP in November 1968 [109]. In practice 'instead of postulated decline, the rapid increase in the number of plan directives took place' [74, p. 31].

C *The Number of Plan Indices*

The number of plan indices to which East European enterprises were subjected during different periods always prompted great interest among economists as an important indicator of the level of centralization/decentralization. Unfortunately, this interest was not matched by careful attention to *what* was being measured and at *what level of aggregation*. We have tried to elucidate the former in the section above, so let us turn now to the latter.

According to most Polish sources the number of obligatory targets binding industrial enterprises underwent the following evolution during the 1956–68 period:

(1) In 1956 the number of obligatory targets was at its all time lowest, totalling only eight [51; 72, p. 25; 75, p. 12].

(2) This number was legally increased by several Decrees of 1957–8 [52; 54; 55; 56] and for plan elaboration for 1959 enterprises were subjected to nineteen obligatory targets [75, pp. 13–14].

(3) There soon developed a practice of supplementing obligatory targets by so-called 'informational indices' issued by economic ministries and industrial associations. This was discovered during the investigation carried out in 1958 and concerned the number of indices issued to enterprises subordinated to the Ministries of Chemical Industry, Light Industry, and Forestry and Timber Industry [75, p. 14]. These 'informational indices' remained a standard planning practice ever since their first appearance and in fact are considered by enterprises to be as binding as obligatory targets.[1] Moreover, the tendency developed to use informational indices 'rather unsparingly' [94, p. 411].

(4) Already in 1958 certain economic ministries and/or industrial associations were found to be issuing to subordinate organizations a greater number of obligatory targets than they were legally entitled to.[2] For example, the Motor and Railway Stock Industry Associations received from the Ministry of Heavy Industry twenty-nine obligatory targets for their 1959 plan, whereas at that time the legal limit was nineteen [75, p. 14]. This practice—sometimes disguised, sometimes not—is still present.[3]

(5) The tendency to increase the total number of plan indices continued over the years, in spite of the (half-hearted?) efforts to prevent it. According to one source: 'In 1959 the number of all indices increased to 18–22, but already in 1962 it varied—depending on the branch of industry—between 23 and 35' [72, p. 24]. Recent analysis of the planning practice of 48 industrial enterprises located in Lower Silesia (see fn. 1, p. 105) indicated that in 1967–8 they were subjected to twelve obligatory targets determined by the CM in its yearly decree on the

---

[1] 'At that time [1958] there appeared so-called informational indices which in practice are treated by industrial associations as obligatory targets' [82, p. 41]. 'In addition to obligatory targets, higher authorities fix for enterprises numerous informational indices which, as a rule, enterprises consider to be as binding as obligatory targets' [84, p. 205]. We may note, *en passant*, that in Polish planning terminology the term *wskazniki orientacyjne* ('orientational indices') is used.

[2] 'Economic practice showed a definite tendency towards increasing the number of obligatory targets, even beyond the legal limits' [82, pp. 40–1].

[3] 'In 1960 the freedom of industrial associations to fix plan targets for enterprises was again curtailed ... These limitations did not bring expected results immediately' [82, p. 14]. 'Immediately' in this context means 'over the next ten years', as we try to prove in this section.

national economic plan and—on average—to eleven informational indices in 1967, and thirteen in 1968 [*84*, p. 205]. 'In 1967 over 80 per cent of all informational indices were accepted by enterprises without any change and in 1969 this index increased to almost 90 per cent' [*84*, p. 205].

The above analysis of the number of obligatory targets binding industrial enterprises—which is typical of most Polish economic writing—has three basic weaknesses: (1) It uses a very high level of aggregation in its count of obligatory targets. (2) Moreover, the aggregation level used is never defined and may change from year to year and between authors and/or between different obligatory targets in a haphazard and unpredictable manner, and hence its comparability is questionable, to say the least. (3) It also completely ignores the scope of the central product-mix determination of enterprise output. Let us discuss these three points briefly.

As a rule the number of obligatory targets binding enterprises is arrived at by adding together plan targets as they are enumerated in appropriate documents, ignoring the fact that most of them are subdivided into more specific categories and in fact represent a set of directives rather than a single obligatory target. Most authors also go so far that they count as one even those obligatory targets which in their very formulation contain obligatory sub-targets. The unanimously quoted figure of eight obligatory targets determined by the 704 Decree of the CM (10 November 1956) completely ignores the fact that for example Target No. 1 explicitly contains two targets (Target No. 1 reads: 'value of commodity output in transfer prices [*ceny zbytu*], including value of output for [consumer] market separately').

As from year to year the formulation of obligatory targets varies, it is reflected in the number of obligatory targets—as usually counted—without necessarily indicating the actual change, if a consistent level of aggregation was observed. For example, formally speaking, the number of obligatory targets determined by the CM and concerning wages increased from one (or rather two) in 1956 to three in 1968 whereas the number concerning investment was and remained one [see *51*; and *84*, p. 205]. In fact, however, when each plan target in a given group—be it wages or investment—is counted as one, the number of obligatory targets in 1968 varied from five to sixteen for wages and from seven to fifteen for investments, depending on the enterprise studied (see Table 3.4).

The whole picture of the scope of enterprise authority—as determined by the number of obligatory targets—changes completely if we follow the proper procedure, by which I mean: (1) if we count each plan target separately, instead of limiting ourselves to big aggregates, as production, employment and wages, investments, etc., and/or if we count simply formal plan targets, which represent a different level of

Table 3.4: The Number of Plan Targets received by Four
Polish Industrial Enterprises in 1968

No. Types of Targets	Enterprise			
	A	B	C	D
1. Indices of production, export, and sub-contracting plans	12	29	24	9
of which obligatory targets	4	5	1	3
2. Employment and wage fund	16	16	5	5
of which obligatory targets	3	3	3	2
3. Financial norms and indices	14	18	15	28
of which informational	4	14	11	20
4. Use limits (*limity zuzycia*) and stocks ceilings for certain inputs	—	8	4	8
5. Targets for technical progress together with tasks for economic effectiveness	43	14	26	5
6. Investment expenditures and tasks	9	10	15	7
of which obligatory targets	1	3	2	2
Total	94	95	89	62

Source: [74, p. 25].

aggregation, and always omit most of the sub-targets within a given group; (2) if we define obligatory targets as in 3.2.3 which requires that from formal plan targets we subtract all planning tasks for which there are no material sanctions but add all bonus conditions.

Such an analysis has been recently published in Poland [74] and its results are presented here. The detailed analysis of four centrally planned industrial enterprises revealed that in 1968 they received between 62 and 95 plan targets. They are presented in Table 3.4. In addition the enterprises studied received approximately 80 bonus tasks every quarter and this figure remained pretty stable over the year, in spite of the fact that numerous bonus tasks changed from quarter to quarter (see Appendix 3.2). Approximately 50 per cent of bonus tasks simply repeat plan targets but assign to them specific bonus value (see 6.2.2). Taking this into account we can arrive at the approximate figure of plan targets, which every enterprise received, by adding to the number of formal planning tasks, as enumerated in Table 3.4, 50 per cent of the total number of bonus tasks, which represent—in fact—additional plan targets. As a result of this calculation we can see that the enterprises studied received in 1968 between 102 and 134 different plan tasks, the average being 125. Out of these plan tasks we can arrive at an approximate number of obligatory targets by adding to the number of bonus tasks those plan targets which are connected with material sanctions and as such are—as a rule—not repeated in bonus tasks. These plan targets concern employment and wages and financial norms and indices. As can be seen in our Table 3.4 (lines 2 and 3) those plan tasks average 29.

Adding this figure to the number of bonus tasks we get 109 as an average number of obligatory targets binding Polish enterprises in 1968. A rather different picture from those usually presented.

Even this analysis is—in my opinion—still insufficient as it lacks a separate study of one of the most crucial plan targets—the assortment plan, or in the wording of Decree 704 'the quantity of the most important products—according to the evaluation of the higher organization—output of which is safeguarded by centrally allocated inputs' [51; 75, p. 12].

As can be seen from Tables 3.5 and 3.6, the trend towards diminishing the share of centrally determined output in total enterprise production lasted only two years, 1957 and 1958, was never quite clear, and started upward again in 1959. As far as I know, thereafter not a single detailed empirical study was ever published in Poland on this subject, but the

Table 3.5: The Share of Centrally Fixed Product-Mix in Total Enterprises' Commodity Production

		Product-mix of commodity production			
	Total	Centrally determined			
		1956	1957	1958	1959
		in % of all goods produced			
All enterprises which answered the questionnaire	100	79·6	66·6	52·2	55·4
Enterprises subordinated to:					
Ministry of Heavy Industry	100	75·6	61·7	53·8	45·5
Ministry of Chemical Industry	100	54·6	39·9	31·0	39·4
Ministry of Light Industry	100	100·0	87·6	86·6	89·7
Ministry of Food Industry	100	93·9	89·4	49·1	51·2

Source: The Economic Council at the Council of Ministers: 'Results of Questionnaire Concerning the Independence of Enterprises in 1956–9.' Warsaw, 1959. Mimeographed. Quoted after [73, p. 297].

Table 3.6: The Number of Enterprises According to the Share of Centrally Planned Value of Output in the Total Value of Commodity Production

Year	Total no. of enterprise replies	No. of enterprises of which the share of centrally planned value of output in the total value of commodity production is			
		below 25%	26–50%	51–80%	over 80%
1956	315	8	13	17	277
1957	316	8	15	26	267
1958	315	13	20	32	248
1959 plan	313	13	24	27	249

Source: As for Table 3.5.

general picture is evident. The connection between the share of rationed inputs in enterprise supply and the share of centrally determined product-mix in enterprise output was terminated,[1] but the latter remained very high indeed. 'How detailed the product-mix of industrial associations and ministries output plans should be, is determined by [yearly] instructions for elaborating the national economic plan. They indicate which products or their groups must be specified quantitatively in output plans submitted by industrial associations ... In addition there is a general requirement that the product-mix enumerated in the plan in value and physical terms, should constitute 60–80 per cent of the total value of output' [68, p. 253; see also 71, p. 12]. 'The rest of the output, the structure of which is not determined, consists mainly of subcontracted components. Under such circumstances the plan is rigid. Industrial associations and enterprises have very limited possibilities of current product-mix changes' [68, p. 253].

It seems that only a joint analysis of plan tasks and obligatory targets (disaggregated to the level of a single task) plus a comprehensive study of the share of centrally determined products in total enterprise output, together throw sufficient light on the actual scope of enterprise authority in any given moment.

D Technico-Economic Coefficients and the Ratchet Principle

In addition to 'obligatory' and 'informational' plan targets, the planning practice uses also so-called technico-economic coefficients [78, p. 16] or 'accounting indices' [106, p. 72]. Formally speaking, they do not represent plan targets but their technical and/or economic justification [106, p. 73], they 'supplement the yearly plan ... and define enterprise economic effectiveness ...' [78, p. 16]. In Table 3.7 a typical set of technico-economic coefficients in one Polish enterprise is given as an example. As can be easily seen by studying the individual items in Table 3.7, in practice the dividing line between plan targets and technico-economic coefficients is blurred. Many technico-economic coefficients are in fact not only plan targets but even obligatory targets. This is due to the fact that the enterprise plan determines not only what (and how much) to produce, but also prescribes methods of production inclusive of the minimum level of efficiency required.

Plan directives and the enterprise's detailed plan-building are based on elaborated systems of indices—labour, material inputs, and technological. The imperfect knowledge of these technico-economic coefficients and faulty assumptions about their application in planning both contribute to deficient planning.

---

[1] 'In 1964 the list of products planned quantitatively in centrally planned industry included 1,600 items, of which approximately 400 items were centrally allocated' [68, p. 253].

*Table 3.7: Planned Technico-Economic Coefficients for 1967
and their Estimates for 1968**

Polish Industrial Enterprise 'X'

Enumeration	*Units of Measurement*	*1967*	*1968*
I. *Production Results:*			
1. Gross output	m. zlotys in constant prices (as of 1 January 1967)	3,015	3,272
2. Commodity production	transfer prices (*ceny zbytu*)	1,937	2,119
3. Weight of commodity production	metric tons	95,201	96,720
4. Labour intensity of output	'000 work hours	10,635	11,040
5. Balance sheet profit	m. zlotys, current prices	100	96·1
II. *Indices of Global Effectiveness:†*			
1. Fixed capital	gross output in '000 zlotys in constant prices per zloty of net fixed assets	3·63	3·92
2. Production space	gross output in '000 zlotys in constant prices per 1 m₂ of production space	33·6	36·1
3. Employment of production workers	gross output in '000 zlotys in constant prices per production worker	576·9	603·0
4. Working time	gross output in zlotys in constant prices per hour	283·5	296·4
III. *Economic Effectiveness:*			
1. Fixed capital	profit in zlotys per 100 zlotys of net fixed assets	12·05	—
2. Production space	profit in '000 zlotys per 1 m₂ of production space	1·1	
3. Employment of production workers	profit in '000 zlotys per production worker	19·1	—
4. Working time	profit in zlotys per hour	9·40	—
5. Value of commodity production (rentability)	profit in zlotys per 100 zlotys of output in transfer prices	5·16	—
6. Weight of output	profit in '000 zlotys per metric ton of commodity production	1·05	—
IV. *Other Coefficients:*			
1. Actual yearly working time of production workers	actual working hours of production workers per production worker	2,035	2,035
2. Labour efficiency of production worker	gross output in '000 zlotys per production worker	649·9	689·0
3. Average monthly wage of production worker	zlotys per production worker	2,887	2,993

* The appallingly primitive level of 'economic analysis' represented by these coefficients should be noted as a telling illustration of our discussion on enterprise planning.

† Mistake in line II 4 has been corrected.

Source: [*78*, pp. 17–18].

There are three basic types of technico-economic coefficients: so-called technologically determined, i.e. based on technological studies of input–output relations; statistically determined, i.e. based on actual past performance; and estimated indices determined by expert opinion. In spite of strenuous efforts and constant CPB pressure, most technico-economic coefficients in Poland are still of statistical and estimated nature. As enterprises are interested in reporting high input–low output indices—for the sake of easy plan performance afterwards—the CPB counteracts by propounding the theory that in planning so-called 'progressive indices' or 'progressive norms' should be used. By 'progressive' norms or indices such norms are meant which are better (i.e. lower in the case of input, higher in the case of output) than the actual performance in the previous year. Application of this theory for the purpose of formulating the next year's planning tasks means that the enterprise's or branch's previous year's performance is always corrected by some 'improvement coefficient', in most cases established quite arbitrarily and irrespective of real improvement possibilities. This is called planning according to the ratchet principle.

This type of planning has been severely criticized in Polish economic literature during the last fifteen years, but nevertheless it still prevails in practice. 'Research carried out in 48 enterprises in Lower Silesia indicated that in 40 enterprises plan tasks in the period 1966–8 increased from 3 per cent to 5 per cent per year in relation to the plan performance of the preceding year. This type of statistical planning [*statystyczne planowanie*] leads to many negative consequences: stimulates concealment of reserves, gives preferential treatment to badly working enterprises, precludes planning based on the real production capacities of enterprises. It is not accidental that industrial associations know the production capacities of their enterprises only very superficially in spite of the fact that this knowledge should be a basis for planning' [*84*, pp. 205–6].

The purpose of the 'progressive norms' theory is to counterbalance the information distortion with its permanent 'low-efficiency' bias and to prevent too much 'slack' developing in the system. Planners seem to believe—and not without justification, given existing management mechanism—that their system needs administrative pressure to perform. Because—as noted above—the industrial association's knowledge about an enterprise's real production possibilities is limited, both too 'tight' and too 'loose' plan directives are issued to subordinate enterprises. Lack of scientifically determined technico-economic co-efficients, further distorted by application of the ratchet principle, adds to the unreliability of planning tasks and supplies.

E *The Form of Plan Directives*

Plan directives are formulated in the form of different indices, in which output indices play the most important role. Output plan is the basis of the whole structure of an enterprise's T-E plan and output indices are used as a basis for planning an enterprise's wage fund and as its success indicator or—at least—main bonus condition (see 7.5). All output indices used in East European industry can be divided into three basic groups: (1) indices in physical terms (kg, m², cal. etc.); (2) gross value indices, as e.g. gross output, commodity output, output sold; and (3) net output indices, as e.g. value added, value of labour costs only, output in planned man-hours, etc.

As we shall see in Chs. 4–7 the choice of output index is of considerable importance, because of the impact of the *form* in which a planning target is formulated on enterprise behaviour. Generally speaking if output indices have to be used at all, net output indices are the least harmful. This thesis has been long advocated by East European economists—in Poland as early as the mid 1950s—but nevertheless gross value indices still play a considerable role in those East European countries which still adhere to yearly planning targets. In 1964 in Poland gross value indices were still used in 82 per cent of all industrial enterprises, producing 77 per cent of total industrial output. Physical and net output indices were used in the remaining 18 per cent [*97*, pp. 149–50]. The Polish experience indicates how difficult it is to get rid of gross value indices within the framework of more or less traditional planning systems. Its ease of calculation, its additivity at all levels of the administrative hierarchy, its universal applicability in the whole industry, and its role at all levels of traditional planning means that if demoted in one function it reappears in another. In Poland, gross output was finally abolished as a success indicator in the early 1960s but remained as a necessary bonus condition in all, and as basis for wage fund determination, in most, branches of Polish industry. The negative economic effects of this situation will be discussed in the chapters which follow.

3.2.4 MATHEMATICAL PROGRAMMING AT THE ENTERPRISE LEVEL

In the decade 1960–70 there was rapid progress in both mastering the knowledge of mathematical programming and in acquiring experience of its application to concrete planning problems at enterprise level. In a sense this progress can be seen by comparing [*95*] and [*91*]. The first, published in 1960, consists mainly of translations from foreign sources and devotes considerable space to the exposition of basic principles of linear programming; the second (1968) describes *Polish* experience in its numerous applications in industrial enterprises. This progress—to a substantial degree—is due to the work of the Central Commission for the Application of Mathematical Methods in the State Committee of Science and Technology. The first Chairman of this Commission was Professor Oskar Lange.

Mathematical programming at enterprise level—as at any other level, say of industrial branch or of national economy—can be applied to partial problems, e.g. how to determine the optimum size of a production run or how to minimize the use of input X in a given industrial process, or to more complex problems such as the construction of the enterprise production plan. Our remarks will be confined mainly to Polish experience in the latter sphere.

A *Plan Construction*

Polish experience gained in the process of applying linear programming to enterprise production planning, reflects the fact that it is being used under conditions of detailed planning from above and under a specific management mechanism. The former severely restricts enterprise freedom of choice, the latter influences management behaviour in a particular way. These together give rise to a number of specific problems and difficulties, which a mathematical programmer in the West usually does not face.

1. The Criterion Function. As the plan requires meeting simultaneously several main targets (from the viewpoint of bonus maximization and/or criteria used in actual evaluation of management performance) it is almost unanimously suggested that the programme should be solved for several different criterion functions [*92*, p. 7; *101*, p. 27]. These maximands must be chosen (from the main plan targets) by taking into account specific features of a given enterprise and/or branch of industry. In the machine-building industry, for example, the following four maximands are recommended: (1) capacity utilization, (2) value of commodity production, (3) gross output value, (4) volume of profit [*101*, p. 27].

It is claimed that experience of production programming shows that '. . . the volume of output of individual products indicated by different optimal programmes (based on different maximands [those indicated above]) is in many cases almost the same, and in some—even identical. From this one can conclude that it is possible to arrive at a "compromise" solution, i.e. to elaborate the yearly production plan, which meets approximately all criteria' (i.e. all main plan targets) [*101*, p. 35].

The need to choose a 'compromise solution' is almost universally suggested by Polish programmers [*85*, p. 26; *92*, p. 7; *101*, p. 35]. It is hardly astonishing, as this is the only practical way out when one has to satisfy simultaneously several conflicting plan targets. Dr. Radzikowski's statement seems to me, however, unduly optimistic and hence misleading. There is not enough evidence that different maximands do lead to a similar production structure. For example, Table 3.8 below indicates that the opposite may be the case. Secondly, Dr. Radzikowski's conclusion is certainly due to the fact that—contrary to the author of Table 3.8—he used with all his maximands

Table 3.8: Optimum Level of Output of Milling Machines (pieces)

Type	Demand for milling machines	Volume of output planned for 1969	Optimal plan variants for 1969*			
			A	B	C	D
1	230	50	165	50	226	—
2	60	50	60	60	60	11
3	350	110	125	—	350	110
4	330	140	330	—	27	140
5	370	130	—	370	—	130
6	230	100	—	230	—	100
7	50	30	—	—	—	32
8	20	20	20	20	—	—
9	45	40	45	7	45	443
10	60	50	60	—	60	30
11	60	50	—	—	60	30
	Total	770	805	737	828	1,026

The enterprise studied was *Zaklady Przemyslowe im. 1-Maja* in Pruszkow. Calculations were carried on 'Elliott 803b' in I Electronic Institute in Warsaw.

* Maximands used: A—commodity production, B—profit, C—gross output, D—gross output but with the demand for type 9 taken as a minimum. For all other maximands and for all other types (except 9) under maximand D the volume of demand was taken as a ceiling (upper constraint).

Source: [85, p. 26; and 86, pp. 264–5].

rather numerous constraints. The latter are responsible for his different maximands producing very similar results. Needless to say, constraints can easily be expanded to the point that the solution becomes in fact predetermined and no 'compromise' will be needed. Optimization procedure will then always produce the exact replica of the plan determined in advance by higher authorities. But this is hardly the purpose of optimization calculation. In short, Dr. Radzikowski fails to indicate that the similarity of the results he obtained under different maximands are due to severe constraints introduced into the programmes, and he fails to point out the price which it entails: small scope of choice, i.e. small scope for optimization (improvements).

2. *Constraints.* Here the picture is not completely clear to the present author. In a recent article, again by Dr. Radzikowski, who is one of the leading Polish authorities on the subject,[1] there are two contradictory statements concerning the necessary minimum of constraints to which an enterprise production plan has to be subjected. To begin with we are told that in preparing the programme one has to take into account all basic plan targets, and the author lists nineteen of them, quoting—as is customary, see 3.2.3.C—from appropriate decrees, i.e.

[1] See p. 93, fn. 1.

Table 3.9: *Results of Yearly Production Plans Calculated with the Help of Mathematical Programming (on EMC National Elliott 803b)**

Result of Optimization

No.	Name of the Enterprise	Commodity output ('000 zlotys)		Costs of production ('000 zlotys)		Accumulation ('000 zlotys)		Employment of directly productive workers ('000 hours)	
		Enterprise plan	Optimal result	Enterprise plan	Optimal result	Enterprise plan	Optimal result	Enterprise plan	Optimal result
1.	*Kasprzak* Factory								
	(a) Maximum of commodity production	379,311	380,223	334,025	334,026	45,280	46,197	1,769	2,186
	(b) Minimum of costs	379,311	379,314	334,025	333,131	45,280	46,183	1,769	2,186
	(c) Maximum of accumulation	379,311	380,223	334,025	334,026	45,280	46,197	1,769	2,186
	(d) Minimum of employment	379,311	379,311	334,025	334,025	45,280	45,286	1,769	2,169
	(e) Minimum of wages	379,311	379,311	334,025	334,025	45,280	45,286	1,769	2,171
	(f) Maximum utilization of working time	379,311	379,311	334,025	334,025	45,280	45,286	1,769	2,195
2.	*Locomotive Factory Chrzanow*								
	(a) Maximum of commodity production	470,000	562,830	400,000	488,239	70,000	74,590	2,922	3,048
3.	*Lodz Clock Factory*								
	(a) Minimum of costs	91,365	91,345	62,742	62,742	28,603	28,603	784	766
4.	*Warsaw Photo-optical Factory*								
	(a) Maximum of commodity production	81,285	103,663	—	—	2,915	3,073	—	—
	(b) Maximum of accumulation	81,285	73,837	—	—	2,915	4,250	—	—
	(c) Maximum utilization of working time	81,285	103,663	—	—	2,915	3,073	—	—
	(d) Maximum of gross output	81,285	103,388	—	—	2,915	2,978	—	—

Result of Optimization

No.	Name of the Enterprise	Wages of directly productive workers		Utilization of machine-time ('000 hours)		Gross output ('000 zlotys)	
		Enterprise plan	Optimal result	Enterprise plan	Optimal result	Enterprise plan	Optimal result
1.	*Kasprzak* Factory						
	(a) Maximum of commodity production	17,490	17,458	446,888	552,164	—	—
	(b) Minimum of costs	17,490	17,424	446,888	550,779	—	—
	(c) Maximum of accumulation	17,490	17,458	446,888	552,164	—	—
	(d) Maximum of employment	17,490	17,317	446,888	547,712	—	—
	(e) Minimum of wages	17,490	17,279	446,888	548,547	—	—
	(f) Maximum utilization of working time	17,490	17,464	446,888	559,671	—	—
2.	Locomotive Factory *Chrzanow*						
	(a) Maximum of commodity production	34,039	35,662	—	—	—	—
3.	*Lodz* Clock Factory						
	(a) Minimum of costs	9,992	7,175	—	—	—	—
4.	*Warsaw* Photo-optical Factory						
	(a) Maximum of commodity production	—	—	—	690	—	102,506
	(b) Maximum of accumulation	—	—	—	523	—	72,457
	(c) Maximum utilization of working time	—	—	—	690	—	102,506
	(d) Maximum of gross output	—	—	—	684	—	102,842

* All results, except for factory no. 4, are 'pure' results of mathematical programming *per se*, i.e. without any steps taken to broaden existing bottlenecks, etc. If the steps indicated by programming calculation were implemented, the final results would be substantially bigger [*101*, p. 46].

Source: [*101*, pp. 44–5].

without any effort to present them at the same level of aggregation [*101*, pp. 10–11].[1] A few pages later we are told that research work carried out in 1959–63 by the Research Unit of Mathematical Methods at the Institute of Organization of the Machine-building Industry indicated that it is sufficient to take into account ten basic constraints, two of which are identical to previously suggested maximands [*101*, p. 15]. Does it imply that this smaller number of constraints—if met— will assure that the others are automatically met also? This seems rather doubtful. More important, perhaps, is the fact that even the list of nineteen constraints ignores bonus tasks which do not happen to be simultaneously basic plan targets (this, on average, leaves out 50 per cent of bonus tasks). In practice it means that enterprise management is being asked to prepare (to order or to accept) an optimization pro- gramme which ignores—to a large extent—their real criterion function i.e. bonus maximization. This, needless to say, is hardly realistic. Two solutions of this dilemma which come to mind are most unsatisfactory. (1) If one tries to construct a programme which takes into account all presently existing obligatory targets, which we have calculated in 3.2.3.C as numbering on average 109, will not the constraints imposed be so severe and the programmer's freedom of choice so drastically restricted as to put in question the very usefulness of optimization procedure? (2) If, on the other hand, the programme prepared ignores most of the obligatory targets for the sake of having room for optimization—which is the case with all production plan programmes I have studied—how does one prevent enterprise management from deviating from this 'optimal plan' in the course of its implementation? There is a strong incentive to do this in order to take into account those obligatory targets which were ignored in optimization calculations, but have substantial (positive or negative) bonus value. I have been unable to find satisfactory answers to these questions in the relevant Polish literature.

B Potential Benefits

1. Higher Economic Effectiveness. Frequently, mathematical pro- gramming *itself* leads to better economic results—under all or most of maximands used—than results envisaged in enterprise plans elaborated according to traditional methods of planning. The improvements achieved in this way—probably because of the severe constraints imposed (see A.2 above)—are usually not very impressive. This is illustrated in Table 3.9. Mathematical programming, however, also

[1] To illustrate: the constraint 'level of the wage fund' has only a few 'sub- constraints', such as the level of the wage fund for production workers, clerical staff, auxiliary personnel, etc. On the other hand, the constraint 'required product-mix' may have hundreds or even thousands of 'sub-constraints' prescribing in detail not less than 60–80 per cent of enterprise total output (see 3.2.3.C).

indicates basic directions of organizational improvements, desirable plan changes, and effective investments which, if implemented, can produce much higher results than 'pure' optimization calculations. Among other factors, mathematical programming helps to identify:

(i) Maladjustments between required product-mix and the technical and production structure of the enterprise. It does so by indicating so-called 'convenient' and 'inconvenient' products. The former—in the optimal programme—exceed the plan requirements, the latter meet it, and only because their planned volume of output is used as one of the constraints [101, pp. 32–5].

(ii) Taking the above as a starting point it is then possible to identify the basic bottlenecks and to formulate the most effective ways of their elimination by: (a) organizational means (e.g. increased number of shifts on bottleneck machinery); (b) introducing so-called 'round-about' technology, i.e. shifting certain operations to under-utilized equipment (the cost of these operations usually increases, but total costs diminish because of better overall utilization of fixed capital); (c) broadening of subcontracting; and finally (d) eliminating bottlenecks through appropriate investments.

When conclusions from mathematical programming are followed up, then the final results of programming are much greater than the initial ones. This is illustrated in line four of Table 3.9. Most of these improvements, such as introducing changes in the product-mix which will make it better adapted to enterprise production possibilities, cannot be implemented without industrial association approval. The industrial association is usually unable to approve them, because they require re-allocation of targets within the branch, a formidable task, indeed. So we encounter here one of those vicious circles, in which economic problems abound. One cannot effectively use mathematical programming at enterprise level—under conditions of branch planning —if there is no mathematical programming at industrial association level. The latter, however, represents a more difficult problem and—before it is solved—prevents full advantage being taken of the potential benefits which mathematical programming can produce at enterprise level.

2. Improvement of Planning. From the enterprise viewpoint, mathematical programming can be useful at both the stages of plan construction described in 3.2.2.A. It helps to argue the high effectiveness of the extra resources required and—at the second stage—to submit several variants of product-mix (unfeasible under traditional planning because of the time required) and to defend the most convenient one, pointing out that it is also the most effective economically (according to economic calculations at enterprise level) [85; 86]. Mathematical programming shortens considerably the time required for plan construction—which has many obvious advantages—and also helps to improve coordination between different parts of enterprise T-E plans.

For the industrial association, mathematical programming opens the way to increase its economic role and its effectiveness. It can facilitate and improve allocation of plan targets and investment funds among member-enterprises and it can also offer invaluable help in programming *new* industrial enterprises. As we have indicated in 3.1.4, mathematical programming cannot, however, be expected to play this role in the near future.

C *Problems of Application*

Even at enterprise level the application of mathematical programming is plagued by difficulties. These can be classified broadly into two main groups: (1) technical and organizational, and (2) economic and institutional.

1. Technical and Organizational Problems. These are of the well-known type, but their acuteness is frequently strengthened by the low quality of available hardware and software and by the lack of appropriate data in many enterprises.

The lack of data necessary for mathematical programming is the difficulty most universally encountered by Polish mathematical programmers [*85; 86; 91; 93; 100; 101*]. Frequently it is due simply to the unsuitability of existing information. Sometimes, however, more complex reasons are involved. For example, certain operations may have never been performed on a given type of machine. As it should not be assumed *a priori* that doing so would be uneconomical, one has to calculate the appropriate technical coefficients. This is being done with the help of theoretical models (in Polish bloomeries), by experiments (in the cable industry) or by interpolation (in the paper industry) [*93*, p. 49].

The need of aggregation is frequently encountered with all the usual difficulties. For example, the cable industry produces 16,000 specifications which have been finally reduced to 80 aggregates, the number of types of ingots was reduced to 67, etc. [*93*, p. 49].

In spite of aggregation, some models remain too big for solution with the help of existing hardware. It turned out that in the paper industry one cannot go below 270 product groups and 120 types of machinery, which proved too complex for available computers. Under such circumstances the model may be broken into independent 'blocks' or those variables of which the solution is dictated by common sense may be eliminated, or both.

2. Economic and Institutional Difficulties. Mathematical programming—giving overall better results—leads frequently to a number of economic problems, which cannot be easily accommodated by the rigid structure of the present planning practice. These are encountered at both enterprise and branch levels, e.g. the branch optimum is frequently accompanied by the worsening of the economic results of some member-enterprises (under the existing price structure). This happened, for example, in the Polish paper industry. Affected enterprises found themselves in a difficult position. 'The plan fulfilment, factory fund, etc. were all at stake. When we reach the stage of elaborating plans of optimal allocation for the whole year, the solution will be simple. In the yearly plan all the consequences of optimal [branch] allocation will be taken into account. Meanwhile, when changes have to be made during the year, the resulting losses must not be considered as the enterprise's fault, and should not affect enterprise rights to the factory fund' [*93*, p. 50].

Mathematical programming, as a rule, leads to longer production runs. In one enterprise of the paper industry, the number of specifications produced diminished by 60 per cent. Longer production runs frequently result in stock increases. Again, if this is not envisaged in the enterprise financial plan, it can lead to serious difficulties with the supervising bank and worsen enterprise planned (as opposed to real) performance [*93*, p. 51].

Some of the existing planning and management practices are also directly responsible for the difficulties encountered in applying mathematical programming. One of the most serious is frequent plan changes imposed from above. They can make invalid the whole basis of a given optimal plan. On the other hand, the existing management mechanism frequently makes enterprise management reluctant to use mathematical programming because it may expose weaknesses in enterprise functioning, such as the lack of certain basic data, low and/or uneven level of capacity utilization, etc. Moreover—as a consequence— mathematical programming may reveal enterprise reserves and lead to the increase of planning tasks with all the dangers involved. To this one has to add understandable psychological resistance to new and difficult methods, which are frequently beyond the comprehension of the managerial staff asked to collaborate in their introduction [see *85*, p. 27].

D *Remedies Proposed*

Leaving aside the obvious technico-organizational suggestions for improvements which follow from the logic of the problems under analysis, the remedies proposed are of two types: one assumes fundamental changes in existing planning and management practice, the other does not. Frequently the same author advocates both, the latter as a second best or rather palliative solution. Here is a typical example.

'It seems that the present system of directives does not induce the search for economic reserves and hence creates no incentives for the application of mathematical methods and EDP . . . Elimination of

6*

these obstacles . . . could be achieved by the abolition of obligatory targets, as has been done in Hungary . . .' [85, p. 27].

If obligatory targets are here to stay, then the author suggests that '. . . optimization programming should be carried out at industrial association level—on the basis of enterprise data—but before fixing obligatory targets for enterprises'. This should give a better chance for arriving at the optimal plan because 'at industrial association level, the "localism" of individual enterprises disappears, and it will be possible to achieve a rational allocation of investment funds allotted to a given branch' [85, p. 27].

There is no need to go beyond pointing out the obvious weaknesses of the author's 'second best' solution: (a) the problem of distortion of data received from enterprises; (b) the 'localism' of the industrial association itself; and—most fundamentally—(c) the contraction of the programming task from production planning to the mere allocation of investment funds (the latter probably reflects the author's implicit recognition of the impossibility of more comprehensive branch programming at present).

More important, however, is the author's explicit admittance of the close interrelation of mathematical programming and institutional reforms (see 2.2.4D and E). Here again it is recognized that effective application of mathematical programming is not a substitute for an institutional, 'guided market' type of reform, but one of its many potential benefits.

APPENDIX 3.1

Simplified Structure of Enterprise T-E Plan

Production Plan
  of main products in physical terms;
  of commodity production in transfer prices;
  of gross output in comparable prices;
  of export;
  of domestic sales;
  of sub-contracting;
  of production capacity.
Plan of Technical Development
  of technical and organizational improvements;
  of elaborating new products;
  of research and experimental work;
  of technico-economic indices.
Maintenance Plan
  of capital repairs;
  of current repairs.

Plan of Input Supplies
   of raw material requirements;
   of input norms;
   of stocks of inputs and of semi-finished and finished goods.
Employment and Wage Plan
   of necessary labour time and its utilization;
   of average employment;
   of additional employment;
   of intra-shop training;
   of average norms fulfilment;
   of labour productivity;
   of wage fund together with average wages by main groups of employees.
Cost Plan
   of planned costs of commodity output;
   of unit costs.
Financial Plan
   of profitability, total accumulation, and total profit;
   of profit distribution;
   of working capital required;
   of bank credits;
   of depreciation fund distribution;
   of total revenue and expenditures.
Investment Plan
   of different types of investment (central, industrial association, and
      enterprise's own);
   of construction works.

Sources: 66, pp. 10–11; *76*, pp. 33–6 and *passim*; *94*, pp. 415–18.

APPENDIX 3.2

List of Quarterly Bonus Tasks Received by Four Polish Enterprises in 1968

   I. *Planned Tasks*
         1. Production plan according to prescribed product-mix
         2. Selected tasks of technical progress
         3. Tasks concerning quality improvements
         4. Investment tasks
         5. Subcontracting tasks
         6. Export plan
         7. Labour productivity per employee
         8. To fulfil commodity production target
         9. Not to exceed the last year's level of stocks of raw materials
        10. To put into service machine X
        11. To meet the tasks enumerated in Section 5 of yearly plan targets.

  II. *Above the Plan Targets* (Additional Tasks)
        12. To produce additional output according to delivery dates
        13. Investments and capital repairs tasks

14. To revise all types of norms and coefficients and to achieve lower labour inputs
15. Export tasks
16. To start the output of new components
17. To put into service certain equipment (according to given enumeration)
18. To start second shift on equipment X
19. To put into service equipment Y and to produce the amount Z of specified components
20. Technical progress tasks
21. Subcontracting tasks
22. To lower the index of complaints from customers (*reklamacje*)
23. Tasks in quality improvements
24. To prepare labour input norms for all products produced by the enterprise
25. To prepare the list of so-called 'cost of processing' prices for all products being produced.

III. *Supplementary Conditions*
26. To adhere to planned monthly output flow within a given quarter (measured either in gross or commodity output) in constant prices (*rytmicznosc produkcji*)
27. To obtain export orders according to specified markets and totalling X 'zl. dewizowy' (zl. dewizowy is an accounting unit. 1 zl. dewizowy = 0·25 US $)
28. To lower labour inputs resulting from technical progress totalling Z '000 working hours
29. To submit the plan of stocks of raw material not later than t_1
30. To implement fully the Instruction of the Ministry of Heavy Industry concerning increased control of the use of silver and precious metals
31. To implement postulates resulting from the resolution of the VIIth Plenum (of the Central Committee of PUWP)
32. Subcontracting tasks
33. Export plan
34. Not to exceed the planned unit costs of the specified products
35. To improve (in relation to the previous year) the index of industrial accidents
36. To verify fully input coefficients as required by the Instruction of Ministry of Heavy Industry
37. To elaborate input norms for product Y
38. To implement the 'normative' cost accounting according to the approved timetable
39. Investment tasks
40. To keep stocks of raw material and certain final goods within approved limits
41. To increase employment in section X
42. To fulfil the X percentage of capital repairs
43. Technical progress tasks
44. To analyse the structure of output

45. To analyse the effectiveness of technical progress undertaken
46. To analyse the functioning of economic incentives in the sphere of subcontracting.

Source: [*74*, pp. 26–7].

Notes:

1. The distribution of bonus task into three groups enumerated above is in accord with the then valid regulation on the incentive system for enterprise management. For a full discussion of economic incentives see Ch. 6.

2. Each enterprise received 3–5 tasks from group I, 1–3 from II, and 3–10 from group III, i.e. from 7 to 15 tasks altogether.

3. The bonus tasks are either single or aggregated, i.e. consisting in fact of many single tasks, as e.g. tasks nos. 1, 2, 13, 17, 28, 32.

4. In the enterprises studied the aggregated tasks constituted approximately 80 per cent of all bonus tasks. The detailed analysis revealed that, on average, the aggregated task consists of 10 single tasks. Because on average each enterprise received 10 tasks, of which 8 are aggregated, it means about 82 single bonus tasks per enterprise ($8 \times 10 + 2 = 82$). This is how we arrived at the rounded figure of 80, which is used in our discussion in 3.2.3.C. (Source for Notes: [*74*, *passim*]).

References to Chapter Three

3.1

1. Bilinski L.: 'Optimal Decisions under Conditions of Multiple Goals', *E*, 3, 1969.
2. —— *Rachunek ekonomiczny w planowaniu i zarzadzaniu* (Economic Calculation in Planning and Management), Warsaw, 1969.
3. Blass B.: 'Success Indicators of the Industrial Enterprise and the Wage Fund', in [*9*].
4. Bratkowski S.: 'Electronic Data Processing—Decisions Needed,' *ZG*, 12, 1970.
5. —— Szwarc K.: 'Electronic Data Processing: Let Us Start by Formulating the Programme'. Part I, *ZG*, 46, 1969; Part II, *ZG*, 47, 1969.
6. Decree of the Chairman of the Planning Commission of the CM of 5 May 1964 concerning the elaboration of general investment requirements, *MP*, 34, 1964.
7. Decree No. 225 of the CM, dated 29 July 1964, concerning the organizational and technical reconstruction of branches and sub-branches of the socialized economy and of regions, *MP*, 55, 1964.
8. Decree No. 276 of the CM, dated 28 October 1965, concerning the financial rules of centrally planned industrial associations and their member-enterprises *MP*, 61, 1965.
9. Dudzinski W., Misiak M., eds.: *Mierniki oceny dzialalnosci przedsiebiorstwa przemyslowego* (Success Indicators of the Industrial Enterprise), Warsaw, 1964. Mimeographed.
10. *Ekonomika przemyslu* (Economics of Industry), Warsaw, 1966.
11. 'Electronic Computers: Where We Are, Where Do We Go?' Discussion by a Panel of Experts. *ZG*, 23, 1969.
12. Fiszel H.: 'Taking into Account more than One Criterion Function in Optimizing Calculation', *PS*, 1964.
13. Gajda J.: *Programowanie produkcji przemyslowej* (The Programming of Industrial Production), Warsaw, 1966.

14. Halak G.: *Rekonstrukcja branz, galezi i regionow gospodarczych* (The Reconstruction of Sub-branches, Branches, and Economic Regions), Warsaw, 1967.
15. Kalecki M., Rakowski M.: 'A Generalized Formula of the Efficiency of Investment', in [*40*, pp. 189–203]. In English.
16. Kierczynski T.: 'The Functioning of the Profitability Index', *ZG*, 42, 1968.
17. Knyziak Z., Lissowski W.: *Ekonomika i programowanie inwestycji przemyslowych* (The Economics and Programming of Industrial Investments), Warsaw, 1964.
18. Komisja Planowania przy Radzie Ministrow (The Economic Commission at the Council of Ministers): *Instrukcja ogolna w sprawie metodyki badan ekonomicznej efektywnosci inwestycji* (General Instruction concerning the Research Methodology of the Economic Effectiveness of Investment), Warsaw, 1962.
19. Komitet Nauki i Techniki (The Committee on Science and Technology): 'Instruction concerning the Ways and Methods of Elaborating the Organizational and Technical Reconstruction Programmes of Sub-branches, Branches, and Economic Regions', *MP*, 68, 1964.
20. Krajski K.: *Ekonomiczne podstawy planowania rozwoju galezi przemyslu maszynowego* (The Economic Principles of Development Planning in a Branch of the Machine-building Industry), Warsaw, 1967.
21. Kuzinski S.: 'On Investment Criteria during 1971–5', *ND*, 10, 1969.
22. Lange O.: *Optymalne decyzje* (Optimal Decisions), Warsaw, 1964.
23. Lesz M.: *Nauka i gospodarka* (Science and the Economy), Warsaw, 1968.
24. Lipinski J.: 'The Informational Functions of Prices', *E*, 2, 1964.
25. Lagowski T.: 'The Macroeconomic, Dynamic System of Electronic Data Processing for the Iron and Steel Industry "Centrostal-11" ', *EOP*, 7, 1967.
26. —— 'The Use of the Multicriterion Method of Optimalization within the System of Automatic Planning and Management (based on the experience of the Iron and Steel Industry)', *EOP*, 8, 1968.
27. Los J.: 'Remarks on the Joint Optimization of Several Magnitudes', *PS*, 3, 1965.
28. Misiak M.: 'Productivity, Modern Technology, and the Economic Mechanism (Some Problems in the Implementation of the Decisions of the IInd Plenum)', *ND*, 11, 1969.
29. —— 'The Industrial Associations' Proposals', *ZG*, 11, 1970.
30. Olenski J.: 'Problems of the Multicriteria Optimization of the Production Plan' (based on the Experience of Allocating Orders among Grinders in Iron and Steel Industry), *EOP*, 9, 1967.
31. Pietrzkiewicz T.: *Model bilansowy branzy przemyslowej* (The Balance Model of the Industrial Branch), Warsaw, 1968.
32. Plichcinski E.: 'Economic Relations in the 1971–5 Plan Proposals of Industrial Associations', *GP*, 11, 1969.
33. Poljak E. M.: 'The Matrix Model of Enterprise Production and Economic Activities', *Ekonomika i Matiematiczeskije Mietody*, 2, 1966.
34. Radzikowski W.: *Ekonomiczny rachunek repartycji zadan i srodkow zjednoczenia przemyslowego* (The Economic Calculation of the Allocation of Tasks and Resources within the Industrial Association), Warsaw, 1967.
35. Rakowski M., ed.: *Efektywnosc inwestycji* (The Effectiveness of Investment), Warsaw, 1961.
36. —— *Optymalizacja programow rozwoju* (The Optimization of Development Programmes), Warsaw, 1968.
37. Karlin S.: *Mathematical Method and Theory in Games, Programming, and Economics*, London-Paris, 1959.
38. Secomski K.: *Podstawy planowania perspektywicznego* (Principles of Perspective Planning), Warsaw, 1967.

39. Skolka I., Wierzek I.: 'The use of matrix models for enterprise and branch planning in Czechoslovakia', *Planovoe Khozyaistvo*, 9, 1963.
40. *Studies on the Theory of Reproduction and Prices.* (Problems of Economic Theory and Practice in Poland), Warsaw, 1964.
41. Targowski A.: 'The Costs of Using Electronic Data Processing', *Maszyny Matematyczne*, 2, 1969.
42. —— 'The Key Problems of Using Electronic Computers in the National Economy', *GP*, 12, 1969.
43. *Wybor ekonomiczny w projektowaniu inwestycji* (Economic Choice in Investment Programming), Warsaw, 1969.
44. *Teaching Materials for Studying the Polish Method of Investigating the Economic Effectiveness of Investments.* The Higher Course of National Economic Planning. Warsaw, 1962. Mimeographed.
45. 'The Technological Gap.' Interview with Professor J. Tymowski, *ZG*, 39, 1969.

3.2
46. Appendix to [53]: 'Instruction concerning the Changes of Organizational Structure of Centrally Planned State Industry'.
47. Bill of 16 February 1960 changing the decree of 1950 on state enterprises. *DU*, 18, 1960.
48. Byrski B.: 'New and Traditional Industrial *Kombinaty*', *ZG*, 21, 1970.
49. Dabrowski S.: 'The Industrial Enterprise in the System of Programming Reconstruction of Industry', *EOP*, 5, 1968.
50. Dabrowski W.: 'The Solution of Financial Disagreements in *Kombinaty*', *PUG*, 7, 1970.

DECREES OF COUNCIL OF MINISTERS
51. 704 of 10 November 1956 concerning broadening the sphere of authority of state industrial enterprises, *MP*, 94, 1956.
52. 199 of 30 May 1957 concerning the remuneration of the employees of state industrial enterprises.
53. 128 of 18 April 1958 concerning the changes of organizational structure of centrally planned state industry. Unpublished. Cf. *PUG*, 6, 1958.
54. 392 of 13 October 1958 concerning profit distribution, equalization payments (*roznice wyrownawcze*), covering of losses, financing of working capital, investments, and capital repairs in industrial enterprises, and financial principles of industrial associations for 1959, *MP*, 88, 1958.
55. 450 of 26 November 1958 concerning employment limits in state industrial enterprises (unpublished).
56. 451 of 26 November 1958 on the national economic plan for 1959 (unpublished)
57. 308 of 17 November 1960 on leading enterprises, *MP*, 94, 1960.
58. 426 of 19 December 1960 concerning the elaboration and approval of yearly technico-economic plans of units of the socialized economy, *MP*, 3, 1961.
59. 193 of 23 October 1969 concerning industrial and construction *kombinaty*, *MP*, 46, 1969.

DECREES OF THE ECONOMIC COMMITTEE OF THE COUNCIL OF MINISTERS
60. of 12 May 1950, *Biuletyn PKPG*, 12, 1950.
61. 210 of 17 July 1966 (unpublished).
62. Doberski W.: 'Results of the Economic Council's Questionnaires in Industry', *GP*, 10, 1961.
63. Dudzinski W., Misiak M., eds.: *Mierniki oceny dzialalnosci przedsiebiorstwa przemyslowego* (Success Indicators of the Industrial Enterprise), Warsaw, 1964. Mimeographed.
64. Economic Council: 'Theses concerning Certain Changes in the Economic Model', *ZG*, 22, 1957.

65. Economic Council: *Results of a Questionnaire concerning Enterprises' Independence in 1956–9*, Warsaw, 1959. Mimeographed.
66. *Ekonomika przedsiebiorstw* (Enterprise Economics). Part II, Lodz, 1968.
67. *Ekonomika przedsiebiorstwa przemyslowego* (The Economics of the Industrial Enterprise), Warsaw, 1965.
68. *Ekonomika przemyslu* (The Economics of Industry), Warsaw, 1966.
69. Fedorowicz Z.: 'The Financial System and Obligatory Targets', *F*, 8, 1968.
70. 'The Financial Principles of Industrial *Kombinaty*', *F*, 2, 1970.
71. Gajda J.: *Programowanie produkcji przemyslowej* (The Programming of Industrial Production), Warsaw, 1966.
72. Glinski B.: 'The Socialist Industrial Enterprise', in [*67*, pp. 9–37].
73. —— *Teorie i praktyka zarzadzania przedsiebiorstwami przemyslowymi* (Theories and Practice of the Management of Industrial Enterprises), Warsaw, 1966.
74. Golinowski K.: 'Directive Indices in Enterprise Management', *GP*, 3, 1969.
75. Gradowski T.: Kiernozycki A.: 'Planned Directive Indices and Enterprise Independence', *GP*, 10, 1959.
76. Grossman A., ed.: *Organizacja i planowanie w przedsiebiorstwie przemyslowym* (Organization and Planning in the Industrial Enterprise), Warsaw, 1968.
77. Grzybowski S.: 'The Structure of Final Products in Planning the Organizational System of the *Kombinat*', *EOP*, 12, 1969.
78. Haus B.: *Planowanie produkcji w przedsiebiorstwie przemyslowym* (Production Planning in the Industrial Enterprise), Warsaw, 1969.
79. Hentschel H.: 'On the Legal Position of *Kombinaty* in GDR', *PUG*, 7, 1970.
80. Jakubowicz S.: 'The Principles of the Functioning of *Kombinaty* in GDR', *ZG*, 16, 1970.
81. Jarosz M.: *Samorzad robotniczy w przedsiebiorstwie przemyslowym* (Workers' Self-management in the Industrial Enterprise), Warsaw, 1967.
82. Jezowski K.: *Zarzadzanie przemyslu* (The Management of Industry), Warsaw, 1970.
83. J.W.: 'How do we "Plan" and "Fulfil" Plans', *ZG*, 7, 1970.
84. Kaleta J.: 'Financial Planning in Industrial Enterprises', *RPES*, 4, 1970.
85. Kierczynski A.: 'The Difficulties of Applying Optimization Methods in an Enterprise', *GP*, 1, 1970.
86. —— 'The Application of Electronic Data Processing to Production Planning', *EOP*, 6, 1970.
87. Kierczynski T.: 'The Functioning of Profitability Index', *ZG*, 42, 1968.
88. —— 'The Functioning of the System of Financing and Crediting Stocks', *ZG*, 43, 1968.
89. Kubisiak J.: 'Certain Problems of Enterprise Technico-Economic Planning and the Participation of Workers' Self-management in Plan Construction', *EOP*, 5, 1969.
90. Kwejt J.: *Metody i strategia zarzadzania przedsiebiorstwem przemyslowym* (Management Methods and Strategy of the Industrial Enterprise), Warsaw, 1968.
91. Lesz M., ed.: *Optymalizacja planow* (The Optimization of Plans), Warsaw, 1968.
92. —— 'Introduction', in [*91*, pp. 5–8].
93. —— 'Certain Problems of the Optimal Allocation of Output', in [*91*, pp. 47–51].
94. Lisikiewicz J.: 'The Construction of the Technico-Economic Plan', in [*67*, pp. 406–33].
95. *Metody matematyczne w organizacji i ekonomice przedsiebiorstwa* (Mathematical Methods in Organization and Enterprise Economics), Warsaw, 1960.
96. Morawski W.: 'The Functions of Workers' Self-management in the Management System of Industry', in [*107*, pp. 243–62].

97. Party-Government Commission created by the Prime Minister's Order No. 35/1963: 'Criteria for Evaluating the Performance of Industrial Enterprises', in [*63*, pp. 130–72].
98. Plonski A.: 'On Enterprises' Reconstruction and Development Programmes', *EOP*, 8, 1970.
99. Przymusinski Cz.: 'Industrial and Construction *Kombinaty* in the Light of Legislation'. Part I, *PUG*, 1, 1970; Part II, *PUG*, 2, 1970.
100. Radzikowski W.: *Ekonomiczny rachunek repartycji zadan i srodkow zjednoczenia przemyslowego* (The Economic Calculation of the Allocation of Tasks and Resources within the Industrial Association), Warsaw, 1967.
101. —— 'The Production Planning of Machine-building Enterprises by Means of Linear Programming', in [*91*, pp. 9–46].
102. —— 'Industrial *Kombinaty* as a Particular Form of the Concentration of Production in the Machine-building Industry', *EOP*, 3, 1970.
103. *Rocznik polityczny i gospodarczy, 1958*, Warsaw, 1958.
104. *Rocznik polityczny i gospodarczy, 1959*, Warsaw, 1959.
105. Samecki W.: *Ryzyko i niepewnosc w dzalalnosci przedsiebiorstwa przemyslowego* (Risk and Uncertainty in the Activity of the Industrial Enterprise), Warsaw, 1967.
106. Spruch W.: 'Production Planning', in [*67*, pp. 62–91].
107. Szczepanski J., ed.: *Przemysl i spoleczenstwo w Polsce Ludowej* (Industry and Society in People's Poland), Wroclaw-Warsaw, 1969.
108. Theses of the Central Committee of PUWP for the Vth Congress, *ND*, 8, 1968.
109. *Uchwala V Zjazdu PZPR* (Resolution of the Vth Congress of PUWP), Warsaw, 1968.
110. Winter E.: *Wplyw finansow na rozwoj przedsiebiorstw socjalistycznych* (The Role of Finance in the Development of Socialist Enterprises), Warsaw, 1967.
111. Wojciechowski T.: 'The Planning of Material Supplies—Tradition and Reality', *GP*, 5, 1970.
112. Zabkowicz L.: 'The Creation and "Modelling" of *Kombinaty* in GDR', *EOP*, 4, 1970.
113. *IV Plenum KC PZPR. 27–28 lipca 1965 r. Podstawowe dokumenty* (IVth Plenum of the Central Committee of PUWP. 27–28 July 1965. Basic Documents), Warsaw, 1965.

PART TWO
THE MANAGEMENT OF PLAN IMPLEMENTATION

CHAPTER FOUR

THE MANAGEMENT MECHANISM OF SOCIALIST INDUSTRY[1]

4.1 The Enterprise as Consisting of, and United by, Feeding, Information, Stimulation, and Steering Systems

In order to analyse management in a socialist enterprise it is convenient to consider the enterprise from a cybernetic point of view[2]

[1] Part Two represents an effort to overcome what I consider the inadequacy of the previous attempts of Professor Wakar and myself to analyse the mechanism of plan implementation with the help of the so-called tripartite management formula: incentives—prices—methods of accounting (see references [*17*] and [*21*, pp. 48–85] in the Preface). As the main weakness of this approach I consider that (1) It combines elements of the enterprise 'rules of the game'—incentive systems and methods of accounting—with prices, which are one of the CPB's information carriers. Prices (and administrative orders) are not part of the management formula, if by the latter we understand the principles of the functioning of the enterprise. (2) The management formula in its original formulation does not distinguish between incentives and success indicators. Success indicators are the *basis* of the incentive system, but there is frequently a long and complex set of stimulation system principles between the success indicator and management bonuses. As a result, the type of success indicator used does not determine unequivocally the character of the stimulation system, and hence, the enterprise behaviour. The success indicator may be synthetic, and the incentive system mixed, if narrowly defined bonus conditions are used. (3) The management formula is too aggregated for the detailed analysis of the enterprise 'rules of the game'. For a proper understanding of enterprise behaviour a much more detailed approach seems necessary. (4) The formula ignores the whole problem of resource flow to and from the enterprise and its regulation, i.e. what I now call the dependent and independent feeding systems. (5) Finally, it seems necessary to distinguish enterprise 'rules of the game' from the management mechanism, which is a much broader concept. If, as a criterion for distinguishing between different management mechanisms, we use the type of main information carrier used by the CPB for guiding plan executants, then it follows that the enterprise 'rules of the game' cannot be either 'parametric' or 'non-parametric'. These concepts refer only to the type of feedback between the CPB and plan executants. Enterprise 'rules of the game' can however be more or less suitable for either type of management. The present book tries to remedy these weaknesses in our previous approach.

[2] O. Lange wrote: 'Cybernetics have proved to be an indispensable instrument of the planning and management of a national economy. Cybernetics fulfils a particularly important role in a socialist economy . . . The role of cybernetics is twofold in a socialist economy. It constitutes an apparatus for precise analysis and precise calculation which ensures that economic processes are directed with the desired effectiveness, precision, and reliability. However, apart from providing a basis for

as a structure consisting of feeding, information, stimulation, and steering systems.

This is graphically presented in Diagram 4.1.[1]

Each of the systems and their interrelationships are discussed in detail in later chapters. The following is a brief introduction to the subject.

The Feeding System (13). An enterprise is endowed with certain amounts of fixed and working capital (1), and with the help of this capital organizes its production process (2). The production process in turn gives the product or services (3). The enterprise sells the product at buyer prices (4)[2] and receives a total revenue (5). The revenue from the sales undergoes a twofold process of regulation before it is re-fed into the enterprise: (a) the first process determines the amount of financial resources which will remain at the disposal of the enterprise (7R); (b) the second determines, within the constraints set, the use to which the resources being re-fed into the enterprise may be put (7D).

The total revenue is first divided between the enterprise and the state. There are two basic stages in this division. In the first place the total revenue is converted into seller prices (6). Ignoring cases where the buyer prices (BP), i.e. the transfer prices (*ceny zbytu*), and the seller prices (SP), i.e. the ex-factory prices (*ceny fabryczne*), are the same, the total revenue of the enterprise is either reduced (BP > SP) and the surplus (for example in the form of turnover tax) is fed into the financial system (8); or vice versa, (when BP < SP) the revenue is increased, for example by a subsidy. In the second stage of regulation, the revenue,

[1] The individual systems are marked by different lines in the diagram and the elements of which the systems consist have been numbered. The numbers in the text indicate which element of the systems is under discussion.

[2] Buyer prices are the prices at which an enterprise acquires the means of production. Seller prices are the prices which an enterprise actually receives for its output.

---

precise analysis and precise calculation, cybernetics creates a specific way of thinking, which one can call cybernetic thinking, and a specific method of defining and solving problems. This cybernetic way of thought is important apart from the results it provides through specific methods of analysis and calculation, in a similar manner to mathematical or statistical ways of thought' [*15*, pp. 165–6]. In applying cybernetic thinking to the management theory of socialist industry, much is owed to J. Wieckowski's work 'The Role of Profit in Production Management' [*20*] in which cybernetic analysis is applied in an analysis of the information system in socialist industry. Where possible, J. Wieckowski's terminology and definitions have been used in this study in order to avoid increasing the chaos in terminology which exists in economic studies using cybernetic instruments. However, since the sphere of this work is much wider than that covered by J. Wieckowski's study, and from the point of view of the merits of each individual case, it has been found necessary to introduce a wide range of new concepts and to redefine many others.

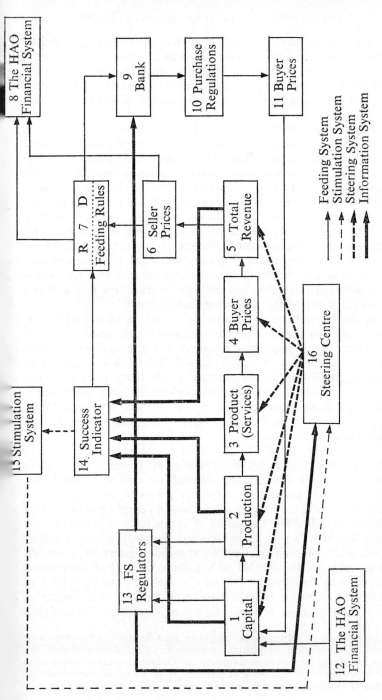

HAO = Higher Administrative Organs
R = reduction   D = distribution according to end-use

——— Feeding System
- - - Stimulation System
━━━ Steering System
▬▬▬ Information System

Diagram 4.1   The socialist enterprise as a cybernetic system   (a simplified diagram)

having undergone the first stage of correction, undergoes a further division based on feeding rules (7), which define other financial obligations encumbent on the enterprise, such as payments to the industrial association. On passing through these two stages the amount of revenue remaining in the enterprise is determined, and is termed the 'enterprise revenue'.

The enterprise is not at liberty to dispose of its retained revenue at will. Two types of constraints are imposed on the use of the revenue remaining in the enterprise. The first constraint stems from the feeding rules, on the basis of which the enterprise revenue must be allocated within the enterprise. These feeding rules define the type of special funds (*fundusze celowe*) which the enterprise is obliged to set up. The size of these funds, however, is decided yearly by industrial associations. The second constraint stems from the regulations (10) pertaining to the purchase (hire) of certain factors of production, such as the labour force and some means of production, which the enterprise may not acquire at will. Within these constraints the enterprise reproduces and increases its resources according to buyer prices (11) and this closes what is termed the 'dependent feeding system'.[1]

Since the socialist enterprise is state property, an additional feeding system exists. On the basis of macro-economic calculation, the HAO may decide that the amount of resources of a given enterprise, which have been determined by the dependent feeding system, should be increased. The HAO may, for example, decide that a given enterprise should be substantially expanded or modernized. Such undertakings are financed from central or industrial association investment funds, and the inflow from such funds is termed the 'independent feeding system' (12).

The Information System (14). Economic events continually take place in an enterprise, for example, raw materials are used in the production process, a given amount of output is produced and sold. These economic events in the enterprise are recorded according to methods of accounting which define the nature of events to be recorded and the manner in which they are to be recorded. Economic events or certain characteristics of economic events grouped together in a specific manner, and usually provided with a norm, or basis of comparison, constitute what are termed 'analysers'. Analysers can be defined as performance indicators for an enterprise, or for parts of an enterprise, such as a department, section, brigade, or workshop. The analysers

---

[1] This system is termed the dependent system, since the inflow of resources is the function of the results of the enterprise performance. The definition of what constitutes the results of enterprise performance, and the type of functional relationship between this result and the inflow of resources to an enterprise, depends on the structure of the management mechanism and will be discussed in later chapters.

serve to compare the actual state of enterprise activity, such as, for example, the amount of steel used per unit of output or a profit volume with the model appropriate to this aspect, such as steel input norm or a planned profit.

A large number of analysers of different types are in use in each enterprise. The roles fulfilled by the analysers are of two types: roles general to all analysers, and roles specific to certain groups of analysers.

The general purpose of all analysers is to 'observe' the economic events taking place in an enterprise, in order to reveal any irregularities, in which case they present the enterprise management, or, in cybernetic terminology, the steering centre, with a basis for decision-making. The general characteristics, therefore, of this role of the analyser consist in its feedback to the steering centre.

The specific functions which analysers fulfil may be used as criteria by which to divide the analysers into groups. Depending on the purpose or function of different analysers, or, in other words, on the type of system to which they are linked, all analysers in an enterprise can be divided into three groups:

(1) The success indicators (14) are analysers which serve as the basis for the management stimulation system (15). Within the constraints set, these analysers exert a decisive influence on the enterprise's product-mix policy and its choice of method of production. Examples of enterprise success indicators recently introduced in Poland are: rate or volume of profit, decrease of unit costs of production, and 'level of final costs.'[1] Previously, accumulation, ratio of cost of production to total revenue, decrease of losses, gross output, commodity output, and various indices of profitability (see 5.5), were used, among others, as success indicators.

(2) Feeding system (FS) regulators (13) are linked to the feeding system and serve to control and regulate the flow of resources into an enterprise and their use within it. The most important type of FS regulators are 'output indices' (*mierniki produkcji*). Output indices constitute the basis on which the labour force and the wage fund of an enterprise or industrial association are planned. Examples of output indices used in Poland are: gross output, commodity output (termed

---

[1] All were introduced by [6]. See [17, p. 14] and [10, pp. 375–81]. The final cost level (FCL) is calculated according to the following formula:

$$FCL = \frac{TR - P}{TR} \times 100$$

where TR = total revenue and P = profit. For details see [10, pp. 375–6] and [12]. The implementation of Decree [6] was 'postponed' early in 1971 (see [2, p. 1]) and the necessary changes introduced in Decree [7]. It is not yet clear, however, if it also means the return to the success indicators introduced in 1966 [5].

gross output indices), value added, output measured in cost of processing prices,[1] output measured in normative labour inputs (termed net output indices).

(3) Technical-economic analysers inform the enterprise management about the efficiency achieved in specific spheres of production and marketing. They take the form of a wide variety of norms and indices, such as input norms, normative costs, or value of claims indices. The technical-economic analysers are used to control the work of the middle and lower categories of the enterprise management, and frequently serve as the basis of the bonus system for these categories of personnel. Technical-economic analysers are linked to top management solely by the information system. When indices for specific aspects of enterprise activity are used to stimulate top management, they then cease to be technical-economic analysers, and become, *ex definitione*, specialized success indicators. These are discussed in greater detail in Ch. 5.

It should be stressed that an analyser may fulfil more than one function at any given time. The same analyser may be an FS regulator and a success indicator, if the analyser is directly linked both to the feeding system and to the stimulation system. For example, for a considerable period of time, gross output fulfilled such a double role in the enterprise. As an FS regulator it functioned as the basis for labour force and wage fund planning; and as a success indicator it functioned as the basis for the management bonus scheme.

Diagram 4.1 shows only two of the three types of analysers, namely success indicators (14) and FS regulators (13). It should be noted that in order to give a full presentation of the complex problem of analysers a much more fully developed classification of the analysers is necessary, a classification based on criteria which are discussed in Chs. 5 and 6.

The Stimulation System (15). Some of the analysers (one or more) are linked to the stimulation system, for example, to the enterprise management bonus system.[2] The structures of stimulation systems vary considerably. The simplest stimulation system consists of three parts: (a) the success indicator (SI) which is also the source of the bonus fund (BF); (b) the bonus coefficient (BC) which determines the relationship between SI and BF; (c) the distribution coefficient (DC) which deter-

---

[1] Cost of processing price (*cena przerobu*) differs from ex-factory price in that it excludes the costs of material inputs.

[2] The stimulation system of an economic unit should be distinguished from its bonus system. The former consists of all bonus systems of the economic unit. Where only one bonus system exists, then, obviously, the stimulation system and the bonus system are one and the same. In East European countries, however, in practice, the stimulation system normally consists of several bonus systems. See 6.2.2.

mines how the bonus fund is to be divided between the members of the enterprise management.

Therefore: $BF = SI \times BC$

and the individual bonus (BFi):

$$BFi = SI \times BC \times DC$$

which gives

$$BFi = BF \times DC.$$

An example of the simplest stimulation system is a management bonus system based on the volume of profit (SI), where BF is directly proportional to SI, and DC directly proportional to the share of the individual basic wage in the wage fund. ($DC = Wi/\Sigma Wi$, where Wi represents the basic individual wage, and ΣWi the total wages of persons entitled to receive a bonus.)

In practice the stimulation system is frequently exceedingly complex and is made up of the following elements (the latter, in turn, also being of greater or lesser complexity) which determine: (1) the size of the bonus fund for the enterprise; (2) the sources from which the bonus fund is to be financed; (3) the conditions on which the enterprise may set up a bonus fund (as a rule a specified level of success indicator must be achieved); (4) the conditions under which part or all of the bonus fund may be paid out (*uruchomiony*, 'activated'); (5) the principles by which the bonus fund is divided among the members of the enterprise management.

It should also be kept in mind that the stimulation system often consists of several bonus funds, running parallel to one another, such as the bonus fund and the factory fund (*fundusz zakladowy*) each of which has its own system of rules, again of varying degrees of complexity, by which it is set up, paid out, divided, and so forth.

The influence of the stimulation system on the behaviour of an enterprise depends on: (1) the manner in which the various elements of the stimulation system are set up and coordinated; (2) the absolute level of a bonus and its relative level in relation to the basic salary of the management personnel; (3) the type of feeding system and information system functioning in the enterprise; (4) the degree to which, on a macro-economic scale, the general conditions of efficient production are fulfilled.[1]

[1] The problem of the effectiveness of a socialist enterprise or of parts of its management mechanism, such as the stimulation system, cannot be examined in isolation from certain general social-economic conditions of efficient production. A number of such general factors exist which have an important influence on the effectiveness at the enterprise (and/or industrial association) level (see e.g. [22, pp. 102–8]). An extensive separate study of this question would be required in order to discuss the subject adequately. One of the factors, however, cannot be ignored in an analysis of the management mechanism, namely, the nature of the market. This factor will be taken into account in this study.

The Steering System (16). The steering system, that is, the behaviour, strategy, and tactics of an enterprise, is determined by the nature of the feeding, information, and stimulation systems, when the three factors: the qualifications of the management personnel, the degree of their integration with the formal goals of the enterprise, and the economic conditions external to the enterprise have been taken into account.[1] The steering system, therefore, can only be subjected to analysis when the detailed description of the other three systems is known. Since the steering system is determined by the specific type of feeding, information and stimulation systems in an enterprise, it, in turn, serves as a control over their effectiveness. If certain irregularities, from the point of view of the CPB, arise in the behaviour of an enterprise which cannot be accounted for by the level of the professional qualifications of the management personnel or by the general economic situation in which the enterprise is functioning, the conclusion must be drawn that one (or all) of the three remaining systems, or the coordination between them, is faulty. One of the main functions of economic analysis is to reveal such faults and to indicate appropriate remedies.

Since different types of feeding, information, and stimulation systems are discussed, enterprise behaviour as a whole will not be analysed separately, but will be dealt with in the analysis of the various types of each kind of system (see, however, 9.1.1.C).

4.2 The Concept and Role of the Management Mechanism

The CPB requires a management mechanism in order to direct effectively plan fulfilment in state enterprises. The management mechanism may be defined as a system of interrelated instruments of economic policy used to direct the activities of economic units of the same form of ownership and administratively subordinated to a given management hierarchy. The role of the management mechanism in socialist industry is: (1) to steer enterprises in plan fulfilment and/or to ensure that the economic guidelines set down by the CPB are followed; (2) to stimulate plan executants to economic behaviour both within the process of plan fulfilment and outside it.

However, although formally the role of the management mechanism consists in directing the process of plan fulfilment, it should be remembered that the structure of a management mechanism also influences the enterprise at the planning stage. Enterprises not only implement plans but also, to some extent, participate in the drawing up of these plans. In the first place, the greater part of the information

---

[1] Apart from the general conditions governing efficient production, the methods by which the remaining elements of the management mechanism are resolved are also to be taken into account here. The concept of the management mechanism and its component parts are analysed in 4.2 and 4.3.

necessary to draw up a plan, of necessity, comes from the enterprise itself. In the second place, the enterprise takes part in drawing up the plan, by putting forward plan proposals and then adapting these according to guidelines set down by higher administrative organs. Thirdly, the enterprise, within a certain limited sphere, may make its own decisions. The quality of the information and the nature of the plan proposals put forward by an enterprise are determined, to a great extent, by the existing management mechanism. This constitutes an additional factor in defining the key importance of the management mechanism in the efficient functioning of the national economy.

4.2.1 THE COMPONENT PARTS OF THE MANAGEMENT MECHANISM

The management mechanism consists of three basic elements: (1) the system by which information is transmitted from the CPB to the enterprise and vice versa; (2) the principles on which the enterprise functions, also termed the 'management formula' in this study; (3) the macro-economic feeding system, which consists of a financial-credit system and the rules governing transactions involving factors of production.

It should be noted that the information system and the feeding system influence the enterprise by the principles on which the given enterprise functions, as is illustrated in Diagram 4.2.

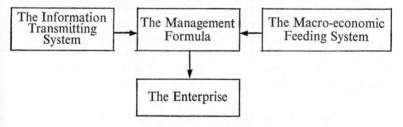

Diagram 4.2 The management mechanism of a
socialist enterprise

The principles on which a given enterprise functions, therefore, determine the manner in which the enterprise reacts to change in price policy or to changes in feeding-in policy. Any underestimation of this fact can lead to serious misconceptions. For example, if management bonuses are based on fulfilment of planned gross output, then a price policy which assumes the 'traditional' relation of price and demand (increase in price brings about a decrease in demand) cannot give satisfactory results, since the introduction of a gross output success indicator radically changes the interdependence of price and demand. An increase in price of input, under the prevailing practice of individual cost-plus pricing (see 5.4.2), leads to greater gross output, and, therefore, lies in the interest of the enterprise. As a result, the demand for the dearer input does not decrease but, in fact, increases. It should, therefore, be continually kept in mind that by changing the principles on which an enterprise functions, the traditionally known categories no longer function in the manner expected on the basis of the experience of enterprises functioning on other principles [*25*, pp. 48–71; *20*, pp. 81–95].

This thesis is presented in a general form in the following section.

4.2.2 THE INTEGRATED NATURE OF THE MANAGEMENT MECHANISM

A close functional interrelationship exists between the three parts of the management mechanism. On the one hand, the reaction of the enterprise, as has been pointed out, to changes in price policy or to changes in the feeding system is determined by the principles on which the enterprise functions, for example, by the character of its success indicators, or its stimulation system. On the other hand, the price system and the feeding system determine the activity of the enterprise to a great extent. The feeding system regulates the amount of resources and the degree to which the enterprise is free to dispose of these resources. Prices, in turn, given the principles on which an enterprise functions, influence the decisions of management in a clearly defined manner.

A full comprehension of the integrated nature of the management mechanism is of great practical importance, since it explains the necessity of strict coordination of changes in any part of the mechanism. The close interdependence of all the parts of the management mechanism and its great internal complexity is also the cause of the theoretical and practical difficulties faced in the construction of an internally consistent and effective management mechanism.

4.2.3 THE MANAGEMENT MECHANISM AND THE INFLUENCE MECHANISM

The national economy of all East European countries consists not only of state enterprises but also of economic units of other types of ownership, which are not administratively subordinated to the state management hierarchy. These economic units are households, small commodity producers (in Poland mostly peasants), small private businesses, and cooperative enterprises. These units cannot be directly managed by the state, although the CPB does exert extensive influence over their activities.

The CPB influences the behaviour of non-state economic units by the 'influence mechanism'. The influence mechanism consists of a set of interrelated instruments of economic policy of *two* types only, rather than the three of the management mechanism. In contrast to the management mechanism, the influence mechanism does not contain a management formula, since the CPB is not in a position to determine the principles on which the non-state economic units are to function. The *modus operandi* of the latter is determined either by the economic nature of the unit concerned, as is the case in the household or the small commodity sectors, or by the appropriate superior organs, as in the case of cooperative enterprises.

It should be noted that in many cases the CPB bypasses the framework of the management or influence mechanisms and resorts to what may be termed 'direct intervention'. Direct intervention is defined here as introduction of a physical change by the CPB into the economic environment. These physical changes in economic environment cannot be placed within the framework of either the tripartite management mechanism or dual influence mechanism, which consists of rules of behaviour, information carriers, and constraints.

Direct intervention on the part of the CPB takes three basic forms. The first is the creation of new enterprises or state institutions, such as research institutes or agricultural services. These new enterprises or institutions constitute instruments influencing certain areas of activity of existing economic units, such as technical progress or designing. The second form of intervention consists of changing the relative scarcity of a given input or output by a direct increase in imports or a change in the level of state reserves. The third form of direct intervention is infrastructure investments.

The scope of the CPB's direct intervention and the share of the latter in overall investment activities is usually affected if substantial changes of the management mechanism are taking place (see 2.1).

4.2.4 THE STEERING MECHANISM OF THE NATIONAL ECONOMY

A number of management mechanisms exist in the national economy. The specific type of mechanism introduced into an enterprise depends on the sphere in which the given enterprise functions and the type of ownership in question. In the state-owned sector, there are, for example, separate management mechanisms for centrally planned and for regionally planned industrial enterprises, for state agricultural enterprises, and for enterprises for foreign and for retail trade. In the cooperative-owned sector management mechanisms for trade and industrial enterprises are subordinate to a given type of cooperative organization. Each of these mechanisms contains common characteristics and at the same time has characteristics individual to itself. The latter require separate analysis. In addition to the management mechanisms, the national economy is equipped with influence mechanisms which extend over households, small commodity producers, private businesses, and cooperative enterprises.

The national economy steering mechanism consists, therefore, of a number of management and influence mechanisms with which the CPB

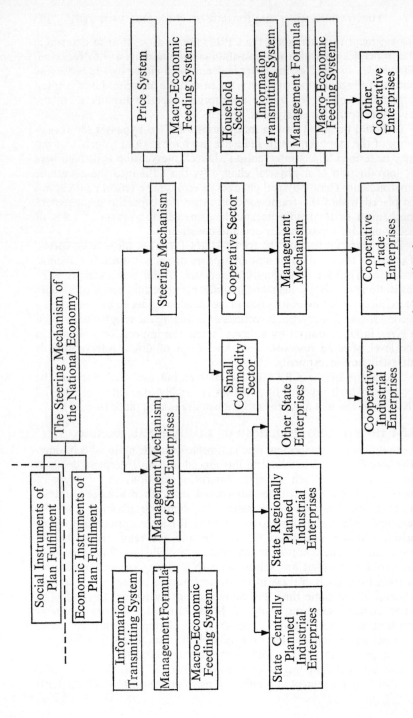

Diagram 4.3   The steering mechanism of the national economy

either directly manages state enterprises or exercises influence over other economic units. Some of these units, such as, for example, cooperatives, are in turn equipped with their own management mechanisms with which they direct economic units subordinate to themselves.[1] This is graphically presented in Diagram 4.3.

The steering mechanism discussed should, in fact, properly be defined as the economic steering mechanism since the CPB not only employs economic instruments of plan fulfilment, but also *social* instruments of plan fulfilment [*19*, pp. 179–218; *21*]. Social instruments of plan fulfilment consist mainly of motivational techniques and the organization of consumer education. Despite the potential importance of social instruments of plan fulfilment, they do not constitute the subject matter of this study, and it should, therefore, be kept in mind that in dealing with steering or management mechanisms, plan fulfilment instruments of an economic nature are to be understood.

The principle of the integrated nature of the management mechanism outlined in 4.4 is equally relevant to the steering mechanism of the national economy. The national economy also requires properly inter-coordinated management and influence mechanisms if effective steering is to be achieved. The household influence mechanism, for example, which is based on consumer freedom of choice, must be coordinated with the management mechanisms of enterprises producing consumer goods in a manner ensuring proper sensitivity on the part of the enterprises to changing consumer demand, since otherwise, market disequilibrium with all the accompanying negative, economic, and social consequences takes place.

The economic and social instruments of plan fulfilment must also be properly coordinated. Certain management mechanisms are more favourable to processes of social integration in production and to consumer education than others. On the other hand, skilful use of social instruments of plan fulfilment increases the effectiveness of economic instruments. For example, the greater the degree of social integration in production, the smaller the negative consequences of misdirected incentives, whereas effective consumer education, i.e. the changes brought about in consumer preferences, allows the achievement of planned change in demand by smaller price changes [*19*, pp. 206–18; *22*, pp. 172–7, 191–225].

The management mechanism of centrally planned state industrial enterprises is analysed in the sections following. Since all management mechanisms have many common structural and functional characteristics, the analysis of the management mechanism of centrally planned state industrial enterprises should provide the reader with a

[1] If the management mechanism of cooperative enterprises is, *de facto*, strictly defined by the CPB, then the difference between directing state enterprises and influencing cooperative enterprises is formal rather than real.

7

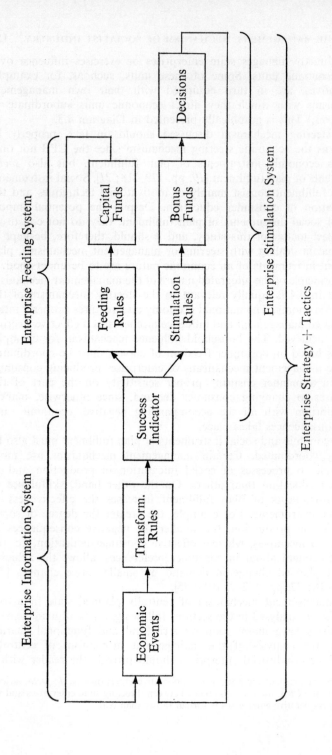

Diagram 4.4   A simple management formula

basis for the analysis of other management mechanisms in all types of state and cooperative industrial and trade enterprises.

4.3 Management Formulae

A more detailed discussion of the principles on which an enterprise functions, i.e. the management formula, is now in order. The main function of a management mechanism is to influence economic events. The course of economic events in an enterprise depends on two sets of factors: (1) the volume and quality of the human and material resources of the enterprise; (2) the decisions taken by the enterprise management.

Given the volume and quality of the human and material resources of an enterprise, the decisions of the enterprise management depend on the type of information, stimulation, and feeding systems functioning in an enterprise.

The role of the management formula consists, therefore, in defining information, stimulation, and feeding systems best suited to effective plan fulfilment and which are generally conducive to economic behaviour on the part of the enterprise. It is evident that management formulae can only be properly constructed in conjunction with the other basic elements of management mechanisms (the principle of the integrated nature of management mechanisms). For example, the use of enterprise cost-plus pricing, that is, what are termed internal prices (see 5.4.2), undermines the working of management formulae whose success indicator is enterprise profit.

4.3.1 THE COMPONENT PARTS OF SIMPLE, COMPLEX, AND HIGHLY COMPLEX MANAGEMENT FORMULAE

Every management formula consists of the following elements: (1) methods of accounting (transformation rules) which transform certain characteristics of economic events into success indicators and FS regulators; (2) one or several success indicators and one or several FS regulators; (3) principles on which the stimulation system is based, which determine the interrelationship of the success indicators and the bonus funds; (4) bonus funds; (5) principles on which the feeding rules are based, which determine the relationship between the success indicators and the FS regulators, and what is termed enterprise special funds; (6) enterprise special funds.

The structure of management formulae depends mainly on the construction of the second of the above elements of a formula, i.e. on the number of success indicators and FS regulators. Three basic types of formulae can be distinguished:

Type 1. A simple management formula consisting of one success indicator, which at the same time serves as the only FS regulator. This is illustrated in Diagram 4.4.

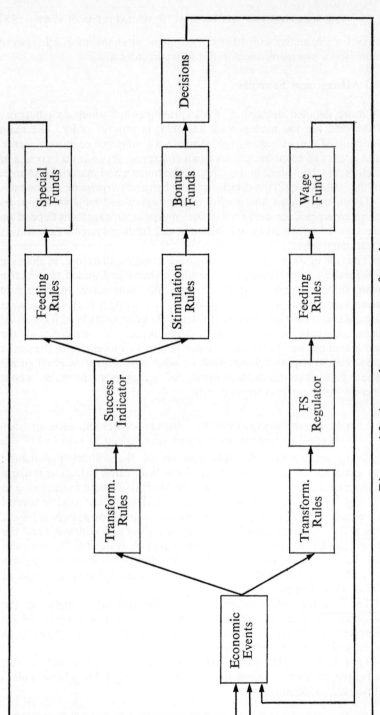

Diagram 4.5 A complex management formula

Type 2. A complex management formula consisting of one success indicator which is also an FS regulator plus a separate FS regulator. This is illustrated in Diagram 4.5.

Type 3. A highly complex management formula consisting of more than three success indicators and FS regulators. This is illustrated in Diagram 4.6.

Type One above is representative of the management formula of a capitalist enterprise where profit fulfils both the role of success indicator and of FS regulator. Yugoslav enterprises function in this manner and Czechoslovakia proposed reforms of this kind (gross income fulfilling both the functions of success indicator and FS regulator). An example of Type Two is a system in which the only success indicator of the enterprise is profit, whereas the inflow of resources is partially regulated by an output indicator such as value added—where the wage fund is concerned—and partially by profit—where investment and working capital are concerned. An example of a highly complex formula is the formula in current use in Polish enterprises. The highly complex formula differs from Type Two in so far as several specialized bonus funds operate in addition to profit and a number of output indices, rather than one, operate as FS regulators.

4.4 Two Socialist Enterprise Management Models

The structure of the management formula defines the aim of the enterprise (which can, for example, be the achievement of a maximum volume of profit, or of a maximum gross output), outlines the limits of its freedom of choice,[1] and determines, to a great extent, the manner in which information on changes in the economic situation external to the enterprise[2] is fed into the enterprise.

There is a feedback between the CPB and the plan executants through the information system. The basic information carriers to the CPB from the plan implementors are: (1) reports on the level of stock of individual products or type of products which provide a general picture of the so-called 'balance equilibrium' (*rownowaga bilansowa*) during the implementation of a plan; (2) reports on the degree to which success indicators have been achieved, which provide information on the quality of the performance of plan executants; (3) other statistical and questionnaire data which illustrate individual aspects of the financial and physical implementation of a plan and/or the work of the plan executants.

The basic information carriers from the CPB to the enterprises are:

[1] The problem of the relationship between the system of management and the character of the management formula is discussed in 4.11.

[2] The enterprise management is continually informed about the internal economic situation in the enterprise by the technical-economic analysers.

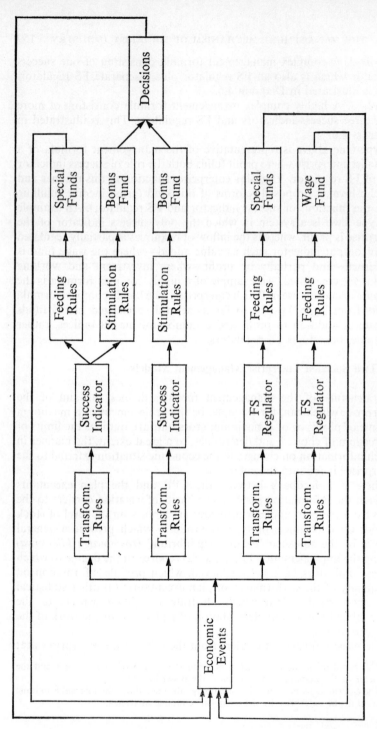

Diagram 4.6   A highly complex management formula

(1) operative prices; (2) the amount of bonus attached to individual parts of the plan, or to 'bonus tasks' (cf. 3.2.3); (3) obligatory plan indices (administrative orders) and information plan indices; (4) changes in the principles on which an enterprise functions, particularly changes in its information and stimulation systems; these changes are used as quasi-operative instruments in directing enterprise activities.[1]

The information carriers from the CPB can be divided into two basic groups; (1) ciphered information carriers, such as prices and bonus levels; (2) open information carriers (direct information) such as plan indices and changes in the principles on which an enterprise functions.

To facilitate clarity, let us assume for the present that only two information carriers are being used, prices and administrative orders. Problems arising in the use of other information carriers will be discussed in later chapters.

Depending on the method by which the CPB feeds information to an enterprise, two systems or models of management[2] can be distinguished: (1) the parametric model which is also termed the decentralized model; (2) the non-parametric model which is also termed the command economy or centralized model.[3]

Parametric management is a ciphered method of transmitting information; non-parametric management, an open or direct method.

The ciphered information carriers are, as has been stated, prices in the wider sense of the word, that is, the prices include the prices of capital, of natural resources, and of labour. It should be noted that the concepts of price and parameters are considered as equivalents in this study and are used interchangeably. Open information carriers are administrative orders (obligatory indices, instructions).

The working of parametric management is presented in Diagram 4.7. To facilitate clarity the simple management formula is used and the feeding system ignored.

For example, the increase in price of product X changes the impact of the economic event (level of output) on the success indicator. If the success indicator is profit, then the increase of output becomes more profitable than before and through the stimulation system encourages the enterprise management to decide on an increase in production.

[1] For example the CM Decree 130 of 4 May 1964 [4] empowered industrial associations to make quarterly changes in what are termed 'branch tasks', which constitute the basis on which enterprise management bonuses are calculated. This is an example of the use of variable enterprise success indicators as quasi-operative management instruments. These problems will be discussed more fully in Ch. 6.

[2] The terms 'system of management' and 'management model' are used synonymously in this study.

[3] This classification, however, overlooks the important question of the method by which the parameters are to be determined—whether by the CPB or by the market. The answer determines whether the given parametric management is state-parametric or market-parametric (see [26, pp. 279–84]).

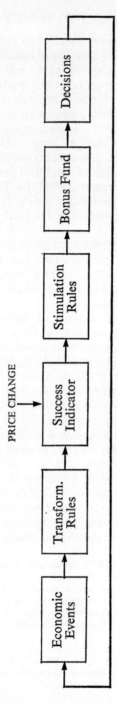

Diagram 4.7   Parametric management

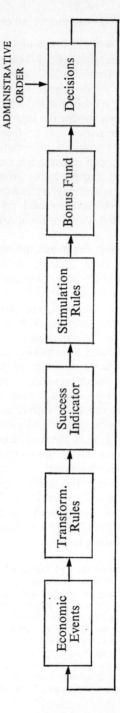

Diagram 4.8   An incorrect representation of non-parametric management

The working of non-parametric management might seem to appear as shown in Diagram 4.8.

Diagram 4.8 illustrates a situation in which the administrative order directly influences the decision taken by the enterprise management and this decision, in turn, influences the economic events. So to define the situation, however, does not take into consideration the fact that, even in a non-parametric management system, the management formula also contains a stimulation system which influences the reaction of the enterprise to plan directives. It is well known that, in practice, many administrative orders are not, in fact, carried out by enterprises,[1] and this is not entirely due to factors external to the enterprise. This phenomenon is to a great extent created by the type of management formula currently in use. This formula frequently gives rise to a contradiction between the economic interests of the enterprise, which are determined by the management formula and existing prices, and the plan targets. The interrelationship of administrative orders and enterprise decisions is, therefore, not as simple as is shown in Diagram 4.8. The correct interpretation is illustrated in Diagram 4.9.

The administrative order influences the future level of the enterprise success indicator and the amount of the management bonus, and the decisions of the enterprise management reflect to some degree—theoretically from 0 to 100 per cent, but, in practice, in a smaller but still important range—the fact that such influence is exerted.[2]

[1] See Ch. 3, p. 94, fn. 1.

[2] This thesis can be illustrated by the following table from an article by M. Lesz [16, p. 19] then the Minister of Internal Trade:

Table 4.1 The Fulfilment of the Product-Mix Plan in 1962 by the Myszkow Factory of Metal Products

Products	Value of output per hour of work (in zlotys)	% of fulfilment of planned supply
Soup ladles 8 cm.	52·6	69·0
Soup ladles 10 cm.	57·4	56·7
Lids 12 cm.	45·4	60·5
Lids 28 cm.	97·5	95·4
Bowls 40 cm.	170·8	173·9
Bowls 45 cm.	177·6	179·8
Bowls 50 cm.	189·2	170·2
Pans 24 cm.	205·2	157·2

This table is accompanied by the following comment: 'We have here a certain proportionality, necessity, law: the degree of fulfilment of a given product is directly proportional to the value of output per hour of work, or, what amounts to the same thing, inversely proportional to the labour intensity.' The reason for this 'law' is not difficult to determine, and is a result of the then current type of stimulation (and feeding) system, where the management bonus and the volume of the wage fund were based on or related to the same analyser—the gross output—which fulfilled a simultaneous role of success indicator and FS regulator. See 7.5 for a more detailed analysis of this problem.

7*

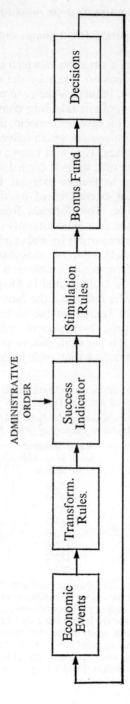

Diagram 4.9 Non-parametric management—a correct representation

Both the parameters and the administrative orders are instruments of operative economic management. The aim of both is, above all, to direct the enterprise towards plan fulfilment. The difference between them lies in the methods used to achieve this goal.

In the first place, parameters are organically connected to the stimulation system, and only function by a parameter/incentive link-up. A break in this link-up serves to make the parameters ineffective as operative management instruments and, at the most, allows them to fulfil certain other functions such as those of aggregative or control instruments. Administrative orders are also far from neutral as far as incentives are concerned. This interrelationship is, however, normally indirect. It is usually not immediately apparent to higher authorities to what extent a given administrative order is consistent with, or in contradiction to, the economic interests of the enterprise as defined by the existing incentive and price systems. Parametric management, therefore, functions directly *through* a stimulation system; management based on administrative orders, on the other hand, should, in theory, function *alongside* the stimulation system. Practical experience shows, however, that the inconsistencies arising between administrative orders and incentives are always present in non-parametric management.

In the second place, parametric management is based on independent evaluations and decisions by enterprise management. A change in the size of a parameter constitutes merely information for an enterprise. Accordingly it entails independent evaluation on the part of the enterprise management and, therefore, relies on the knowledge, experience, and self-interest of those directly involved in plan implementation for a decision on how to react to any given change in the size of a parameter. This is of great importance to an enterprise and carries many implications for social integration in production, since it allows initiative to be used in the enterprise. It is also important for the quality and speed of the reaction of the economic apparatus to changes in economic conditions and to the functioning of the information system of the national economy. It may facilitate both, particularly if combined with the wider use of market determined parameters.

In the third place, the above-mentioned benefits are to a great extent the result of those features of parametric management which allow horizontal information, fed in from the market and received by direct contact between supplier and buyer, to be exploited to a far greater degree. In a non-parametric system of management, the vertical information flow, from the plan executants to the CPB and vice versa, is a dominant one. In contrast, in a parametric system of management, only the most important information is collected and coded by the CPB and transmitted to the plan executants in the form of changes in the size of parameters. In parametric management the greatest part of the information is acquired by the plan executants from horizontal contacts, which shortens the information circuit, lessens the possibility of the distortion of information, and speeds up decisions.

4.4.1 THE EXTENT OF THE AUTHORITY SPHERE OF AN ENTERPRISE IN PARAMETRIC AND NON-PARAMETRIC MODELS OF MANAGEMENT

For the purpose of management theory it is useful to distinguish the following concepts: (a) the sphere of enterprise activity (activity sphere), which covers all economic events within the enterprise; (b) the sphere of enterprise authority (authority sphere), which covers those economic events over which the enterprise has the power or the right to command (see 5.3.2).

In all multi-level economic structures—from capitalist business corporations to socialist industrial associations—the enterprise activity sphere is broader than the authority sphere. Parametric and non-parametric management define, however, different ranges of powers for the enterprise management. Parametric management is accompanied by management formulae conferring a wide range of powers, that is, *a wide authority sphere*; non-parametric management confers a narrow range of powers, that is, *a narrow authority sphere*. The authority or powers of the manager at a given level are those delegated to him by superiors. The delegation of authority encompasses the allocation of tasks, the authority necessary to implement them, and the responsibility for fulfilling the tasks. The basic principles in delegating powers require consistency between the tasks, authority, and responsibility assigned to plan executants.

A broad or narrow range of power may be delegated to subordinate units. The delegation of a broad range of powers is termed decentralization in textbooks on management, and the delegation of a narrow range of powers is termed centralization.

'There is seldom absolute centralization or decentralization. Absolute centralization in one person is conceivable, but it implies no subordinate managers and no organization. Therefore, it can be said that some decentralization characterizes all organizations. On the other hand, there cannot be absolute decentralization, for if a manager should delegate *all* his authority, his status as manager would cease; his position would be eliminated; there would, again, be no organization. Centralization and decentralization are, therefore, tendencies; they are qualities like "hot" and "cold".

'As one management expert [3, p. 107] has explained the nature of decentralization, the degree of decentralization is greater:

'(1) The greater the number of decisions made lower down the management hierarchy.

'(2) The more important the decisions made lower down the management hierarchy. For example, the greater the sum of capital expenditure that can be approved by the plant manager without consulting anyone else, the greater the degree of decentralization in this field.

'(3) The more functions affected by decisions made at lower levels. Thus companies which permit only operational decisions to be made at separate branch plants are less decentralized than those which also permit financial and personnel decisions at branch plants.

'(4) The less checking required on the decision. Decentralization is greater when no check at all must be made; less when superiors have to be informed of the decision after it has been made; still less if superiors have to be consulted before the decision is made. The fewer people to be consulted, and the lower they are on the management hierarchy, the greater the degree of decentralization' [13, pp. 317–18].[1]

The extent of the authority sphere outlined in a management formula is closely correlated to the method of management in use. The greater the authority sphere allowed by the management formula, the more parametric the control of the plan executants, and vice versa. The dependence is, therefore, two-sided. In the first place, parametric management is not possible if the enterprise does not have a fairly wide range of powers. Where an enterprise cannot undertake decisions on investment, then there is no place, and, of course, no necessity for, influence to be exerted by the level and ratios of the prices of means of production and by the rate of interest charged on the enterprise investment. In the second place, where there is no parametric management system, plan executants cannot be allowed a wide range of delegated powers since the CPB then has no instruments with which to influence the decisions allowed the enterprise. Only a correctly constructed system of parameters allows both plan fulfilment to take place in accordance with the requirements of the CPB, and also, simultaneously, allows the enterprise a fairly wide sphere of authority, since parameters allow the decisions of the plan executants to be steered in the desired direction without formally narrowing their range of powers. This gives rise to the known thesis that the main condition for decentralization (that is, of increasing the authority sphere of an enterprise) is the correct construction of a system of prices for all the factors of production, including capital and natural resources.[2]

In discussing the interdependence of the management formula and the system of management, one other important factor should be taken into account. In non-parametric management the authority sphere of

[1] P. Drucker similarly defines the American motor-car firm 'General Motors' as a decentralized organization, on the basis of an analysis of the division of functions and division of decisions between the top management and the executive committees of the thirty divisions which make up the corporation [8, pp. 41–71].

[2] The concepts of centralization and decentralization are used here in a strictly defined sense. The concepts relate to the different methods of transmitting information and to the different authority spheres of the plan executants. In speaking of centralization or decentralization only the different methods of plan *implementation* are meant. The problem of plan *construction* is a closely related but separate one in the sense that the method of plan construction does not completely predetermine the method of plan implementation. See [25, pp. 110–14].

an enterprise is not only narrow but is also usually *variable* in scope. The enterprise does not have a permanent range of powers and responsibilities. Responding to the requirements of economic changes external to the enterprise, the HAO increase or decrease the range of powers of an enterprise management. For example, a building enterprise in a given area is obliged at one period of time to use silicate bricks, and in another period the order is rescinded. In parametric management the authority sphere of an enterprise is not only wider but its scope is generally *stable*. The parametric system of management eliminates the necessity of change in the range of powers of an enterprise during operative management, since the enterprise is informed about current economic changes by the parameters. The authority sphere of the enterprise, therefore, remains comparatively stable. Changes occur infrequently, when, as part of the process termed 'the perfecting of planning and management methods', the whole management formula undergoes change.

The degree of stability or variability in the authority sphere of an enterprise management is of basic importance to the effective working of the enterprise and to the behaviour of management. Where the range of powers of an enterprise is in constant flux a certain style of management termed the 'administration' of production arises, and undermines the basis of economic calculation in the enterprise. This thesis is supported by many cases of enterprise directors complaining of continual 'intervention' from above.

4.4.2 MIXED MANAGEMENT MODELS

Pure models of centralized, or administrative, management and decentralized, or parametric, management can be defined as follows:[1]

The pure centralized model assumes (1) the existence of more than one level in the industrial hierarchy, (2) that decisions are undertaken only by the highest level (the CPB). Lower levels do not undertake economic decisions, that is, decisions regarding choice of product-mix or methods of production. There are no examples of such types of management models on the macro-economic level since, even apart from the social consequences they would bring about, such models cannot be put into effect from a technical point of view because of the problem faced in amassing the immense amount of information involved and in transforming this information efficiently and quickly into decisions.[2]

The pure decentralized model may be a model consisting of one level

[1] See [23] and [25, pp. 102–15] for the author's early formulation of this problem.

[2] On the micro-economic scale examples of this type of management can only be found in very small enterprises in which the number of workers does not exceed what in management theory is termed 'span of management', that is, the range of the effective management of a group of people by one person. In such enterprises there are no, *ex definitione*, intermediate levels of management and, therefore, there is no organization, as understood in the terms of management theory.

or several levels, provided, however, that the higher level directs subordinate levels solely by the use of parameters.[1] The classical example of a fully decentralized model is a pure competitive market, and an example of a fully decentralized socialist economic model is the model presented by O. Lange in 1937 [14] in which the CPB directs the national economy solely by the use of parameters, with the exception of the total volume of investment which is determined directly.

In practice only mixed management models have been used to date in East European countries. These management models use both administrative orders and parameters in directing enterprises. It is, however, obvious that mixed management models may use administrative orders or parameters in varying degrees, and, therefore, the models may be more parametric or less parametric in character. The character of a mixed management model, that is, the degree to which it is centralized or decentralized, and the type of changes which may take place within it, can be analysed in two ways: directly and indirectly.

Direct analysis of the character of the management model consists in analysing the role of parameters in the management of an enterprise. Two questions should be examined.

First of all, which instruments ensure the equilibrium of the national economic plan: administrative orders or parameters? Here the centralized and decentralized models represent two different approaches to the method of organizing management. In the centralized model the main instrument for balancing the plan is the system of 'obligatory plan indices and resources necessary for the implementation of the plan, laid down for individual ministries, local government (*Rady Narodowe*) and the more important industrial associations', which in turn lay down obligatory indices for enterprises subordinate to them.[2] In the decentralized model the level and ratio of parameters guide plan fulfilment of the enterprises. If the role of the parameters in balancing the plan increases, then according to the definition accepted in this study, the management model assumes a more decentralized character: and if the role of the parameters decreases, the model is more centralized.[3]

[1] It should be stressed that the present discussion is wholly limited to relationships *between* the various levels of the given organizational structure of the national economy, and does not deal with management within these levels [25, p. 103].

[2] Applying directives to ministries is somewhat difficult if the ministries do not have the power to send directives to industrial associations subordinate to them. The same applies to industrial associations [24, pp. 136-9].

[3] The first attempt to analyse this problem empirically and to establish a suitable methodology for doing so is the subject of an article by Z. Frank and J. Waelbroeck [11]. The methodology presented in this article was applied—after some changes—to Polish economic policy by M. Strzyzewska and R. Pazura of the Research Unit on Price and Incentive Theory of the Central School of Planning and Statistics, Warsaw, under the direction of J. G. Zielinski. The results are presented in [18].

The second question to be asked is: what methods are employed to correct the plan? It is obvious that, since information can never be perfect, the current implementation of a plan demands constant change, in order to ensure balance equilibrium and market equilibrium. If the parameters are 'frozen' during the implementation of a given plan, if they are not changed in order to influence enterprises' behaviour or are 'neutralized', that is to say, the influence of changes in the size of the parameters on the success indicators of the enterprise is eliminated by the methods of accounting, as, for example, by subtracting what are termed 'independent profits',[1] then administrative orders become the main instruments for transmitting current information to the enterprise on changing economic conditions, and the management mechanism acquires the characteristics of a centralized model.

Indirect analysis of the method of management consists of an analysis of the management formula of the enterprise. The authority sphere defined by the management formula is closely correlated to the parametric or non-parametric nature of the method of management. If the enterprise management formula is characterized by a narrow and variable authority sphere, then the extent of parametric management is small; a wide and stable authority sphere is evidence of predominantly parametric management. A parallel argument applies to the analysis of changes brought about in the management formula in the process termed the perfecting of planning and management methods.

4.5 Operative Prices as Instruments of Parametric Management

In East European countries there are four basic types of prices [*24*, pp. 98–104], two of which are used in plan construction, and two in plan implementation.[2]

4.5.1 PRICES USED IN PLAN CONSTRUCTION

Aggregative prices are used as the main tool with the help of which the CPB endeavours to construct a feasible and consistent plan. They serve, as the term indicates, as an instrument of aggregation. In the real world, even such 'homogeneous' commodities as coal or cotton are of numerous kinds and grades. The use of prices enables planners to aggregate, that is, to add together different commodities. Technological units such as calories or horsepower, which are also used for planning purposes, have considerably narrower spheres of application. Large aggregates are necessary in planning since the CPB has a limited capacity to handle information and process it into planning decisions.[3]

---

[1] This term is defined and analysed in 5.3.2.

[2] The complex problem of agricultural prices also fits into this classification, but the analysis of the numerous features specific to these prices lies outside the scope of this book.

[3] The use of modern computers only pushes this barrier upwards. It does not eliminate it.

In actual planning practice the 'operative' and 'consumer goods prices' (see below 4.5.2 and [25, pp. 48–69]) at a given time, for example at 1 January 1965, are used as aggregative prices. Operative and consumer prices may change in the given period, but as aggregative prices they remain constant for at least an entire five-year period. Aggregative prices in conjunction with technological units such as calories and ton-kilometres, are the main planning instruments and are used in most planning calculations.

It should be stressed that aggregative prices do not play an active role in planning choices. The planning goals and the ensuing allocative decisions of the CPB have been derived directly from the balance calculations of the plan in which the aggregative prices were only a tool for trying to meet the feasibility and consistency requirements of the plan.

Programming prices, also called 'shadow' or 'accounting prices', or 'objectively determined valuations' are used for partial optimization calculation in the process of plan construction.[1] Optimization of the national economic plan is at present impossible, mainly owing to technical difficulties. Even the construction of a feasible and consistent plan cannot as yet be attained in practice. At the same time, however, it is possible to try to arrive at partial optimal and/or 'quasi-optimal' solutions. In socialist countries, these partial optimization procedures are mainly confined to two spheres, namely, calculation of economic effectiveness of investment, and foreign trade transactions. A number of programming or 'shadow' prices have been calculated for these purposes. Programming prices, in contrast to aggregative prices, are used by the CPB as instruments of economic decision-making. For example, shadow prices used in investment calculations help the CPB to decide which production methods to use. Shadow prices, however, do not apply to decisions on the nature of output to be produced, these decisions being directly derived from the plan targets based on the forecast of domestic or foreign demand and/or on CPB preferences.[2]

4.5.2 PRICES USED IN PLAN IMPLEMENTATION

Consumer goods prices, in conjunction with wage and incomes policies, constitute the main instrument used by the CPB in implementing the *consumption* plan, that is, in selling consumer goods and services produced by the socialized sector to households. Consumer goods prices at present are, as a rule, set at market clearing level, the differentiated turnover tax, positive or negative, constituting the main instrument in achieving equilibrium in the consumer goods market. The main function of consumer goods prices is to influence household purchasing patterns,

---

[1] See e.g. [25, pp. 10–32] and literature quoted therein.
[2] See e.g. M. Kalecki's arguments quoted in [25, p. 36].

since freedom of choice exists in this sphere, in a manner ensuring that the entire consumer goods output, minus any necessary changes in stock levels, of course, is sold. The basic question of the manner in which the consumer goods plan is determined and by whom, lies outside the scope of this study.[1]

Operative prices constitute one of the instruments used in implementing the *production* plan. The main functions they fulfil are as follows:

(1) They constitute information carriers of changes in transformation ratios in the national economy and changes in CPB preferences. The degree to which they carry out this function depends on the character of the operative prices used (see below, p. 173).

(2) They are elements of an incentive system aimed at stimulating plan implementors to fulfil plans, since the success indicators for an enterprise, such as volume of profit, or profit/cost ratio, on which the bonuses for management and white and blue collar workers depend, are usually calculated according to operative prices.

(3) They function as instruments which divide resources between the enterprise and the state by a system of separate prices for sellers and buyers; the difference between the two prices, in the form of turnover tax, being fed off to the state budget. Operational prices are also instruments of resource redistribution, since they are used in the calculation of output indices and success indicators which, in their function as FS regulators, control the flow of resources being fed into an enterprise, for example, to the wage fund or the development fund (see 7.4 and 7.5).

The systems of operative prices in use in Poland and most other East European countries at present have the following characteristics:

(1) Operative prices constitute only one of numerous information carriers. Even the same information is frequently simultaneously transmitted by other information carriers. For example, information on the required type of product-mix is transmitted simultaneously to the enterprise in the form of (a) an obligatory plan target; (b) prices—by differentiating the prices of individual products; (c) incentives—by bonuses awarded for fulfilling the plan for a particular product-mix and by implicit trade-offs between a product-mix bonus and bonuses for other plan tasks, fulfilment of which could be facilitated by violating the product-mix target.

(2) The range of information transmitted through prices, or rather entirely by prices, is normally relatively narrow. A greater part of information on product-mix, volume of output, or methods of production is transmitted to the enterprise by the CPB in a direct (open) form, that is by obligatory and information plan targets (see 3.2.3).

(3) Several types of operative prices such as ex-factory prices, transfer prices, cost of processing prices, operate simultaneously. These prices are used to calculate the various success indicators and output indices of

[1] This problem is discussed in [24, Ch. IV] and [25, pp. 86–101].

plan executants. In other words, different price systems are used for 'controlling' different aspects of enterprise activity.

(4) A great part of the operative prices are not equilibrium prices. The widespread use of central allocation and use-control[1] of the means of production is an open admission of this fact.

(5) In directing the activity of investment project bureaux and foreign trade enterprises, some application of programming prices (prices of partial optimal calculation) as operative prices is present.

The characteristics of the existing system of operative prices, as defined in points 1 to 4, restrict the possibilities and practicability of using operative prices on a wider scale—as terms on which alternatives are offered for the enterprises. For the same reason, existing operative prices cannot be used by the CPB as an effective instrument in directing the economic activities of the plan executants. The role of operative prices in the management mechanism depends on their character. If they are not equilibrium prices, if they neither reflect the existing transformation ratios nor even CPB preferences correctly, then application of the operative prices must, of necessity, be restricted. This thesis is generally accepted. In practice it means that if operative prices are to be efficient CPB information carriers, i.e. if management by administrative orders is to be limited and parametric management increased, then a radical improvement of the price system must take place.

4.6 The Interrelationship between Enterprise and Industrial Association Management Formulae

Industrial associations in Poland play an important role in economic management (see Ch. 8). The industrial association, being part of the plan implementation apparatus, is itself directed and stimulated by the previously described highly complex management formula. This formula, which defines among other things the success indicator of the industrial association, and the principles by which its management is to be stimulated, to a great extent determines the behaviour of the association, and, as a result of the powers it wields, also influences the activities of enterprises subordinate to it. Consequently, the necessity of coordinating enterprise and industrial association management formulae arises, since a correctly structured formula on the enterprise level may be neutralized by a faulty industrial association management formula; or, vice versa, the correct policies of the industrial association, stimulated by a proper management formula, may be frustrated when the management formula of an enterprise is faulty. The problem of the interrelationship of enterprise and industrial association management formulae will be raised in further chapters.[2]

[1] Defined and discussed in 7.7.

[2] In particular see Ch. 8. For comparative analysis see [27, pp. 49–86].

References to Chapter Four

1. Blass B.: 'Industrial Enterprise Success Indicators and the Wage Fund', in [*9*, pp. 173–81].
2. 'Changes in the Financial System of Industry', *F*, 3, 1971, pp. 1–2.
3. Dale E.: *Planning and Developing the Company Organization Structure*, New York, 1952.
4. Decree 130 of the CM of 4 May 1964 on incentives to industrial state enterprise white collar workers, *MP*, 32, 1964.
5. Decree of the Chairman of the Planning Commission of the CM and the Minister of Finance on the principles of setting profitability indices, *MP*, 42, 1966.
6. Decree of the CM and the Trade Union Central Council of 1 July 1970 on the incentive system of employees of centrally planned enterprises and associations for the years 1971–5, in [*14*, pp. 5–29].
7. Decree 176 of the CM of 9 November 1970 on the financial system in centrally planned state enterprises, *kombinaty* and industrial and construction associations, *MP*, 40, 1970.
8. Drucker P.: *The Concept of the Corporation*, Boston, 1960.
9. Dudzinski W., Misiak M., eds.: *Mierniki oceny dzialalnosci przedsiebiorstwa socjalistycznego* (Success Indicators in Socialist Enterprises), Warsaw, 1964. Mimeographed.
10. Fick B.: *Polityka zatrudnienia a place i bodzce* (Employment Policy and Wages and Incentives), Warsaw, 1970.
11. Frank Z., Waelbroeck J.: 'Soviet Economic Policy since 1953. A study of its structure and change', *SS*, 1, July 1965.
12. Instruction No. 16 of the Minister of Finance, Warsaw, May 1970.
13. Koontz H., O'Donnell C.: *Principles of Management*, New York, 1964.
14. Lange O., Taylor F. M.: *On the Economic Theory of Socialism*, Minneapolis, Minn., 1952.
15. Lange O.: *Wstep do cybernetyki ekonomicznej* (Introduction to Economic Cybernetics), Warsaw, 1965.
16. Lesz M.: 'Incentives and Success Indicators of Industrial Enterprises and Requirements of the Market', in [*9*, pp. 17–28].
17. *Nowy system bodzcow materialnego zainteresowania. Zbior podstawowych dokumentow* (The New System of Material Incentives. Collected basic documents), Warsaw, 1970.
18. Strzyzewska M., Pazura R.: 'Les instruments de la politique économique de la Pologne au cours des années 1961–1965. Structure et changements'. *Revue du Centre d'Etude des Pays de l'Est et du Centre National pour l'Etude des Etats de l'Est*, 1–2, 1968.
19. Wakar A., ed.: *Zarys teorii gospodarki socjalistycznej* (Outline of the Theory of Socialist Economy), Warsaw, 1965.
20. Wieckowski J.: *Rola zysku w kierowaniu produkcja* (The Role of Profit in Production Management), Warsaw, 1965.
21. Wiszniewski E.: 'Consumer Education in a Socialist Economy', *Handel Wewnetrzny*, 2, 1964.
22. Zielinski J. G.: *Big Business. Z problematyki nowych technik zarzadzania* (Big Business. Problems of New Management Techniques), Warsaw, 1962.
23. —— 'Centralization and Decentralization in Decision-Making', *EP*, 3, 1963.
24. —— *Rachunek ekonomiczny w socjalizmie* (Economic Calculation in a Socialist Economy), Warsaw, 1967.
25. —— *Lectures on the Theory of Socialist Planning*, Ibadan-London, 1968.
26. —— 'Economics and Politics of Two Types of Economic Reforms', *EP*, 3, 1969.
27. —— 'Planification et gestion au niveau de la branche industrielle en Europe de l'Est', 1, 1970.

CHAPTER FIVE

THE INFORMATION SYSTEM OF A SOCIALIST ENTERPRISE

5.1 The Functions of Success Indicators

Success indicators usually fulfil the following functions in an enterprise:
(1) signals to the CPB on the performance of the enterprise; (2) a basis
for decision-making within the enterprise; (3) a basis for the enterprise
management stimulation system; (4) a basis for the regulation of the
feeding system of the enterprise.

5.1.1 SUCCESS INDICATORS AS INFORMATION SIGNALS TO THE CPB

The duties of the CPB include: observation of plan fulfilment at
macro-economic level, and evaluation of, and control over the work of
individual plan executants. It is important to distinguish these two roles
of the CPB and to be aware of the fact that each of the roles is carried
out, or should be carried out, with the aid of different instruments. The
two roles are frequently considered identical and attempts are made to
execute them with the same instruments of economic policy.

The observation of the process of plan fulfilment should be carried
out by the CPB by analysis of material and other balances. The analysis
of individual material balances, that is, the level of stocks, informs the
CPB whether the balance equilibrium has been maintained. If, for
example, the stock of steel falls below the planned norms, this serves as
a signal that the supply or demand for steel is different from that foreseen in the plan, and that intervention is required to deal with the situation. This may be done by the CPB directly changing steel supplies, or
through the feeding system, or by a change in the size of parameters,
such as the price of steel, or by a combination of all these methods.

The observation of the process of plan fulfilment through balances
concerns the development of the economy at macro-level. Analysis of
the performance of individual plan executants must also be simultaneously carried out, since the observation of balances does not provide direct evidence of the quality of their performance. A situation may
arise, for example, where normative stock levels are falling rapidly and
yet the plan executants are working efficiently. For example, the output
plan may in fact be overfulfilled, the demand, however, being greater
than foreseen because of incorrectly set parameters. The opposite
situation may also arise, namely, that balance equilibrium is maintained

and yet the plan executants are not working efficiently. Inefficient performance on the part of one of the plan executants is not necessarily reflected in the balances, since it may be compensated for by particularly efficient work on the part of other enterprises involved in the given plan. We can conclude, therefore, that analysis of the performance of plan executants should be carried out *parallel* to observation of the process of plan fulfilment, even when the fulfilment of any given part of the plan, for example, supply and demand for steel, gives no apparent basis for anxiety.

In the management formula the success indicators should fulfil the role of criteria of enterprise performance. The level of success indicators should be an *information signal* to the CPB on the situation in individual plan implementing units. If a negative signal is received analysis is necessary with a view to measures being undertaken to deal with the situation. Success indicators should not serve as a basis for the analysis of the implementation of an enterprise output plan. They should instead serve as information to the CPB on the quality of the performance of the enterprise. This is illustrated in the following examples. It is assumed that the success indicator of the enterprise is profit, and that the enterprise has no influence on the price level of its inputs and outputs.

Example 1. Observation of the balances does not reveal any divergence from the plan. At the same time the profits of individual enterprises are checked. An increase in profit needs no action on the part of the CPB. A fall in profit, however, serves as information that certain enterprises are not working correctly, and that their performance should undergo analysis. Since in this example it has been assumed that balance equilibrium has been maintained, the parameters, therefore, do not need to be changed. Technical-organizational measures, however, must be taken in order to ensure that the performance of enterprises in which profits are falling, becomes more efficient.

Example 2. Observation of the balances shows that demand is greater than supply, since stocks have fallen below the norm. Measures must be taken to restore equilibrium, either by direct intervention or through the feeding system, e.g. credit restrictions, and/or a change in parameters, which would limit demand and in time increase supply.

Balance disequilibrium does not neutralize the role of success indicators as signals of enterprise performance, although it does complicate the situation to some extent. Enterprises which maintain their profits still do not require special attention on the part of the CPB. Analysis of enterprises with declining profits may, however, show that the reasons for the fall are to a great extent external to the enterprise, and are due, for example, to lack of supplies. At the same time, it should be realized that in a situation where demand is greater than supply, the average level of current, for example, monthly or quarterly, profitability of a given branch of industry will probably rise, since suppliers are selling more than normally, thereby decreasing their stock norms, whereas their customers' profitability will decline (at first only for a few of them, later for an increasing number) since they will be faced with work stoppages as a result of shortage of supplies.

Where balance disequilibrium occurs because supply exceeds demand, that is, stocks increase above normative level, such an external situation will have no influence on the profit signals of the customers. The suppliers' profit, however, will fall owing to lack of demand. Profit, nonetheless, will still be an effective indicator of which enterprises should be analysed, even though the level of the profit index will reflect the influence of the external situation to a great extent.

The conclusions which can be drawn from the above are as follows:

(1) The CPB should constantly observe fulfilment of planned output by analysing the balances. From the macro-economic point of view the degree to which the output plan is fulfilled by individual enterprises is not important as long as balance equilibrium is maintained. If a single enterprise is the only producer, or the most important producer of a given article, then that enterprise's performance will immediately be reflected in the balances. An intra-branch allocation of output, different from the allocation planned, may be evidence, when profits are rising that, in aiming to maximize profit, a better, more effective allocation of production has taken place than had been anticipated. (2) The level of the success indicator, profit, serves as a signal to the CPB on the performance of individual plan executants. It does not inform the CPB of the reasons for the unsatisfactory level of the success indicator, nor, therefore, of the measures required in the given situation. It does, however, point out which enterprises need attention.

Enterprise success indicators have been presented here, using the profit success indicator as an illustration, in their role of signals to the CPB of the performance of enterprises. The same analysis applies in full to other success indicators such as value of gross output, decrease in costs, or quality of product. These indices differ from profit in that they inform the CPB solely on individual aspects of enterprise performance. They are similar to profit in that they neither show the reasons for their movement nor do they free the CPB from the necessity of analysing each individual case, at enterprise or branch level, before deciding on measures to improve the situation.

An analysis of the comparative merits of various success indicators, including that of their efficacy as signals to the CPB of the performance of plan executants, is to be found in 5.6.

5.1.2 SUCCESS INDICATORS AS THE BASIS OF CHOICE IN ENTERPRISE DECISION-MAKING

Success indicators define the tasks which an enterprise management has been set, and, therefore, constitute the compass by which decisions are taken within the authority sphere of the enterprise (see 4.4.1). The success indicator serves both as the basis for decision-making and later as a verification of the correctness of the given decision of the enterprise. 'An enterprise which does not have an analyser [a success indicator is meant here] would require to have all its decisions approved by higher authorities. Information on proposed decisions would have to be transmitted to the HAO. The decision itself could only be undertaken on HAO acceptance or correction of the proposals put forward by the enterprise' [22, p. 16]. It is obvious that such a management model—outside the decisions which are pertinent to the HAO only—would be very costly and hardly feasible.

The success indicators as a criterion of choice may be accompanied by a number of constraints. In the current management formula the constraints mainly take the form of what are termed the conditions of activating (paying out) bonuses (bonus conditions). These are: fulfilment of planned product-mix and what are termed branch tasks, set yearly by ministers for individual industrial associations. For example, the bonus conditions may be: meeting certain export targets, better utilization of production capacity, decrease in material costs, maintaining or reducing the level of stocks, see [1]. In such a situation, the criterion of choice—*formally* speaking—is the maximization of the success indicator on the condition, however, that the constraints are not violated. Actual enterprise behaviour is presented in 5.6.

5.1.3 SUCCESS INDICATORS AS THE BASIS OF THE ENTERPRISE MANAGEMENT STIMULATION SYSTEM

Since success indicators define the tasks set for an enterprise, logic requires that they should also constitute the basis of financial rewards, or penalties for the enterprise management. Financial interest on the part of management and workers in the degree to which a success indicator is fulfilled should ensure that maximization of the success indicator constitutes a behaviour motive to plan executants.

It is also of importance that the success indicators should not only be the basis of the bonus system but also the basis of overall-evaluation on the part of the HAO. This fact must be stressed since the two may not necessarily coincide, as frequently happens in the initial period following a change in success indicators. For example, when a management bonus system based on planned profitability[1] was introduced in Poland in 1964 [1] the level of fulfilment of gross output or commodity output remained for a long time, and to a great extent still remains, the *de facto* criterion of overall evaluation on the part of the HAO.

It should be added that the role of profit as the basis for evaluation

---

[1] By profitability [*rentownosc*] is meant the ratio of the volume of accumulation or profit to the cost of output sold.

of the performance of an enterprise is also undermined by the fact that in the current management formula the main technical economic indices of the plan, as will be shown in 6.2.2, are simultaneously the management bonus conditions. This means that the achievement of a given level of success indicator is a necessary but not a sufficient condition for the award of a bonus, and also for approval of superiors.

5.1.4 SUCCESS INDICATORS AS THE BASIS OF REGULATING THE ENTERPRISE FEEDING SYSTEM

The final role of the success indicators consists in the partial or complete regulation of the feeding system, the success indicators also serving as FS regulators in this case. As has been pointed out in 4.3, success indicators in the majority of management formulae to some extent regulate the feeding system. Therefore, if the enterprise increases the level of a success indicator this fact is not only reflected in the management (and workers) bonuses, but also entitles the enterprise to a greater amount of resources. In other words, success indicators not only constitute the basis for the creation of what are termed enterprise consumption funds (bonus fund and factory fund, see Ch. 6), but also constitute the basis of what are termed development funds, that is, funds necessary for investment and to increase working capital (see Ch. 7).

The role of regulating the feeding system constitutes an important function of success indicators, although it should be remembered that the role of this function varies in importance in various types of management formulae. In simple management formulae this role is at its greatest, in highly complex formulae, at its lowest (see again 4.3).

5.2 Conditions Enterprise Success Indicators Should Fulfil

If success indicators are to define the *ciphered tasks* of socialist enterprises effectively, they must fulfil several basic conditions [see *24*, pp. 151–7].

(1) The first condition is that the maximization of a given success indicator should simultaneously serve to maximize the goals, however defined, of the national economy as a whole. There is still considerable controversy in Eastern Europe as to how this condition is to be achieved. Numerous questions arise, such as, what should constitute the success indicator and whether this success indicator should in fact be a single indicator or a group of indicators, the latter being the current practice. Above all, there is the question of the nature of the external conditions which should be created. This includes the problem of the type of management mechanism (inclusive of appropriate price system) which should be constructed, and the wider question of the economic situation as a whole, such as the character of the market. The external conditions

created should ensure that success indicators correctly reflect the contribution of a given enterprise to the national economic goal.

The fulfilment of this first condition alone demands much from economic policy makers and Polish economic reforms have not, as yet, made any substantial progress towards meeting it, as will be demonstrated in subsequent pages.

(2) The enterprise success indicator must be strictly measurable. If this condition is not met, the effectiveness of all the functions fulfilled by success indicators (described in 5.1) is endangered. Ignoring other aspects for the time being, the formal condition that the enterprise success indicator be measurable, means that the usefulness of a group of indicators for defining the enterprise tasks is questionable, since if the marginal rates of substitution are not specified as in Polish planning practice, the results of the performance of an enterprise are not commensurable. For example, it becomes impossible to state what percentage of plan fulfilment is constituted by a 120 per cent fulfilment of the commodity output plan, a 90 per cent fulfilment of the product-mix plan, and a 105 per cent fulfilment of the cost reduction plan.

(3) Of no less importance is the condition that the calculation of the success indicator should be simple and unequivocal. Where this condition is not fulfilled the workers and sometimes even the management cease to understand the correlation between their work and the size of the success indicators. The result is the commonly held opinion that the whole thing depends on the accountants. The practical importance of this problem will be seen later, in the discussion of the methods used in comparing the levels of a success indicator over time, under dynamic conditions (see 5.4 and 7.5.2).

5.3 The Reception Sphere of Enterprise Success Indicators

Depending on the aim of the analysis, classification of success indicators may be based on a variety of criteria. From the point of view of management theory the following divisions of success indicators are of decisive importance: (1) by the criterion of what is termed the reception sphere of the indicator, (2) by the criterion called the 'basis of comparison' of the indicator. The first criterion will be discussed now. Discussion of the second will follow in Ch. 6.

By reception sphere is meant the number and types of characteristics of economic events registered by the success indicator and influencing its level.[1] The reception sphere of different success indicators may reflect a greater or smaller number of characteristics of the various economic

---

[1] J. Wieckowski introduced the concept of the reception sphere into economic literature [22, p. 34]. Taking his definition as a starting point, we had to expand it here in order to present a full picture of the problem of the management of economic processes.

events, that is to say, the 'range of reception' may be broader or narrower.[1]

Characteristics of economic events are determined by the influence of: (a) the enterprise's own performance; for example, decrease in the steel input per unit of output; (b) information transmitted from the CPB to the enterprise; for example, an increase in the price of steel raises the money costs of the given steel input; (c) information transmitted by customers; for example, late delivery results in an enterprise incurring contractual fines.

Success indicators should react both to internal information on the activity of an enterprise, and to external information transmitted from the CPB and from customers. Information from the latter to a certain extent verifies or supplements incorrectly registered or initially unregistered information in the success indicator on the quality of the performance of an enterprise, for example, goods returned by customers dissatisfied with the quality of the product or repairs under guarantee change an enterprise's cost calculation; and to a certain extent they provide a new type of information on the relation of the size and structure of enterprise output to actual demand.

A discussion of the factors determining the range of the reception sphere of success indicators is now in order.

5.3.1 THE SENSITIVITY OF SUCCESS INDICATORS TO CHANGES IN THE QUALITY OF ENTERPRISE PERFORMANCE

This sensitivity mainly depends on: (1) the construction of the success indicator, (2) the completeness of the price system, (3) the rules governing price-setting.

Points 2 and 3 only apply to value success indicators.

(1) The dependence of the reception sphere on the structure of the analyser is obvious. For example, the analyser of 'grade of output' only reacts to the relative share of different grades in total output, whereas the analyser of 'value of gross output' reacts in addition to the amount of output and to the product-mix chosen.

(2) If the analyser is a value success indicator, such as profit, then its reception sphere also depends on the comprehensiveness of the price system, namely: (a) capital; is interest charged on all resources being used by the enterprise, that is to say, on fixed capital, on working capital, and on natural resources? (b) means of production; does the price system include the price of land and the price of exploiting natural resources, in other words, is ground rent or mining rent to be paid? (c) economic events; does the price system include (and if so to what extent) what are termed 'prices of economic events'? These are prices which usually arise in special situations, such as increased cost of power

---

[1] The concept of the reception sphere analysed here in respect of success indicators, relates to all three groups of analysers described in 4.1.

in peak hours, higher interest on overdue credit, fines for overdue accounts, fines for late unloading of rail consignments, fines for pollution of air and water [see *22*, pp. 75–6, 112–13, 335–6].

(3) The range of the reception sphere of value analysers also depends on the principles governing price-setting. For example: (a) whether the prices of new products in demand on the market are set at a higher level than would result from the normal principles of price-setting; (b) whether the cost of labour is constant, i.e. payment is for hours worked, or variable, i.e. payment is for piece work. Where payment is for hours worked an increase in productivity serves to lower unit cost and is reflected in the profitability analysers. Where payment is for piece work an increase in productivity does not lower unit cost and, therefore, may not be registered by the analysers [see *22*, pp. 269–72].

5.3.2 THE SENSITIVITY OF SUCCESS INDICATORS TO INFORMATION TRANSMITTED FROM THE CPB

From the point of view of management theory not only the range of the reception sphere of the analyser in respect of internal information is of basic importance, but also its sensitivity to information transmitted from the CPB. If economic processes are to be steered effectively, the enterprise information system must be constructed in a manner which allows signals about changes in the external economic situation transmitted from the CPB to be received, and which ensures correct reaction on the part of the enterprise to these signals. The latter question is discussed in 5.4.

The sensitivity of success indicators to information sent from the CPB depends mainly on: (1) the structure of the analyser, (2) the methods of accounting, i.e. the principles of transforming external information into quantitative changes in success indicator, (3) the principles of price-setting.

This is illustrated in the following examples.

(1) The analyser 'decrease of cost of production' does not react to information on prices of final output. The analyser 'value of gross output', given the prices of final output, does not react to information contained in input prices. Since it is impossible to send parametric information in areas not covered by the reception sphere of the analyser, open information must of necessity be used. This means that a strict correlation exists between the type of information system of a given management formula and the management model. The narrower the reception sphere of the success indicator, the wider must be the range of the open, obligatory information and vice versa. Referring to the notions of the enterprise activity and authority spheres introduced in 4.4.1 it can be said that the use of parametric management *cannot go beyond the range of the reception sphere and the authority sphere*. In properly constructed management formulae, the reception sphere is

equal to the activity sphere and the parametric management is confined to the authority sphere. This means that there are two basic prerequisites for wider use of parametric information: a broadening of the reception sphere of success indicator(s), and a broadening of the sphere of the enterprise authority.

The above relationships are presented in Diagram 5.1.

In actual practice we frequently encounter violations of these relationships. The reception sphere of success indicators is often narrower than the authority sphere, omitting—for the time being—some activities which are not steered by the CPB. This leads to efforts to broaden the reception sphere, frequently by adding new specialized success indicators and/or—if these are unsuccessful—to extend the sphere of open information and, as a result, to diminish the enterprise authority sphere. These problems are further discussed in 5.6.

(2) Accounting methods may eliminate the influence of certain types of information transmitted from the CPB on the size of the analysers. For example, what is termed the profit verification rule, currently in practice in Polish state industrial enterprises, eliminates the influence of changes in prices, wages, depreciation costs, etc., on enterprise profits in calculating management bonuses in the year in which the changes are introduced.[1] The result is such that—theoretically speaking—changes

---

[1] Decree 176 of the CM of 9 November 1970 states:
'(1) Prior to final settlement of profit, profit must be verified in order to eliminate: (a) profit independent of enterprise activity; (b) incorrectly achieved profit (*zysk nieprawidłowy*).
(2) Profit independent of enterprise activity is profit achieved as a result of changes in prices, salaries and wages, depreciation, insurance, and tax rates, if the decision on these changes states that the [resulting] profit should be considered as independent, as well as profit resulting from methodological and organizational changes.
(3) Incorrect profit is profit achieved by an enterprise in a manner which is considered contrary to social interest or infringes regulations, for example, using incorrect prices and wages scales, lowering output quality by violating the obligatory norms, standards, or specifications, neglecting current repairs of fixed assets and/or safety precautions and work hygiene. Excessive profit, defined by separate regulation, is also considered as incorrect profit. [The present author has not been able to locate this separate regulation.]
(4) Profit independent of enterprise activity is fully transferred to the state budget.
(5) A sum equal to 150 per cent of incorrectly achieved profit must be transferred: (a) at the rate of 85 per cent to the [state] budget and 15 per cent to the industrial association reserve fund, if the incorrectly achieved profit is revealed by the industrial association; (b) at the rate of 100 per cent to the state budget if the incorrectly achieved profit is revealed by external control bodies, by banks, or by financial departments of local government . . .
(6) If incorrect profit is revealed by the enterprise itself, the sum equal to 100 per cent of this profit must be transferred to the [state] budget.' [5, section 8]. We may note, *en passant*, that the above formulation is—in several respects—more severe than the formulation of 1965 on the same subject [2, section 36], but there are no changes of real importance. This is, unfortunately, true of many 'new' regulations which the abortive reform of 1969–70 intended to introduce.

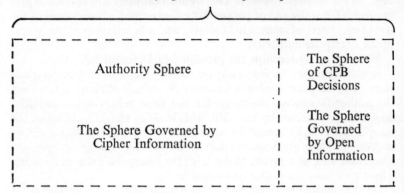

Activity Sphere = Reception Sphere

Authority Sphere

The Sphere of CPB Decisions

The Sphere Governed by Cipher Information

The Sphere Governed by Open Information

Diagram 5.1 The reception sphere and parametric management

in price in a given year only begin to influence the verified profit (and management bonuses) of the enterprise in the following year.

The profit verification rule could be interpreted as an allowance by the CPB of a given period of time to enterprises in which to adjust to price changes. Practice, however, does not substantiate such an interpretation. As a general rule the profit plan for the year 't_2' is adjusted on the basis of changes in price in the first year 't_1', as a result of which increase in price does not necessitate changes in methods of production in an enterprise in order to maintain the original level of the bonuses. The correct interpretation of the profit verification rule would seem to indicate that the rule constitutes the end product of the line of thought that the role of profit should only be that of a narrowly defined *performance* indicator. The influence, therefore, of changes in price on the success indicators should be eliminated since, it is argued, price changes distort actual enterprise performance.

Those opposed to this line of thought claim that, in the first place, the main role of the success indicator should be that of criterion of choice. In this case, the function of a change in price is precisely to influence the level of the success indicator and as a result the enterprise decisions. A change in price which is not allowed to influence the success indicator is tantamount to sending blank messages. Furthermore, it should be noted that allowing price changes to influence the level of the success indicator does not deprive it of its role as a performance indicator. On the contrary, it includes in performance evaluation one additional and very important element: the enterprises' ability to react to changing choice alternatives. It should also be borne in mind that in the case of parametric management, changes in price are usually multi-directional and gradual in character.

(3) The sensitivity of success indicators to information transmitted from the CPB also depends on the price-setting system. Some price-setting systems result in certain types of price information transmitted from the CPB not being registered by analysers. This question will be discussed in detail in 5.4.

5.3.3 THE SENSITIVITY OF SUCCESS INDICATORS TO INFORMATION TRANSMITTED BY CUSTOMERS

The effectiveness of an economic system depends not only on efficiency of production methods, but also on whether production satisfies demand. The information system in an enterprise, therefore, must be constructed in a manner which allows information from customers to be taken into account.

The sensitivity of success indicators to information transmitted by customers mainly depends on: (1) the structure of the analyser, (2) the completeness of the price system.

(1) The success indicators should be constructed in a manner allowing the degree of consistency between the structure of the enterprise's production and effective demand to be registered. While value of gross output does not react to either volume or structure of demand, the value of output sold does register effective demand for enterprise output, and the analysers of profitability react to demand for both output and inputs. Success indicators constructed in this manner theoretically enable customers to exert pressure on suppliers. In practice the effectiveness of this pressure depends on the nature of the market (it is only effective in the case of a buyer's market) and on the comprehensiveness of the existing price system.

(2) The more comprehensive the price system is and particularly the price system of economic events (5.3.1), the greater opportunity the customer has to influence the quality of the supplier's work. This influence is exerted by means of various types of economic sanctions such as fines for late delivery, reduction in payment for goods of lower quality than specified by obligatory standards or contracts, or the supplier's bearing the cost of repairs under guarantee.

In the light of the preceding analysis, any success indicator can be said to be a type of receiving-transmitting mechanism, which on the one hand receives certain internal and external information and on the other transmits information to the enterprise steering centre and to the HAO and the banking system. Diagram 5.2 illustrates this concept of the success indicator.

5.4 The Reaction of Success Indicators to Economic Events

The range of the reception sphere apart, a question of considerable

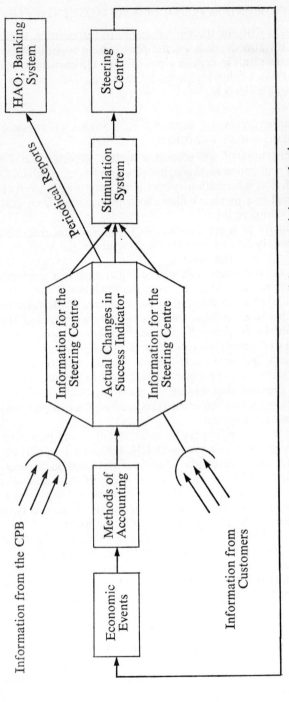

Diagram 5.2   The success indicator as a receiving–transmitting mechanism

importance in the construction of enterprise success indicators is the manner in which they react to economic events. It is not sufficient in itself that a given characteristic of an economic event is within the reception sphere of a success indicator. In order to 'guide' properly the choice of enterprise management, the success indicator must react 'correctly' to changes in economic events. By correct reaction we mean here that changes in economic events which are considered as 'desirable' by the CPB, bring about changes in the success indicator which are 'desirable' from the viewpoint of enterprise management.[1]

The manner in which success indicators react to economic events mainly depends on: (1) the structure of the success indicator, (2) the principles of price-setting, (3) the methods of accounting for economic events.

5.4.1 THE STRUCTURE OF THE SUCCESS INDICATORS AND THEIR REACTION TO ECONOMIC EVENTS

The variation in the reaction of success indicators of different construction to the same economic event (external information) can be shown in an example based on two profitability analysers: increase in volume of profit (ΔPf) and 'the coefficient of economic effectiveness', i.e. the proportion of total costs in the value of output sold $\left(\dfrac{C}{R}\right)$, where total costs $= C$, and income from sales $= R$. Let us assume that a new article is being produced and that the price of the new article is internal and has a normative (constant) coefficient of profitability.[2] The influence on the level of each of the two profitability analysers of an increase in price of a given factor of production is then as follows.[3]

(A) *Changes in volume of profit* (ΔPf). This profitability analyser reacts positively to an increase in the price of factors of production according to the following formula:

---

[1] Desired changes in success indicators may carry a positive sign ($+$) if the success indicator represents the maximization of a given effect such as profit or commodity output, or a negative sign ($-$) when the success indicator represents the minimization of costs or input of a specific type, for example, ratio of costs in gross value of sales, level of unit costs, or the level of raw material costs. What constitutes the 'desires' of enterprise management is analysed in 5.6.

[2] The internal price is the price based on costs of a given enterprise plus the centrally determined profit margin which is normally set as a certain percentage of cost of production. This profit margin is called the normative coefficient of profitability. Internal and external prices and profit coefficients are discussed below in 5.4.2.

[3] All equations in this section are adapted from [22, pp. 260–90]. Only the present author is responsible, however, for their adaptation, interpretation, and analytical application as presented in this study.

8

$$\Delta Pf = C \times \Delta P \times Cm \times PfCn \qquad (1)$$

where C = total costs

Cm = part of direct material costs which are affected by the price increase

ΔP = increase of price index $\left(\dfrac{P_2 - P_1}{P_1}\right)$

$PfCn$ = the normative coefficient of profitability

Thus a rise in input prices, given new products and the internal price with normative coefficient of profitability, creates a positive change in the volume of profit.

The reaction of the coefficient of economic effectiveness, to an increase in input price is as follows:

(B) *Changes in the coefficient of economic effectiveness* $\left(\Delta\dfrac{C}{R}\right)$.

This analyser does not react to an increase in input prices, since, under our assumption of new products and internal prices, costs and revenue rise in the same proportion as a result of increase in input prices.

These examples serve to show that the same information—increase in input prices—may bring about different changes in success indicators, depending on their construction. Detailed analysis [see *22, passim*] shows that some success indicators react in an opposite direction, but more frequently the degree of reaction of success indicators to the same economic events (information)[1] is different: some react more, some less, strongly.

Economic policy-makers try to take advantage of this feature of success indicators in their choice of enterprise information system. For example, the coefficient of economic effectiveness was used in Poland in branches of industry where decrease of cost was considered of particular importance, and volume of profit was used where output expansion was given priority.

5.4.2 THE PRINCIPLES OF PRICE-SETTING AND THE REACTION OF SUCCESS INDICATORS TO ECONOMIC EVENTS

From the point of view of the problem under discussion two types of price-setting principles are relevant: (1) those based on factors external to the enterprise, such as average branch costs, the price which clears the market, or the use value of the product; (2) those based on cost of production of the enterprise itself.

Prices set on the basis of point 1 are termed *external prices* in this study, those set on the basis of point 2, *internal prices*. Products produced in a previous planning period, for which prices have been set for some time, should be distinguished from newly introduced products,

[1] It should be remembered that *information* influences analysers only *via* economic events. Information, however, influences management decisions *directly* by their hypothetical or possible influence on analysers.

the prices of which have only recently been set. The former are termed 'standing products' in this study, the latter, 'new products' [see *22*, pp. 86–95]. It should be stressed that an internal price once approved, affects the 'standing products' in the same manner as external prices, that is to say, as independent of the actual level of costs of production. Contrary to widespread belief, a large number of prices in the Polish economy are set on the basis of the costs of production of individual enterprises.[1]

The reaction of success indicators to a particular economic event is decisively influenced by whether prices are external or internal. This can be illustrated by examining the influence of an *increase in prices of factors of production* on the analysers previously discussed.

(A) *Changes in volume of profit.* With standing products and an external, constant price, profit will fall according to the following formula:

$$\Delta Pf = C \times \Delta P \times \frac{Cm}{C} \qquad (2)$$

With new products and internal prices with a normative coefficient of profitability, an increase in profit will result according to formula (1).

(B) *Changes in the coefficient of economic effectiveness.* With standing products and external prices a positive, i.e. undesirable change of the coefficient takes place:

$$\Delta \frac{C}{R} = \Delta P \times \frac{Cm}{R} \qquad (3)$$

With new products and internal prices with a normative coefficient of profitability, an increase in the price of factors of production will *in no way influence* the coefficient of economic effectiveness, as has already been explained in 5.4.1.B.

These examples show that the principles of price-setting have a decisive influence on the manner in which a success indicator reacts to economic events. The generally accepted thesis that there is no pre-determined functional relation between costs and revenue and profit is only valid in the case of external prices. Where the price is internal.

---

[1] The basic reasons that individual rather than branch average cost-plus pricing is so extensively used in the socialist countries are: (a) high degrees of specialization do not allow average branch costs to be calculated for many products; (b) prices for goods supplied by sub-contractors are fixed by agreements between seller and buyer on a cost-plus basis; (c) the planned profit/cost ratio is differentiated individually for each enterprise in a manner ensuring profitability; this practice is tantamount to individual cost-plus pricing even if prices are formally based on branch average costs; (d) price subsidies of various types are extensively used; (e) prices of new products are, as a rule, set at a profitable level, even if it cannot be justified by the utility/cost ratio of a new product to its closest substitute; (f) intra-branch 'accounting prices' are used (see 8.2.2.A).

the volume of revenue and profit is a function of costs according to the profitability coefficient used. This is a result of the principles on which internal prices are set.

The reaction of a success indicator to economic events also depends on the principles on which the internal prices are set. Current Polish economic practice uses three types of coefficients of profitability, which are added to the costs of production of individual enterprises: (1) a normative coefficient (PfCn); (2) a coefficient based on actual profitability in similar production at the time of planning (PfCp); (3) a coefficient based on actual profitability in similar production at the time of sale of the new products (PfCa).

Depending on the manner in which the coefficient of profitability is set, the same economic event may create multi-directional changes in success indicators, since the various coefficients generally have different percentage levels. As a rule the lowest is the normative coefficient, the highest—the coefficient PfCa [see *22*, pp. 138–9].

The decisive influence of price-setting principles on the manner in which success indicators react to economic events can be clearly seen in the above examples. They also further illustrate the integrated nature of the management mechanism, in this case the close interrelationships between the principles of price-setting and the manner in which the information system of an enterprise functions. Important practical conclusions can be drawn on the basis of these interrelationships. In the first place, they must be taken into account both in formulating the principles of price-setting and in the construction of the success indicators. For example, a coefficient of profitability in constructing internal prices cannot be chosen without giving due consideration to the influence which it will exert on the functioning of the enterprise information system. In the second place, since the freedom of choice of the CPB in the sphere of prices and success indicators can, for technical reasons, vary, it is possible that certain defects which cannot be avoided in the price system, may be *partially neutralized* by a correctly constructed information system and vice versa. For example, if internal prices cannot be dispensed with, the success indicator 'coefficient of economic effectiveness' only blocks certain price information, whereas volume of profit reacts perversely.

5.4.3 THE METHODS OF ACCOUNTING AND THE REACTION OF SUCCESS INDICATORS TO ECONOMIC EVENTS

The reaction of success indicators also depends on the methods of accounting employed in respect of economic events. In the situation previously under consideration the same economic events produced *different reactions* in enterprise success indicators. The situation, however, can also arise, in which different economic events create *analogous changes* in the analysers. This means that the information system is *not sufficiently selective,* which at times may lead to behaviour on the part of plan executants considered harmful to the national economy. This can be illustrated taking as an example the influence of an increase in sub-contracting on changes in volume of profit and in the coefficient of economic effectiveness.

(A) *Changes in volume of profit.* The impact of an increased share of sub-contracting on increase of profit is:

$$\Delta Pf = C \times \frac{\Delta Cs}{Cs} \times \frac{Cs}{C} \times PfCn \tag{4}$$

where Cs = cost of sub-contracting.

If the enterprise's real production capacity remains unaffected by increased sub-contracting or diminishes less than the latter—extension of sub-contracting is an easy way of increasing profit. The Polish experience indicates that both HAO and enterprise managers are well aware of the functional relationship presented in (4).

(B) *Changes in the coefficient of economic effectiveness.* An increase in sub-contracting causes an increase in the total cost equal to the costs of sub-contracting. Since revenue also rises by the amount equivalent to the value of the sub-contracting plus a constant coefficient of profitability, an increase in sub-contracting leaves the coefficient of economic effectiveness unaffected.

The current methods of accounting do not 'differentiate' between the cost of production of an enterprise and the cost of sub-contracting. As we have shown, this creates the possibility of improving certain analysers of profitability by increasing the ratio of cost of sub-contracting in total costs. Since internal cost-plus prices are widely used, this possibility has far-reaching economic consequences [see *22*, pp. 296–9]. First of all, enterprise management is induced to seek 'short contact with the product' because limiting enterprise input and expanding the share of sub-contracting improves—as a rule—most profitability analysers. Secondly, the strategy called 'moving closer towards the final product' becomes advantageous. The further the enterprise is from processing the raw material and the closer to assembling the final product, the greater the share of the product produced by its predecessors it can ascribe to itself.

Implementation of these tactics is limited by the rigidity of technical processes. 'Short contact with the product' and 'moving closer towards the final product' require changes in the organization of production. These changes, however, are not too difficult if the enterprise is simultaneously engaged in producing the final product and some of the sub-components which are marketed separately as spare parts. A gradual limitation of the production of spare parts increases the share of final products in the enterprise output. Similar results can be achieved when an enterprise produces both components for sub-contractors, and its 'own' final products. A decrease in the production of components usually increases enterprise capacity in respect of the final product.

The tendencies described above result in the constant shortages of spare parts and sub-components which are so characteristic of all East European countries. In turn they give rise to two phenomena. First, there is a tendency to self-sufficiency within each enterprise, industrial association, and ministry. This increases unit cost owing to lack of specialized equipment and the loss of economies of scale[1] and, *en passant*, is one of the causes of lack of consistency in horizontal organizational integration prevailing in most East European countries. Secondly it prompts the CPB to take special measures both to reduce economically unjustified sub-contracting and to enforce fulfilment of planned output of spare parts and sub-contracting deliveries (*dostawy kooperacyjne*). These measures can take the form of making fulfilment of sub-contracting plan a bonus condition (see 6.2.2) or of introducing appropriate changes in the enterprise information system—either in the methods of accounting or in the construction of success indicators. These changes, however, should not take the form of *narrowing* the reception sphere of the enterprise success indicator, for example, by excluding the costs of sub-contracting from the reception sphere, since the enterprise management should be interested in economizing *all* inputs, both its own and those bought. Introduction of economic differentiation between the enterprise's own costs and the cost of sub-contracting, may represent the best feasible improvement within the framework of the existing management mechanism. The simplest manner in which this economic differentiation can be achieved is, however, not through the enterprise information system but by changing the principles of price-setting. There are two possibilities here. The first is to differentiate the normative coefficient of profitability of final products (a lower coefficient) and of sub-component and spare parts (a higher coefficient) on the basis of the general principle that the greater the proximity to the final product, the higher the ratio of cost of sub-contracting. The second possible solution is, when setting internal prices, to calculate the coefficient of profitability solely in relation to the cost of processing (value added). In this way an increase in production achieved by increasing the share of sub-contracting costs in total costs would not cause an increase in the volume of profit, and would also lead to a positive, i.e. undesirable, increase in the coefficient of economic effectiveness. The second

[1] For example, the cost of tools produced in enterprises' own 'tools divisions' (*narzedziownie*) exceeds the cost of the same tools produced by specialized enterprises by 200–500 per cent. This applies even to very big enterprises such as the *H. Cegielski* machine-building factory in Poznan [*11*, p. 82].

solution, however, could possibly strengthen the tendency to autarky in enterprises (now a result of uncertainty of supplies) which would be just as undesirable as the artificial increase in sub-contracting.

The discussion in 5.3 and 5.4 can be summarized by the following table.

Table 5.1   Main factors determining the reception sphere and type of reaction of success indicators

Factors	Construction of Success Indicator	Methods of Accounting	Comprehensiveness of Price System	Principles of Price Setting
Sensitivity to the activity of the enterprise itself	×		×	×
Sensitivity to the information transmitted from the CPB	×	×		×
Sensitivity to the information transmitted by customers	×		×	
Type of reaction to economic events and/or external information	×	×		×

5.5 Synthetic and Specialized Success Indicators

The reception sphere of analysers is used here as the criterion for dividing success indicators into two sub-groups.

(1) Analysers which take into account both cost and revenue are—*ex definitione*—in the profit category. They have the widest reception sphere of all analysers and are termed here *synthetic* success indicators.

Profit analysers may be constructed in various ways. The 'classical' success indicator and simultaneously the goal of a capitalist enterprise is *volume of profit*. Socialist countries use a large number of synthetic success indicators. For example, the resolution of the IVth Plenum of the CC of PUWP (July 1965) stated that for the period 1966–70 the main synthetic success indicator for enterprises and industrial associations should be the *coefficient of profitability*. It is the ratio of profit to cost of production of output sold. In certain branches of production *rate of profit*, i.e. ratio of profit to value of fixed and working capital, was to be used [*27*, p. 152].[1]

The incentive system which was planned to be introduced on 1 January 1971 [*4*] but withdrawn after the events of December 1970 (see Glossary), allowed enterprises the choice of the following four indicators: decrease of unit cost of production; final cost level (*wynikowy poziom kosztow*); volume of profit; rate of profit.[2] With the exception of the first, all the indicators are synthetic in character, according to the definition used in this study.

The indices enumerated above are by no means identical as far as reception spheres and manner of reaction to economic events are concerned. All of them, however, cover *both* revenue and costs and because of this feature deserve to be considered as a separate group (see 5.6 below).

It should be noted that most of the synthetic success indicators tried in Poland were constructed in the form of a *ratio* of two different magnitudes, say, profit to costs (coefficient of profitability) or profit to capital assets (rate of profit), rather than in the form of *absolute* magnitude, e.g. volume of profit. As operational research experts indicated in the early 1950s [*10*] and repeated later on many occasions [*12*], any maximand in the form of a ratio of benefit to costs (however

---

[1] The following four industrial profitability indices (*wzkazniki rentownosci*), depending on the branch of industry, were introduced on 1 January 1967:
(a) net profitability—R_n;   (b) gross profitability—R_b;
(c) profitability of processing—R_p;   (d) rate of profit—R_z.
These indices are calculated according to the following formulae:

$$R_n = \frac{z_w}{c_{qt}}$$

$$R_b = \frac{z_w + f_o + f_n}{c_{qt}}$$

$$R_p = \frac{z_w}{q_{tp}}$$

$$R_z = \frac{z_w}{S_c + O_s}$$

where z_w = profit or loss as shown in the enterprise balance
c_{qt} = cost of production of commodity output sold by the enterprise
f_o = turnover tax
f_n = tax on non-commodity operations (*podatek od operacji nietowarowych*)
q_{tp} = enterprise commodity output according to cost of processing prices for the given year
S_c = fixed assets of the enterprise
O_s = working capital of the enterprise
At the same time the coefficient of economic effectiveness was dispensed with [*3*].

[2] For details of how these success indicators are constructed see [*7*, pp. 375–81]. See also p. 147, fn. 1.

costs and benefits are defined) is very misleading, can easily lead to undesirable behaviour, and, therefore, should not be used.[1] The basic weakness of all decision criteria formulated in the form of a ratio, is that they do not specify the desired *scale* of operation. If, however, the

[1] Let us take as an example the superficially sensible criterion of maximizing profit/cost ratio. The examination of the diagram below will show its fallacy:

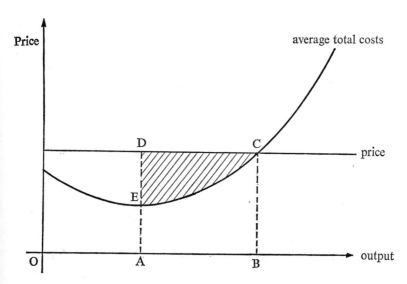

Diagram 5.3   The Optimum Volume of Output under Profit/Cost Ratio and Volume of Profit Success Indicators

As can easily be seen from the diagram, the enterprise maximizing profit/cost ratio will produce only CA volume of output. By doing this it is sacrificing, however, the great potential profit to be made and represented in our diagram as a shaded area E-C-D. It may be worthwhile to note that the critique of success indicators in the form of a ratio does not apply to maximands in the form of marginal increments of benefits which are also a ratio, e.g. increase of profit/profit achieved in base year (see 6.4, where such a criterion function is recommended). The reason is that the constraint introduced is given (base year profit) and not arbitrarily introduced and as the maximand is the ratio of *profit* (increased) to *profit* (achieved in base year) it is tantamount to the maximand 'volume of profit' with one extra constraint, namely that there is a penalty for not achieving the base result. This does not change enterprise behaviour in any significant or negative direction. For example, under the maximand of incremental profit the enterprise would immediately try to increase its output to OB level. One can argue that constraint in the form of base profit may inhibit the enterprise from risk-taking, but the danger seems to be rather slight (management always tries to avoid lessening its previous achievements) and can be made still slighter by introducing a number of special devices (see 6.4 *passim*).

8*

scale element is introduced as a constraint, say in the form: 'maximize profit/cost ratio but profit should be at least £1,000', how do the HAO know beforehand if a £1,000 target is feasible and, moreover, optimal? It is quite astonishing to the author that in Poland with her quite sophisticated economics, the CPB adheres to success indicators in the ratio form. It is combined with profit target in absolute terms, but, as we have said above, it only eliminates the most extreme potential negative consequences of such a success indicator, without eliminating its inherent weakness.

(2) All other analysers will be termed *specialized* success indicators. The characteristics of these indicators are: (a) that their reception spheres are narrower than those of success indicators based on profit, (b) that their reception spheres cover certain characteristics of economic events, *either* from the sphere of input *or* of output; *ex definitione*, their reception spheres do not cover both.

The specialized success indicators can be sub-divided according to the range of their reception spheres, if each succeeding success indicator contains the reception sphere of the preceding indicator plus an extra reception sphere, for example, quality of production—gross output; material costs—cost of production.

This classification, however, cannot be fully comprehensive, since many specialized success indicators have different reception spheres which do not overlap, and which cannot be said to be wider or narrower than each other. They are simply different, as, for example, value of commodity output and index of decrease in cost of production. These indicators reflect various aspects of enterprise activity: the first reflects output, the second input.

Specialized success indicators may also be sub-classified according to the sphere of economic activity they reflect in the enterprise. This classification may go into any given degree of detail as, for example: (a) input—material costs, wage bill, cost of production; (b) volume of output—value of commodity output, value of gross output, value of gross turnover;[1] (c) quality of output—index of quality grades, value of repairs under guarantee or value of returned goods per X zlotys of output sold; (d) management of inventories—indices for various kinds of stock, norms of working capital; (e) exports—the share of exports in total revenue, economic effectiveness of exports; (f) changes in product-mix—the share of new products in total revenue.

[1] Gross turnover is an output indicator (see 4.1) which is a variation of the value of gross output index. Gross turnover constitutes the sum of the value of internal turnover in an enterprise in certain semi-processed goods, plus the value of output sold. It should be added that this indicator contains most of the flaws characteristic of gross output and commodity output indices. It does, however, have, in comparison, one positive feature, since it eliminates any interest enterprises may have in unnecessary sales of certain semi-processed goods to one another [see *8*, pp. 22–3].

5.6 Selection of the Reception Sphere of Enterprise Success Indicators

The criteria which define the reception sphere of value success indicators were discussed in 5.4. The following discussion covers the nature of the reception sphere required if success indicators are to fulfil their roles (discussed in 5.1) in the management mechanism efficiently.

5.6.1 SYNTHETIC AND SPECIALIZED SUCCESS INDICATORS AS SIGNALS TO THE CPB OF ENTERPRISE PERFORMANCE

Signals of enterprise performance transmitted to the CPB through a set of specialized success indicators frequently do not cover the whole sphere of enterprise activity. If this is the case, the CPB is unable to obtain a proper picture of enterprise performance since certain spheres of enterprise economic activity (and all spheres of economic activity are important, as all use scarce resources) are not covered by specialized success indicators. As a result, although considerable amounts of information are transmitted—which is costly—the sum of all the signals is insufficient to keep the CPB informed of the quality of performance of the plan executants.

It is, of course, possible to cover the whole sphere of enterprise activity by a set of specialized success indicators such as total costs and total revenue. This, however, is an uneconomical method of achieving the desired result, not only because this can be done by using *one* synthetic success indicator but also for a number of more important reasons, which are discussed below.

5.6.2 SYNTHETIC AND SPECIALIZED SUCCESS INDICATORS AS THE BASIS OF ENTERPRISE DECISION-MAKING

Specialized success indicators have several basic flaws as a basis for decision-making in an enterprise. Let us assume that specialized success indicators cover the *full* sphere of enterprise activity (Model I). The existence of a set of specialized success indicators frequently results in the enterprise being presented with several contradictory tasks.

The pursuit of contradictory goals is a characteristic of *homo sapiens*. Contradictory goals can only be reconciled with one another if the problem is considered as a search for an optimum solution. For example, if instead of attempting to maximize both income and leisure, which are self-contradictory goals, their optimum proportions are sought. In order to define these optimum proportions a supreme goal (meta-criterion) is necessary, such as maximization of satisfaction (or utility). Income and leisure then become partial goals, pursuit of which maximizes the supreme goal.

The existence of a supreme goal allows the marginal rates of substitution of partial goals to be determined, however imperfectly. If, however, the marginal rate of substitution between total revenue and total costs were set by the CPB, this would mean that, *de facto*, a synthetic indicator for the activity of the enterprise has been set, namely a coefficient of economic effectiveness.

If the marginal rate of substitution is *not* set by the CPB the enterprise must set it, since if a marginal rate of substitution between the specialized success indicators is not determined, the enterprise has no criterion of choice between various types of activities. In order to set the marginal rate of substitution the enterprise must formulate its own criterion function. Observation of the behaviour of Polish enterprise managers reveals that their goal is to maximize the volume of bonuses for a given volume of effort exerted. The enterprise criterion function can, therefore, be formulated as follows:[1]

$$G = \frac{\sum_{z=1}^{n} B_z}{\sum_{s=1}^{m} N_s} = \max. \left(\text{for the given bonus intensity} \sum_{s=1}^{m} N_s = \text{const.} \right) \quad (5)$$

[1] When the author presented this view in 1967 in Poland [*25*] it met with hardly any serious opposition [see *17* and *26*] and was later reprinted without change (in 10,000 copies) in what—at that time—was generally expected to become one of the leading university textbooks on the political economy of socialism [*18*]. In this context it is worthwhile noting the characteristic evolution which views on the goal of socialist enterprises have undergone in the last seventy years in Western economics and in the last fifteen years in East European economic literature. During the initial idealistic (or self-deceiving?) period it was maintained in West and East that under socialism the goal of the enterprise was not the production of exchange value and surplus value but of *use* value. Professor L. J. Gordon [*9*] for example, maintained that under socialism 'production for satisfaction of needs will replace production for profit' and the view of Polish Marxist economists was the same till approximately 1955–6. As a plan was considered a representation of social needs, in 'operational' terms the goal of the socialist enterprise was 'to fulfil and overfulfil the planned tasks'. Such (or similar) formulations of the socialist enterprise's aims are still predominant in most *official* decrees and pronouncements. What is characteristic of the present, more realistic stage in Polish economic thinking is the realization that there might exist and indeed that there does exist a difference between the *formal* goal of the socialist enterprise and the *de facto* goal of enterprise management. The latter is now almost universally considered as maximization of managerial bonuses. See numerous proceedings from Polish symposia on the socialist enterprise, such as [*13*] and [*20*] for ample illustration. Instead of an idyllic picture of the socialist enterprise as a selfless seeker of social welfare, these symposia portray the enterprise as a focus of many conflicts, both external, between the enterprise and society as a whole, other enterprises, and consumers, and internal, between management and employees and different groups of employees as well. The best proof, however, that socialist enterprises are maximizers of managerial bonuses is provided by enterprise behaviour, strategy, and tactics. The latter are analysed throughout most of the present volume and summarized briefly in 9.2.1.B.

where

G   = the goal of the enterprise;

B_z (z = 1, 2, ..., n) = bonuses awarded for different specialized success indicators;

N_s (s = 1, 2, ..., m) = efforts exerted by management in order to achieve the bonuses awarded for various specialized success indicators.[1]

The criterion function defines—within the given internal and external constraints the optimum proportions of achievement of individual specialized success indicators, according to the condition that: G = max., when

$$\frac{\Delta B_1}{\Delta N_1} = \frac{\Delta B_2}{\Delta N_2} = \cdots = \frac{\Delta B_n}{\Delta B_m} \tag{6}$$

This means that the level of achievement of individual specialized success indicators by the enterprise is influenced by two factors: (a) the level of the bonuses set by the CPB for individual specialized success indicators, (b) the degree of difficulty faced by the enterprise in their achievement.

The comparison of equation (6) with the condition of maximizing volume of profit immediately shows the weak points of specialized success indicators, even if these cover the whole reception sphere of the synthetic success indicator.

Profit is at a maximum where the following condition is fulfilled:

Pf = max., when

$$\frac{\Delta z_1}{\Delta c_1} = \frac{\Delta z_2}{\Delta c_2} = \cdots = \frac{\Delta zn}{\Delta cn} \tag{7}$$

where

$\Delta c_{1, 2, \cdots, n}$ = the marginal cost of increasing or decreasing any factor influencing profit, such as volume of output, quality, costs;

$\Delta z_{1, 2, \cdots, n}$ = marginal profit resulting from the increase or decrease of any factor influencing profit.

Where volume of profit is the success indicator, the denominator consists of the marginal costs of various activities which influence maximization of profit, and the numerator consists of marginal profits

[1] Formula (5) requires comment. The number of activities bringing bonuses (Ns) may be greater than the number of bonuses ensuing from the different success indicators (Bz)—z > s—since some N may have *indirect* bonus effects. For example, there may be no bonus for quality, but one for volume of revenue. Nonetheless, quality may be taken into consideration, depending on its B/N ratio, in the actual Ns, if there is price/quality differentiation. Therefore, since z > s, then also m > n and should be read accordingly.

achieved as a result of incurring these costs. When prices are correctly set, it can be assumed that the marginal costs represent the social costs of achieving the given results, and profit represents their social utility. When specialized success indicators are used, the denominator of the equilibrium equation of the enterprise represents the effort exerted by management in order to achieve the individual indices, while the numerator represents the bonus for their achievement. It is not difficult to prove that maximization of equation (6) does not result in activity in the interests of the national economy. Whereas the bonus increase (ΔBz) can be accepted as the social evaluation of the achievement of a unit of a given task, the efforts exerted (Ns) cannot be considered as a correct proxy for the social costs of fulfilling these tasks. For example, the social costs of a marginal increase in output may be very high—the marginal costs may be greater than the increased value of output—whereas the effort exerted by the enterprise in achieving this increase may be small. Conversely, the social cost of decrease in costs may be very low[1] whereas the effort necessary to achieve this end may be considerable.

Since:

$$\frac{\Delta B_1}{\Delta N_1} : \frac{\Delta z_1}{\Delta c_1} \neq \frac{\Delta B_2}{\Delta N_2} : \frac{\Delta z_2}{\Delta c_2} \neq \ldots \neq \frac{\Delta Bn}{\Delta Nm} : \frac{\Delta zn}{\Delta cn} \qquad (8)$$

the maximization of equation (6) is not equivalent to maximization of equation (7). Therefore, given our assumptions, the award of bonuses for specialized success indicators does not lead to optimum results from the viewpoint of the national economy. This is tantamount to stating that specialized success indicators are not a suitable criterion for choice in an enterprise.

Undesirable enterprise activity, which results from the use of specialized success indicators, generally consists of maximizing certain indices—where the ratio $\dfrac{\Delta Bx}{\Delta Nx}$ is favourable—and neglecting other indices where this ratio is less favourable. Since we can reasonably assume that consecutive 'N' are increasing, an enterprise will not concentrate solely on one indicator, but after exhausting the easiest way of maximizing bonuses will turn to other indicators with the aim of maximizing the enterprise goal. The enterprise equilibrium resulting from this tactic (see equation (6)) is not, however, optimal from the national economy viewpoint.

There are two basic methods of improving the manner in which specialized success indicators function. The first consists of interrelating

---

[1] Decrease in costs is not costless itself. There is, however, substantial evidence that the input necessary to decrease costs is frequently characterized by a high degree of effectiveness.

the various specialized success indicators *via* the bonus conditions. The second consists of 'proper' differentiation of bonuses for the achievement of various tasks (see below under paragraph 2).

(1) Suppose that the enterprise has two specialized success indicators: value of gross output (B_1) and average cost per unit (B_2). According to equation (6) an enterprise will only turn its attention to decreasing costs when:

$$\frac{\Delta B_1}{\Delta N_1} \leq \frac{\Delta B_2}{\Delta N_2} \qquad (9)$$

In practice this can mean that for a considerable period of time, while $\frac{\Delta B_1}{\Delta N_1} > \frac{\Delta B_2}{\Delta N_2}$, the enterprise may concentrate entirely on increasing output. A change in the situation may be brought about by introducing a condition that the bonus for fulfilling the gross output plan will not be awarded unless at least 95 per cent of the planned reduction in costs is achieved. As a result, equation (9) may be attained considerably earlier than if the bonus condition had not been introduced.

This solution, however, is relatively ineffective. The system described, in contrast to synthetic success indicators, does not create a natural tendency for plan executants to reduce costs. The cost reduction plan has to be set by HAO, and efforts will be made by enterprises to ensure the plan is set as low as possible, since the necessity of reducing costs is considered one of the main obstacles to maximizing bonuses by maximizing value of gross output or commodity output.

(2) The manner in which specialized success indicators function can also be improved by introducing the differentiation between the bonuses awarded for fulfilling various tasks such as will lead to a situation in which:

$$\frac{\Delta B_1}{\Delta N_1} : \frac{\Delta z_1}{\Delta c_1} = \frac{\Delta B_2}{\Delta N_2} : \frac{\Delta z_2}{\Delta c_2} = \ldots = \frac{\Delta Bn}{\Delta Nm} : \frac{\Delta zn}{\Delta cn}. \qquad (10)$$

Differentiation of bonuses should, therefore, aim at neutralizing the difference between marginal costs and marginal managerial efforts necessary to achieve the same economic event.

In practice this means that indices which an enterprise will find difficult to achieve but which are economically effective, such as costs reduction, should be awarded high bonuses, whereas indices which are simple to achieve but of low economic effectiveness, such as increase in output for which there is little demand, should be awarded low or no bonuses. Theoretically speaking, such differentiation is possible. Experience has shown, however, that in practice it is very difficult to implement effectively. It should, moreover, be stressed that this constitutes a very complicated method of achieving an end which could be more easily attained by using synthetic success indicators.[1]

If the situation is such that the specialized success indicators used *do not cover* the whole activity sphere of an enterprise (Model II) then the situation is different and considerably inferior to that of our Model I discussed thus far. Let us assume again that two specialized success indicators are in use but the sum of their reception spheres is smaller than the enterprise activity sphere. The condition of equilibrium in the given enterprise is then as follows:
G = max., when

$$\frac{\Delta B_1}{\Delta N_1} = \frac{\Delta B_2}{\Delta N_2} = \frac{\Delta (B_1 + B_2)}{\Delta N_3} = \ldots = \frac{\Delta (B_1 + B_2)}{\Delta Nm} \qquad (11)$$

where
  N_1 and N_2 = efforts exerted in areas covered by success indicators;
  $N_3, N_4, \cdots, Nm$ = efforts exerted in areas not covered by success indicators.

This means that activities not covered by the reception sphere of success indicators are relegated to the role of instruments aiding the fulfilment of indices for which bonuses are paid. The enterprise is interested in them only in so far as any improvement in these activities brings about an improvement in results in areas covered by a bonus. If, for example, only decrease in average total costs were awarded a bonus and value of output carried none, then, assuming increasing marginal costs, an enterprise—as the textbooks tell us—would decrease output to the point at which marginal costs would equal average total costs. An output policy of this kind would be adopted irrespective of the demand situation and the ratio of enterprise marginal costs to price of its product.

It therefore seems clear that Model II is inferior to Model I. Enterprise equilibrium in Model II diverges to an even greater extent

---

[1] At given prices and marginal costs, profit (Pf) will bring about specific equilibrium in an enterprise or branch between the various profit-determining factors, for example, between volume of output and level of costs. This equilibrium may not, however, be acceptable to the CPB. The CPB may, for example, prefer enterprises in branch X to exert more effort in decreasing costs, rather than increasing output. By a suitable price change, for example, by decreasing the output prices of branch X, the CPB changes the internal structure of the profit-determining factors in branch X, as a result of which:

$$\frac{\Delta Pf_1}{\Delta c_1} < \frac{\Delta Pf_2}{\Delta c_2}$$

where c_1 = costs of increasing value of output,
  c_2 = input necessary to decrease costs,
which will result in inputs for increase of output being transferred to decrease of costs.

than the equilibrium achieved by a synthetic success indicator, since it can be assumed that:

$$\frac{\Delta B_3}{\Delta N_3} : \frac{\Delta z_3}{\Delta c_3} < \frac{\Delta (B_1 + B_2)}{\Delta N_3} : \frac{\Delta z_3}{\Delta c_3} \qquad (12)$$

where B_3 is the *direct* bonus effect of activity N_3, which has only *indirect* bonus effects (through its impact on B_1 and/or B_2) according to Model II.

Our discussion has been based so far on the implicit assumption that the enterprise information system is *constant* from the viewpoint of day-to-day management. In practice, however, in a non-parametric management model, a change in the information (stimulation) system by the introduction of *new* specialized success indicators (or new bonus conditions) is frequently an instrument used in influencing enterprise decisions.[1] The role of these new specialized success indicators is to draw the attention of enterprise management to those aspects of enterprise activity which have taken on special significance in the current economic situation.

This form of information transmission by the CPB mainly results from a policy of keeping prices unchanged for long periods although economic conditions are in continual flux. When prices are frozen only the following forms of information transmission can be used: administrative orders, changes in bonus levels, introduction of new bonus conditions, or introduction of new, specialized success indicators.

The latter form of information transmission is highly deficient, since its use brings about a proliferation of specialized success indicators, which in turn gives rise to the problem that the enterprise activity sphere is not fully covered by success indicators and also causes the information system to become too complex for effective day-to-day management.

The introduction of new specialized success indicators is simple to effect. It is considerably more difficult to cancel those already in existence. The difficulty lies in the fact that each specialized success indicator represents the income of the management personnel. Any attempt to decrease the nominal income is, as is well known, an undertaking of considerable difficulty. The elimination of any specialized success indicator is further made difficult in so far as every area covered by an indicator—and for that matter every area not

---

[1] Instead of introducing new specialized success indicators, the same effect can be achieved by empowering the HAO to introduce periodic, for example quarterly, changes in bonus conditions according to the requirements of the current economic situation. This system was introduced in Poland in 1965 by [*1*]. This question is discussed more fully in Ch. 6.

covered by an indicator as well—is important. An argument, therefore, that specialized success indicator X should not be eliminated since area X is economically important is very easily substantiated. Besides this, it is difficult to cancel a bonus for any activity if the activity is still being carried out as efficiently as before. As a result, proliferation of specialized success indicators ensues, since new ones are added as occasion demands without the previous indicators being cancelled. In 1960 when the greatest number of specialized success indicators was in force, at least fifty were being used simultaneously in Polish industry [see 5, pp. 109–21].[1]

Proliferation of specialized success indicators has two serious consequences as far as their role of criterion for choice in an enterprise is concerned. In the first place, as soon as specialized success indicators of a *narrow* reception sphere, such as for individual aspects of input, output, or use of resources, are introduced, the creation of a group of specialized success indicators covering the whole activity sphere of the enterprise becomes in practice, impossible, since a vast number would be necessary. The examples previously taken of value of output and level of costs as two specialized success indicators covering the whole reception sphere of a synthetic success indicator were not chosen at random. The use of specialized success indicators *as information carriers* from the CPB leads directly to Model II with all its negative consequences.

In the second place, proliferation of specialized success indicators also makes enterprise information systems highly complex. The more complex the information system of the enterprise, the greater the deficiency of specialized success indicators in their function as a decision-making criterion in an enterprise. In addition, the more complex the system the more difficult the evaluation of the economic performance of the enterprise; the greater the cost of collecting and processing information; and the more difficult it becomes to forecast enterprise behaviour correctly.

5.6.3 SYNTHETIC AND SPECIALIZED SUCCESS INDICATORS AS THE BASIS OF THE ENTERPRISE MANAGEMENT STIMULATION SYSTEM

All specialized success indicators contain inherent weaknesses as a basis for the management bonus system. This weakness lies in their very construction, since their reception sphere only covers certain characteristics of economic events, either from the input or output side.

[1] B. Fick points out that the proliferation of specialized indicators was a result of many different factors. In his opinion 'the initial and most important factor was the pressure exerted to raise wages and salaries and also the necessity of increasing differentials' [6, pp. 109–10] particularly in favour of enterprise management. 'New bonuses were normally introduced in cases where employees were expected to carry out certain [additional] economic tasks or expected to fulfil normal duties with particular care' [6, p. 115].

Increase in output cannot be correctly judged and rewarded if the input necessary to achieve the increase is unknown; nor can decrease in input be rewarded without information about its influence on output. It can be assumed that the bonus awarded for increasing the output of product X by a million zlotys reflects the social evaluation of this achievement. The given increase, however, in the output of product X may be the result of economic activity of different effectiveness. For example, the marginal cost of additional output may be higher, lower, or the same as the average cost. The bonus awarded on the basis of a specialized success indicator does not take this aspect of the matter directly into account. The link between output and input can only be created indirectly by prescribing that the bonus awarded on the basis of one success indicator may only be paid out on fulfilment of other success indicator(s).

The second weakness of specialized success indicators as a basis for the management stimulation system is that they frequently decrease the effectiveness of a bonus. For example, as a rule the total amount of bonus the management receive is limited to some maximum level, such as 80 per cent of their basic yearly salary. There are several reasons for setting such a ceiling, the main one being to ensure the proper proportion between management and workers' pay. If, however, the limited bonus fund is divided—and, moreover, unevenly divided—between numerous indicators, then the bonuses for achieving some specialized success indicators may represent a sum too small to be of any incentive value.[1]

The third weakness of specialized success indicators lies in the effect they have on the information system, which they render highly complex. Every specialized success indicator, of which there can be a considerable number in an enterprise, has its own reception sphere, its own rules regulating the size of the bonus funds, principles governing the sources from which the bonus may be paid, conditions for setting up and paying-out the bonus, and principles for dividing it among the management personnel. In this situation it becomes virtually impossible to differentiate the various bonuses properly in order to direct the allocation of management effort between rival tasks according to changing economic requirements or CPB preferences.

5.6.4 SYNTHETIC AND SPECIALIZED SUCCESS INDICATORS AS THE BASIS OF REGULATING THE ENTERPRISE FEEDING SYSTEM

The regulators in a dependent feeding system (see 4.1) may fulfil two roles.

In the first place an increase in the inflow of resources into an

---

[1] For example, the lowest bonuses awarded for the more important specialized success indicators in 1963 were: 23 zlotys (maximum 17,000) for 'economic progress', 23 zlotys (maximum 49,000) for 'technical progress', 31 zlotys (maximum 17,600) for volume of export [6, p. 113].

enterprise may be a function of the quality of enterprise performance. In this case the enterprise's success indicators should also fulfil the role of FS regulators. The success indicators would then play a dual incentive role, first directly through the stimulation system, and secondly indirectly through the feeding system. This interrelationship is illustrated in Diagram 4.4. The success indicators in their role of FS regulators simultaneously fulfil the function of allocation on the macroeconomic scale, for example, within an industrial association or ministry. The function of allocation consists in regulating the dependent flow of resources between enterprises and eventually also between industrial associations, on the basis of the greatest effectiveness, measured by the degree to which the success indicator in force is achieved.

In the second place, the increased inflow of resources to an enterprise may be a function of the 'real needs' of the enterprise, defined by the tasks set for the enterprise multiplied by the appropriate technical coefficients. In this case a division of the functions of success indicators and FS regulators between different analysers is normally recommended. It is argued that the analysers regulating the feeding system should only fulfil one function, that of allocation, and, moreover, that the criterion of allocation should not be the effectiveness of enterprise performance but the 'real needs' of the enterprise as defined above. It is also stressed that these analysers should not function as incentives. This is held to be of particular relevance in regulating the volume of the wage fund.[1]

It should be stated that the recommendation for constructing FS regulators of a non-incentive character is unfeasible. Separate FS regulators which would not simultaneously function as the formal basis for the management bonus system, i.e. as success indicators, could be

---

[1] B. Fick states that: 'The search for perfect production indices [success indicators and output indices] is of considerable importance, since they are indispensable to the achievement of two basic objectives. The first is to provide an objective measure of economic effectiveness and results of enterprise performance, which would constitute the basis of material incentives. Indices [success indicators] introduced for this task simultaneously determine the direction in which the enterprise exerts effort . . . The indicator which determines the enterprise wage fund defines a completely different task. The sole role of this indicator is to provide an objective measure of the size of the wage bill necessary to carry out production tasks. Therefore, while the indicators introduced into the mechanism of economic incentives are to define the desired direction of management's efforts, the purpose of the indicator defining the size of the wage bill is completely different. It can, therefore, be concluded that both types of indicators should be fundamentally different . . . The index defining the wage fund should not contain any incentives to specific types of behaviour nor should it negatively influence other behaviour. The wage bill indicator should have no incentive effect. It would be nonsensical to set tasks for an enterprise and to guarantee a given increase in the wage fund and in the average wage for fulfilling them . . .', since for the fulfilment of these tasks '. . . there may be no objective necessity to increase the wage bill at all' [6, pp. 308–9]. The terms 'wage bill' and 'wage fund' are used as synonyms of the Polish term *fundusz plac*.

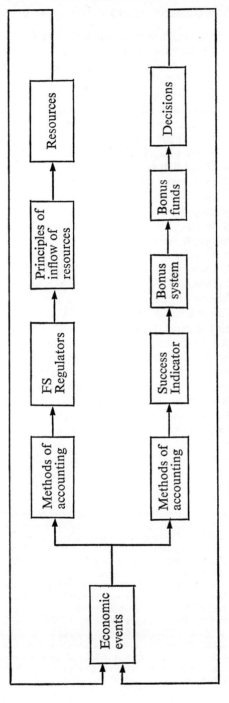

Diagram 5.4 The indirect incentive role of FS regulators

introduced. FS regulators, however, which do not function indirectly as incentives by influencing economic events according to the interrelationship presented in Diagram 5.3 cannot be constructed.

FS regulators which define the size of the wage fund must, of necessity, fulfil both a direct and an indirect incentive role, since the wage fund constitutes the main source of income of all enterprise employees including management.[1] All these questions, however, constitute a separate problem which will be discussed later in Ch. 7. At present the question of specialized success indicators functioning simultaneously as FS regulators requires attention. It is not difficult to prove that specialized success indicators do not function effectively as FS regulators.

In the first place, as we have already tried to prove in 5.6.3, specialized success indicators do not reflect the quality of enterprise performance correctly. If, therefore, a dependent feeding system is to be regulated by the economic effectiveness of the enterprise, specialized success indicators provide a wrong basis for regulating the inflow of resources.

In the second place, the degree to which the specialized success indicators are achieved—in most cases—is not a correct indication of the real needs of an enterprise for resources. A vivid illustration is to be found in the value of gross output index which for many years always fulfilled, and even now frequently fulfils, the dual role of specialized success indicator and wage fund regulator. Originally this was through the direct relationship between fulfilment of the value of gross output plan and the planned wage fund (with an extra 1 per cent added to the enterprise wage fund for every 1 per cent overfulfilment of plan); after 1960 a coefficient of less than one was used.[2] This indicator, however, does not reflect correctly the enterprise's 'real needs' for labour. It is well known that the cost of labour per unit of output depends primarily on the labour intensity of output and not on the value of the output expressed either in constant or in transfer prices. Attempts to use other specialized success indicators simultaneously as indices of the

---

[1] I am pleased to note that the validity of these arguments has been accepted: 'One has to agree with J. G. Zielinski that complete incentive neutrality of [output] indicator cannot be achieved. One cannot construct FS regulators which would not function indirectly as incentives, due to the influence they exert on economic events. These regulators must fulfil an indirect as well as a direct incentive function, since the wage fund constitutes the main source of income for employees and for management [see 25]. Since as experience to date shows, J. G. Zielinski's thesis seems to be correct, those who postulate the necessity of ensuring the incentive neutrality of output indices must revise their views' [7, pp. 219–20].

[2] 'An attempt to eliminate the automatic correction of the planned wage fund by reforming the methods of controlling the fund took place in 1963. It was, however, limited to certain branches of industry only ... The new system was based on the wage fund reserves created in ministries and industrial associations to be used to increase enterprise wage funds' [6, p. 266, see also pp. 259–79]. This reform is analysed in some detail in Ch. 7.

real needs of an enterprise for resources also proved unsuccessful, since numerous basic flaws came to light (see Ch. 7).

Since it was found impossible to construct specialized success indicators which would provide a correct basis for both the stimulation system and the feeding system—other solutions were sought. Two types of solution were considered: (1) The construction of separate FS regulators whose incentive functions would be as neutral as possible or would be correctly directed, and whose main function would be to serve in the optimum control of resources, according to the principle that the flow of resources should be a function of the real needs of an enterprise. (2) Numerous attempts were made to find what was termed a universal indicator on which the financial incentive to the enterprise management could be based, and by which the wage fund could be regulated both at the planning and plan implementing stage, and which, moreover, would regulate the whole dependent feeding system. Both these approaches are discussed in Ch. 7.

5.7 Problems of Application

5.7.1 THE CONDITIONS NECESSARY FOR THE EFFECTIVE FUNCTIONING OF SYNTHETIC SUCCESS INDICATORS

The preceding analysis of synthetic and specialized success indicators in their role of criterion in enterprise decision-making might well be considered somewhat one-sided if the difficulties in applying synthetic success indicators were not dealt with. These difficulties are, mainly although not entirely, due to the fact that conditions in which the synthetic success indicators can function effectively are not easy to create under the present circumstances in East European countries.

A *The Problem of Prices*

In order that equation (7)—see 5.6.2—should not only govern enterprise equilibrium but also ensure enterprise behaviour advantageous to the national economy, prices must reflect correctly the marginal rates of transformation. If this is not the case, the results of micro- and macro-economic calculation will diverge.[1] The construction

---

[1] J. Mujzel rightly points out that '. . . the direct objective of an enterprise can only be provided by a synthetic success indicator . . . However, certain conditions must be established if profit is to be used effectively. Above all a proper system of economic data, determining the enterprise behaviour, must be constructed . . . If these conditions are not fulfilled the enterprise objective of profit maximization causes serious disruptions and losses' [*14*, pp. 73–4]. And later: 'It seems that by disregarding the above, certain economists have been able to use empirical evidence against the role of profit as the direct enterprise objective, and, in turn, as the main performance indicator and basis of material incentives. By pointing out the negative consequences of profit maximizing behaviour in cases where the conditions for effective functioning of profit as a success indicator were lacking, these economists have made their criticisms and observations into general theoretical formulae which cannot be justified' [*14*, fn. 58, p. 74].

of a correct system (or systems) of prices, which would function properly in both micro- and macro-economic calculation is a difficult task. Until this problem is solved a management formula based on a synthetic success indicator may give rise to numerous negative side-effects, and the use of specialized success indicators may be economically unavoidable.

B *The Nature of the Market*

Profit maximizing behaviour leads to socially beneficial results only where a competitive buyers' market exists. The competitive buyers' market exerts economic pressure as a result of which, in order to maximize profit, cost must be systematically decreased, new, more attractive goods must be produced, and the product-mix must be constantly adapted to customers' demand. Conversely, as experience shows, where there is a sellers' market, easier methods exist of maximizing profit, mainly by increasing prices. Even when prices are set or controlled by the state, enterprises which have a secure market for their output have no incentive to decrease costs, introduce new products, or adapt their product-mix to buyer demand, since there is no difficulty in achieving sales objectives—and therefore the rate of profit which has been calculated into the price—without undertaking these measures, which demand considerable management effort.

A buyers' market is not easily achieved in a rapidly developing economy, which, as a rule, has a sellers' market or at best what is termed a 'shallow buyers' market', which exerts only limited economic pressure on producers.

5.7.2 THE FLAWS INHERENT IN SUCCESS INDICATORS

Although the main obstacle in introducing synthetic success indicators lies in the difficulty of creating conditions in which they can function effectively, it should also be kept in mind that these indicators are not free of the weaknesses inherent in all success indicators.

(1) Synthetic success indicators—like all others—leave the problem of the time horizon of decision-making by plan executants open. The problem is important, since maximizing profit may, and as a rule does, give rise to different behaviour in the long and in the short term. It should also be remembered that profit in the short term is frequently contrary to the interests of the national economy, since, for example, repairs are ignored or resources to cover innovation and technical progress are not budgeted for.

An enterprise management cannot be guaranteed a sufficiently long-term horizon in undertaking economic decisions solely on the basis of a correctly constructed success indicator, synthetic or specialized. A whole series of factors is necessary, of which the most important are as follows. (a) The principle must be accepted that the basis on which an enterprise management is awarded bonuses is not changed annually but is set for a long period. This principle is called the comparatively constant basis of comparison of a success indicator (see 6.2.1). (b) The conditions in which an enterprise functions must be stabilized. This relates primarily to: the principles on which the enterprise functions, the level of enterprise obligations to the state, i.e. the setting of what are termed long-term financial norms (see 7.2), and supply conditions. (c) The role and importance of long-term planning both in enterprises and in industry as a whole must be increased.

(2) Synthetic success indicators, like all success indicators, do not resolve the problem of what are termed external effects in production (see [24, pp. 37–43] and literature quoted therein). Some of the external effects can be 'internalized' by a suitable price policy. If, for example, an enterprise is obliged to pay fines for polluting air and water, then these side-effects of production activity become 'internal' since they are included by the enterprise in calculating costs. The majority of external costs, however, are difficult to introduce into the economic calculations of an enterprise. As a result, where an activity has pronounced external effects the necessity arises, either for the CPB to take decisions instead of the enterprise, or for a method of correcting enterprise micro-economic calculation, in order to eliminate the gap between the results of micro- and macro-economic calculations.

The following conclusions can be drawn from the preceding discussion of success indicators.

(1) The superiority of synthetic success indicators can only be proved in practice in certain economic conditions. If these conditions are not fulfilled, specialized success indicators may constitute the most effective practical solution to the problem. However, since the use of synthetic success indicators is potentially much more advantageous, an attempt to create conditions which would allow them to function properly is economically justifiable.

(2) When the external conditions which would allow synthetic success indicators to function effectively are only partially fulfilled, a practical solution may be to use a synthetic success indicator as the enterprise goal, but with the imposition of certain constraints in the form of administrative rules. These constraints would supplement or replace imperfect price information, providing the pressure normally exerted by a buyers' market or by competition. For example, a constraint could take the form of a planned target of introduction of new products or fulfilment of technical progress tasks. It would seem, however, that if the synthetic success indicator is still to remain the real goal of the enterprise the constraints should be (a) few, (b) only those which cannot be easily transmitted parametrically, (c) relatively constant, (d) different in various branches of industry.

Points b, c, and d require brief explanations.

The constraints (point b) should not take the place of information which can be relatively simply transmitted parametrically by price differentiation. The function of constraints is to supplement parametric information in situations when the use of parameters presents difficulties, i.e. when a considerable price differentiation, unacceptable for other reasons, would have to be introduced if the parameters were to function effectively. A new product serves as a good example. Where a secure and easy market exists for a given product and where there are considerable possibilities of increasing profit by decreasing costs, it is difficult to encourage an enterprise to innovate by means of prices. Economic pressure in this case could only be achieved by allowing foreign competition, frequently unacceptable for a variety of reasons. In this situation, a constraint in the form of a planned task for introducing new products, for example, as a bonus condition, may be justified.

The necessity of relatively constant constraints (point c) results from the above discussion of point b. Constraints should be introduced as a result of specific economic situations in enterprises or branches of industry where, for example, there is a lack of effective competition. Their function is to induce a desired type of enterprise behaviour, such as the production of a new product, which would not take place solely on the basis of profit maximization. The specific conditions in which a given enterprise or groups of enterprises function are relatively constant as a rule. Constraints, therefore, should also be constant. Frequent changes of constraints, such as, for example, quarterly changes of bonus conditions (see 6.2.2) are evidence that the constraints are being used in place of, rather than as a supplement to, parameters in situations where, because of specific economic conditions, steering is difficult to effect by means of ciphered information.

The necessity of differentiating constraints (point d) is evident from discussion of points b and c. Constraints must be differentiated since their role specifically requires that they reflect the particular conditions of a given enterprise or branch of industry. It should be noted that the use of constraints in conjunction with synthetic success indicators can also be justified in cases where pronounced external effects arise which cannot be internalized by the price system.

(3) The discussion in paragraph 2 leads to the conclusion that the enterprise's information system, and looking ahead to Ch. 6, the stimulation system, require constant analysis and improvement according to the requirements of the changing economic situation. The thesis that a success indicator can be constructed which would, by itself, radically improve enterprise behaviour is, of course, unrealistic. Where a synthetic success indicator is used, the need for consistency between the micro- and macro-economic calculations remains, but the method by

which consistency between the two calculations is ensured, radically changes. Instead of administrative orders and changes in the management formula, parameters become the main carriers of information on changes in economic conditions and CPB preferences.

(4) Whatever the form of the management model and information system, the price system always plays a leading role. Constant efforts are necessary to perfect it and adapt it to the function it fulfils. In a *mixed* management model there is a problem of frequent inconsistency of open information and parametric information. Some Polish economists believe that a possible solution might lie in constructing a system of neutral prices, that is, of prices which do not create preferences for any particular product-mix or for any particular production method, or at least minimize these. Neutral prices, therefore, would cause plan executants to be particularly sensitive to open information transmitted from the CPB and also to customers' demand [see e.g. *15* and *23*].[1] The question of what prices fulfil the condition of neutrality most effectively depends in turn to a large extent on the success indicators used [see *21*]. In a *parametric* management model, however, it is important to ensure that prices transmit correct information to an enterprise on changes in external economic conditions, since agreement between the results of macro- and micro-economic calculations depends on them. In this model, the range of the reception sphere of the success indicator defines the range of information which may be transmitted parametrically.

References to Chapter Five

1. Decree 130 of the CM of 4 May 1964, on bonuses for white collar workers in state industrial enterprises, *MP*, 32, 1964.
2. Decree 276 of the CM of 28 October 1965, on the financial system of centrally planned industrial associations and enterprises, *MP*, 61, 1965.
3. Decree of the Chairman of the Planning Commission of the CM and Minister of Finance of 10 August 1966, on the principles of setting profitability indices, *MP*, 42, 1966.
4. Decree of the CM and the Central Council of the Trade Unions of 1 July 1970, on economic incentives for employees of centrally planned industrial enterprises and associations for the period 1971–5 in [*16*, pp. 5–29].
5. Decree 176 of the CM of 9 November 1970, on the financial system in centrally planned state enterprises, *kombinaty*, and industrial and construction associations, *MP*, 40, 1970.
6. Fick B.: *Bodzce ekonomiczne w przemysle* (Economic Incentives in Industry), Warsaw, 1965.
7. Fick B.: *Polityka zatrudnienia a place i bodzce* (Employment Policy, Wages and Incentives), Warsaw, 1970.

[1] The scope of this book does not leave room for more extensive discussion of the theory of prices or—more broadly—information carriers, under different management mechanisms. The author, when feeling optimistic, hopes to return to this subject at some future date.

8. Glowczyk J., ed.: *IV Plenum KC PZPR. Zmiany w systemie planowania i zarzadzania. Slowniczek pojec* (IVth Plenum of CC of PUWP. Changes in the System of Planning and Management. Small Glossary of Terms), Warsaw, 1965.
9. Gordon L. J.: *Economics for Consumers*, New York, 1944.
10. Hitch Charles J.: 'Sub-optimization in Operations Problems.' *Journal of the Operations Research Society of America*, 1, May 1953.
11. Kierczynski T., Wojciechowska U.: *Finanse przedsiebiorstw socjalistycznych* (Finances of Socialist Enterprises), Warsaw, 1967.
12. McKean R. N.: *Efficiency in Government through Systems Analysis*, New York, 1967.
13. Misiak M., ed.: *Bodzce ekonomiczne w przedsiebiorstwie przemyslowym* (Economic Incentives in the Industrial Enterprise), Warsaw, 1963.
14. Mujzel J.: *Przedsiebiorstwo socjalistyczne a rynek* (The Socialist Enterprise and the Market), Warsaw, 1966.
15. Nowicki J.: 'The Impact of Prices on the Functioning of Industrial Enterprises' in [*20*, pp. 226–64].
16. *Nowy system bodzcow materialnego zainteresowania. Zbior podstawowych dokumentow* (New System of Economic Incentives. Collection of Basic Documents), Warsaw, 1970.
17. Plichcinski E.: 'Comments on the Goal Function of Socialist Enterprise', *E*, 4, 1967.
18. Pohorille M., ed.: *Ekonomia polityczna socjalizmu* (The Political Economy of Socialism), Warsaw, 1968.
19. *Problemy teorii gospodarki socjalistycznej. Pamieci Profesora Dra Aleksego Wakara* (Essays on the Theory of Socialist Economy. *In memoriam* of the late Professor Aleksy Wakar), Warsaw, 1970.
20. *Przedsiebiorstwo w polskim systemie spoleczno-ekonomicznym* (The Enterprise in the Polish Socio-Economic System), Warsaw, 1967.
21. Wakar A. and Zielinski J. G.: 'Socialist Operational Price Systems', *AER*, March 1963.
22. Wieckowski J.: *Rola zysku w kierowaniu produkcja* (The Role of Profit in the Management of Production), Warsaw, 1965.
23. —— 'The Functions of Synthetic Indicators in the Management Mechanism' in [*19*, pp. 419–54].
24. Zielinski J. G.: *Rachunek ekonomiczny w socjalizmie* (Economic Calculation in a Socialist Economy), Warsaw, 1967.
25. —— 'Success Indicators in a Socialist Enterprise', *E*, 1, 1967.
26. —— 'Reply to E. Plichcinski's "Comments" ', *E*, 4, 1967.
27. *IV Plenum KC PZPR. 27–28 lipca 1965 r. Podstawowe dokumenty* (IVth Plenum of the Central Committee of PUWP. 27–28 July 1965. Basic Documents), Warsaw, 1965.

CHAPTER SIX

THE STIMULATION SYSTEM OF A SOCIALIST ENTERPRISE

6.1 Economic Incentives

6.1.1 THE CONCEPT OF ECONOMIC INCENTIVES, TYPES OF INCENTIVES AND THEIR FUNCTIONS

An extensive system of incentives is essential for effective performance by plan executants. By incentives we mean ways of motivating people to realize a given objective. Two main types of stimuli are used: economic, where the encouragement is material, and non-economic, also termed non-material or moral incentives, where the encouragement is non-material, such as medals, diplomas, or honours.

The basic economic incentive is pay. The pay of any particular employee depends on the category to which he or she belongs. This in turn depends on the skill grading and pay scales in force. If a promotion system is functioning efficiently it activates the incentives contained in the wage and salary scales, encouraging employees to improve their qualifications and undertake more difficult, responsible work, on which promotion is based.

The basic wage is, on the whole, not subject to variation, in order to ensure a certain minimum stability of the household budgets. However, this weakens the interrelationship between an employee's performance and his material situation. The interrelationship can be strengthened by providing for dismissal for unsatisfactory performance, but this has a number of weaknesses: (a) it is not particularly effective under full employment, since a dismissed employee has no difficulty in finding similar work in another enterprise; (b) is frequently unjust, since a single set of unsatisfactory results is not necessarily proof that an employee is unsuitable for the job; (c) involves a certain social cost, since a dismissed employee will as a rule be unemployed for a transition period even when demand for labour is high.

In order to ensure the proper relationship between performance and level of remuneration without affecting the principle of stability of basic pay, what is termed the variable part of pay was introduced by the CPB.[1] This variable part of pay is related to performance. The system

[1] The first such attempt in Polish industry took place as early as 1946 when a collective bonus for the whole labour force was introduced as an element in the division of enterprise profit [see *17*, p. 25].

of the variable part of pay has been called the stimulation system (see 4.1) in this study. Henceforth, by incentives we mean those in the variable part of pay, unless otherwise stated.

In a planned economy the object of a system of economic incentives is to encourage: (1) 'optimal planning', i.e. taut but realistic planning (see 6.2.1); (2) economic behaviour in the process of plan fulfilment.

The direction in which the planning and implementation efforts are made depends, however, on the tasks for which the variable part of pay is awarded. These tasks are defined by the information system of the enterprise. Success indicators, as we have seen, constitute the link between the information and stimulation systems. As a result, if the incentive system is misdirected, a situation can arise in which it operates effectively, that is to say, employees are stimulated to considerable effort, yet negative economic results are achieved, since plan executants are pursuing the wrong goals. This was frequently the case with the numerous incentive systems tried in Polish industry during the last twenty-five years and remains one of the basic weaknesses of the present management formula.[1]

If the incentive system does not fulfil one of its functions efficiently, for example, does not encourage optimal planning, then other economic instruments, as a rule administrative orders, must be used. We see, therefore, the close interrelationship between the effectiveness of the incentive system and the management model; the more effective the incentive system, the more parametric the management of the national economy can be and vice versa.

6.1.2 CONDITIONS FOR EFFICIENT OPERATION OF THE INCENTIVE SYSTEM

For an incentive system to operate efficiently, several conditions must be fulfilled, and above all: (1) the correct degree of 'intensity of incentives' must be found; (2) consistency between different information carriers and incentives must be ensured; (3) conditions permitting and/or enforcing activity consistent with the direction of incentives must be created; (4) consistency between economic and moral incentives must be ensured; (5) sufficient time must be allowed for employees to become adjusted to the incentive system; (6) the incentive system must be properly coordinated at all levels of the plan implementing apparatus.

(1) The optimal degree of bonus intensity is difficult to determine and in practice has to be found by trial and error. The only guideline which theory and experience can give is a warning against too low or too high

---

[1] Abundant illustration of this thesis can be found in [2; and 18, passim] for the period till 1967, and in [20 and 34] where a description of the latest incentive system, which was to be introduced in 1971 but which was abandoned after the December 1970 events, will be found (1.4.2.D).

bonus intensity. Too low intensity does not provide real encouragement to greater effort; too high intensity, on the other hand, also has certain negative consequences: (a) if the bonus becomes a decisive factor in the household budget of an employee, for example when it reaches 30 to 50 per cent of basic pay, a tendency to achieve the bonus at any cost results, which frequently leads to uneconomic behaviour; (b) at the same time a tendency arises for the HAO to try to justify non-fulfilment of plans and to award bonuses where planned results have not been achieved in order to avoid disrupting the household budgets of employees. Once this practice becomes established, any incentive system ceases to be effective.

A certain threshold exists, therefore, above which an increase in bonus intensity brings a strong reaction, and also a ceiling, above which there is no further improvement. The problem of economic policy is to choose the correct degree of bonus intensity, between the two extremes, according to the particular tasks and prevailing conditions in a specific branch of industry and in the national economy as a whole.

(2) The effectiveness of an incentive system requires the elimination of inconsistencies within the system itself and also between the incentives and other information carriers. Where a system contains many success indicators, as described in Ch. 5, inconsistencies frequently arise between different types of incentives. For example, bonuses for value of gross output tend to cause a rise, and bonuses for cost reduction a fall, in costs of production. The effects of such contradictory stimuli on the equilibrium of an enterprise have been discussed in 5.6.

A second factor which can limit the effectiveness of an incentive is inconsistency between the actions indicated by the incentive and open information. Where an economic unit is faced with a situation in which administrative orders are inconsistent with incentives, the consequence, as described in 4.4, is a compromise between the two, the product of both forces, and difficult to foresee with any degree of accuracy. The result of such inconsistencies is a decrease in effectiveness of both incentives and administrative orders. It should be stressed that in a situation in which the same information is transmitted by several methods, for example, when information on the desired product-mix is transmitted simultaneously in the form of a plan indicator, through price differentiation, and through a bonus for fulfilling the product-mix plan, the danger of inconsistencies between the various types of information arises, since it is difficult to ensure that each of the information carriers contains exactly the same information. In the above situation the result can be that the plan indicator defines one product-mix, the price system a variation of this product-mix, and the bonus system another variation. The consequence of using three different carriers for transmitting the same information is that not only is the reliability of the system not improved, but it is, in fact, decreased. The situation would be entirely different if a substitute information carrier were introduced when a given carrier proved ineffective. For example, with a constant cost curve, price is not sufficient to determine volume of output. In this case, open information from the industrial association, such as, 'we can guarantee X volume of sales of your output', can really improve the effectiveness of the price system, since it does not provide an inconsistent version of information previously transmitted by the price system, but additional relevant information. An improvement in the reliability of the system can, therefore, be ensured where additional information carriers are held in reserve to deal with situations in which the existing carriers are ineffective. Where the information carrier is functioning effectively, however, the reserve information carrier should have zero value, that is, should not be used.

It should also be kept in mind that the stimulation system does not constitute the sole source of incentives for an enterprise. Incentives are also created by the wage system and the feeding system. Incentives generated by one system may offset the deficiencies of another to some extent. Inconsistencies, however, between incentives set by different systems can also arise. The stimulation system, for example, may encourage different activity from the feeding system (see Ch. 7). The necessity, therefore, of coordinating incentives is not limited to those within the stimulation system, but extends to all incentives in the enterprise.

(3) The conditions permitting and/or enforcing activity consistent with incentives can be divided into internal and external. Internal constraints means primarily the authority sphere of an enterprise, which should not constitute an obstacle to the activity indicated by the stimulation system.[1] External constraints, which can paralyse the effectiveness of the incentive system, stem above all from the feeding system. The central allocation and use control of factors of production has the same result as the constraints on the wage fund, namely, to prevent substitution encouraged by the incentive system. The nature of the market is of particular importance. As we have already pointed out several times, where there is a sellers' market, no incentive system can function effectively. Experience proves that, where buyers have no effective control, even the most sophisticated stimulation system cannot ensure a high standard of performance on the part of producers.

(4) The next condition for efficient operation of economic incentives is consistency between economic and other incentives. Even a correctly constructed economic incentive system cannot function effectively if it is inconsistent with current political and social objectives. It is particu-

---

[1] For example, an enterprise might be able to reduce total costs quite considerably with a small increase in the wage bill. The authority sphere of the enterprise, however (the wage fund limit), may not permit this.

larly difficult to ensure consistency between economic and 'moral' incentives in the initial period after a change in success indicators (see 5.1.3). The problem of changing success indicators leads to our next condition.

(5) It is generally accepted that no incentives can be effective in the short term, and require a considerable period of time to allow employees to adjust to them [see *18*, p. 148]. Incentives are effective when employees as a rule act in ways consistent with them. All radical changes in the incentive system involve basic changes in the criterion of choice of economic activity. It is obvious that an operationally meaningful acceptance of a new criterion of choice by employees cannot be achieved easily or rapidly.[1] Each change requires time to take root and for employees to adapt to it. This time can only be shortened by two methods: either by increasing the material attractiveness of the incentives, which is not always possible, or by intensive propaganda which implies consistency between material and moral incentives. In order to achieve this, however, success indicators must constitute not only the basis of the bonus system but also the basis of approbation on the part of superiors and society in general. Synthetic success indicators never achieved such 'status' in communist Poland.

(6) An essential condition for the effective operation of economic incentives is proper coordination of incentives at different levels of the plan implementing apparatus, that is, in enterprises and industrial associations. Two situations must be distinguished here: (1) where the incentives in an enterprise are fulfilling all their functions efficiently, that is, are encouraging taut and realistic planning and effective plan fulfilment, then the incentives in the industrial association must be consistent with those in the enterprise; (2) where the incentives in an enterprise do not fulfil all their functions efficiently, the creation of certain conflicts of interest between enterprises and industrial associations in spheres not covered by bonuses in the enterprise may be justified.

The following example illustrates the latter. If the incentives in an enterprise are based on *plan* indices (see 6.2.1), for example on a planned profit index, then there is a natural tendency on the part of the enterprise to try to get the lowest possible plan indices. The negative consequences of this tendency can be considerably reduced if the industrial associations are *not* awarded bonuses for planned profit but for actual increase in profit in the given branch of industry compared with the

---

[1] This was highly important in the period 1960–3. 'For fifteen years there had been a set of powerful incentives to maximize value of output and, as a result, employees were convinced of the prime importance of the output plan above all other tasks. The introduction of the financial result as the synthetic success indicator, therefore, constituted a basic change in the direction of incentives . . .' [*18*, p. 149].

9

preceding period. The creation of this conflict of interest is a way of severing the mutual interest of industrial associations and enterprises in minimizing planned tasks.

Practical experience in Poland has clearly shown the key importance of ensuring proper coordination of incentives in enterprises and industrial associations. An incentive system partly based on a synthetic success indicator and containing a mechanism stimulating taut planning was introduced into industrial enterprises in 1960. The system awarded higher bonuses for achieving declared additional targets than for corresponding plan overfulfilment. The aim of the system was to encourage enterprises to put forward what were termed counter-plans, higher than the obligatory indices received from the industrial associations. This reform, however, was not accompanied by changes in the stimulation system of industrial associations, which were still awarded bonuses for fulfilling the value of gross output plan and for not exceeding the planned cost of production [see *18*, pp. 151–65]. A basic contradiction was thus introduced between incentives in industrial associations and in enterprises. The consequences of the contradiction are vividly described by B. Fick, economic adviser to the Minister of Finance: 'This contradiction above all paralysed the incentives for enterprises to raise plans themselves. This incentive system gave them an understandable interest in being set the lowest and easiest targets of accumulation [i.e. profit plus turnover tax] by the industrial associations, so they could increase their bonus fund by raising the targets. Since the influence of enterprises in determining this target was not decisive, the consequences would not have been serious had the industrial associations, for their part, been interested in setting high plan tasks. The industrial associations, however, also had an interest in setting low planned levels of accumulation and output for enterprises, since the bonus of the industrial association employees depended on their fulfilment . . . At the stage of setting plan directives the interests of industrial association and enterprise coincided. At the following stage, when enterprises were working out their technical-economic plans, their interest lay in raising the level of the tasks received. To the industrial association, however, this represented danger to their own quarterly bonuses. At the same time, the risk of not fulfilling a plan was less serious for an enterprise than for the industrial association. The enterprise, at most, would have its bonus fund reduced, the industrial association would lose it completely' [*18*, pp. 157–8]. This inconsistency between the incentives for industrial associations and enterprises was one of the basic reasons for the failure of the 1960 reforms of the bonus system, which was abandoned three years later [see *18*, pp. 131–2 and 146–50]. This means that, as a rule, it is essential to use the same success indicator for both enterprises and industrial associations. When enterprise incentives are not fulfilling all their functions effectively and this cannot be remedied then—as a temporary measure—the use of different success indicators at industrial association and enterprise level may be justified. Its purpose would be the conscious introduction of conflict of interest between these two levels of the industrial hierarchy in an effort to counterbalance the negative side-effects of the defective incentive system in the enterprises.

6.1.3 MISDIRECTED AND UNINTENDED INCENTIVES

One of the basic difficulties in constructing an incentive system and, more generally, a management mechanism, is the problem of eliminating misdirected incentives (*antybodzce*) inherent in the system. For brevity's sake they will be termed misincentives. By misincentives we understand those side-effects of incentives which are not in the interests of the national economy [see *18*, pp. 10–11; *29*, p. 18]. The misincentives created by a bonus system can sometimes be so strong that their elimination or at least neutralization can become the main condition for improving the efficiency of the economy.[1]

The side-effects of an incentive system take many different forms, sometimes entirely unanticipated by the inventors of the system. An example of misincentives is where employees try to get their bonus without exerting greater effort, for instance by increasing sub-contracting (see 5.4.3), or where a particular bonus condition is fulfilled at any cost, even to the detriment of performance in areas where no bonus or only a relatively low bonus is paid (see 5.6.2).

The history of bonus systems in Polish industry in the last twenty-five years abounds in examples of powerful misincentives. For example, the application of value of output in transfer prices as a success indicator stimulated a tendency to distort the product-mix in favour of products with a high accumulation rate.[2] The tendency to maximize value of output—irrespective of whether the output is calculated in ex-factory prices or transfer prices, and whether it is gross output or commodity output—leads to neglect of production costs.

---

[1] 'Whatever our view of the effectiveness of material incentives, one factor is surely indisputable: misincentives, that is, incentives operating contrary to the desired aims, must be eliminated' [*29*, p. 18].

[2] For example, according to the 1963 report of the Highest Chamber of Control on the Sira knitwear factories in Sieradz, in comparison to plan targets output of baby clothes decreased by 30,000 items (accumulation rate 8·4 per cent) and output of men's underwear by 120,000 items (accumulation rate 27·3 per cent). Output of ladies' cardigans and blouses together increased by 135,000 items (accumulation rate 63 per cent). The incentives to overfulfil the accumulation plan were so strong that representatives of all the relevant organizations in the enterprise supported these changes which, from the point of view of market supplies, were, of course, undesirable. As the above report states, these changes were introduced by a decision of the Workers' Self-management Conference '. . . in order to guarantee fulfilment of annual tasks' [*29*, p. 21]. Accumulation is turnover tax plus profit.

The danger of misincentives arises in *all* incentive systems, both those based on specialized success indicators and those based on synthetic indicators. For instance, where bonuses are awarded for volume of profit the following tendencies may arise: to increase prices, for example by presenting price-setting organs with inflated cost calculations; to concentrate on production of the most profitable product-mix; to worsen quality of goods with fixed prices; to make cuts in investment needed to reduce pollution such as treating sewage, and investment necessary for safe and hygienic standards of work. Any new stimulation system therefore requires detailed analysis to determine whether side-effects (misincentives) will arise, so that counter-measures can be taken. These measures can take various forms ranging from the introduction of an extended system of prices for economic events, such as fines for decrease in quality, to the administrative enforcement of sewage treatment. If disincentives are to be avoided, a radical change is frequently necessary in the economic conditions in which an enterprise functions, for example, a buyers' market may have to be created to ensure that the customer can effectively exert pressure on the supplier in respect of quality, specification, delivery dates, and prices.

Although all stimulation systems generate negative side-effects, these can be eliminated more easily from some types of system than others. As we have already indicated in Ch. 5, incentives based on synthetic success indicators can in principle be freed from negative side-effects, although the conditions necessary for this may be difficult to fulfil, since, for example, internal prices may have to be eliminated or a buyers' market created. Where the incentive system, however, is based on specialized success indicators, misincentives cannot be eliminated, owing to the very nature of these indicators and the type of stimulation system by which they must be accompanied. It is, however, possible, in some cases particularly, to reduce their misincentive effects.

Beside the misincentives created by a stimulation system, the management mechanism frequently generates 'unintended incentives'. Unintended incentives can be defined as incentives arising spontaneously from certain aspects of a management mechanism and not intended by the constructors of the system. The classical example of an unintended incentive usually quoted is the automatic bank correction of the enterprise wage fund which will be discussed in greater detail in Ch. 7. In creating the system, the aim was to ensure that any increase in the wage fund of an enterprise would be proportional to the increase in the real labour requirements of the enterprise. The system, in fact, proved to be one of the most powerful incentives in the Polish economy, stronger than many specially created bonus systems. Moreover, its effect was negative, and had far-reaching repercussions.

Unintended incentives usually appear because the interrelationships within a management mechanism have been overlooked or underestimated. Unintended incentives, as a rule, arise in the feeding system of an enterprise or the information transmission system from the CPB. If the interrelationships in the management mechanism are fully appreciated, the unintended incentives can be foreseen and correctly directed, though, as a rule, unintended incentives cannot be entirely eliminated—because of the high degree of interrelationship existing between the various elements of a management mechanism—and it is frequently very difficult to redirect them. As we have pointed out, all types of feeding systems have an incentive function, through the relationship: resources → economic events → success indicators. This interrelationship cannot be broken, but the consequences can be foreseen and the system suitably modified *ex post* if not always *ex ante*. The same applies, for example, to the price system. The level of prices and the principles on which they are set influence the quantitative expression of economic events and the reception sphere of the success indicator, and thus the relationship: success indicators → bonus funds → management bonuses. This interrelationship also cannot be broken as a rule, but again its results can be foreseen and, consequently, price ratios and the principles on which they are set can be constructed so as to ensure that the incentives they create encourage behaviour which is in the interests of the national economy.

It should be stressed that many misincentives could be avoided if economic models were set up and examined before a change in the management mechanism is put into effect. For example, the basic principles of a given incentive system could be formulated in a model which would permit: (a) definition of the reception sphere of the success indicator in the light of factors which influence it (see Table 5.1); (b) research into the manner in which the success indicator reacts to economic events and external information; (c) definition of the direction and intensity of the proposed incentives; (d) a check on the degree to which the conditions necessary for the incentive system to function efficiently are met (see 4.5, 5.7, and 6.1.2); (e) definition of the expected misincentives and unintended incentives, on the basis of points a to d, and thus of the probable strategy and tactics of enterprise management; (f) comparison of the latter with the management behaviour which the new incentive system was expected to bring about; (g) formulation of any corrective measures needed before putting the new system into operation.

The most likely aspects which may require improvement are: the construction of the success indicator; the factors influencing the reception sphere (or manner of reaction) of the success indicator; the intensity of the incentives; the conditions in which the incentive system is to function.

6.2 Different Types of Stimulation Systems

A great variety of stimulation systems exists both in economic theory and in practice. From the point of view of the theory of management mechanism, the most useful classification is by the following three criteria:

(1) What is termed the basis of comparison of the success indicator. This criterion divides stimulation systems into those founded on (a) a relatively constant basis; (b) a variable basis of comparison; (c) the achievement of planned tasks; (d) actual improvement of results.

(2) The type of success indicator which is the basis of the stimulation system. This criterion distinguishes systems founded on (a) a synthetic success indicator; (b) specialized success indicators; (c) both synthetic and specialized success indicators. The first two systems can be termed 'pure systems', the third a 'mixed system'.

(3) The means of relating the bonus to the basis for the bonus, that is to the success indicator. This criterion distinguishes stimulation systems in which (a) the achievement of the success indicator is a necessary and sufficient condition for the award of the bonus; (b) the achievement of the success indicator is a necessary, but not a sufficient condition for the award of the bonus.

Since stimulation system 3b is a mixed, and system 3a a pure system, and since the systems based on specialized success indicators do not differ in substance from mixed systems, discussion can be limited to points 2a and 2c.[1] First of all, however, incentive systems founded on different bases of comparison will be discussed.

6.2.1 INCENTIVES TO TAUT PLANNING IN AN ENTERPRISE

A *Formulation of the Problem*

The creation of incentives to taut planning (*napiete planowanie*), i.e. planning which will ensure that the level of 'reserves'[2] in an enterprise is economically justified, constitutes one of the main objectives in constructing an effective management mechanism. Incentives to taut planning should stimulate the enterprise: (1) to work at full capacity and reduce costs of production; (2) to reveal the extent of reserves at the planning stage; this is often a necessary condition for bringing them

---

[1] Many bonus systems also prescribe in greater or lesser detail the rules for the intra-enterprise bonus system. The function of the latter is to transmit incentives to individual organizational and working units in the enterprise by making fulfilment of specific tasks a bonus condition. Definition of these tasks in a way that permits effective control is frequently both difficult and time consuming. These problems, however, are not discussed in this study.

[2] Enterprise 'reserves' in East European terminology mean those possibilities of improving enterprise performance—output, costs, quality of product—which do not, in principle, require investment of fixed capital.

into use, and as a rule, is essential if they are to be efficiently deployed in the context of the national economy as a whole.

B *The Classification of Bases of Comparison in Information-Stimulation Systems*

From the point of view of the theory of the management of the national economy, the sub-division of success indicators not only according to the range of their reception sphere (see 5.3), but also according to their so-called basis of comparison, is fundamental, since the bases of comparison to which the success indicators relate are of decisive importance for the problem of incentives to taut planning.

In our discussion we shall take as the basic criterion of division of types of information-stimulation systems the relative stability or variability of the basis of comparison used. We can thus distinguish: (1) relatively stable types, by which we mean those where the basis of comparison does not change for perhaps three to five years; (2) variable types, where the base is subject to change every financial year.

Our second criterion of sub-division is the base with which the results achieved by an enterprise in a given financial year are compared. Here we can distinguish: (1) planned types, i.e. bases set for the enterprise by the HAO in the form of obligatory planned indices. The use of these leads to comparison of performance with plan and to bonuses for fulfilment or overfulfilment of plan tasks; (2),bases in the form of actual results in some previous period—as a rule although not necessarily, the preceding financial period. This leads to comparison of current achievements with past performance, and to bonuses for actual improvement in results.

The use of relatively constant bases means, *de facto*, that actual improvement in results is rewarded. In this situation, even if an enterprise were set annual tasks for improving results, these tasks would merely be informative in character and, *ex definitione*, no bonus sanctions would be attached to them as long as the enterprise at least achieves the base result. Combining the two criteria defined above leads to the following classification of bases of comparison in information-stimulation systems: (1) relatively constant types—results achieved in previous periods; (2) variable types—(a) planned targets; (b) results achieved in previous periods.

C *The Influence of the Base of Comparison Adopted on Incentives to Taut Planning*

The use of a base of comparison, which changes every year, whether in the form of plan tasks or the results of the previous year, has several negative consequences. In incentive systems the enterprise management bonus is generally made up—*de facto* if not *de jure*—of two parts: a basic bonus and an additional bonus.

The basic bonus is awarded for either: (a) fulfilment of the obligatory plan index of the success indicator, such as profit or increase in profit; this is what is termed a bonus for plan fulfilment; or (b) the achievement of results equivalent to those achieved in the preceding year; this is what is termed a bonus for results achieved.

The additional bonus is awarded for one of the following: (a) what is termed a counter-plan, if the enterprise declares and achieves an improvement over its planned profit; (b) overfulfilment of its planned profit without prior declaration in the form of a counter-plan; (c) an actual improvement in results, not declared as an addition to the plan; (d) an actual improvement in results, declared as an addition to the plan.

If the base of comparison of the success indicator is variable the enterprise tends to conceal reserves and to be very cautious about over-fulfilment of plans or previous results. The reason for this stems from fear of endangering or losing the basic bonus. The economic justification for such behaviour from the point of view of the enterprise is evident. The basic bonus is always considerably greater than the additional bonus and the interests of the enterprise management are primarily to ensure their regular basic bonus. If it reveals its full reserves the enterprise risks an increase in the level of the base of comparison of the success indicator to a level at which there is serious danger of not receiving the basic bonus.

Where the base is variable, whether it be a plan indicator or the results achieved in the preceding period, the enterprise has no interest in either declaring the possibility of improving past results, or in increasing plan targets, or in actually overfulfilling the plan. This tendency cannot be eliminated however the incentive system is constructed; at best it can be weakened.

Such behaviour by enterprises causes serious losses to the national economy, since the failure to make use of reserves in a particular period is equivalent to a loss to the community of part of the social product which could have been achieved and which cannot be regained. Even if reserves are revealed and exploited in period t_1, the fact still remains that the total product for periods $t_0 + t_1$ will be lower by the amount of reserves not exploited in period t_0.

If the variable base takes the form of a variable obligatory index then it results in bargaining between enterprises and the HAO over the level of plan tasks. If the variable base takes the form of results achieved in the previous period, then the tendency to great caution in improvement of results arises, in order to avoid endangering the basic bonus in the following period.

Adoption of a relatively constant base of comparison for success indicators eliminates these negative consequences. As a rule, for a given period, such as three to five years, this solution awards the basic bonus for achievement of results equivalent to those of the initial period, and the additional bonus is awarded for any improvement above this level. At the end of the given period the base of comparison is changed, and may be calculated, for example, as the arithmetic mean of the results achieved in the three-year period, whereupon the basic bonus will be increased correspondingly, being set as the arithmetic mean of the actual bonuses achieved over the given period. Elimination of the fear that the base of the success indicator on which the basic bonus depends will be increased following an improvement in enterprise performance and of the fear that the benefits achieved will later be lost (an increase in the base of comparison after the given period is accompanied by a pro-portional increase in the basic bonus) gives the enterprise an interest in revealing its reserves and systematically improving its results. It is necessary, however, to create incentives which will ensure that reserves are revealed at the planning stage rather than during plan fulfilment (see 6.2.1.A). The problem can be solved by setting the additional bonus higher for planned and achieved results than for achieved, undeclared results. There must also be no further sanctions for failure to achieve declared improvements in results. Should the enterprise not achieve the declared improvement—it should be awarded the same bonus as for achieved, undeclared results. Sanctions should only come into force where results are below the initial period t_0 on which the basic bonus is awarded.

The use of a relatively constant base of comparison in incentive systems creates three problems: (a) the comparability of results; (b) the exhaustion of scope for improvement in results as reserves are ex-ploited, thus diluting the effectiveness of the additional bonuses; (c) excessive increase in bonuses, with consequent disturbance of the relationship between management's and workers' pay, and a threat to market equilibrium.

Since stimulation of the enterprise to maximize a success indicator is economically justified only when the indicator is a synthetic one, these problems are discussed in 6.4 where the incentive model based exclusively on profit is presented.

6.2.2 MIXED INCENTIVE SYSTEMS

Mixed incentive systems can be of three basic types: (1) the synthetic success indicator is accompanied by several specialized success indi-cators which are parts of separate bonus systems; (2) the specialized success indicators constitute the bonus condition and/or the regulators of a bonus calculated on the basis of the synthetic success indicator (variant I), or the synthetic indicator is the regulator and/or bonus condition for bonuses calculated according to specialized success indicators (variant II); in addition, beside the basic bonus system, there are a number of specialized bonuses; (3) as in 2 but without the addi-tional specialized bonuses.

9*

We shall concern ourselves mainly with type 2 since an incentive system combining both synthetic and specialized success indicators is, firstly, the most interesting theoretically and, secondly, is the type of system in force in Poland over the last decade; in 1960–3 variant I and from 1964 onwards variant II.

As we have already said, from the point of view of formal structure mixed bonus systems, of types 2 and 3, represent a combined use of specialized and synthetic indicators in a single system. There are two basic variants of mixed bonus systems, depending on the position of the success indicators.

Variant I. The specialized success indicators are subsequent to the synthetic success indicator (see Diagram 6.1). In this system the specialized success indicators are the bonus conditions and/or the regulators of the bonus awarded on the basis of the synthetic success indicator and act as constraints.

Variant II. The specialized success indicators are followed by the synthetic success indicator as shown in Diagram 6.2. The synthetic indicator acts here as the bonus condition and/or regulator of the bonus awarded on the basis of the specialized success indicator.

Variant I is frequently contrasted with variant II, the former being treated as a synthetic and the latter as a specialized bonus system [see *18*, p. 205]. This is not correct since in both variants the achievement of a particular level of the synthetic success indicator is a necessary but not a sufficient condition for the award of the bonus. In variant I just as in variant II the specialized success indicators must be achieved even though this may not be justified from the point of view of the synthetic success indicator. Variant I, like variant II, creates a tendency to concentrate on areas which are bonus conditions, even at the cost of neglecting others.

The twenty-five years of experience in Poland since the war have not seen any examples of pure incentive systems based on synthetic success indicators. All the systems used have been mixed systems and, on the whole, have been of type 2, variant II. Mixed incentive systems were introduced in an attempt to counteract the negative consequences of stimulation systems based entirely on specialized success indicators, not by abolishing the specialized success indicators but by supplementing them with synthetic success indicators.

The following are illustrations of mixed incentive systems: (1) the bonus system in force in Polish industry in the years 1960–3 [7]; (2) the bonus system enacted in 1964 [9][1] and still in operation, with the minor modifications discussed below. Both systems are variants of type 2; 1960–3—variant I, 1964 onwards—variant II.

---

[1] An excellent description of these systems is to be found in [*18*, pp. 54–228] and [*2*, *passim*].

(1) The bonus system introduced in Poland in 1960 was a double compromise. In the first place the specialized success indicators were retained as bonus conditions for the bonus fund, which was based exclusively on achievement of the synthetic success indicator. In the second place, in addition to the basic incentive system, the extensive system of bonuses for various specialized success indicators, which was independent of the basic system, remained in force. Without going into a detailed description of the complicated construction of this system, we shall present its main assumptions. The creation of a bonus fund was made entirely dependent on the achievement of the synthetic success indicator, which consisted of the so-called 'financial result', i.e. accumulation. The bonus condition, on the other hand, was the fulfilment of a number of specialized success indicators, which may be divided into constant and variable. The constant indicators, which applied to every enterprise without exception, comprised: (a) adherence to the enterprise wage fund, according to the principle of bank control of the wage bill [see 21 and 22]; (b) fulfilment of the value of output plan.

The setting of variable bonus conditions was left to the industrial associations. These conditions were to be operational instruments for steering enterprises to achieving particular economic and technical objectives (see 5.6.2). The tasks which would be bonus conditions were to be indicated to enterprises at the beginning of an accounting period and for a definite time. At the same time, the effect of partial or late fulfilment of the tasks on the basic bonus fund (the degree to which it would be decreased or completely lost) was to be prescribed. Typical supplementary tasks envisaged included among others: fulfilment of the product-mix plan; introduction of new products; elimination of excessive stocks; shortening of the investment cycle.

The extensive system of specialized bonuses was retained alongside the basic bonus system. At the beginning of 1960 about fifty types of rewards and bonuses were in operation in industry, which altogether represented financial resources of over a milliard zlotys annually [18, p. 109]. Owing to the strong opposition to the withdrawal of any of the specialized bonuses, only two were in fact cancelled [18, p. 119]. As a result, the basic bonus system and the system of specialized bonuses operated simultaneously. The strength of the material incentives in each system was relatively similar. The system of specialized bonuses, however, was more attractive to industrial management than that based on the synthetic success indicator. It should also be added that no formal connection existed between the two systems. Diagram 6.1 outlines the basic bonus system.

(2) The stimulation system in current use in Poland is also a variation of type 2. The synthetic success indicator here is one of the regulators of the bonus awarded for specialized success indicators and a system of specialized bonuses operates alongside the basic bonus system. The

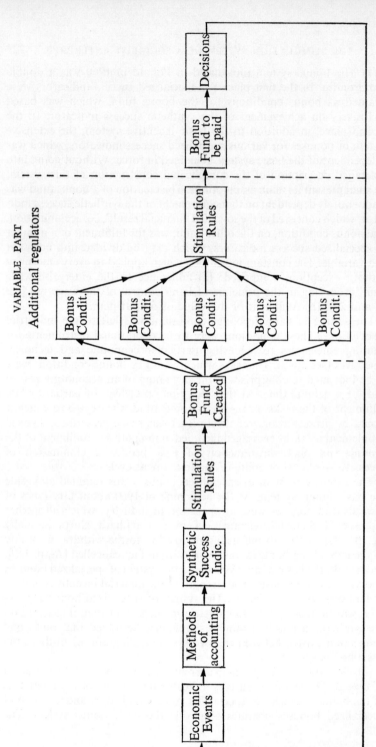

Diagram 6.1   The mixed bonus system—variant 1: Poland 1960–3

current bonus system is based on specialized success indicators, supplemented by a synthetic success indicator, whose intended function is to counteract the defects of the specialized bonus system.

The basic outline of this system is as follows. The basis of calculation, or the bonus condition, for enterprise management consists of general and branch tasks. There is one generally obligatory task and one condition, namely, fulfilment of the prescribed product-mix (the task) and fulfilment of the profitability plan or the coefficient of economic effectiveness (the condition).[1] Branch tasks for industrial associations are set by the appropriate ministers, enterprise tasks by the industrial associations. The Decree lists a number of examples of branch tasks, such as increase of production for export, cost reduction, development of new products. The general obligatory task and the branch tasks are the basis on which the enterprise management bonus is calculated using a points method: each task carries a given number of points, not less than fifteen. The total sum of points for all tasks is 100. The percentage of the bonus fund associated with any one task is proportional to the number of bonus points carried by the task, that is, 15 per cent of the fund is awarded for fifteen points. The achievement of 100 bonus points, therefore, earns 100 per cent of the bonus fund. The total number of tasks cannot exceed five, which is to prevent fragmentation of bonuses and consequent loss of the necessary incentive value. The first regulator of bonuses is the level of achievement of individual tasks. If, for example, task X carries twenty bonus points, worth 10,000 zlotys of bonus fund, and task X is 50 per cent fulfilled, the bonus payable is cut to 5,000 zlotys. The second regulator of bonuses for fulfilment of all tasks (general and branch) is the degree of fulfilment of the bonus condition, i.e. profitability or the coefficient of economic effectiveness. All bonuses for fulfilling individual tasks are subject to reduction by 20 per cent for every percentage point of underfulfilment of the bonus condition; if therefore fulfilment of the condition falls below 96 per cent, no bonus is payable at all.

The introduction of the new bonus system was accompanied by '. . . modifications to specialized rewards and bonuses. The compass of these rewards was greatly limited, thirty individual bonuses were eliminated and the financial resources transferred to the new reformed bonus system. This increased the attractiveness of this system considerably and permitted a substantial rise in individual bonuses. Although these modifications proved to be a considerable achievement in themselves, they were not really radical, since many individual bonuses remained in force, particularly specialized bonuses for various economies' [18, p. 181].

Diagram 6.2 outlines this system.

---

[1] Those coefficients are defined in 5.5.

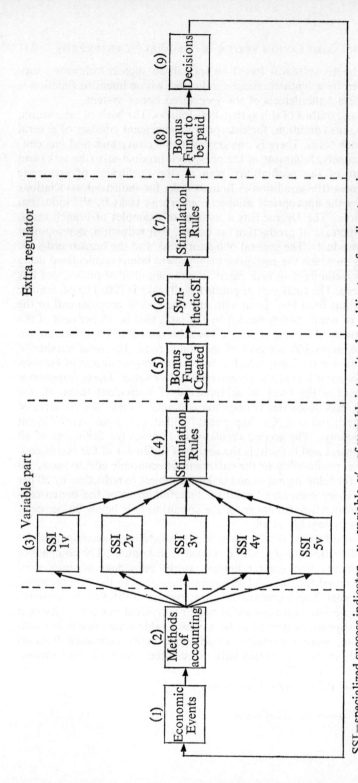

SSI = specialized success indicator, v = variable, v' = of variable intensity but obligatory for all enterprises

Diagram 6.2   The mixed bonus system—variant II: Poland 1964 onwards

The bonus system of May 1964 discussed here was reformed in December 1966 [11]. The essence of the changes is as follows: 'Two new instruments were introduced into the bonus system. The first was a special bonus for meeting sub-contract delivery deadlines, the second, a bonus for regularity of output. These incentives were incorporated within the current bonus system rather than introduced as separate bonuses outside the system.

'The bonus for sub-contractors only applied to enterprises in which such output accounted for 10 per cent to 80 per cent of the value of commodity output. Meeting delivery deadlines in production on sub-contracts became the bonus condition for bonuses for other tasks both for enterprise management and for engineering and technical staff in planning, supply and marketing departments, and in the production on sub-contracts.

'The level of fulfilment of sub-contracts is determined by comparing the value of deliveries within the deadline to the total value contracted to be produced in the given quarter. If this condition is not fulfilled, the bonuses accruing to employees for fulfilment of basic bonus tasks are subject to reduction by up to 50 per cent. Besides the reduction of bonus as a result of underfulfilment of sub-contract deliveries, additional bonuses were provided which increased the bonus fund of the enterprise. This additional fund is calculated as a percentage margin on bonuses, depending on the proportion of output on sub-contract to planned value of commodity output. The higher the proportion, the higher the margin (up to 15 per cent of the bonus). This is intended to encourage the enterprise to increase the proportion of output on sub-contract.

'The bonus for regularity of output operates in a similar manner, and applies to enterprises which produce insignificant amounts on sub-contract and to enterprises in which output on sub-contract exceeds 80 per cent of the value of commodity output. Where the condition of regularity of output in monthly periods is not fulfilled, the bonuses for other tasks are reduced, as with underfulfilment of sub-contract deliveries. If the output tasks, however, are fully and regularly fulfilled, the enterprise sets up a fund for additional bonuses. The size of this additional fund depends on whether regularity of output was achieved in one quarter or several successive quarters. The maximum additional bonus (12 per cent of the bonus for other tasks) is payable if output has been regular for at least four successive quarters.

'The additional bonuses for sub-contracting and regularity of output may justify the planned enterprise bonus fund being exceeded.

'Apart from these additional incentives, further modifications were made in the bonus system. The most important of these was the institution of the bonus fund reserve. This is at the disposal of the industrial associations, to be paid for fulfilment of additional tasks allotted to enterprises during the year' [*19*, pp. 227–9].[1]

It should be stressed that mixed incentive systems represent a certain —however limited—advance from pure specialized bonuses. This is because the introduction of a synthetic success indicator into the bonus system focuses the attention of enterprise management on factors which, although neither the base of a bonus (variant I) nor bonus conditions (variant II), nevertheless influence the synthetic success indicator which in mixed systems is either the base or a regulator of the bonus.

It is difficult to determine the effectiveness of a synthetic success indicator in a mixed bonus system. Evaluation of Polish experience (with variant I in 1960–3 and variant II from 1964 onwards) is complicated since, as we have pointed out, several secondary factors were present, such as the existence of bonuses independent of the system (in both periods) and inconsistencies between the direction of incentives in enterprises and industrial associations (1960–3). Moreover, during all these years, the enterprises were (and are) subject to yearly plan targets, which—in our opinion—undermines the effectiveness of any bonus system.

The use of mixed bonus systems may be a result of the imperfect character of the current price system. If the price system were efficient from the point of view of the objectives of the CPB, and the conditions discussed in 5.7 were fulfilled, then, on the whole, neither constraints nor bonus tasks would be necessary, since enterprises aiming at maximizing the synthetic success indicator would themselves choose the proper product-mix, introduce new products, or attempt to keep stocks at optimum level. Also, instead of changing bonus tasks or conditions as the economic situation changed, the same information could be transmitted to enterprises by appropriate price manipulation and/or other methods discussed in 5.7.

The inherent flaw in specialized and mixed bonus systems stems from the nature of the success indicators on which they are based. As a rule, they lead to excessive expansion of information in the form of commands and/or deliberate weakening of the effect of bonuses.[2] Both these

---

[1] After withdrawal of the Decree [*13*] the incentive system at present operating in Poland is basically as described here. It is going to be changed as a part of the intended new reform of the planning and management mechanism. As we have already pointed out in 1.3.2.D, neither the exact date of introduction nor the substance of the 'new' system—the fourth since 1956—is known at present (March 1972).

[2] The proposal to diminish the intensity of incentives by reducing the proportion of bonuses in pay was put forward by W. Brus [*3*, p. 120] and M. Kalecki [*26*, p. 43]. The proposal was put into effect at the time—the constant part of pay was increased and the share of bonuses in pay limited to a maximum of 30 per cent [see *23*, p. 23]. Enterprise top management bonuses can currently be up to 80 per cent of their basic pay [see *9*].

measures aim to counteract or diminish the unintended effects of incentives. Their use, however, reduces the effectiveness of the stimulation system.

6.3 The Factory Fund

6.3.1 INCENTIVES FOR MANAGEMENT AND WORKERS

Individual groups of employees fulfil different functions in an enterprise, and the nature of the function has a direct bearing on the importance of the different types of incentives applying to the various groups of employees.

In both the theory and the practice of economic incentives the essential distinction is between the following three groups: I top management,[1] II middle management, III production workers.[2]

These groups are ranked according to their influence on the overall results of enterprise activity. They are also inversely related to the measurability of the results of the individual employee's work, which is greatest for production workers and least for the enterprise director.

A different measure of the results of their work and different economic incentives are necessary for each group. Performance may be measured by the results achieved by an individual or a group—group III; by the results achieved by individual organizational units (as long as a sufficiently developed system of intra-enterprise economic accountability, and/or an internal bonus system, exists)[3]—group II; or by the performance of the whole enterprise—group I. Corresponding to these different measures of performance are different basic methods of stimulation for each group: individual or group piece work, bonuses for the results of individual organizational units, bonuses for the overall enterprise results.

Very often, however, the various groups of employees have not one

[1] For example, according to [9] an enterprise management consists of: the director, his deputies, the chief engineer, the head of production, the chief accountant, and the chief specialists.

[2] Enterprise employees of group IV—office/administrative staff—are either awarded bonuses as group III, for example typists working at piece rates, or as group II. Frequently their pay has no variable part and their incentives consist in the possibility of promotion.

[3] 'Intra-enterprise accountability means that: (1) the economic results of the different sections and organizational units are compared with their planned targets, with the aim of discovering any possibility of improvement; (2) the wages of employees in different sections or brigades depend on their results. If intra-enterprise economic accountability is to function effectively, proper intra-enterprise planning is of fundamental importance, so that plan tasks, in particular for economies in inputs, reach sections and lower organizational units. It is also essential that proper work norms are set . . . and that correct accounting is instituted, so the economic results achieved by individual sections can be quickly calculated' [31, pp. 597–8].

but several types of stimulation. For example, in Poland as in many other countries, there are frequently incentives based on overall enterprise results for both middle management and workers. For the latter, incentives based on overall enterprise results are of limited significance. They can, however, play an essential integrating role by showing the worker the relationship between overall enterprise results and his own material situation, and may bring about a decrease in labour turnover. Incentives based on overall enterprise results are used for middle management when measurement of the performance of the individual units of the enterprise is either impossible or impracticable.

6.3.2 INCENTIVES RELATED TO THE FACTORY FUND

The current stimulation system in state industrial enterprises provides three types of incentives for management: (1) bonuses from the bonus fund for white collar workers; (2) specialized bonuses; (3) payments from the factory fund (*fundusz zakladowy*).

Types 1 and 2 have already been discussed, so only the factory fund[1] now requires a brief analysis. The construction of the factory fund [see *10*; *14*; *19*] and the incentives arising from it approximate closely to the functioning of the existing bonus system for white-collar workers described in 6.2 as variant II.[2]

The basis of the factory fund is achievement of the obligatory profitability index or—in 'justified circumstances'—accumulation. The size of the factory fund is defined as some percentage of the planned wage fund for the given year. The percentage for the factory fund is set for industrial associations by the appropriate ministries, and for enterprises by the industrial associations which should vary the percentage according to the tautness of planned tasks but in practice are unable to do this properly [see Chs. 3 and 8]. There is a scale which defines the increase due to the factory fund when the obligatory profitability index or accumulation is overfulfilled, or the reduction when it is not fulfilled. The enterprise loses the right to the factory fund if the profitability plan is less than 80 per cent fulfilled. The regulations governing the factory fund are thus much less stringent in this respect than those for the bonus fund, where the bonus is lost if the profitability index is less than 96 per cent fulfilled.

The factory fund system as reformed in 1965 contains several additional incentives.

---

[1] The institution of the factory fund already has more than a decade of history in Poland. For a fuller discussion of the fund see [*19* and *40*].

[2] The factory fund system, discussed here, is frequently called the 'leading' fund and applies to about 60 per cent of industrial enterprises. The Decree cited lists eight groups of enterprises to which these regulations do not apply. The details of the factory fund undergo frequent—sometimes yearly—changes. Most of these changes are, however, of marginal importance and are ignored in this study.

(1) Incentives to reveal reserves. The enterprise enjoys a 30 per cent increase in the rate of allocation to the factory fund if it declares an increase in profitability above the obligatory planned level in its technical-economic plan. No element of risk is involved, since should the plan not be fulfilled the enterprise loses only the additional percentage.

(2) Incentives to fulfil plans for export and production of goods of a high technical standard. For enterprises specializing in export goods the ministries concerned have the power to increase the factory fund by up to 25 per cent according to the proportion of export output in the gross value of output sold. The right to an increase in the factory fund for production of goods of the highest technical standard (the so-called A group goods) applies to enterprises in the electrical and engineering industries. According to the factory fund regulations, each percentage point of group A products in the gross value of output sold increases the fund by 0·2–0·4 per cent. The percentages are differentiated by the appropriate ministers according to the difficulty of producing the goods or the proportion of their value in the gross value of output sold. The condition governing the increase in the factory fund is fulfilment of the output plan for group A goods [see *14*, p. 31, in *42*].

6.3.3 THE DIVISION OF THE FACTORY FUND

The factory fund consists of two basic parts; a minimum of 25 per cent is earmarked for housing construction, and the remainder is for rewards for employees—with the proviso that this part of the fund may not exceed 8·5 per cent of the wage fund—and investment in social and cultural amenities. According to the regulation [*10*] the rewards paid from the factory fund to individual employees depend partially (up to 50 per cent) on fulfilment of tasks set, on the suggestion of the factory director, by the Workers' Self-management Conference (see Ch. 3, p. 100, fn. 1). There is a close analogy here, therefore, to the principles of intra-factory bonuses laid down by [*9*]. The amount of any individual reward from the factory fund may not exceed the monthly wage of an employee as calculated for holiday pay.[1]

6.3.4 THE INTERRELATIONSHIP BETWEEN INCENTIVES FOR MANAGEMENT AND WORKERS

The factory fund is the source of incentives for both enterprise management and workers. However small the payments from the factory fund to management may be in comparison to those from the bonus fund,[2] its incentive value to management is considerably greater

[1] The reform of the bonus system introduced in 1966 (see 6.3.2) eliminated a number of the previous inconsistencies between the factory fund and the bonus fund. A detailed analysis of the coordination of incentives arising from the bonus system and the factory fund system, and also of the problems still unsolved, can be found in [*19*, pp. 237–52].

[2] This is illustrated by the following table (see next page):

than the purely material interest involved. This is due to the following basic reasons: (a) moral incentives, and the pressure of the factory environment (workers' councils, party organizations, and trade unions) on management to ensure an adequate factory fund, are very powerful; (b) the level of the factory fund has a significant influence on the morale of employees, and management cannot afford to ignore this; (c) the factory fund can play an important role in reducing labour turnover.

The pressure and the necessity to ensure adequate incentive funds for the labour force constitute a powerful incentive to management, even though management derives little or no direct material benefit from these funds.

6.4 Synthetic Stimulation Systems (a Model)

Despite the frequent changes in the stimulation system in the course of the last twenty-five years in Poland, there has never once been a pure system of synthetic incentives. We have no historical example to draw on, therefore, for a synthetic stimulation system and must rely on theoretical discussion. Although this model has not hitherto been used in practice, the superiority of the synthetic incentive system is accepted by the majority of Polish economists [see 15; 32; and 35] and is increasingly being recognized by theoretical and practical economists in other East European countries.

Whilst not claiming to give a full presentation of the problem, we shall outline briefly the basic principles of the bonus model based on a synthetic success indicator. The model described here should be treated as one of many possible ways of basing enterprise management bonuses entirely on profit. The main purpose of this model is to give an example of a feasible stimulation system based on a synthetic success indicator.[1]

Table 6.1: *The structure of the variable part of monthly pay of industrial enterprise management personnel in 1960*

Position held	total	bonuses	awards	payments from factory fund
		Variable part of pay in per cent		
Directors	100	42	53	5
Deputy directors/technical affairs	100	42	51	7
Deputy directors/administrative-economic affairs	100	51	44	5
Chief accountants	100	61	31	8
Chief specialists	100	42	54	4

Source: [36, pp. 192–3].

[1] Bonus systems based exclusively on profit were proposed in Poland as early as 1957. See [17; 4; 5; 27]. A number of works on the possibility and expediency of using profit as a success indicator and as the basis of the enterprise stimulation system appeared in the 1960s. The following deserve particular attention: [1; 6; 18, pp. 330–51; 23; 24; 30; 33; 37; 39; 41].

The model is as follows:

(1) The same success indicator is used in both enterprises and industrial associations.

(2) The success indicator for plan executants is what is termed the index of relative increase in profit, $\dfrac{\Delta Pf}{Pf_b,}$ where Pf_b is profit in the base period.[1]

As described in 6.2.1, the base profit is set for three to five years, and thereafter is changed to the arithmetic mean of the preceding period. If the base is set for three years, then Pf_{b1}, the new base, equals $\dfrac{Pf_1 + Pf_2 + Pf_3}{3}$.

The object of an incentive system with a relatively constant base is to eliminate the negative side-effects of bonuses with a variable base in the form of planned tasks or the previous year's results. As we have pointed out in 6.2.1, the use of a variable base creates a tendency to low plans and caution about overfulfilment of plans or exceeding the previous year's results, so as to ensure favourable conditions for plan fulfilment or improvement of results in future and minimize the risk of loss of bonus.

(3) The bonus fund for enterprise management consists of two parts: (a) the basic bonus for achieving results equivalent to the base period (with bonuses on a reduced scale down to, perhaps, 90 per cent achievement of the base result, and no bonus below that level); (b) additional bonuses for improvement on the base result.

We consider that the level of the basic bonus should change on the same principles as the base. For example, if the base is set for three years, when it is changed the total sum of the basic bonus should equal $\dfrac{B_1 + B_2 + B_3}{3}$ where $B_1 + B_2 + B_3$ is the sum of all the bonuses, both basic and additional, actually achieved in periods 1, 2, and 3. The level of the additional bonus is determined by the degree of improvement over the base, according to a scale set *before* the bonus system was introduced.

(4) The basic instrument for steering the activities of enterprises and industrial associations is ciphered information, i.e. market-type parameters.[2] Open information is only used in limited and strictly

[1] The adoption of the index of profit growth with a relatively constant base differs from the 'pure' bonus based on total profit only in that: (a) the bonus scale does not start from zero but from the base level; (b) the base level itself changes at specific intervals according to the bonus regulations. These differences have no effect on the behaviour of the enterprise as long as the base and the bonus fund remain relatively constant and change according to a predetermined pattern which safeguards enterprises' legitimate interests (see 6.2.1 and point 3 on this page).

[2] By market-type parameters—in contrast to market parameters—we mean prices, rates of interest, exchange rates, etc., *irrespective* of whether they are market- or state-determined (see 4.9).

defined areas. As a result, the authority sphere of plan executants, determined by the management formula, is both broad and constant. The activity of enterprises is steered, according to the requirements of changing external economic conditions, by a flexible system of market-type parameters, not by open information in the form of administrative orders or specialized bonus tasks.

(5) When bonuses are awarded for actual improvement in profit-ability rather than achievement of a planned profit target, the problem arises of the comparability of results in successive periods, with the consequent need to verify balance-sheet profit for independent and incorrect factors. Verification of profit for incorrect factors is, of course, necessary in all systems. In a capitalist economy the tax authorities check that balance-sheet profit conforms to current regulations. The area of verification of profit in respect of incorrect factors is, of course, much wider in a planned economy. This verification, however, should not cover changes of product-mix since with parametric management there is no place for an obligatory product-mix and the profitability of different products is regulated by changing prices. The need to correct profit for exogenous factors such as changes in prices, freight rates, or wages, and for changes in product-mix, stems from certain principles: (a) that profit is to be solely and exclusively an indicator of enterprise performance and not simultaneously a CPB economic steering instrument; (b) that prices are not an active instrument for transmitting information to plan executants. The first principle implies very precise correction for exogenous factors so as to make profits comparable. The second preserves the situation where a change from product-mix A to B in the same enterprise with existing capacity can mean a serious and economically unjustified rise or fall in profitability.

When both the success indicator and prices are used as steering instruments by the CPB, the situation is fundamentally changed. The object of price changes in this case is precisely to influence the level of profit in an enterprise, and thus the decisions of the plan executants, concerning products and techniques. This applies equally to changes in input prices, which influence enterprise production costs and thus choice of techniques, and to changes in output prices, which influence the profitability of different product-mixes and thus the products produced.

(6) The system must not only provide incentives working in the right direction but they must also be sufficiently strong. This problem is solved by establishing the bonus funds—both basic and additional—and individual bonuses on the correct principles.

The basic bonus for enterprise and industrial association management is conditional on achievement of the level of profitability of the base period. The size of the additional bonus fund, however, is determined by the improvement in results compared with the base, according to a predetermined scale. This scale is defined on the basis of practical experience and current economic conditions.

The relationship between the growth of the bonus fund and the improvement in profitability is set for a long period. This stability is an essential condition for drawing out all the enterprise's reserves. Otherwise plan executants may fear that substantially exceeding the actual result of the base period will lead to a change in the division of profit, to their disadvantage. We may add here that setting the relationship between results achieved and the bonus fund for a long period should be part of a general change over to long-term financial norms, the advantages of which have been discussed for many years [see 28, pp. 333–4 and 7.2]. The division of profit should be set by ministries for industrial associations and by industrial associations for enterprises, since profitability and possibilities of increasing it vary greatly. A cautious division of profit should effectively counter excessive growth of the bonus fund in the initial period of the new system, when the extent of reserves for increasing profitability is not precisely known. Once the majority of accumulated reserves has been drawn out, the division of profit can be altered *in favour* of plan executants without fear of the total bonus fund in the national economy becoming excessive and threatening the principles of incomes policy.

(7) Basing plan executants' bonuses on profit growth creates the long-discussed problem of whether this leads to a progressive decline in the strength of incentives when reserves for improving profitability gradually become exhausted. There is also the problem that '. . . change in profit [is] extremely sensitive to every kind of chance phenomenon, such as the regularity of supply of raw materials' [27, p. 32]. One method proposed for solving both these problems simultaneously was that the basis of the bonus should be '. . . not increase in verified profit over the previous year [in the model presented here—over the base year] but the arithmetic mean of the corrected increases of, for example, the previous three years . . . Clearly, calculated in this way . . . the effect of the increase in profit achieved in the given year is more permanent, since it influences awards over the next two years' [27, p. 32].

If this solution were adopted, the index of profit growth would be calculated as follows:
In the first year

$$\frac{Pf_1 - Pf_b}{Pf_b}$$

In the second year

$$\frac{\dfrac{Pf_1 + Pf_2}{2} - Pf_b}{Pf_b}$$

In the fourth year

$$\frac{\dfrac{Pf_2 + Pf_3 + Pf_4}{3} - Pf_{b1}}{Pf_{b1}}$$

where Pf_{b1} is the arithmetic mean of profits in the initial three years.

A different variant is also possible:

In the first year

$$\frac{\dfrac{Pf_{t-1} + Pf_b + Pf_1}{3} - Pf_b}{Pf_b}$$

where Pf_{t-1} is profit in the year preceding the introduction of the reform (Pf_b).

In the second year

$$\frac{\dfrac{Pf_b + Pf_1 + Pf_2}{3} - Pf_b}{Pf_b}$$

In the fourth year

$$\frac{\dfrac{Pf_2 + Pf_3 + Pf_4}{3} - Pf_{b1}}{Pf_{b1}}$$

(8) In order to provide additional safeguards for the interests of enterprise and industrial association employees in case of temporary setbacks and deterioration in economic results, and particularly in order to encourage them to undertake long-term technical-economic measures which could cause a temporary slackening of the rate of improvement of results as the price of a substantial increase later, bonus fund reserves at the disposal of enterprises and associations could be established. These would provide (1) bonuses in cases where the current bonus fund cannot be set up because of a temporary deterioration in profitability; and particularly (2) extraordinary non-recurring rewards over longer periods. A reserve bonus fund would also constitute a long-term success indicator of the performance of individual enterprises and industrial associations [see 18, pp. 347–8].

(9) As for individual bonuses, it is proposed that the ceiling on these should be abolished, since it decidedly weakens the incentives provided by the bonus system.[1] Instead, '. . . a constant relation between the bonuses for standard positions or jobs or a constant share in the total bonus fund for specific positions or jobs [is suggested]. In this way an increase in the bonus fund would mean an equivalent increase in bonuses

[1] See [18, p. 346] and also S. Gora [23, pp. 104–58] who states that 'The reward ceiling is, *ceteris paribus*, the productivity ceiling' [p. 113].

for all employees. The whole labour force would then have an interest in the growth of the bonus fund and, at the same time, the established relationship between individual bonuses could not be disturbed' [*18*, p. 347].

(10) It is important not only to stimulate employees to achieve a high level of economic results, but equally to encourage taut and realistic planning, which is essential for correct balance relationships and maintenance of reserves at the economically justified level. In order to create incentives to taut planning, a method of awarding bonuses which has been known for several years could be introduced, in which stronger incentives are provided for planned growth of profitability and weaker ones for growth of profits not declared in the plan and where actual profit is lower than planned.[1]

(11) The conditions for effective functioning of the model described are an integral part of the model. We have two groups of conditions in mind here: (a) conditions for the effective functioning of incentives; (b) conditions for the effective functioning of synthetic success indicators. Both these groups of conditions have already been discussed in 6.1.2 and 5.7 respectively.

References to Chapter Six

1. Czerwinska E.: *Metody regulowania zysku. Analiza instrumentow finansowych* (Methods of Controlling Profit. The Analysis of Financial Instruments), Warsaw, 1971.
2. Borkowska S.: *Wspoldzialanie nakazow i materialnych bodzcow w przemysle lekkim* (Interrelationship between [Administrative] Orders and Material Incentives in Light Industry), Warsaw, 1969.
3. Brus W.: *Prawo wartosci a problematyka bodzcow ekonomicznych* (The Law of Value and the Problem of Economic Incentives), Warsaw, 1956.
4. —— 'The Concept of Incentives Based on Profit', *ZG*, 25, 1957.
5. —— 'An Attempt to Construct an Incentive System Based on Profit', *ZG*, 26, 1957.
6. Burzymowa E.: *Pomiar i ocena rentownosci przedsiebiorstw przemyslowych* (The Measurement and Evaluation of Rentability of Industrial Enterprises), Warsaw, 1971.
7. Decree 24 of the CM of 25 January 1960 on bonuses for white collar workers in centrally planned state industrial enterprises, *MP*, 9, 1960.
8. Decree 186 of the CM of 2 June 1960 on the principles and procedure of bank control of the wage fund in enterprises functioning according to the principles of business accounting, *MP*, 54, 1960.
9. Decree 130 of the CM of 4 May 1964 on bonuses for white-collar workers in state industrial enterprises, *MP*, 32, 1964.

[1] Such a system was introduced for the first time in Czechoslovakia in 1960. It provided differential norms for sharing in increased profit. For example, where planned increase in profit was 1 million crowns, the share was 20 per cent, 2 million crowns—40 per cent, and 3 million crowns—50 per cent. In order to encourage realistic planning, norms were lower for both underfulfilment and overfulfilment of planned profit [*28*, p. 322, first ed.].

10. Decree of the CM of 28 October 1965 on the factory fund in state industrial enterprises, *DU*, 45, 1965.
11. Decree 380 of the CM of 6 December 1966 on changes in the previous decree on bonuses for white-collar workers in centrally planned state industrial enterprises, *MP*, 71, 1966.
12. Decree 381 of the CM of 6 December 1966 changing the previous decree on the principles of remuneration of employees of state industrial and construction associations, *MP*, 71, 1966.
13. Decree of the CM and the Central Council of Trade Unions of 1 July 1970 on the incentive system of employees of centrally planned enterprises and associations for the years 1971–5, in [*34*].
14. Druska H.: 'The Factory Fund', in [*42*].
15. Dudzinski W. and Misiak M., eds.: *Mierniki oceny dzialalnosci przedsiebiorstwa przemyslowego* (Success Indicators in the Industrial Enterprise), Warsaw, 1964.
16. *Dyskusja o polskim modelu gospodarczym* (The Discussion on the Polish Economic Model), Warsaw, 1957.
17. Economic Council: 'Theses Concerning Certain Changes in the Economic Model', *ZG*, 22, 1957. Reprinted in [*16*].
18. Fick B.: *Bodzce ekonomiczne w przemysle* (Economic Incentives in Industry), Warsaw, 1965.
19. —— *Fundusz zakladowy* (The Factory Fund), Warsaw, 1967.
20. —— *Polityka zatrudnienia a place i bodzce* (Employment Policy, Wages, and Incentives), Warsaw, 1970.
21. Firlejczyk A.: *Kontrola funduszu plac jako narzedzie zarzadzania* (The Control of the Wage Fund as a Management Instrument), Warsaw, 1969.
22. —— 'The Enterprise Financial Results and the Bank Control of the Wage Fund', in [*41*].
23. Gora S.: *Bodzce ekonomiczne w gospodarce socjalistycznej* (Economic Incentives in a Socialist Economy), Warsaw, 1961.
24. Kaczmarek Z.: *Rentownosc jako wskaznik gospodarnosci przedsiebiorstw* (Rentability as an Indicator of Enterprises' Efficiency), Warsaw, 1970.
25. Kalecki M.: 'Outline of the New System of Incentives and Directives', *ZG* 29, 1957. Reprinted in [*27*].
26. —— *Szkice ekonomiczne* (Economic Essays), Warsaw, 1958.
27. —— *Z zagadnien gospodarczo-spolecznych Polski Ludowej* (On Some Social-Economic Problems of People's Poland), Warsaw, 1964.
28. Kierczynski T., Wojciechowska U.: *Finanse przedsiebiorstw socjalistycznych* (Finances of the Socialist Enterprises), 1st ed., Warsaw, 1965, 2nd ed., Warsaw, 1967.
29. Lesz M.: 'Incentives and Success Indicators in an Industrial Enterprise and the Requirements of the Market', in [*15*].
30. Madej Z.: *Zysk w gospodarce socjalistycznej* (Profit in a Socialist Economy), Warsaw, 1963.
31. *Mala encyklopedia ekonomiczna* (Short Economic Encyclopedia), Warsaw, 1961.
32. Misiak M., ed.: *Bodzce ekonomiczne w przedsiebiorstwie przemyslowym* (Economic Incentives in Industrial Enterprise), Warsaw, 1963.
33. Mujzel J.: *Przedsiebiorstwo socjalistyczne a rynek* (The Socialist Enterprise and the Market), Warsaw, 1966.
34. *Nowy system bodzcow materialnego zainteresowania. Zbior podstawowych dokumentow* (The New System of Material Incentives. Collected Basic Documents), Warsaw, 1970.
35. 'On the Functioning of Economic Incentives', *ND*, 1, 2, 3, 1962.
36. Pasieczny L.: *Kierownik a bodzce materialnego zainteresowania* (The Director and Material Incentives), Warsaw, 1963.

37. Popkiewicz J.: *Stopa zysku w gospodarce socjalistycznej* (The Rate of Profit in a Socialist Economy), Warsaw, 1968.
38. Resolution of the CM and the Central Trade Union Council of 28 October 1965 on the principles of the division of the factory fund in respect of awards, *MP*, 61, 1965.
39. Sliwa J.: *Rola zysku w funkcjonowaniu handlu socjalistycznego w Polsce* (The Role of Profit in the Functioning of Socialist Trade in Poland), Warsaw, 1969.
40. Wojciechowska U.: *Problemy tworzenia funduszu zakladowego* (The Problems of Constructing the Factory Fund), Warsaw, 1961.
41. *Wynik finansowy przedsiebiorstwa. Zagadnienia dyskusyjne* (The Financial Result of the Enterprise. The Controversial Issues), Warsaw, 1970.
42. *Zasady nowego systemu finansowego przemyslu, budownictwa oraz inwestycji* (The Principles of the New Financial System in Industry, Construction, and Investment Activity), Mimeographed, Warsaw, 1966.

CHAPTER SEVEN

THE FEEDING SYSTEM OF A
SOCIALIST ENTERPRISE

7.1 The Functions and Main Instruments of the Feeding System

The course of economic events in an enterprise depends basically on three groups of factors: (1) the quantity and quality of labour, (2) the quantity and quality of enterprise resources, (3) management decisions.

A dependent feeding system fulfils the following basic functions in an enterprise: I. it defines the quantity of resources to remain in the enterprise; II. it defines the enterprise authority sphere over the resources left at its disposal; III. it creates economic incentives to stimulate the enterprise to efficient activity.

The feeding system fulfils these functions by: ad I. defining the principles of division of total revenue and financial results[1] of an enterprise between the state, the enterprise and its employees, ad II. defining the principles of allocation of the resources left at the enterprise's disposal, ad III. devising principles of division and allocation of resources which create incentives to economically rational behaviour by the enterprise.

The three main groups of economic instruments of the feeding system are: (1) financial norms, (2) enterprise funds, (3) FS regulators.

(1) The financial norms define the division of the enterprise's revenue between the state, the enterprise, and its employees. The financial norms may be constant, i.e. independent of the financial results of the enterprise, or variable, i.e. related to those results.

(2) The enterprise funds define, in varying degrees of detail, the authority sphere a given enterprise has in the use of the resources left at its disposal.

(3) The FS regulators influence the level of the variable financial norms, and also determine the maximum resources which the enterprise can allocate in any given area, for example they define the size of the wage bill.

---

[1] 'The financial result of the socialist enterprise's operations is . . . the difference between income from sales and cost of production . . . Since certain types of revenue and expenditure are excluded from the financial result and, for others, different levels from the actual ones at the time are taken, accounting uses a number of concepts of financial results' [29, p. 46]. A general definition of the concept of financial result, however, is sufficient for the purposes of the present study.

It can be concluded from the above that (a) financial norms are the economic instruments used to fulfil function I; (b) enterprise funds are the instruments used to fulfil function II; (c) FS regulators are used to fulfil functions I and II. Depending on the particular construction of these instruments and their practical application, the incentive function III of the feeding system is fulfilled.

7.2 Financial Norms

Financial norms determine the division of enterprise revenue between the interested parties. As a rule, the norms are set in the form of a percentage of, for example, total profit, cost of production, turnover, value of fixed assets, or the wage fund.

Irrespective of particular institutional solutions, the division of enterprise revenue, in conjunction with the principles of allocation of bank credit, should ensure: (1) reproduction of the resources of the enterprise; (2) finance for technical-economic progress and so-called 'enterprise investments' (as opposed to industrial association or CPB investments, see 8.2.2); (3) the employees' interest in the enterprise's results; (4) the planned development of the given branch of industry; (5) the amount due from the enterprise to the state budget.

(1) The reproduction of resources used in the production process, both fixed and working capital, means that, except in special cases, at least that part of the depreciation fund necessary for simple reproduction should remain in the enterprise.[1]

(2) Technical-economic progress and investment in modernization which pays for itself quickly are necessary for an enterprise to fulfil its function of innovation, to increase the flexibility of the production complex, and to implement the principle that decisions be taken at the level which has the largest amount of relevant information. At the same time this type of feeding system provides an additional stimulus to enterprise management to improve performance by the relationship: resources→economic events→methods of accounting→success indicators→stimulation system.

(3) Employees' interest in the enterprise's results can be considered as the material expression of the social ownership of the means of production and is an important way of getting employees to identify with the objectives of the enterprise.

(4) Planned development of the branch of industry of which the enterprise is a part is necessary to ensure correct intra-branch co-ordination and to achieve economies of scale. For example, expenditure

---

[1] The depreciation fund is not only the source of simple reproduction but also of expanded reproduction. As a result, only part of the depreciation fund need remain in the enterprise for simple reproduction. The excess of this fund over the needs of the enterprise may be transferred to the HAO for investment and capital repairs anywhere in the given branch of industry.

for long-term technical progress is frequently best concentrated at branch level rather than dispersed among enterprises, which would lead to duplication of effort and the slowing down of the quality and pace of research and experiment (the need to concentrate highly-qualified personnel and equipment).

(5) The amount due from the enterprise to the state budget is the enterprise's contribution to the resources needed for financing the basic economic development of the country and for non-economic activities, such as culture, education, and defence.

The proper division of revenue should ensure stable conditions for an enterprise's operation, which, in turn, would extend the time horizon for its decision-making. This implies that long-term, for example, five year, financial norms should be introduced. Where long-term financial norms are set, an enterprise management knows what resources it has at its disposal for a number of years and this knowledge is an essential condition for the economic use of resources. Continual variation of enterprise obligations (financial norms) introduces an element of un-certainty into financial resources and makes it difficult for an enterprise to plan for any period longer than a year. Long-term financial norms also eliminate the enterprise management's interest in concealing reserves, since they remove the risk of losing these reserves in the next plan year if the HAO increases the financial norms.

The division of revenue should also create incentives to effective enterprise performance. This implies that those financial norms which determine the share of the enterprise and its employees in profit should be dependent on the enterprise performance. Relating financial norms to improvement in results, and setting financial norms for several years, are, of course, in no way inconsistent. Long-term financial norms do not mean that the actual percentage norms have to be independent of enterprise results, but that the rules governing them are defined for several years, for example that the enterprise's share in overplan profits will be determined by a defined scale which is fixed for a five-year period.

The details of the division of revenue in Poland and other socialist countries change with the level of economic development and the evolution of methods of planning and management. The financial system of centrally planned industrial associations and enterprises contains three groups of financial norms:[1] (1) norms relating to fixed assets; (2) norms for the division of profit; (3) mark-ups on costs of production.

(1) Two norms relate to fixed assets: the percentage division of

---

[1] The system as described here, based on [14], was formally replaced by [19]. This change did not invalidate our basic presentation and, moreover, the new system hardly warrants any lasting attention since it is a part of the abortive reforms of 1969–70, has already been modified [5], and—as new reforms are now being actively prepared—will probably vanish before, or soon after, this book is published.

depreciation and the percentage charge on fixed capital. The percentage division of depreciation defines what part of depreciation allowances is to be transferred to the industrial associations to create the industrial association investment fund, and what part is to remain in the enterprise to form the capital repairs fund (see 7.4). The percentage charge on fixed capital (see 7.3) serves to calculate the amounts the enterprise is obliged to pay the state for the use of the fixed assets allocated to the enterprise, such as buildings, machinery, and equipment which constitute the basic part of what is termed the enterprise 'statutory fund' (*fundusz statutowy*).

(2) There are also two financial norms relating to the enterprise's profit:[1] the norm for deductions for the factory fund and the norm for payment of profit to the industrial association. The norm for deductions for the factory fund serves to calculate the employees' share of profit. This norm is set as a percentage (3·5 to 5·5) of the wage bill. The norm for payment of profit to the industrial association serves to divide the remaining profit between the state and the enterprise. The profit which finally remains in the enterprise constitutes the 'development fund' (see 7.4). The division of profit in an enterprise can be illustrated by the following example. Given that the enterprise profit is ten million zlotys, the wage bill twenty million zlotys, the norm of deductions for the factory fund 5 per cent, and the norm of payment to the industrial association 80 per cent, then the division of profit is as follows:

Table 7.1: Division of Enterprise Profit (in million zlotys)

Profit	10	
Norm of deductions for the factory fund (5 per cent of wage bill of 20 m. zlotys)		1
Norm of payment of profit to the industrial association (80 per cent of 9 m. zlotys)		7·2
Development fund (the remainder)		1·8
Total	10	10

The profits paid by enterprises to the industrial association are the source of the industrial association's funds, the remainder being passed on to the state budget.

(3) The enterprise and industrial association financial system provides two mark-ups on costs of production: for maintenance of the industrial association and for the technical-economic progress fund. The mark-up for maintenance of the industrial association is a percentage

---

[1] The so-called 'balance sheet profit' (*zysk bilansowy*) is meant here. It encompasses both the results of the enterprise's basic operations and of other activities such as housing and welfare programmes, and also extraordinary profits and losses (*zyski i straty nadzwyczajne*) [see *29*, p. 47].

of, and is included in, planned costs of production. This follows from the accepted principle that the enterprises forming an industrial association finance the association. The mark-up for the technical-economic progress fund, also included in costs of production, is the source from which the fund is set up at industrial association level, and also, via redistribution by the industrial association, at enterprise level (see 7.4).

The enterprise and industrial association financial system provides that financial norms must be set for at least a two-year period, and the norms of division of depreciation for five years. The need for setting long-term financial norms has long been recognized. The official position is that practical difficulties, connected with changes in the conditions in which enterprises operate, do not allow at present all financial norms to be set for five-year periods. The introduction of two-year financial norms was intended as a first step towards stabilizing the conditions in which enterprises operate. In practice this attempt was entirely unsuccessful since financial norms are still revised several times a year (see 2.2.2).

7.3 The Interest Charged on Fixed and Working Capital

Centrally planned industry has large and continually increasing capital resources available for producing goods and services.[1] The problem of the economic effectiveness with which these resources are used is, of course, of major importance. (1) Better use of resources gives the same increase in output with less investment, or raises the rate of growth, allowing the investment funds thus freed to be used elsewhere. (2) More intensive use of fixed assets, for example by working two or three shifts, reduces their recoupment period which is very important in view of the rapid obsolescence of machinery owing to the current pace of technical progress.

In order to stimulate enterprises to use capital effectively, a system of material incentives is essential. These incentives are created by setting a price for capital and relating the cost of capital to success indicators and the enterprise management stimulation system.

The price of capital, as a separate factor of production, is the interest paid on it.[2] Charging interest on capital may have two purposes; it may: (1) be an element of correct economic calculation at macro- and

---

[1] For example, on 31 December 1969 the gross value of the fixed assets of socialized industries amounted to 822·1 milliard zlotys, at prices of 1 July 1960, and working capital amounted to 393·7 milliard zlotys at current prices. With these resources the value of gross output for 1969 was 1017·5 milliard zlotys (at 1 July 1960 prices) [47, pp. 110, 550, and 120].

[2] The functions of interest in capitalist and socialist economies are discussed in [61, pp. 24–9].

micro-economic level, (2) be simply an element in an incentive system to stimulate effective use of capital.

If interest is to be a factor in economic calculation, the following principles need to be strictly observed: interest must affect prices and be universally applied, the rate must be uniform and equate supply and demand for capital. The cost of capital should be one of the elements forming the price of a product. Only such prices can correctly reflect the total outlay, including capital, necessary to produce a given product, and correctly inform consumers of the real rates of transformation. Universal interest means that all economic units must pay for the capital they employ, and all capital, fixed and working, is liable to interest. A uniform interest rate means that the price of capital, i.e. the interest charged, is the same for all uses.[1] The use of capital involves costs for the national economy which are the same irrespective of the branch of industry in which the capital is used. If the interest rate equates supply and demand for capital, it means not only that the cost of capital is recognized in economic calculation and in the choice of methods of production and product-mix, but that it is fully taken into account, so as to prevent a less effective decision being taken instead of a more effective decision. A universal uniform rate is not in itself sufficient to ensure this, but only a rate which also equates supply and demand for capital.

These well-known principles of economic theory must be adhered to if effective investment policies are to be followed both by the CPB and the plan executants. At the same time, interest is not only an instrument of economic calculation but also, like all prices, an instrument which steers production, and thus implements particular social preferences. The use of interest as a CPB steering instrument in practice involves differentiating the rate, in order to give preference to those branches of production where a disparity exists between the CPB's and consumers' evaluation.

The introduction of a lower interest rate for branches of industry given special preference by the CPB may be operationally more convenient than, for example, subsidizing the branch. Obviously, at the plan implementation level, the interest rate actually charged is simultaneously a parameter of decentralized investment calculation. For planning purposes, however, the CPB should use a uniform equilibrium rate, in order to obtain an undistorted picture of the cost of favouring certain branches or products.

Charging interest on capital may also have a less ambitious objective. It may simply constitute one of the parameters used in a given management formula as an incentive to greater effectiveness in the use of

---

[1] Throughout this discussion the 'pure' interest rate is meant, i.e. risk is disregarded or—in other words—interest differentiation reflecting varying risks does not invalidate the postulate of a uniform capital charge.

252 THE MANAGEMENT OF PLAN IMPLEMENTATION

resources. In this case it is enough to establish a sufficiently strong relationship between effective use of resources, and the success indicators and the size of the enterprise management bonus in order to achieve the desired improvement in the use of resources.

The introduction of a price for capital and the relation of its cost to success indicators and enterprise management bonuses can, theoretically, achieve the following effects: (a) stimulate enterprises to dispose of both fixed and working capital they do not need, which frees them from paying interest on this capital; (b) improve the utilization of existing capital by encouraging enterprises to obtain more output from it than hitherto, which, *ceteris paribus*, increases their profit through the relationship: decrease in interest per unit of output → increase in profit rate → increase in total profit; (c) improve the quality of enterprise investment decisions; interest, which is the fixed cost of tying up resources, stimulates the enterprise to maximize economic results per unit of capital employed; (d) equalize the economic conditions of enterprises with different quantities and quality of capital.[1]

The last problem requires a brief comment. Where the interest rate is correctly set, the economic consequences of differential endowment of enterprises with fixed and working capital are to a great extent eliminated by differential interest burdens. Enterprises with more, or more modern, machinery and equipment must pay proportionately higher interest.

If interest is to equalize the economic conditions of various enterprises correctly, it is essential to: (a) calculate interest on the net value of fixed assets, that is, after depreciation has been subtracted; (b) calculate depreciation correctly, taking into account not only physical deterioration, but also obsolescence; (c) revalue fixed assets when, for reasons external to the enterprise, such as an invention or a shift in demand to new substitute goods, a substantial decrease in the economic effectiveness of fixed assets is brought about, which could not be foreseen when the amount of depreciation to be written off was originally set.

In practice [15; 16][2] interest is intended to be used only as a parameter in a system of incentives for more effective use of capital. This is obvious from the fact that not one of the four essential principles for the use of interest as an instrument of economic calculation is fulfilled.

(1) Interest on fixed assets is not paid by all branches of industry, but only in branches in which (a) charging interest is expected to bring about a decisive improvement in the utilization of means of production, (b) charging interest will not entail financial difficulties.

---

[1] See 9.2.2 for a discussion of the reasons why these expectations were not realized.

[2] The changes introduced by [20]—a uniform 5 per cent interest rate with *universal* application—are in practice meaningless, since the Minister of Finance has been granted unrestricted discretion to waive either of them.

THE FEEDING SYSTEM OF A SOCIALIST ENTERPRISE   253

As a result, a large number of branches of industry, such as mining, enterprises with seasonal production, the power, refrigeration, and cement industries, escape interest charges.

Also, not the whole of an enterprise's capital bears interest. In the current regulations interest is charged on all fixed capital (except in those branches of industry which are exempt) and on the part of working capital covered by bank credit. Since a minimum of 60 per cent of the permanent working capital of an enterprise must be found from its own resources, this means that only 40 per cent, the part covered by bank credit, is charged interest, as is 100 per cent of credit provided to cover seasonal and special stocks.[1]

(2) Two different interest rates are charged in different branches of industry, namely 5 per cent and 2·5 per cent. From the point of view of incentive value, the proportion of interest in gross profit is decisive. In view of the varying relation of gross profit to fixed capital in individual branches of industry, a differential rate was adopted.

(3) The interest rate was set at a level which was considered to provide sufficient incentive, rather than at the level equating demand and supply of capital even within individual branches of industry. It should be noted that the interest rates used in calculating the economic effectiveness of investment are considerably, and in some cases many times, higher than the rates currently charged on fixed and working capital.[2]

(4) Interest is not included in costs, nor, therefore, in product prices but is directly deducted from results. As long as interest has only an incentive function, this solution is both correct and simple.

It should be noted that in improving the existing management mechanism the proclaimed aim is to create conditions allowing fuller use of interest as an effective factor in economic calculation, not only in calculating the effectiveness of investment, but in the day-to-day decisions taken by enterprises and industrial associations. Achieving this goal would require, however, changes in the management mechanism of a magnitude which the CPB is not likely to implement in the near future (see [20] and 9.2.2).

[1] Enterprises set up by the CPB are allocated both fixed and working capital. There seems to be no economic justification why (a) enterprises should pay interest on fixed assets but not on working capital which they also receive from the CPB; (b) since any increase in fixed assets from enterprise funds is charged interest, increases in working capital should not be treated similarly. The alternative solution is to charge interest only on resources received from the CPB, and capital, both fixed and working, financed by the enterprise itself would constitute opportunity costs, since instead of increasing existing material resources an enterprise could receive interest if it deposited financial resources in the bank.

[2] In the official formula of effectiveness of investment, the coefficients of 'freezing' fixed and working capital are 16 per cent and 12 per cent respectively. [See 62, pp. 44–5.] For recent changes in Polish investment planning and calculations of investment effectiveness, see [46].

7.4 Enterprise Funds

The function of enterprise funds is to define the degrees of freedom of the enterprise in the use of financial resources at its disposal. The authority sphere of the enterprise management is to a great extent determined by the nature of the enterprise funds. In financial literature a great deal of attention is rightly paid to the problem of centralization and decentralization of financial decisions. Analysis of this problem involves the concepts of the quantitative and qualitative limits of decentralization [see *29*, pp. 163–4].

The quantitative limits of decentralization of financial decisions are based on the division of revenue between the HAO and the enterprises. If we take sales in factory prices, the main instruments used in defining this ratio are financial norms and FS regulators, which are discussed in 7.5.

The qualitative limits of decentralization are based on the authority sphere of management in the use of financial resources, that is, on what is termed the 'sphere of financial disposition' of the enterprise. The regulations governing enterprise funds are the main instrument of definition of this sphere.

Constraints on the financial autonomy of management may take many different forms. (1) Constraints on the right of choice of what to spend resources on. The very fact of the existence of several enterprise funds indicates the constraints on allocation of financial resources among different uses. The more complex and detailed the regulations governing the transfer of resources between these funds, the smaller the degree of freedom. (2) Constraints on the material purposes for which the individual funds may be spent, such as prescribing the use of the investment fund. (3) Confirmation by HAO of plans for the use of special enterprise funds. The practice of official confirmation of plans frequently turns into direct allocation of funds by higher authority.

Where the qualitative limits of decentralization are extremely narrow, the disposal of resources is a mere formality as far as enterprise management is concerned, since the method of allocating both enterprise resources and resources transferred from the enterprise to higher bodies becomes one and the same.[1] The financial regulations introduced on 1 January 1966, aim at widening both the quantitative and qualitative limits of decentralization of financial decisions. This aim, however, was not achieved owing to the limited character of the reform measures of 1965–6. This was admitted, among other things, in the course of the

[1] 'In essence there is no economic difference between allocating an enterprise a subsidy from centralized funds for a specific expenditure and detailed prescription of the purposes for which the enterprise may use its own funds' [*29*, p. 164].

debate[1] on the 'new' financial system of state enterprises, the draft of which was published in December 1969 [40] and the final version in November 1970 [19]. The 'new' financial system was not formally withdrawn after the December 1970 events, but its merits and demerits are now of little consequence since another extensive reform of the planning and management system is at present being prepared (see 1.4.2.E).

In the system currently in use in Poland and several other socialist countries, centrally planned state industrial enterprises create the 'statutory fund' and what are termed the 'special funds'.

The enterprise statutory fund reflects the value, and changes in value, of its fixed and working capital. The size of the statutory fund should be equal to the sum of the net value of fixed capital plus 60 per cent of the value of working capital less seasonal and special stocks.[2]

Special funds are financial resources left at the disposal of the enterprise for set purposes. The current enterprise financial system provides for the following basic special funds: the development fund, the capital repairs fund, the technical economic progress fund, the factory fund.[3]

The development fund. This fund is formed from the part of the profit remaining in the enterprise after the amount due to the factory fund and the industrial association has been deducted. The development fund serves to cover the enterprise's need for working capital and its own productive investment. First of all the enterprise must finance the working capital it needs, to the obligatory extent of 60 per cent, from its development fund (the remainder may be covered by bank credit). The remainder of the fund may be used for the enterprise's own investment.

---

[1] This debate took place in 1970 in *ZG* (Nos. 2–8 and 11), in *GP* (No. 2), *Bank i Kredyt* (Nos. 3, 5, 6), and *F* (No. 5). Altogether in those four journals alone 21 articles appeared. The discussion was terminated rather abruptly by the Editorial Board of *ZG*, which in No. 11 formally announced that it would not continue the debate but would pass all the articles it had directly to the Ministry of Finance. (The evaluation of the discussion by Mr. Trendota, Minister of Finance, appeared in *ZG*, No. 19.) No reasons for this decision were given, but they are fairly obvious. In the same number the basic principles of the new incentive system were published and the discussion was of course duly switched to this new subject. It started in the very same issue (No. 11) and some participants, e.g. T. Kierczynski, immediately proclaimed the new incentive system as of 'historic importance' and some, e.g. M. Mieszczankowski, as a result of the 'relatively high level of wages and incomes' already achieved. Both were 'right' in a sense neither of them meant or expected: the new system became of 'historic importance' as a significant step leading to the workers' revolt of December 1970, and the same revolt indicated that the wage level of Polish workers could be called 'high' only very *relatively* indeed. The second reason for interrupting the debate on the new financial system was probably the fact that the new incentive system, if introduced, would have had numerous repercussions on the former, and thus would already have made part of the debate irrelevant.

[2] 100 per cent of special and seasonal stocks and 40 per cent of the value of permanently necessary working capital is covered by bank credit.

[3] The factory fund is discussed in 6.3.

The object of this division of the development fund is to encourage rational use of working capital.

The financial system introduced on 1 January 1966 provided for greater self-financing of enterprises. Whereas, for example, in 1965 only 10 per cent of financial accumulation remained in the enterprise for its own use, the new system allows up to 22 per cent [see 57, p. 22]. This formal extension of self-financing had no practical consequences for two reasons. First of all, industrial associations increased enterprise financial contributions to their own investments. Secondly, a substantial part of financial resources left for *bona fide* enterprise investments was 'frozen' by the banks, since the sum of enterprises' development funds left for investment purposes far exceeded the banks' quota for decentralized investments. When the frozen sums on enterprise investment accounts started to grow, they were simply taken over by industrial associations and/or by the state budget.

To put the whole question in proper perspective we should note how the level of enterprise self-financing of fixed capital was falling steadily from 1955 onwards (see Table 7.2, column 8) and by 1962 was already below 50 per cent of their depreciation fund.

Table 7.2: *Enterprises' Fixed Investment as a Share of their Depreciation Fund, in '000 zlotys*
(Poland, representative sample)

| Year | Depreciation Fund | | | | | | |
	Calculated	Left at enterprise disposal	E'prise investment	Capital repairs	Total 4 + 5	$\frac{6 \times 100}{2}$	$\frac{6 \times 100}{3}$
1	2	3	4	5	6	7	8
1955	140,865	52,153	2,752	49,986	52,738	37·4	101·1
1958	338,153	107,987	98,465	93,658	192,123	56·8	177·9
1961	425,418	202,303	203,026	113,122	316,148	74·3	156·3
1962	536,704	151,161	156,567	164,306	320,873	59·8	212·3

Source: adapted from J. Szyrocki *Samofinansowanie przedsiebiorstw* (Enterprises' Self-financing), Warsaw, 1967, p. 228.

This is not surprising because about 80 per cent of enterprise profits and two-thirds of depreciation funds are still being siphoned off to higher authorities [29, pp. 135 and 265]. This reflects two phenomena: (a) the small share of enterprise investments in total investments, which in the Polish FYP, 1966–70, was fixed at 9 per cent (in contrast to 21 per cent in 1961–5) [29, pp. 245 and 249]; (b) the subordinate role of enterprise funds in financing investments. For example, analysis of a representative sample of Polish state industrial enterprises revealed that in 1962 out of total investments in *existing* enterprises only 39·2 per cent was self-financed, 9·6 per cent was borrowed from the banking system, while the remaining 51·2 per cent came from the state budget or industrial association funds [*53*, pp. 225–7].

The repair fund. This fund is formed from the part of the depreciation allowances left to the enterprise by the industrial association and from revenue from scrapping fixed assets. The percentage norms of division of depreciation are set for a five-year period and subdivided for individual years. The repair fund finances capital repairs.[1] If capital repairs are not economically viable, new machinery and equipment may be financed from the fund. If the fund is temporarily insufficient for capital repairs, an enterprise may be granted short term credit by the bank against future depreciation allowances.

The technical progress fund. This fund is allocated to the enterprise by the industrial association to cover expenses in respect of certain planned technical or organizational-economic development work and rewards for the fulfilment of these tasks. An enterprise may also increase its technical economic progress fund by selling fixed assets originally acquired, or created from, the development fund in previous periods. The size of the fund in any enterprise depends, therefore, above all, on the plan tasks for technical progress, the resources necessary to carry out these tasks, and the resources the industrial association has at its disposal. The aim of the fund is to ensure appropriate financial conditions and incentives for innovation in an enterprise. We shall return to this problem in 7.6.

7.5 FS Regulators

7.5.1 ALTERNATIVE TYPES OF FEEDING SYSTEMS

One of the basic problems which the management mechanism of socialist industry must solve is the formulation of the principles of the enterprise feeding system. It is generally considered that the inflow or increase of resources should be governed by two groups of factors [see *29*, p. 171]: (1) the real needs of the enterprise resulting from the tasks it has been set, and also implementation of its own initiatives, such as decentralized investment, or improvements; (2) the economic results of the enterprise's operation, as expressed by the degree of fulfilment of the relevant success indicator.

The feeding system, therefore, should: (a) ensure the inflow of resources into the enterprise in accordance with its production needs, (b) use the principles of inflow of resources as material incentives for the maximum results, by creating a relationship between the enterprise success indicators and the amount of resources remaining in the enter-

---

[1] The current financial system differentiates between medium repairs, which may not exceed 30 per cent of the historical cost of the asset, and capital repairs, which may not exceed 70 per cent of the asset's historical cost.

prise: success indicators → principles of inflow of resources → resources.
Three basic types of feeding system may be distinguished.

(1) A universal analyser may be used which simultaneously serves as
a success indicator and as the single FS regulator. In this system one
analyser determines both the 'enterprise consumption fund' (the basic
wage fund plus rewards and bonuses) and the amount of resources left
in the enterprise to augment its fixed capital (decentralized investment)
and working capital. The simple management formula described in 4.3,
Diagram 4.4, is used in this type of feeding system.

The reforms in the management system in Czechoslovakia proposed,
among other things, the introduction of this type of feeding system. The
gross income of the enterprise is the universal analyser in this system,
and regulates the entire dependent feeding system. Total revenue is the
source from which all expenses incurred by the enterprise are paid.
When material costs are subtracted from total revenue, gross income is
obtained. The enterprise pays its obligations to the state, such as payments into the budget and interest on fixed capital, and repays credit,
from its gross income. From the remaining resources the basic wage and
rewards and bonuses fund is formed, and increases in fixed and working
capital are financed.

(2) The feeding system may also use two separate FS regulators
relating to different sections of enterprise resources. For example, the
allocation to increase fixed and working capital is regulated by the
success indicators in force, which also function as FS regulators, whereas
the size of the basic wage fund is regulated by a separate FS regulator
such as a specific output indicator. This type of feeding system involves
the use of a complex management formula (see 4.3, Diagram 4.5).

(3) The inflow of resources into an enterprise may also be regulated
by an extended system of FS regulators (one employing more than two
FS regulators) in which resources for different purposes, for example
fixed and working capital, technical progress, basic wages, or bonuses,
are regulated by different FS regulators (such as profitability, export
plan fulfilment, or labour intensity of production) and/or by decisions
taken by higher authorities (for example, the association). In this case
we are dealing with a highly complex management formula (see 4.3,
Diagram 4.6).

The solution employing a universal analyser has many advantages.[1]
A universal analyser, in conjunction with the incentives it creates to
optimize the wage fund, eliminates the necessity of setting and regulating the enterprise wage fund by HAO. This is very important since, in

[1] As a result of these advantages Yugoslavia has been using the universal analyser
for several years and Hungary introduced it as part of her 1968 reform. The universal
analyser was experimentally applied in Bulgaria and formed a part of Czechoslovak
pre-invasion reforms. For details see appropriate (forthcoming) volumes in this
series.

practice, major difficulties are encountered in planning and regulating the wage fund and, to date, no fully satisfactory system for doing so has been found. In addition, the universal analyser means using a simple management formula. This can facilitate a more effective economic policy since it simplifies the relationships within the management formula, which in turn facilitates prediction of enterprise reactions to changes in the information it receives. The simple management formula also considerably simplifies enterprise economic calculations, since it means maximization of one rather than several conflicting magnitudes (which involves setting marginal rates of transformation and substitution between them; see 5.6).

The use of a universal analyser does, however, require the existence of a specific model of planning and management of the national economy, in which the conditions for its proper functioning are fulfilled. The universal analyser creates, among other things, the complicated problem of how to ensure effective central incomes policy. One of the essential measures is to set up strict principles governing the permitted increase in wages in enterprises, for example by linking it to growth of labour productivity.

At the same time it should be stressed that the general view is that with present planning and management methods in Poland the introduction of a universal analyser is not possible [see *28*, pp. 9–10; *9*, pp. 149–52; *22*, pp. 279–85]. In this situation detailed regulation of the inflow of resources into an enterprise by complex or highly complex formulae is essential.

The following problems arise with all types of detailed regulation of the feeding system: (a) which kinds of resources require separate regulation; (b) how to define the real needs of an enterprise for each particular kind of resources; (c) how to reconcile provision for the real needs of an enterprise for resources with the incentive function of the feeding system which produces a particular type of enterprise behaviour.

In practice, in planning and management in Poland and most other socialist countries, two problems are of fundamental importance: (1) separate regulation of the enterprise wage fund, which is generally done by output indicators; (2) separate regulation of fixed and working capital, which is done primarily by use as FS regulators of the success indicators in force.

7.5.2 OUTPUT INDICATORS AS FS REGULATORS

The correct regulation of the enterprise wage fund is one of the most difficult and crucial problems of the feeding system.

(1) The wage fund defines the employment potential of the enterprise. The results of the production process depend decisively on the size and quality of the labour force. Labour is undoubtedly the most universal

factor of production with the broadest substitution possibilities. An increase in labour input frequently compensates for the quality and quantity of material factors of production, both machinery and equipment and raw materials. Hence the great importance of the correct regulation of enterprises' employment policy for economic efficiency.

(2) The total national wage fund has a decisive influence on the equilibrium of the consumer market. Market equilibrium is, in turn, of great economic, social, and political importance.

(3) The correct planning and regulation of the enterprises' wage funds becomes particularly important when enterprises have no incentive mechanism to optimize the wage bill.[1] It is often stressed that '. . . wage costs are the only costs of production which enterprises make no effort to decrease on their own initiative but on the contrary aim to maximize' [22, p. 317]. The basic reason for this seems to lie in the coincidence of the interests of workers and management in wage bill maximization. The contradiction between, on the one hand, achieving a prescribed success indicator and receiving the bonus due, and, on the other, maximization of the wage bill, only appears after a planned wage fund and rules governing changes in it have been set. Prior to this an enterprise management is primarily interested in maximizing the wage bill, since: (a) this is in accord with the pressure exerted by employees and their representatives; (b) a high average wage decreases undesirable labour turnover and increases the competitiveness of the enterprise on the labour market in which supply is normally short; (c) a high wage fund allows recruitment of better qualified labour; (d) to increase the labour force is a natural professional ambition of management where its size still decides the importance of an enterprise and the category to which it is graded (and the category of the enterprise determines the basic pay of management); (e) above all, however, labour reserves are of decisive importance in reducing the risk of non-fulfilment of production plans,[2] on which both managers' bonuses and their standing in the eyes of their superiors depend.

In conditions where a tendency arises in the enterprise to maximize the wage bill, contrary to the interests of the national economy, a mechanism to regulate the size of enterprises' wage funds according to their real needs must be set up. This immediately poses the problem of assessing these needs, and changes in them, objectively.

There are two basic conceptions here: (1) that the enterprise wage fund should be set and corrected *automatically* by an FS regulator; (2) that automatic setting and correction of the wage fund should be replaced by directives from the HAO, in particular from the industrial associations, which would determine the wage fund and any changes

---

[1] 'Wage fund' and 'wage bill' are treated here as synonyms.

[2] I have already stressed that the labour force is the most universal factor of production.

really necessary for the given plan period on the basis of economic analysis.

We shall examine these two conceptions in turn.

In the first conception the FS regulator which determines the wage fund should be the output indicator, since the labour requirements of the enterprise are a function of the volume and product-mix of its output and its methods of production. It is generally agreed that the size of the enterprise wage fund should be related to the labour intensity of production, since labour intensity is the sole factor which determines the wage fund really necessary for the enterprise to fulfil its output plan with given production methods. As a result, recent work on output indicators has tended to concentrate on construction of indicators based on labour intensity, also termed net indicators (value added in ex-factory prices, output in cost of processing prices, or output measured in normative labour costs).

These indices undoubtedly represent progress in comparison with the so-called gross output indicators which were once in general use. They do not, however, solve the problem completely, and this raises the question of the validity of the whole concept of automatic setting and correcting of the wage fund. The use of net indicators as wage fund regulators encounters the following fundamental difficulties.

Theoretically the wage fund regulator should have no incentive effect. Use of the wage fund as an incentive to achieve specified tasks is not justified, since the enterprise would use the increase in wage fund to promote staff and upgrade workers. Such processes are more or less irreversible. In the above situation each task fulfilled would lead to an increase in the average wage, which in turn would be bound to cause infringement of the wage and salary scales and labour norms in force.

Although the wage fund regulator in principle should have no incentive effect, in practice this cannot be achieved since: (a) every FS regulator has an incentive effect through the relationship: FS regulator → principles of inflow of resources → resources → economic events → methods of accounting → success indicators → bonus system → bonus funds (see 5.6.4); (b) the wage fund regulator has additional significance as an incentive since the 'resource' itself, the wage fund, constitutes the main source of income for enterprise employees.

If the wage fund regulator does fulfil an incentive role, then it may bring about enterprise behaviour which is not in the interest of the national economy. The use of output indicators based on labour intensity produces the following phenomena in the enterprise.

(1) At the planning stage the enterprise aims at maximizing the labour intensity of production as a means of increasing the wage fund, since it will enable it to increase the average wage during plan implementation. If actual labour intensity were the basis of the planned wage fund, this

could put a brake on technical progress, the main method of reducing labour intensity and, therefore, the wage bill.

(2) If the enterprise aims at maximization of an output indicator based on labour intensity, this is bound to lead it to make undesirable changes in its product-mix. Enterprises will obviously be interested in maximization of output of those products for which the relationship of the real level of labour intensity to the level of labour intensity used as the basis for planning the wage fund is to their advantage.[1] Wage fund reserves are created as a result and can be used by the enterprise either to increase its labour force or raise the average wage.

(3) Analysis of 'juggling' with product-mixes (*manewr asortymentowy*) where the wage fund regulators are based on net indicators, leads to the problem of measurement of labour intensity. This is both technically and economically complex. The problem is relatively simple in the case of mass production using similar types of machinery, since average branch norms can be established. Average *branch* norms, however, create particularly favourable conditions for 'juggling' with the product-mix. The establishment of average *enterprise* norms, on the other hand, raises the problem of who is to set the norms. Experience shows that enterprises cannot be trusted to set labour norms themselves.[2] Since in addition the norms require continual revision because of technical and organizational progress, these are serious obstacles to the use of wage fund regulators based on labour intensity. It should be added that the use of enterprise norms does not eliminate 'juggling' with the product-mix. With time, differential divergences between real labour intensity and enterprise labour norms will arise and the possibility will again arise of maximization of the wage fund by 'juggling' the product-mix, according to the equation 2 in footnote 1 below.

[1] For the enterprise the lowest ratio possible of actual to normative labour intensity $\dfrac{(LI)}{LI'}$ is the most advantageous. If

$$\frac{LI_1}{LI'_1} < \frac{LI_2}{LI'_2} < \frac{LI_3}{LI'_3} < \cdots < \frac{LI_n}{LI'_n} \tag{1}$$

then the first product is more advantageous to the enterprise than the second, the second more than the third and so forth. The enterprise's product-mix, in the absence of constraints, is determined by equating the ratio of actual to normative marginal labour intensity for all products:

$$\frac{\Delta LI_1}{\Delta LI'_1} = \frac{\Delta LI_2}{\Delta LI'_2} = \cdots = \frac{\Delta LI_n}{\Delta LI'_n} \tag{2}$$

$\Delta LI'_1, \Delta LI'_2, \ldots, \Delta LI'_n$ are, of course, constant between revision of labour intensity norms.

[2] 'Evidence to date indicates that enterprises would rather aim to get incorrect norms set, in order to ensure a large wage fund. This tendency can be seen in the plan proposals enterprises put forward and in their demands for the most favourable ratio of volume of output to wage fund' [22, p. 318].

(4) Output indicators closely related to labour intensity create serious problems in planning the wage fund. Since these are micro-economic indicators they are not suitable for the planning and control of the wage fund at macro level. A solution to this problem is sought in construction of an output 'super-indicator', which would aggregate the growth of output calculated by various specialized indicators [see 22, pp. 321–6].

All this casts doubt on the validity of the conception of automatic adjustment of the wage fund according to a particular output indicator and provides ammunition for the advocates of the second conception, which would replace the automatic regulation of the wage fund by HAO decisions based on economic analysis of each individual case.

The protagonists of the second conception advance the following basic arguments.

(1) The conception of automatic regulation of the planned wage fund according to a particular output indicator does not take into consideration that not every overfulfilment of a plan is desirable and advantageous. It does not ensure economic analysis of the usefulness of increasing output as expressed by the particular output indicator but automatically increases the enterprise wage fund if an increase in output takes place. There is no output indicator maximization of which would always be desirable from the national point of view. The analysis of output indicators based on labour intensity has proved that net indicators are no exception. They can, for example, be maximized by undesirable 'juggling' with the product-mix.

(2) An enterprise can maximize a given output indicator by: (a) increasing the labour force; (b) increasing the hours worked; (c) increasing labour intensity for workers; (d) introducing new techniques; (e) improving the organization of production. Only a, b, and c require an increase in the enterprise wage bill. There are, however, no output indicators which react only to a real increase in labour intensity. This also applies to net indicators if the purely theoretical possibility of continuous revision of enterprise labour intensity norms is ignored.[1] In reality, with given labour intensity norms, the growth of output achieved by technical and organizational progress is registered as an increase in the labour intensity of production and makes additional wage funds available.

(3) As a result the advocates of this conception hold that: (a) the system of automatic regulation of the wage fund on the basis of a particular output indicator is not suitable for precise determination of the wage fund really necessary for the enterprise; (b) the system can

[1] 'The value of the correction coefficient [of the wage fund] actually necessary should only take into account additional payment for direct growth of labour productivity after eliminating the effect of technical-organizational factors in overplan increases in output. This coefficient, however, cannot be set, since it would have to be adapted to individual enterprises and, moreover, changed with time [22, p. 265].

thus cause shortages, and, in particular, increases in the wage fund unjustified by real needs; (c) in addition, the system cannot be freed from the economic misincentives it embodies, which encourage enterprise behaviour, both at the planning stage and in plan implementation, which is directed at maximizing the wage fund.

(4) The proposed alternative is to replace the automatic regulation system by an economic analysis of the justification and necessity of an increase in the wage fund in each individual case. The analysis would be carried out by industrial associations in respect of enterprises; economic ministries in respect of industrial associations; and the CM in respect of ministries. There would be a system of wage fund reserves at all levels. The reserves would only be made available in the case of enterprises when: (a) overfulfilment of the output plan for a given product-mix is economically justified; (b) a higher level of labour intensity than planned is necessary; (c) the replacement of material input by labour input is justified.

An increase in the wage fund would only take place in this system for specific purposes, fully justified economically. The increase would not be automatic but would constitute a production-steering instrument. The system of reserves would simultaneously fulfil a second function, of a constant alarm signal, since the depletion of reserves at any given level and in any given branch would indicate where and by what amount the wage bill had increased. Requests for additional wage funds could then be evaluated, both from the point of view of the economic justification of the particular case and of the eventual effect they may have on general market equilibrium (for example, whether the output to be achieved by increasing the wage bill takes the form of consumer or producer goods).

The system of reserves was introduced into some branches of industry in Poland in 1964 [12] and considerable hopes have been placed on the effectiveness of the system. According to some economists [see e.g. 22, p. 270]: (a) it allows control of the amount of the aggregate wage fund, since it eliminates the possibility of enterprises automatically generating additional wage fund requirements; (b) it ensures the necessary flexibility in making reserves available for economically justified overfulfilment of plans; (c) it removes the incentive to achieve additional wage funds by plan overfulfilment.

It must be stressed, however, that the system of wage fund reserves has a number of drawbacks, the seriousness of which its proponents tend to forget or at least to underestimate. First of all, it assumes that industrial associations are able to evaluate correctly and *impartially* their enterprises' claims for additional wage funds. In the light of industrial associations' performance over the fifteen years of their existence, this is simply not the case. Secondly, it ignores the unavoidable time lags involved in the essentially bureaucratic procedure of making additional wage funds available. As each application is supposed to be judged on its merits, the time required for conducting such evaluation would at best be considerable and it would be naïve to suppose that the applicants will not try to 'dress-up' their cases to their advantage. In any case, the system of wage fund reserves did not expand significantly during the eight years after its selective introduction and most effort went into constructing 'correct' net output indicators.

To conclude our discussion of output indicators, it should be added that, even if the superiority of the system of reserves over automatic wage fund regulation were to be recognized, it would not mean a diminution of the importance of establishing correct output indicators, since only *automatic* regulation of the wage bill on the basis of these indicators and not the indicators themselves, would be discarded. An accurate output indicator based on labour intensity, would still be needed to facilitate setting the wage fund necessary to fulfil additional economic tasks, and hence to simplify decisions to make available wage fund reserves. Both are essential if the system of reserves is to function effectively.

7.5.3 SUCCESS INDICATORS AS FS REGULATORS

As we have already pointed out in our discussion of alternative feeding systems, in the absence of a universal analyser regulating the total flow of resources to the enterprise, there arises the problem of separate regulation of different types of resources, distinguished according to the relevant criteria. The most important division of resources—of all those which are used in practice—is between those for basic wages on the one hand and for increases in fixed and working capital on the other. The latter are normally regulated by success indicators functioning as FS regulators. The justification of this use of success indicators is twofold [see *29*, pp. 133–4]: (1) when success indicators become not only the basis of enterprise management bonuses, but also of the inflow of some resources, their incentive value is strengthened; (2) a certain decentralization of control of resources, by leaving them in the enterprise, ensures their more effective use, since enterprise management has the greatest amount of information on which to take correct decisions in such spheres as modernization requirements or product improvements.[1]

At the same time, by setting individual norms for each enterprise for payments from profit to the industrial association, the HAO retains the possibility of regulating the inflow of these resources to individual enterprises in accordance with the general branch development policy. On the other hand, the setting of the share of self-financing in the total enterprise accumulation determines the shares of centralized and

---

[1] The shortcomings and advantages of centralized and decentralized investment and their relation to the historical development of the socialist economy are discussed in some detail by Z. Madej [*35*, pp. 261–81].

266   THE MANAGEMENT OF PLAN IMPLEMENTATION

decentralized use of resources which is recognized by the CPB as optimal in the given circumstances.

In the current financial system, the dependent inflow (see 4.1) of fixed and working capital to the enterprise is regulated by the volume of profit, which determines the size of the development fund (see 7.3). It should be noted that, although volume of profit is the basis of the development fund in *all* enterprises, in *most* enterprises it does not form the basis of management bonuses.[1] Current regulations [*19*] specify the following four success indicators: decrease of unit cost of production, the final cost level, the rate of profit, the volume of profit (see Ch. 4, p. 147, fn. 1 and 5.5, esp. p. 197.)

Three out of the four success indicators in force are relative magnitudes and may change in the opposite direction from the volume of profit. The use of different indicators for the development fund and the bonus fund creates incentives which frequently operate in different directions. We can obviously have a situation where the success indicators which are relative magnitudes, move in the same direction as the volume of profit, but this is not necessarily the rule. If the management formula is to function effectively, success indicators should simultaneously function to the highest degree possible as FS regulators.

7.6 Financing Technical Progress

Economic development is not so much repeating on a larger scale what is already known but rather 'the creation of new combinations of productive factors' [see *50*, p. 66]. This concept, according to J. Schumpeter, embraces the following five elements: (1) the introduction of a new good, or good of a new quality; (2) the introduction of a new method of production or marketing in a branch of manufacture concerned; (3) the opening of a new market; (4) the conquest of a new source of supply; (5) the carrying out of the new organization of any industry.[2]

These changes, which are the principal driving force of economic progress, are not, as a rule, the result of change in demand, but are initiated by producers. One of the main objectives of the industrial management mechanism, therefore, is to create incentives and conditions ensuring a steady flow of these 'new combinations of productive factors', a flow sufficiently extensive and intensive to ensure that the technical-economic level of national production does not lag behind world progress and that domestic products are competitive on world markets.

[1] The same inconsistency existed in previous financial systems.
[2] Under socialism the acquisition of new markets and new sources of supply is rather the task of industrial associations or foreign trade enterprises than of industrial enterprises. Nonetheless, this does not lessen their role in economic development.

In discussing the problems of technical-economic progress, it is useful to distinguish the following concepts [*33*, p. 30]: (1) a scientific discovery: an addition to knowledge; (2) an invention: a tested combination of existing knowledge to a useful end; (3) an innovation: an initial and significant application of an invention to economic production; (4) an improvement: a minor beneficial change in a known invention in the course of its application; (5) the spread of an innovation either through extensive imitation or internal growth.

It should be stressed that Schumpeter's five elements constituting 'new combinations of productive factors' embrace not only innovations and improvements in Kuznets's sense but also what we can term economic innovations in marketing, supply, and organization.

The task of the management mechanism is to create incentives and conditions for innovations, improvements, both technical and economic, and their propagation. Scientific discoveries and inventions are, to a great extent, the result of the development of fundamental research. This does not mean that inventions, in particular, cannot be financed by industry. The problem of invention, however, extends beyond the sphere of the management mechanism *per se*.

A talent for innovation is something comparatively rare in any social system [see *50*, pp. 84–7].

In the first place, the creation of something new is of a different order of difficulty from the performance of even the most complex activities which are already known and mastered.[1] Considerable risk is involved. This can be of two types [see *52*, pp. 318–19; *2*, p. 408]: (a) The probability of what is termed insurable risk can be mathematically calculated, according to the law of large numbers, and can be insured against. Such risks can relate, for example, to fire, theft or loss of goods in transit. (b) Economic activity, however, is characterized by what is termed uninsurable risk, which is unique and cannot be insured against. This means primarily the possibility of losses.[2]

In the second place, objective difficulties apart, people, as a general rule, instinctively resist the new and the unknown. This is related, among other things, to the difficulty of breaking down routine thought and action.

In the third place, the community can frequently be unwilling or even opposed to innovation. In economic life this antagonism can be expressed: (a) in the reaction of groups whose interests are threatened by an innovation; (b) in the difficulty of ensuring the necessary co-operation by others, for example, suppliers of individual components;

---

[1] 'Carrying out a new plan and acting according to a customary one are things as different as making a road and walking along it' [*50*, p. 85].

[2] Sometimes, following F. H. Knight, only insurable risk is called risk, and uninsurable risk is termed uncertainty (see, e.g. [*35*, p. 288]).

(c) in the necessity of convincing customers of the advantages of a new product or method of production.

All this causes great difficulty in ensuring a strong flow of innovation in any social economic system. The majority of Western economists have long discarded the thesis that socialism, in comparison with capitalism, contains inherent obstacles to innovation and discovery.[1] Some East European economists go further and claim that, from the macro-economic point of view, a socialist economy creates conditions more favourable to technical progress than a capitalist economy: '(1) The general objective of economic activity under socialism (the satisfaction of social needs) generates unlimited interest in the most effective possible methods of production and products . . . (2) Economic calculation on a national scale allows (at least potentially) so-called external economies to be taken fully into account . . . (3) The planned socialist economy operates with a long time horizon. This makes it possible to take into consideration [also] those types of technical progress whose benefits are relatively distant . . . (4) The social ownership of the means of production creates a basis for dissemination of modern production methods . . . (5) There is the possibility of planning the development of science and technical progress . . . (6) In the sphere of education and professional training, a socialist economy is free of the limitation which results from the tendency in a private economy for only those outlays to be made which bring results to the given economic unit [i.e. which can be internalized]. This also applies to point 5 . . . Socialist production relations encourage invention among employees, and a general tendency to rationalization' [4].[2] The advantages enumerated above are, at best, purely theoretical. The conversion of these potential advantages into a management mechanism favouring continuous, vigorous technical-economic progress has proved very difficult in practice in all East European countries.

Research into the influence of the management mechanism on technical-economic progress in Poland has shown that at present it has a large number of shortcomings [see 26, pp. 238–309; 58, passim].[3] Disincentives to technical progress are due, to a great extent, to the fact that the enterprise incentive system is based on annual plan targets. This creates a short time horizon for management decisions

---

[1] J. Schumpeter had already come to this conclusion in 1911 [49, p. 94]. Returning to the same question thirty years later, J. Schumpeter fully maintained his earlier point of view [see 50, 1st edn., 1942, Part III 'Can Socialism Work?', in particular, Ch. 18 'The Human Element'].

[2] At the same time W. Brus admits the fact that the problem of incentives for technical progress at micro level is a far from satisfactory solution.

[3] Those interested more deeply in the problems of research and development in centrally planned economies may wish to consult the following basic Polish works on this subject: [6; 10; 27; 31; 36; 38; 39; 43; 44; 51].

and causes a reluctance to innovate, since it frequently threatens fulfilment of current annual plan indices.

Disincentives appear already in the period of preparation for a new product. This requires, obviously, a certain outlay of labour and materials. For many years the only form of finance for this outlay was working capital, which was later recovered out of revenue from sales of the new product. This created a brake, since certain resources had to be withdrawn from current production, on which the management bonus was based, to be used for uncertain future output.

An attempt to resolve this problem was undertaken in 1958 by creating a special technical progress fund (currently termed the technical-economic progress fund) from which enterprises can finance part of the work involved in implementing technical progress, instead of tying up their own working capital. Technical progress, however, requires not only the employment of material resources but also of human resources. As we pointed out when discussing output indicators functioning as FS regulators, the current Polish system of regulating the enterprise wage fund is related to fulfilment of the output plan. The implementation of technical progress, however, often has a negative influence on fulfilment of the output plan in the initial period, whereas the wage bill required remains unchanged, and frequently even temporarily increases.[1]

A number of measures were introduced in order to deal with this problem. The most radical was the experiment in 1964 in the electrical-machinery industry. The enterprise wage fund was divided into the technical progress wage fund and the current production wage fund, the aim being to separate wages for technical progress from wages for fulfilment of current output plans. This policy, however, is by no means simple to put into practice, since it is difficult to divide employees between implementation of technical progress and current production, and it is also difficult to guard against the danger of resources for financing technical progress being reallocated to wages for current output.

A second group of problems arises in the initial period of production of a new product. As a rule, cost of production in this period is higher than the target level and the enterprise wishes to escape the economic consequences of this. The financial system faces a dilemma here. If (as was the case in the period 1952–60) the introductory and initial production costs are separated and amortized during normal production (basically over a three-year period), then there is no incentive to cut the initial period and the costs involved. If (as in the system introduced in 1960) the learning costs arising *after* full-scale production

---

[1] For example, the introduction of a new product frequently involves the necessity of transferring the workers concerned from piece-work to pay by the day, with a bonus system, in order to avoid a fall in earnings.

has commenced, are not recoverable in a certain time, then enter-prises will avoid introducing new products, fearing the risk involved. Among other suggestions to solve this problem is the idea that the initial period of a new product should be isolated in the enterprise plan, and the excess cost of production in this period over target level should be predetermined, and treated as a planned loss. In this case, the initial period would only influence the profitability of an enterprise to the extent that the loss was greater or less than planned [see 37].

A separate group of disincentives relates to price policy for new products. Since a profit norm of 5 to 10 per cent of cost of production is used in setting prices of new products, whereas the profitability of current output, owing to the decrease in cost of production, is considerably higher, the introduction of a new product, as a rule, brings about a fall in the economic results of an enterprise.[1] Attempts to resolve this problem by allowing the factory prices of new products, produced by new techniques, to include a rate of profit up to 50 per cent above the normative coefficient of profitability for the particular group of products [see 11],[2] failed to make new products as attractive as current output, which still remained more profitable. As has been rightly pointed out in economic literature [see 26, p. 258], in order to resolve this dilemma the prices of both new and current products should be simultaneously manipulated: (1) new products must be ensured a higher profitability than current products; (2) in order to ensure this, prices of current products should be systematically reduced when, owing to declining costs of production, their profitability becomes considerably greater than the normative level.[3]

The last set of problems to be discussed relates to the question of incentives to undertake risk and of covering the possible losses on unsuccessful innovations. Although there is a lack of comprehensive studies on the subject, there is abundant evidence that the current

---

[1] The problem is made even more acute by the fact that the prices of new products are normally set on the basis of target costs, which means the enterprise does not even achieve normative profit in the initial period of production.

[2] This decree [11] as J. Gordon rightly notes, does not take into account new products produced by existing techniques.

[3] An attempt to resolve a number of the problems discussed here was made by the Decree [17], see also [59]. The guidelines of this decree recommend, among other things, that: (1) When setting the prices of products, rates of profit should be differentiated, within a certain range, expressing a definite economic policy. Relatively higher rates should be set for new or specially attractive products, or products of a high technical level, etc.; (2) A category of so-called 'temporary factory prices' should be introduced in order to create favourable conditions for production of important new products despite the initial high costs (higher than selling prices) involved. These products are to have temporary ex-factory prices, different for each half year of the period of build-up of production, in accordance with the expected rate of decrease of costs. The period for which temporary factory prices can be used i.e. in which a new product is to be subsidized, should not exceed three years.

management mechanism creates reluctance on the part of enterprises to undertake risk, and, as a result, the number of technical and economic innovations and improvements is small. To try to remedy this, enterprises have been given the right to be allocated resources from the HAO to cover losses, where the failure of an innovation or improvement is due to factors independent of the enterprise. The regulations on the technical-economic progress fund give financial precedence to undertakings involving a greater degree of risk. These regulations even, in some cases, allow a refund of working capital used by an enterprise for work on technical progress, if this work ends in failure through no fault of the enterprise. On the whole, however, enterprises rarely make use of these possibilities. The reason is that it is difficult to prove that the failure of an innovation or improvement is a result of independent factors exclusively. On the other hand, excessive liberalism in covering losses incurred by unsuccessful attempts at innovation can lead to thoughtless expenditure.

Solution of the problem of uninsurable risk in a centrally planned economy is complicated and requires extensive research before any useful policy recommendations can be offered. Such research is—as yet—almost entirely lacking.[1] There is no doubt, however, that in most—if not all—East European countries, including Poland, the potential benefits of a risky venture are too small in relation to the costs involved and the consequences of failure. Both costs and benefits should be broadly defined. On the cost side managerial effort and the consequences of failure for promotion prospects should be included. We must not forget either that under the current Polish management and administrative mechanism there are no economic penalties for *not* innovating—as there is no competition—nor are there negative consequences for managerial (as opposed to purely technical) careers. Innovations and improvements cannot—by their very nature—be required, so there can be no administrative punishment for not supplying them.

The conclusion from this discussion is that, to solve the problem of innovation and improvements and to ensure that they are properly encouraged, the management mechanism must be fundamentally changed and in particular yearly plan targets for enterprises should be completely abolished (see 9.1.1.C). The technical-economic progress which is undoubtedly taking place, even if at too slow a pace, is to a great extent the result of action and pressure by the HAO rather than of enterprise initiative. One of the basic aims of the various reforms in the

---

[1] Polish literature on the subject—as far as we are aware—basically consists of [*45*; *35*, Ch. IV; *48*; and *41*]. Samecki's interesting work deals only with the sources of risk in socialist enterprises and does not analyse incentives and disincentives to undertake risk, while Nietyksza's monograph is concerned exclusively with risks involved in *technical* innovations and its legal treatment.

planning and management mechanism currently taking place in all East European countries, is to establish effective conditions and incentives for technical-economic progress. The effects to date, however, are by no means satisfactory, at least in Poland.

7.7 The Macro-Economic Feeding System

The dependent feeding system of the enterprise is linked to the circulation of resources in the national economy by (1) the independent feeding system; (2) the finance and credit system; (3) the supply and marketing system.

The connection is, of course, two-way. Resources flow to and from the enterprise. Only the inflow of resources from the macro-economic feeding system is discussed here. The outflow was considered in 7.4.

(1) With the exception of Yugoslavia and Hungary, the greater part of investment in East European countries has hitherto not been financed from enterprise funds, but from central or industrial association resources.[1] The shares of these three basic investors in the gross accumulation fund vary at particular stages of economic development (see 8.2.2). The independent feeding system is, above all, the instrument of long-term economic growth, rather than current operation and short-term adjustment. As a result the analysis of this system belongs to the theory of economic growth which lies beyond the scope of the present study. The theory of the management mechanism can only provide very general guidelines to the criteria which should govern the division of the gross investment fund between the dependent and independent systems (see 7.4). Its main objective is to indicate conditions in which investment processes can function efficiently.

(2) The connection between the dependent feeding system and the credit system is: (a) for control, (b) to increase mobility of resources, (c) to increase the flexibility of feeding.

An example of the control function is the permanent provision of part of the enterprise working capital by bank credit. This facilitates bank control over enterprises.

Increased mobility of resources is achieved by the principle that temporary enterprise needs (for seasonal stocks, for example) are covered entirely by bank credit. This allows the immediate release and transfer of resources to other uses when the particular need has passed.

The basic purpose of linking the dependent feeding system and the credit system, however, is to increase the flexibility of feeding into enterprises. The credit regulations define the cases in which an enterprise may undertake certain expenditure, for repairs, for example, beyond the limit of its own resources for this purpose. The credit

[1] Financial regulations differentiate between enterprise, industrial association, and central investments.

regulations also allow enterprises to undertake certain expansion on credit if it is sufficiently effective. For example, regulations on financing investments yielding quick returns [*13*] require that: (a) the outlay must be recouped within three years from the time of the investment; (b) the estimated value of the investment must not exceed 1 million zlotys; (c) the percentage of construction-assembly work must not exceed 15 per cent of the total cost of the investment; (d) the investment must be completed within one year.[1]

Greater flexibility of feed-in and possibilities of expansion beyond the limit permitted by enterprises' own resources are a basic factor in increasing the operating efficiency of economic units.

(3) Smooth circulation of resources in an enterprise depends, to a large extent, on the conditions of supply, while the conditions of supply reflect the current character of the market. In a buyers' market the only constraint on supply is the amount of financial resources available. In a sellers' market, availability of material resources becomes of prime importance. Lack of materials can make it impossible for an enterprise to carry out an investment even though it has been provided with the appropriate financial resources. Lack of materials can also force the choice of technically less effective methods for which materials are available, and may ultimately make the possibility of a particular undertaking dependent on prior allocation of the given factors of production.

With a sellers' market for capital goods, certain constraints have to be set on trade in supplies. In the management mechanism currently in force in Poland, these constraints relate both to the legal subjects negotiating delivery contracts, and to the objects of the transactions.[2]

The first set of constraints on transactions in capital goods apply to non-state units. The constraints cover: (a) the provision of supplies and services for state units; certain conditions, less rigorous for cooperatives, and considerably more rigorous for privately-owned economic units, must be fulfilled; (b) the purchase of material supplies from state units; here too the constraints are less severe for cooperatives than for private enterprises.

The second type of constraints take the form of central allocation (*rozdzielnictwo*) and use control (*reglamentacja*) of capital goods.

Central allocation makes the buyer's right to enter into a contract subject to prior allocation. Constraints apply to transactions in specific products only in a year when they appear on the list of centrally

---

[1] In 1969 an extensive revision of investment regulations appeared [*46*]. Since far-reaching work on a new reform blueprint started in 1971, the 300 pages of the 1969 investment decrees and instructions are mainly of historical interest and need not concern us here.

[2] For further information on material supply, see [*1*], which is a series of pamphlets begun in 1968 and still appearing. Also [*7*; *8*; *23*; *25*; *32*; *34*; *54*; and *55*].

allocated products. When a product is omitted from the list, trade in it is free. The basis of the list of scarce and centrally allocated products is the material balances worked out by the Planning Commission and economic ministries, or by the particular marketing unit (*centrala zbytu*) on the instructions of the former. A scarce product may be listed for central allocation only if it has certain characteristics which make its central distribution feasible. Namely, demand for the product must be known already in the period when the balances are being drawn up and the central allocation list prepared. Such advance determination of demand is only possible for groups of products whose production methods allow supply and demand to be balanced without the product-mix being defined in detail. Examples of such product groups are rolled steel products, castings, and forgings.

A stricter constraint on transactions in capital goods is use control. This is where specific economic units have the exclusive right to trade in centrally allocated articles and, frequently, the power to control the use to which these articles are put by buyers. For example, the distributors of non-ferrous metals not only have the sole right to trade in these metals, but are also obliged to control the use to which they are put. They are also obliged to ensure that these metals are *not* used to produce certain specific articles. Use control applies mainly to scarce industrial raw materials (raw hides, raw and semi-processed textiles, timber, non-ferrous metals, etc.) and scrap materials. Use control regulations are backed by penal sanctions.

Efforts are made to a greater or lesser extent in all socialist countries to limit the sellers' market as much as possible, not only for consumer goods, but also for capital goods. These efforts take the form of reducing the number of centrally allocated goods and the range of use control, and increasing direct contacts between suppliers and buyers. This tendency is understandable since the existence of a sellers' market for capital goods: (a) weakens the effectiveness of the management formula in improving quality, decreasing costs, etc.; (b) weakens incentives to innovation and invention; (c) complicates economic calculation in the enterprise.

It should be stressed, however, that the creation of a buyers' market for capital goods is a complex problem, still far from being solved in Poland (see 2.1.2).

Economic theory [see e.g. *3*, pp. 116–47; *56, passim*] differentiates between what is termed active money and passive money. As we have pointed out, money fulfils an active role when the economic units have sufficient independence to take decisions, within a given range, on the use of the financial resources at their disposal. Money fulfils a passive role when it is not '. . . an instrument influencing the flow of material factors of the reproduction process, but is, on the contrary, a passive reflection of this process' [3, p. 137]. This is not to say that passive money does not fulfil useful functions. The functions it fulfils, however, are in the recording and checking of plan fulfilment. Passive money does not act as a means to permit independent decision-making.

The type of feeding system used to a great extent determines the function of money within the state sector. The broader the qualitative limits of decentralization of financial matters (see 7.4), i.e. the greater the enterprise's freedom of choice in the use of financial resources, the more active is the role of money. The broader the quantitative limits of financial decentralization, i.e. the greater the share of total investment funds at the disposal of enterprises, the greater the percentage of total resources covered by active money. The nature of the macro-economic feeding system obviously has great bearing on the real qualitative and quantitative limits of financial decentralization. A sellers' market for capital goods with the accompanying factors of central allocation and use control, may, as we have already pointed out, reduce the enterprise authority in financial decisions, to a purely formal function.

References to Chapter Seven

1. *Biblioteka Gospodarki Materialowej* (Library on Planning and Management of Supplies), Warsaw, from 1968 on.
2. Bober M.: *Intermediate Price and Income Theory*, New York, 1955.
3. Brus W.: *Ogolne problemy funkcjonowania gospodarki socjalistycznej* (General Problems of Functioning of a Socialist Economy), Warsaw, 1961.
4. —— 'Economic Incentives for Technical Progress and Changes in the Planning and Management System', *ZG*, 15, 1966.
5. 'Changes in the Financial System of Industry', *F*, 3, 1971.
6. Charkiewicz M.: *Programowanie i projektowanie modernizacji przedsiebiorstwa przemyslowego* (Planning and Programming of Modernization of Industrial Enterprise), Warsaw, 1970.
7. Cholinski T.: *Zapasy w przedsiebiorstwie przemyslowym* (Stocks in an Industrial Enterprise), Warsaw, 1969.
8. Cholinski T., Michajlow G., and Milewski S.: *Gospodarka zapasami w krajach socjalistycznych* (Management of Stocks in Socialist Countries), Warsaw, 1967.
9. 'Criteria Governing Industrial Enterprises' Success Indicators. Conclusions of the Party-State Commission on Industrial Enterprise Success Indicators', in [21].
10. Chwieduk R.: *Warunki efektywnego zastosowania automatyzacji w przemysle* (Conditions for the Effective Use of Automation in Industry), Warsaw, 1970.
11. Decree 170 of the CM of 15 May 1960 on profitability of output produced by new techniques in centrally planned industries (*przemysl kluczowy*). Unpublished.
12. Decree 417 of the CM of 23 December 1963 on principles of wage fund control in centrally controlled state industrial enterprises, *MP*, 4, 1964.
13. Decree 100 of the CM of 27 April 1964 on principles of financing investment, *MP*, 23, 1964.
14. Decree 276 of the CM of 28 October 1965 on the financial system of centrally planned industrial associations and enterprises, *MP*, 61, 1965.
15. Decree 279 of the CM of 28 October 1965 on interest charged on fixed assets in certain state enterprises, *MP*, 61, 1965.

16. Decree of the Minister of Finance of 11 November 1965 in respect of interest charged on fixed assets in centrally planned state industrial enterprises, *MP*, 61, 1965.
17. Decree 30 of the CM of 1 February 1966 on the principles and procedures of setting and on the application of ex-factory prices and accounting prices in nationalized industries, *MP*, 7, 1966.
18. Decree of the CM and the Central Council of Trade Unions of 1 July 1970 on the incentive system of employees of centrally planned enterprises and associations for the years 1971–5, in [*42*].
19. Decree 176 of the CM of 9 November 1970 on the financial system in centrally planned state enterprises, *kombinaty* and industrial and construction associations, *MP*, 40, 1970.
20. Decree 178 of the CM of 9 November 1970 on interest charges on fixed *i*assets of state enterprises, *MP*, 40, 1970.
21. Dudzinski W., Misiak M., eds.: *Mierniki oceny dzialalnosci przedsebiorstwa przemyslowego* (Success Indicators in the Industrial Enterprise), Warsaw, 1964.
22. Fick B.: *Bodzce ekonomiczne w przemysle* (Economic Incentives in Industry), Warsaw, 1965.
23. Gadomski K., ed.: *Podstawowe zagadnienia zbytu w przemysle* (Basic Problems of Planning and Management of Supplies in Industry), Warsaw, 1967.
24. Galeski B., ed.: *Zmiany spoleczne i postep techniczny* (Social Change and Technical Progress), Wroclaw, 1971.
25. Garlinski B.: *Metody ksztaltowania zapasow* (The Methods of Determining Stock Levels), Warsaw, 1971.
26. Gordon J.: *Zarys ekonomiki postepu technicznego* (An Outline of the Economics of Technical Progress), Warsaw, 1966.
27. Holdowska E.: *Czynnik organizacyjny w postepie technicznym* (The Organization Factor in Technical Progress), Warsaw, 1968.
28. Jedrychowski S.: 'Basic Problems of Industrial Enterprise Success Indicators', in [*21*].
29. Kierczynski T. and Wojciechowska U.: *Finanse przedsiebiorstw socjalistycznych* (Finances of Socialist Enterprises), Warsaw, 1967.
30. Knight F. H.: *Risk, Uncertainty, and Profit*, London, 1933.
31. Krol A.: *Postep techniczny a kwalifikacje* (Technical Progress and Qualifications), Warsaw, 1970.
32. Krygier K., Witkowski H.: *Zaopatrzenie i gospodarka materialowa w przemysle* (Planning and Management of Supplies in Industry), Warsaw, 1970.
33. Kuznets S.: *Six Lectures on Economic Growth*, New York, 1961.
34. Kwejt J. ed.: *Zarzadzanie gospodarka materialowa* (Planning and Management of Supplies), Warsaw, 1970.
35. Madej Z.: *Zysk w gospodarce socjalistycznej* (Profit in a Socialist Economy), Warsaw, 1963.
36. Marlewicz M.: *Finansowanie postepu technicznego w krajach socjalistycznych* (Financing Technical Progress in Socialist Countries), Warsaw, 1968.
37. Moszczynski J.: 'Financial Implications of Starting Production' (*uruchomienie produkcji*), *F*, 3, 1962.
38. —— *Koszty rozwoju techniki* (Costs of Technical Progress), Warsaw, 1966.
39. Nalecz-Jawecki A.: *Spoleczne dzialanie na rzecz postepu technicznego* (Social Action to Encourage Technical Progress), Warsaw, 1970.
40. 'The new financial system in industry. The draft of the Decree of the Council of Ministers'. *ZG*, 50, 1969.
41. Nietyksza B.: *Eksperyment, ryzyko, odpowiedzialnosc karna* (Experiment, Risk, Penal Responsibility), Warsaw, 1967.
42. *Nowy system bodzcow materialnego zainteresowania. Zbior podstawowych*

dokumentow (New System of Material Incentives. Collected Basic Documents), Warsaw, 1970.
43. Ostrowski Z.: *Badania naukowe i prace rozwojowe w gospodarce narodowej* (Research and Development in the National Economy), Warsaw, 1968.
44. Pilawski B.: *Obliczanie efektow ekonomicznych postepu technicznego w przedsie- biorstwie* (Calculation of the Economic Effects of Technical Progress in the Enterprise), Warsaw, 1970, 3rd edn.
45. Poplawski H.: *Dopuszczalne ryzyko gospodarcze w przedsiebiorstwie* (Acceptable Economic Risk in the Enterprise), Warsaw, 1970.
46. *Przepisy o planowaniu i inwestycji* (Decrees on Planning and Investments), Warsaw, 1969.
47. *Rocznik statystyczny 1970* (Statistical Yearbook 1970), Warsaw, 1970.
48. Samecki W.: *Ryzyko i niepewnosc w dzialalnosci przedsiebiorstwa przemyslowego* (Risk and Uncertainty in Industrial Enterprise Activity), Warsaw, 1967.
49. Schumpeter J.: *Capitalism, Socialism and Democracy*, New York and London, 1942.
50. —— *The Theory of Economic Development*, Cambridge, Mass., 1955.
51. Staszkow M.: *Wynalazki i ich ochrona w prawie polskim* (Inventions and their Protection in Polish Law), Wroclaw, 1970.
52. Stonier A. W. and Hague D. C.: *A Textbook of Economic Theory*, London, 1956.
53. Szyrocki J.: *Samofinansowanie przedsiebiorstw* (Enterprises' Self-financing), Warsaw, 1967.
54. Tarka Z.: *Zasady obrotu srodkami produkcji* (Principles of Planning and Manage- ment of Supplies), Warsaw, 1963.
55. Urbanek T.: *Efektywnosc procesow zbytu i zaopatrzenia materialowego* (The Effectiveness of Planning and Management of Supplies), Warsaw, 1970.
56. Wiles P.: *The Political Economy of Communism*, Oxford, 1964.
57. Winter E.: 'Changes in the Financial System of Centrally Planned Industrial Enterprises and Industrial Associations', in [60].
58. Wojciechowska U.: *Finansowanie postepu technicznego* (Financing of Technical Progress), Warsaw, 1964.
59. Zachariasz J.: 'Ex-Factory Prices', *ZG*, 26, 1967.
60. *Zasady nowego systemu finansowego przemyslu, budownictwa oraz inwestycji* (The Principles of the New Financial System in Industry, Construction, and Investment), Warsaw, 1966. Mimeographed.
61. Zielinski J. G.: *Rachunek ekonomiczny w socjalizmie* (Economic Calculation in a Socialist Economy), Warsaw, 1967.
62. —— *Lectures on the Theory of Socialist Planning*, Ibadan-London, 1968.

CHAPTER EIGHT

MANAGEMENT AT BRANCH LEVEL

8.1 Different Models of Branch Organization

8.1.1 THREE TYPES OF INDUSTRIAL ASSOCIATIONS

The role of industrial associations in planning—especially operative planning—and management depends on their functions within the industrial hierarchy and the scope of their authority over member-enterprises. Taking these as a criterion the following basic types of industrial associations may be distinguished:

A. *The Industrial association as a government office.* Under this model, industrial associations are in fact part of the CPB and their functions are mainly administrative: to control and supervise the subordinate enterprises in the process of plan fulfilment. The rationale of their existence is explained by the phenomenon of limited span-of-management. Industrial associations have been created to help economic ministries to supervise their respective branches of the economy and—as we said in Appendix 1.1—originally were even part of these ministries as so-called 'branch departments' or 'branch central offices'.

B. *The Industrial association as a business corporation.* Under this model, the industrial association becomes the basic unit of plan-carrying apparatus. The industrial association becomes the enterprise; former enterprises become divisions or firms. Under this structure, the CPB should, practically speaking, deal with industrial associations only, and industrial associations should be left free to decide how to organize their internal structure. According to circumstances, some of them could choose a General Motors type of decentralized structure or a Republic Steel centralized type of organization. Under a corporation model, all plan targets—if any—should be fixed for industrial associations only, which should be fully and solely responsible for meeting them. All instruments and measures of government economic policy should also be directed exclusively at industrial associations.

C. *The Industrial association as an association of independent enterprises.* Under this model, industrial associations are organizations created by independent enterprises as their service organizations for such purposes as: production and technological research, designing, short- and long-term market research, advertising, and the like.

Organizational and functional details of this type of association may be very different indeed, but its basic common feature must be a complete lack of administrative power over member-enterprises, irrespective of whether membership is voluntary or compulsory.

The choice of a particular model of industrial association is closely connected with the type of economic system aimed at. Industrial associations as a part of the CPB are clearly a feature of a centralized system under which the CPB tries to manage and supervise directly the plan executants—industrial enterprises. Such a model of industrial associations was a prevailing practice in all East European countries until mid 1950s and early 1960s. Some economists [10, p. 380] maintain that the choice between our model B and C does not necessarily indicate in itself a preference for a more or less decentralized economic system, but rather the level at which decentralization is to be placed: at branch level—model B, at enterprise level—model C. The correctness or incorrectness of this position depends on the definition of decentralization. It is useful to distinguish not only between administrative and parametric managements, but also between state-parametric and market-parametric management models, depending on *how* the parameters are determined—by the CPB or by the market (see 4.4). If decentralization is defined simply as the use of parametric management, irrespective of how parameters are determined, it is compatible with the business corporation model. If, on the other hand, the concept of decentralization is reserved to the description of the market-parametric model only, then the business corporation model is detrimental to the development of market determined parameters for obvious reasons stated eloquently by the theory of monopolistic competition. It has been noted by Polish economists that the choice between the industrial association as a business corporation or association of independent enterprises reflects also the CPB's readiness to rely on the market mechanism. If the CPB decides 'to entrust the shaping of economic relations between enterprises to the market mechanism (which obviously does not preclude intervening in the functioning of the market through price policy and other measures)'—then it chooses model C. If, on the other hand, the CPB wants 'to create an organized set of relations, in which—alongside with the market—there is a possibility of more direct shaping of the social division of labour and factors of technical and economic development', then it opts for model B (both quotations are from [14, p. 43]).

The above description applies, broadly, to what actually happened in Eastern Europe. The believers in the 'guided market model' have chosen our model C (Hungary) or intended to choose it (Czechoslovakia), while Bulgaria, GDR, Poland, and Rumania—which we shall call 'cautious reformers'—all stick to variants of our model B.

8.1.2 CORPORATION VERSUS ENTERPRISE ORGANIZATION OF INDUSTRY

A Lack of Consistent Policy

The problem of industrial organization is, however, considered by Polish economists themselves as still wide open.[1] The influential economic weekly *Zycie Gospodarcze* together with the Research Institute of the Planning Commission announced on 1 December 1968 a questionnaire for its readers about 'Enterprise in Experimenting Associations' [6]. The editorial article accompanying this questionnaire states frankly that: (1) Polish views on the relative role of industrial associations and enterprises were and are fluctuating considerably over time. In 1956–7 all changes aimed at broadening enterprise autonomy. The Decree of the CM of 18 April 1958 which created the industrial association as a *khozraschyot* organization already indicated a certain change of viewpoint. This decree was not implemented, however, and only the years 1964–6 brought a decisive change of official attitude. The resolutions of the IVth Congress and then the IVth Plenum of the CC of PUWP (27–8 July 1965) together with the subsequent Decree 283 of the CM (November 1965) [3; see also 24] put the main stress on problems of the concentration and specialization of production and hence on industrial associations as a basic level of planning and management. (2) Differences of opinion, however, still persist among experts. If some economists think that the slow progress of the reforms of Polish planning and management in 1956–66 was due to too much stress on enterprises, others ask if 'the reasons for our delays in reform implementation are not the result of a basic assumption, which puts the main stress on the role of industrial associations and neglects the role of enterprises?' [16, p. 9].

Similar fluctuations of opinion (and practice) are evident in other socialist countries as well, as has been already noted. Even in GDR where reforms, like the Polish reforms, put the main stress on industrial associations, there are noticeable changes in emphasis over time. If during the first stage of reform implementation in 1964 and 1965, industrial associations got practically all the attention, recently '. . . the strengthening of enterprises position has taken place as is witnessed by their statutes, without, however, any formal changes in industrial organization' [6].[2]

---

[1] 'The reform of the management mechanism introduced [in Poland] in 1966'—we read in a leading Polish textbook on enterprise finance—'did change the functioning of associations in a number of aspects. It seems, however, that these changes did not increase the economic role of the association to the degree postulated and proposed during the discussions preceding this reform. Bearing this in mind . . . the problem of elaborating the new model of association is, in our opinion, still open in Polish practice' [10, p. 381, fn. 1].

[2] A similar observation was made by M. Gamarnikow in his recent book [8, p. 55].

B. *Theoretical Controversy*

In the circumstances it may be worth while to analyse briefly the arguments for the industrial association solution versus the enterprise solution.

The supporters of the industrial association solution use mainly the economies of scale argument (advantages of concentration and specialization of production, in East European parlance) and the externalities argument. In practical terms the advantages of mass production and the necessity of large expenditures for technical progress—beyond the possibilities of individual enterprises—are most frequently quoted. The advantage of having the industrial association for implementing the CPB's preferences is also sometimes mentioned [*14*, p. 43]. The main strength of industrial association supporters lies, however, in *fait accompli*. As industrial associations not only exist, but are very strongly entrenched in most East European countries, their supporters do not have to exert themselves unduly to justify the necessity of their existence. Such being the case, the main burden of argument lies with the opponents of the industrial association.

(1) The monopoly argument is the one most frequently used by the opponents of the industrial association solution. Proponents of the 'guided market model' complain mainly that existence of branch monopolies undermines the proper functioning of the market and that monopoly prices distort the data for economic calculation and resource allocation. Economists from countries which are 'cautious reformers', put the main stress on lack of external economic pressures for technical progress and losses to consumers owing to quality deterioration and price increases [*14*, p. 46].

It has been duly pointed out that (a) the degree of concentration is very high in most socialist countries,[1] (b) participation of social organizations, such as trade unions or workers' councils, in enterprise management cannot be effective against monopolistic abuses, because their members are themselves materially interested in monopolistic practices, (c) paradoxically the long-term profit motive acts as a less effective self-constraint than in a capitalist economy, because fear of new entries is ineffective[2] and management's time horizon is necessarily much shorter than under private or corporation ownership conditions.[3]

---

[1] The degree of concentration of production in East European countries is usually measured by the share of big enterprises in total employment as in the Table 8.1. Of course the data showing *product* concentration in individual enterprises would be much more useful, but are difficult to obtain, except on a very fragmentary basis.

[2] Basic investment decisions belong to the CPB, which is price insensitive by definition. If the CPB wanted investment decisions to be price sensitive, it would leave them at enterprise or industrial association level.

[3] On all these problems see the excellent book [*13*, Ch. IV and *passim*].

*Table 8.1: The Distribution of the Number of Workers in
East European Countries according to the Size of the Firm*
(data for 1967?)

No.	Country	−500	501–1,000	1,001–5,000	5,001–10,000	10,001–	Total
		Percentage of firms employing the above number of workers					
1.	Czechoslovakia	7·2	8·1	55·4	16·7	12·6	100
2.	Bulgaria	31·8	20·9	39·2	4·3	3·8	100
3.	GDR	42·7	16·8	29·8	8·2	2·5	100
4.	Hungary	9·7	7·9	47·9	20·0	14·5	100
5.	Poland	21·2	16·5	47·2	11·9	3·2	100
6.	Rumania	13·6	20·2	51·9	8·8	5·5	100
7.	Soviet Union	24·2	16·5	37·0	11·1	11·2	100

Source: L. Tüü: 'Concentration of Industrial Activity and Industrial Organization in Hungary', *Kozgazdasagi Szemle*, 9, 1968. (The table was kindly translated for the author by Dr. I. Varallga, from the Research Institute of Agricultural Economics, Oxford University).

There is also abundant evidence that enterprises do behave as *textbook* monopolies, they: (1) restrict output, (2) raise prices, and (3) lower quality. Ample illustrations of all these phenomena are provided daily by the East European press and do not have to be repeated here (see, however, Ch. 9 and esp. [23] for some striking data).

All these problems have been admitted and analysed even by supporters of the industrial association solution. The remedies proposed by them include: (a) central price fixing; (b) resort to imports as a method of forcing domestic (monopolistic) prices down; (c) intra-branch competition; (d) prevention of a fully monopolistic position by leaving some outsiders beyond the industrial association's direct powers; (e) prevention—by legislative means and administrative controls—of monopolistic practices in the market.[1]

It seems to the author that the monopoly argument against industrial associations deserves a few critical comments.

First of all, the remedies proposed are either worse than the illness itself (central price fixing) or completely impractical. Nobody who knows anything about the real functioning of East European economies can seriously think that 'resorting to imports', for example, can be a practical method for forcing down domestic prices. The foreign exchange allocations are most rigidly controlled and any increase in the planned level of foreign exchange spending requires intervention at the level of the Ministry of Finance and the approval of the Prime Minister's Office. As a result, industrial associations, who have spent their foreign exchange allocations and then face an urgent need for components which are usually imported, are willing to pay practically any price in zlotys to have it manufactured domestically. The author

[1] For discussion of (a), see [*13*, pp. 220–45]; for (b) to (e), see [*14*, pp. 45–8].

knows cases when 150–200 zlotys per dollar have been paid by industrial associations for unplanned import-substituting products. To give the reader some idea what this rate of exchange means, let us indicate that transfer prices of imported goods are usually only 10–25 per cent higher than their domestic equivalents (if such exist), the tourist exchange rate is $1 = 24 zl., shadow dollar prices used in investment calculations are 44 zl. per dollar for machinery and equipment and 60 zl. per dollar for raw materials and semi-finished goods [20, p. 43] when the highest marginal-exchange rate for foreign trade transactions varies between 90–100 zl. per dollar.[1] Also, quality deterioration and hidden price increases continue unabated in spite of the flow of legislation trying to prevent them (see Ch. 9), and the belief in the effectiveness of intra-branch competition cannot be taken seriously by anybody who is aware of the horizontal organization of industrial associations, the persistent sellers' market, and the price insensitivity of state enterprises. We are not, of course, denying the potential usefulness of the anti-monopolistic steps advocated by some Polish economists, but we want to stress merely that under the *present* management mechanism they are almost totally useless. The proponents of these measures have failed, however, to specify what changes of management mechanism they deem necessary to make their proposals effective.

Secondly, the anti-monopolistic proposals advanced, failed to analyse the practical possibility of separating actual monopolistic *position* from monopolistic *behaviour* by devising special 'rules of the game' for branch organizations. This possibility was first mentioned by Oskar Lange [11] and then developed by other Polish economists see, e.g. [19, pp. 55–108], but never commanded any attention. It is quite possible that these proposals are also impractical, but they deserve examination on, at least, equal terms with other proposals which have already been proved as of no practical value.

Thirdly, and most importantly, the question arises: is the branch-monopoly type of industrial organization the main reason for the negative behaviour which we are used to associate with monopolistic or oligopolistic competition? It is the present author's opinion that the real reason is first of all the existence of a sellers' market, and secondly the *de facto* monopolistic position of many enterprises. If we are right, then two conclusions follow: (a) Dissolving industrial associations will not much improve enterprise behaviour in branches which have a *de facto* competitive or nearly competitive structure (say in the clothing industry), because the sole existence of a sellers' market is enough to lead to poor quality and highly priced output. (b) The policy of 'concentration and specialization' carried out for the last fifteen or twenty years resulted in an unusual number of enterprises being the

[1] Personal interview.

II

sole or almost the sole producers of certain goods—from railway carriages to sewing machines or detergents. Dissolving the appropriate industrial associations will still leave Poland with an essentially monopolistic structure in very many branches of industry. Breaking *de facto* monopolies is a completely different and much more complicated matter than dissolving *artificial* monopolies created by horizontal integration.

(2) The monopoly argument is the one most commonly used against the industrial association structure but is certainly not the only one. At least two others deserve to be mentioned briefly. One is that the 'concentration and specialization advantages' argument is pushed much too far in Poland. 'It is frequently argued,' writes one of the Polish opponents of the industrial association solution, 'that increasing the role of associations is in accord with modern tendencies towards [industrial] concentration, which is strongly evident, for example, in a capitalist economy. This argument is, however, based on a serious misunderstanding. It is true that in a capitalistic economy there are tendencies towards concentration, but they never include industry as a whole. Supporters of absolute concentration evidently do not realize what is the scope and role of small enterprises in the home countries of the biggest capitalist monopolies ... It is also worth noting that these concerns are based on real advantages of economies of scale or emerge as a result of competitive struggle, but are not created by a mechanistic grouping of firms belonging to the same branch of industry' [*16*, p. 1].

(3) Finally, some authors favour the industrial association solution if, and only if, '. . . it does not undermine the position and responsibility of enterprises ... All advantages resulting from possibilities of more rational economic activities within the framework of big economic groupings, may be jeopardized by bureaucratic, centralized management at industrial association level. Losses resulting from the lack of real economic accountability in the enterprises (owing to the centralization of decisions at the higher level), from undermining their initiative and incentives resulting from the feeling of responsibility for their own decisions, can be much greater than theoretical possibilities of more rational [economic] calculation at the higher level' [*14*, p. 45].

Here the authors quoted raise the important question of the benefits of scale and externalities of the industrial association solution versus efficiency losses at enterprise level. The authors intuitively believe that the former are worth having only if the latter can be avoided. Unfortunately, they fail to prove whether (a) the industrial association solution must always lead to lower efficiency at enterprise level, and (b) if such losses do occur, they must be greater than the benefits under *any* conditions. Obviously the efficiency losses at enterprise level—if any— will depend to a great extent on the *internal* management mechanism of the industrial association. Equally, the benefits of branch level calculation will vary both with the type of intra-branch relationships determining the scale of externalities and with the *quality* of information provided by enterprises, which again depends substantially on the management mechanism used.

Without pretending that we have the ready-made solution—if there is any—to the problem of 'optimal' organization of socialist industry, a few comments may be offered:

(1) It seems rather obvious that only the enterprise and the industrial association models are internally consistent. All attempts to stop half-way between them produce the worst of both.

(2) As in a market economy so in the socialist economies of Eastern Europe there seems to be room for *both* solutions, in different branches of industry. In many cases there is no choice if there are *de facto* monopolies already established. Breaking them up for the sake of better market functioning would be prohibitively expensive.

(3) A proper management mechanism is as important at branch level as it is at national economy level. The result of a benefit-cost analysis of the branch versus the enterprise solution depends significantly on the possibility of designing a branch management mechanism which is characterized by (a) a low level of intra-branch information distortions, (b) strong incentives and a sufficient authority sphere for enterprise management to minimize efficiency losses at enterprise level. It is the author's belief—based on his studies of big American corporations [*18, passim*]—that devising such a branch management mechanism is within the range of practical possibilities.

8.2 Branch Management by Industrial Associations

8.2.1 THE AUTHORITY OVER ENTERPRISES' PLANS

In those East European countries which we called 'cautious reformers', the existing industrial associations are a mixture of our models A and B. Economic reforms in Poland are characterized by efforts to decentralize at enterprise and branch level *simultaneously*. As a result the present 'dual character' of industrial associations emerged. On the one hand they ceased to be pure government offices and became 'economic organizations' based on the 'economic accountability' principle, rewarded according to the performance of subordinate enterprises, etc. On the other hand they did not become industrial corporations *sensu stricto*, at least theoretically, because of the belief that separate enterprises rather than industrial associations should remain the basic form of economic organization in socialist industry. 'However, economic practice [in Poland]—as well as experience in the Soviet Union, Czechoslovakia, or GDR—clearly indicates that in spite of proclaiming the enterprise a basic industrial unit, there develops a tendency towards grouping enterprises into bigger economic organisms' [*17*, p. 5]. We have little doubt that if this tendency has not been conveyed strongly enough by our discussion of branch and enterprise planning in Part I, the analysis of the *functioning* of industrial associations which we shall now undertake will make quite clear that the above opinion of a Polish expert on industrial programming properly reflects the actual changes in economic organization in Poland.

Many Polish economists [*14*, Ch. 4; *12*, Ch. 2; see also *2*] indicate that industrial associations fulfil the following basic functions: (1) mid- and long-term branch planning; (2) operative planning or—as it is most frequently called—'organization of the division of labour and resource allocation between enterprises'; (3) the development of research facilities and the creation of organizational and economic conditions for speedy technical progress; (4) service functions, such as common transportation, warehouses, sales organization, computer centres, etc. It is easy to see that only functions 1 and 4 could be reconciled with really independent enterprises and only on condition that mid- and long-term branch planning is purely indicative and participation in common services purely voluntary. But this is not the case in Polish industrial associations.

The very detailed nature of present-day branch operative planning has been already explained in 3.1. What we want to point out here is that industrial associations are in fact engaged in operative *management* of subordinate enterprises as well. For this purpose they have already been granted a very broad authority over their member-enterprises and this trend seems to continue, in spite of some sporadic protests or reservations [*16*].

First of all, industrial associations have the right to determine the *scope* of obligatory plan indices binding their member-enterprises. The number of plan directives which the association itself receives from its ministry constitutes only the minimum which it has to pass to enterprises. That this minimum is in most cases very substantially exceeded, is documented in Ch. 3.

Industrial associations have also the right to determine the *level* of enterprise planning tasks. Here again, the level of plan targets fixed for the industrial association as a whole is only a lowest level, below which the sum of enterprise targets should not fall. Polish industrial associations use this right for creating so-called association reserves by fixing the sum of enterprise targets above the association total and the sum of their allocated resources below its own allocations. This prevailing practice '. . . enables the association to intervene in enterprises during plan implementation; it is undoubtedly a useful and proper solution, which, however, makes enterprises dependent on the association and diminishes their responsibility for their own economic activity' [*10*, p. 383].

Finally, industrial associations have the right to *change* both the level and the content of enterprise plan targets during the whole planning period, till its very end. This problem has been already discussed in 2.2.2. and 3.2.2.C, so we will add only a few remarks here.

In the case of discrepancies between plan and actual fulfilment, the HAO have two alternatives: (a) they can accept the fact, introduce the necessary factual changes, but leaving the original plan targets unchanged; (b) the same, but with formal plan targets revised.

All socialist countries have chosen alternative b because leaving the plan unchanged would deprive, under the present incentive system, the managers and the workers of their bonuses and premia if there is even slight plan underfulfilment, or it could lead to very high enterprise funds and/or bonuses and premia payments—if there is substantial plan overfulfilment.[1] Changes in plan tasks are also necessary for giving an account of how the wage fund—which is strictly rationed—has been spent.

The right of industrial associations to change enterprise plan targets has been extended so far that it includes their right to annul and/or change by the mutual consent of the industrial associations involved the contractual agreements of their member-enterprises [5]. Annulment of contracts at the order of the industrial association frees the enterprises from any financial penalties if it informs the interested party of contract annulment (or change) within seven days after it itself has been informed about this decision. The industrial associations have also the right to force their member-enterprises to accept contracts which they previously refused to accept. To the above we should add that 'General Conditions of Sales' entitle the suppliers to cancel or postpone their domestic obligations in order to meet export contracts—even if these have been received on a later date [5; see also 1, p. 158]. These regulations, together with general shortages in the producer goods market, explain the serious and widespread deviations from the planned level of supplies to which socialist enterprises are subjected (see Table 3.3).

8.2.2 THE AUTHORITY OVER ENTERPRISES' RESOURCES

A *Industrial Association Redistribution Funds*

The right of industrial associations to fix and to manipulate

---

[1] As we have already discussed in 6.2.2, in Poland the managerial bonuses are reduced 20 per cent for each 1 per cent of underfulfilment of the basic bonus condition, which means that at the 95 per cent fulfilment level there are no bonuses at all. On the other hand the maximum volume of the bonus fund is fixed beforehand and there is no statutory provision for payment for plan overfulfilment, but industrial associations have a reserve bonus fund which they can use for rewarding outstanding achievements. At the same time there are no statutory ceilings for the enterprise development fund and enterprise fund. In practice in relatively rare cases of substantial plan overfulfilment plan targets are revised upward and extra funds are taken over by industrial associations.

enterprise plan targets is the most important but certainly not the only measure at their disposal. Second in importance is the right to redistribute resources between member-enterprises.

In Polish industrial practice there are two basic forms of re-distribution of financial resources: (a) industrial associations create special redistribution funds; (b) industrial associations use their role as intermediary between enterprises and the state budget for the purpose of intra-branch redistribution.

Ad (a) 1. The basic and universal redistribution fund is the industrial association *reserve fund* created from part of enterprise profits. Till 1966 it was created at a uniform level of 10 per cent of each enterprise's development fund. Since 1 January 1966, economic ministries deter-mine for industrial associations only the minimum level of their reserve funds, but each industrial association has a right to fix its actual level as it deems necessary. The industrial association reserve fund is mainly used for: (1) covering enterprise unplanned losses; (2) supplementing their insufficient working capital; and (3) supplementing enterprises' own investment and capital repairs funds [see *10*, pp. 400–1].

In most cases enterprises receive financial help from the industrial association reserve fund as a non-repayable subsidy, but it is also used for granting loans to needy enterprises and as financial backing for association guarantees given to the banks, in cases when the latter refuse to lend to enterprises which are in serious financial trouble. Generally the industrial association reserve fund is a flexible instrument of economic intervention which can be used in a wide range of cases.

2. As a rule, socialist enterprises face a uniform selling price for a given good, whatever their individual costs of production may be [see 5.4.2]. If, however, '(1) Differences in objective conditions of production (technical level of production equipment, geological conditions, etc.) result in sub-stantial and lasting cost differentials between enterprises within a given association, accounting prices may be used. (2) The use of accounting prices requires that at industrial association or selling organization (*centrala zbytu*) level a clearing account of price differentials will be established. This account will be further referred to as a *price clearing account*' [*4*; italics added]. Intra-branch accounting prices are based on an individual enterprise's cost of producing a given article plus the approved rate of profit. The differences between the established accounting prices and the ex-factory (or transfer) price at which the industrial association sells its product are cleared through the account mentioned: low-cost enterprises pay in surpluses over the approved rate of profit, high-cost producers get appropriate subsidies. The difference between these subsidies and surpluses goes to or is received from the state budget.

The price clearing account is an important redistribution fund in those industrial associations where it has been established. It enables the association to keep its high-cost enterprises going (and inefficient ones too!), and the right of fixing accounting prices and of varying the profit rate included in them gives the industrial association a potentially important economic instrument.[1]

Ad (b). The plan financial targets of the industrial association as a whole form the basis of payments between the association and the state budget. As the association has the right—as we have already noted—to fix the sum of enterprise obligation at a higher level than its own financial targets, the *budget account* is also used as an extra redistribution device. Industrial associations have been granted the right to use any surplus from this account for paying subsidies and for covering the unplanned losses of its member-enterprises.

B *Industrial Association Special Funds*

In Polish industrial practice a number of so-called special funds, i.e. funds which must be spent for a given purpose, are created not only at enterprise but also at industrial association level. The most important of industrial association special funds are the *investment fund* (created out of enterprise profits) and the *fund for technico-economic progress* (paid by enterprise fees, which are charged into their cost of production). Both these funds have their exact counterparts in member-enterprises, but both quantitatively and qualitatively, industrial association investment and technical progress funds are of predominant importance.

(1) Association investments are still substantially bigger than enterprise investments, as can be seen in Table 8.2.

Table 8.2: *Industrial Association and Enterprise Investments in Poland* (in million zlotys, current prices)

	1961	1962	1963	1964
Association investments[a]	10,694	12,423	13,000	14,279
Enterprise investments[b]	8,112	7,514	7,850	—

[a] Data of Polish Investment Bank.
[b] Data of Polish National Bank (estimated).

Source: A. Plocica: *Inwestycje w Polsce. Zarys systemu i polityki* (Investments in Poland. Outline of the System and Policy), Warsaw, 1967, pp. 39 and 41.

(2) Moreover, association investments are at present growing much faster than enterprise investments (Table 8.3).

---

[1] The economics of intra-branch accounting prices is an interesting subject in itself —with many arguments both for and against their use—but its analysis would take us too far from our present discussion.

Table 8.3: Relative Growth of Different Types of Investments in Poland

	1965	1966
Central investments	100	90
Association investments	100	138
Enterprise investments	100	110

Source: A. Plocica: op. cit., p. 229.

(3) Association investments are less vulnerable to the lack of capacity of construction enterprises (many industrial associations have their own construction enterprises) and to the lack of bank credits, which, in practice, substantially diminish the enterprise's possibility of investing.[1]

(4) The industrial association determines the overall investment policy, including most of enterprise investment which theoretically is up to enterprises to decide, but in practice requires association approval in most cases.

Industrial associations have even more say in enterprise policy on technical progress, including new product development. The fund for technico-economic progress is created at industrial association level and then allocated between enterprises as the association deems appropriate. Part of this fund is retained at association level for direct financing of research and development on a contractual basis. As there is no necessary correlation between any enterprise contributions to association investment and technical progress funds and its share in their allocation between enterprises, these funds can also be considered as a form of intra-branch redistribution of resources.

The reason why the main initiative in the field of technical progress is retained at branch level in all socialist countries (except Hungary), lies in the lack of adequate incentives to innovate at enterprise level. This has been discussed in 7.6.

C *Intra-branch 'Rational Specialization'*

The right of *financial redistribution* is only one aspect of the much broader powers of the industrial association to redistribute material resources between its member-enterprises. As we have mentioned already, the new legislation enables the industrial association to transfer machines and equipment between enterprises without compensation, and raw materials with compensation. It is done for the sake of intra-branch 'rational specialization', but frequently with total

---

[1] 'Enterprise investments are not limited by state plan. In principle enterprises can engage in investments up to the limits of their own financial resources allocated for investment purposes (according to existing regulations) and the possibilities of getting and repaying bank credits. In practice, however, there are certain constraints in undertaking and fulfilling those investments owing to the country's economic situation, the limits of bank credits for enterprise investments, and also to difficulties in placing orders with constructing-building enterprises' [15, p. 40].

disregard of an enterprise's economic self-interest. For example,
recently the gearbox division of the Starachowice Truck Factory was
moved—including qualified personnel—to Tczew, where a specialized
gearbox plant was being established by the Industrial Association of
Motor-transport. Before long the Starachowice Truck Factory was
informed that the price of the gearbox they were using had almost
doubled, and later deliveries revealed that up to 50 per cent of them
were deficient, endangering plan fulfilment and managerial bonuses and
workers' premia.[1]

8.2.3 INCENTIVE POLICY

Last but not least, is the association right to fix the level of *managerial
bonuses* and *workers premia* (both are fixed as a certain percentage of
so-called basic salaries and wages funds) and to determine quarterly the
bonus conditions for each enterprise's management separately (see
6.2.2).

According to present legislation, the industrial association has the
right to fix the percentage scale of both managerial bonuses and
workers' premia within the total limit allotted to it by its ministry,
differentiating it according to the tautness and difficulty of plan targets
in individual enterprises. In addition, the industrial association should
keep at its disposal certain reserve bonus/premia funds to be used during
the year for rewarding the fulfilment of tasks over and above original
plan targets or for plan changes disadvantageous to a given enterprise.
Such use of reserve bonus/premia funds should diminish enterprise
resistance to accepting more difficult planning targets during the year.
Industrial associations are also given the power to fix and to change
quarterly the so-called branch bonus conditions (see Appendix 3.2),
as well as to change their relative significance by assigning a different
percentage of the total bonus fund for their fulfilment (see 6.2.2). This
practice of quarterly changes of bonus conditions which is tantamount
to constantly pointing out to enterprise management what to do first—
say, during this quarter of the year reduce inventories and attend to
exports, during the next complete your investment project and finish
design work on new products, etc.—undermines the functioning of
profit incentives and is detrimental to the training of creative managerial
staff with an overall view of their enterprises.

The 'dual nature' of industrial associations to which we referred
above at the beginning of this section is clearly perceived by Polish
economists and lawyers [*1*, pp. 160–1; *9*, p. 487; *10*, p. 375; *12*, pp. 41–2],
many of whom support it as inevitable, workable, and advantageous.
Inevitable, because '... economic calculation of individual enterprises
within the framework of the market mechanism cannot solve sufficiently

[1] Personal interview.

correctly the basic economic problem of the rational social division of labour and resource allocation'. Workable, because the 'existence of industrial associations and the delegation to them of certain functions in the sphere of industrial management can be reconciled, it seems, with preserving the significant role and responsibility of the enterprises'. Advantageous, because industrial associations can assure the '... rational division of labour (mainly determination of the direction of specialization) and the [rational] allocation of resources (mainly investments) between their subordinate enterprises' [*14*, pp. 43, 44, and 45].

These—one suspects—officially[1] optimistic views are not shared universally, however. Many Polish economists—including the present author [*21*, pp. 212–14]—indicated the inherent difficulties of maintaining *à la longue* the dual role of industrial associations. It is impossible to decentralize effectively *both* at industrial association and enterprise level. According to official pronouncements, the industrial associations' scope of authority should be broadened at the expense of economic ministries with simultaneous broadening of enterprise freedom of action. The experience of East European countries indicates, however, that the expanding *economic* functions of the industrial association inevitably leads to the diminishing of enterprise independence.

In 8.1.2.B I have already expressed the opinion that only 'pure' corporation or individual enterprise models represent internally consistent solutions. It may be interesting to note here that all efforts to stop halfway between these two models represent an 'unstable equilibrium', with a pronounced tendency to move towards the corporation model managed internally by administrative means. This is due to the fact that what industrial associations lack as a full-blooded corporation, they try to overcome by relying on their prerogatives as government offices which have the right to issue administrative orders to their subordinate member-enterprises. The above-mentioned tendency is quite pronounced not only in Poland but also in other socialist countries which try to maintain a similar dualistic kind of branch management (see [*22*]).

References to Chapter Eight

1. Buczkowski S.: 'Enterprises' Legal Relations with other Units of Socialized Economy' in [*7*, pp. 149–70].
2. Decree 276 of the CM, 28 October 1965, concerning the Financial Rules of Centrally-planned Industrial Associations and their Member-enterprises, *MP*, 61, 1965.

[1] In 1968, when the book quoted was published, J. Pajestka was Director of the Planning Institute of the Polish Planning Commission and K. Secomski the Commission's Vice-Chairman in charge of investment policies. At present both are Vice-Chairmen of the Commission.

3. Decree 283 of the CM, 9 November 1965, concerning the Project of the State Budget and Certain Rules for its Implementation (unpublished).
4. Decree 30 of the CM, 1 February 1966, concerning principles and methods of fixing ex-factory and accounting prices in socialized industry and methods of their application, *MP*, 7, 1966.
5. Decree of the Chairman of the Planning Commission at the CM, 7 October 1966, concerning General Conditions of Sales in the Home Market, *MP*, 57, 1966, with changes announced in *MP*, 6, 1967 and 36, 1969.
6. 'The Enterprise in an Experimenting Association' (editorial comment), *ZG*, 48, 1968.
7. *Przedsiebiorstwo w polskim systemie spoleczno-ekonomicznym* (The Enterprise in the Polish Socio-economic System), Warsaw, 1967.
8. Gamarnikow M.: *Economic Reforms in Eastern Europe*, Detroit, 1968.
9. Glinski B.: *Teorie i praktyka zarzadzania przedsiebiorstwami przemyslowymi* (Theories and Practice of Management in Industrial Enterprises), Warsaw, 1966.
10. Kierczynski T., Wojciechowska U.: *Finanse przedsiebiorstw socjalistycznych* (Finances of Socialist Enterprises), Warsaw, 1967.
11. Lange O.: *On the Economic Theory of Socialism*, Minneapolis, Minn., many editions.
12. Leskiewicz Z.: *Zjednoczenie—organizacja branzowa przemyslu socjalistycznego* (Association—Branch Organization of Socialist Industry), Warsaw, 1961.
13. Mujzel J.: *Przedsiebiorstwo socjalistyczne a rynek* (Socialist Enterprise and the Market), Warsaw, 1966.
14. Pajestka J., Secomski K.: *Doskonalenie planowania i funkcjonowania gospodarki w Polsce Ludowej* (Improvement of the Planning and Functioning of the Economy in People's Poland), Warsaw, 1968.
15. Plocica A.: *Inwestycje w Polsce. Zarys Systemu i Polityki* (Investments in Poland. The Outline of the System and Policy), Warsaw, 1967.
16. Polaczek S.: 'Let us not Forget the Enterprise', *ZG*, 41, 1968.
17. Radzikowski W.: *Ekonomiczny rachunek repartycji zadan i srodkow zjednoczenia przemyslowego* (Economic Calculation of Allocation of Tasks and Resources within the Industrial Association), Warsaw, 1967.
18. Zielinski J. G.: *Big Business. Z problematyki nowych technik zarzadzania* (Big Business. The Problem of New Management Techniques), Warsaw, 1962.
19. —— *Rachunek ekonomiczny w socjalizmie* (Economic Calculation Under Socialism), Warsaw, 1967.
20. —— *Lectures on the Theory of Socialist Planning*, Ibadan-London, 1968.
21. —— 'On the Theory of Economic Reforms and their Optimal Sequence', *EP*, 3, 1968.
22. —— 'Planification et gestion au niveau de la branche industrielle en Europe de l'Est', *RE*, 1, 1970.
23. —— 'On the Effectiveness of the Polish Economic Reforms', *SS*, 3, 1971.
24. Zebrowski E.: 'Changes in the Financial System of Centrally Planned Industrial Associations and Enterprises', *PUG*, 2, 1966.

CONCLUSIONS

CHAPTER NINE

ON THE EFFECTIVENESS OF THE POLISH ECONOMIC REFORMS

9.1 Were the Polish Economic Reforms Successful?

As we have indicated in 1.1.1, the Polish reforms, which started in 1956, included changes in growth strategy, the planning process, the mechanism for plan implementation in the socialist sector, agrarian policy, and the policy towards small private businesses and artisans.

The reforms' objective was to increase the effectiveness of the economy by introducing changes in all the five key spheres of economic policy mentioned above. As for the socialist sector, the following sequence of changes was expected as a result of the introduction of the reforms: (1) desirable behavioural changes at enterprise and industrial association level that would lead to greater economic efficiency and a less distorted information flow; (2) improved consistency of planning and a better plan/performance ratio; (3) a lower share of investment in national income coupled with greater effectiveness; and (4) substantial increases in real wages at the cost of only slightly lower rates of growth.

9.1.1 WAYS OF EVALUATING THE EFFECTIVENESS OF THE ECONOMIC REFORMS

The results of the economic reforms may be evaluated either from the planners' or the consumers' viewpoint. If, however, the *effectiveness* of the reforms is the subject of analysis, as it is here, then planners' preferences must be used as a criterion because planners formulate reform objectives. To the extent that planners' and consumers' preferences coincide, the result of the analysis will answer both questions.

The problem of evaluating the effectiveness of economic reforms is a complicated one. There is, of course, the traditional method of using quantitative evidence only. In a planned economy, however, its use—never easy at best—is further complicated by the fact that the performance level as such is hardly sufficient because a lower (or higher) rate of growth of national income or real wages or capital-output ratio, etc., may be the result of a conscious policy choice. On the other hand, a better plan/performance ratio, without due regard for the performance level, may simply reflect the plan's less ambitious target, such as, say, the planners' acceptance of certain inefficiencies, which may not be inevitable if proper policy measures have been taken. As a result, I suggest that, in addition to quantitative evidence, *behavioural* evidence at CPB and enterprise level should also be used. This means that the evidence on the efficiency of the reforms may be grouped into four categories: (1) quantitative evidence on macro- and micro-performance; (2) behavioural evidence at the Central Planning Board level; (3) behavioural evidence at the enterprise level, and (4) the situation of consumers (if this has been included in reform objectives). Here only a summary outline is intended as most of the evidence is provided in the body of the book and point 4 will be discussed only indirectly (but see Ch. 1).

A *Quantitative Evidence*

In recent years quantitative studies of the efficiency of 'economic working arrangements' have made substantial progress both in refining their methodology and in producing the relevant statistical data.[1] These studies were concerned with national and international comparisons of both static and dynamic efficiency.

Studies of static efficiency produced comparative data of real national income per employed worker and of real national income per unit of the composite of labour and capital, to take into account the differences in the supply of capital available to cooperate with the labour [1, p. 23]. They also stressed that the efficiency of economic working arrangements is closely related to but not the same thing as productivity [1, p. 25]. In the attempt to isolate the impact of economic working arrangements on efficiency from other factors, efforts have been made to adjust the labour and the labour *cum* capital productivity figures, by taking into account the differences in [1, pp. 25–30]: the quality of labour, especially of varying levels of education and of different shares of female workers in total employment; supplies of mineral resources and of usable agricultural land; market size; available technological knowledge; and quality of output structure.

This list, I think, should be extended by taking into account at least two additional factors. First of all, the technological quality (use value) of output produced by discounting output figures of selected commodities by the length of their useful life (number of miles which the average tyre can withstand, average number of light hours which an electric bulb can deliver, etc.). Secondly, the impact of output structure on productivity level. There is no reason to assume that this cancels out either in comparisons between countries and/or over time within one country and, obviously, may have a very substantial impact on productivity figures. It would be a serious mistake to attribute resulting productivity changes to economic working arrangements. This problem is particularly serious in relation to planned economies, where profound

[1] See [1, *passim*] and literature quoted therein.

structural changes are frequently undertaken on a scale rarely rivalled
by market economies under peaceful conditions. For example, a substantial increase of the share of investments going to branches with
high capital-output ratios, such as agriculture, mining, housing, and
others, has taken place in recent years in the Soviet Union and some
other socialist countries, including Poland.

The practical possibility of taking these different factors into account
in a statistically satisfactory, or even acceptable manner, differs greatly,
but nevertheless the overall findings are illuminating and further
refinements will, undoubtedly, be forthcoming.[1]

The same approach has been applied to problems of dynamic
efficiency, and the average annual rate of growth of real national
income per employed worker and per unit of factor inputs (labour and
reproducible capital) have been calculated for different countries and
different post-1950 periods [1, pp. 52–73].

As far as I know, such studies have so far been carried out for different Western countries and the Soviet Union only. It seems to me
that they could be very profitably extended to the study of the comparative efficiency of economic working arrangements between different
Soviet-bloc countries and also used for studying the effectiveness of
economic reforms within individual East European countries. I am not
aware of any such study having been published[2] and this field of research

---

[1] Mr. P. Hanson in [8, pp. 327–43] presented a spirited critique of this type of
study. Being used to the fact that in economic research we must be satisfied not only
with the second- but frequently also with the third- and fourth-best, Mr. Hanson's
arguments have not changed my opinion of the illuminating character of Professor
Bergson's findings. *En passant* we may add that there are no techniques which can
throw any light on 'socialism' *per se*—in the abstract and undefined. Unfortunately,
the argument that we cannot prove the inferiority of such 'socialism' plays a prominent part in Mr. Hanson's paper, who asserts (rightly) that '. . . as long as some
other kind of "socialism" is at least conceivable, evidence about the Soviet Union
is inconclusive about socialism in general'. It is, however, the present author's opinion
that there is no room for scholarly debates on 'socialism in general'. As long as it
remains 'general'—socialism is simply a contemporary name for the utopian society,
free of all evils by definition or rather by faith. It is interesting to note that social evils
immediately reappear in any system—be it existing or theoretical, capitalist or
socialist—the very moment it is defined in operational terms. Moreover, they frequently appear in greater number and/or severity than in existing systems or in the
systems they replaced. Is not Soviet socialism sometimes defined as a system mostly
preoccupied by coping with the problems of its own creation? Needless to say, Professor Bergson studies *existing* Soviet and US 'economic working arrangements' and
calls them 'socialist' and 'capitalist' in accordance with general usage. One can call
these systems differently, but the case for socialism will not be much strengthened by
the comment that 'it is conceivable' to imagine a 'good socialism', as opposed to
existing 'bad' ones. (Professor Bergson's reply and Dr. Hanson's rejoinder appeared
in *SS*, October 1971. Neither, however, addressed himself explicitly to the issue:
is 'socialism in general' a meaningful concept which can be scientifically debated?)

[2] Except [7], but it tries to use Kalecki's growth model to measure the impact of
the traditional system of planning and management on the economic performance of
Czechoslovakia.

is waiting to be undertaken by a statistically inclined, imaginative researcher.

Before comprehensive quantitative studies on the efficiency of the economic reforms in Eastern Europe (and Poland in particular) are available, we have to use existing statistical data. Even these give quite convincing evidence that the economic reforms have so far not produced any satisfactory improvement in Polish economic performance.

As for overall efficiency, it can be seen from Table 9.1 that the rate of

Table 9.1: Average Yearly Growth Rates of Selected
Economic Indicators in Three Subsequent Polish Mid-Term Plans
(in 1961 prices)

1	2	3	4
	1950–5	*1956–60*	*1961–5*
Net National Income (NNI)	9·7	6·6	6·5
Share of Accumulation in NNI	23·3	22·7	25·5
Real Wages per employee	0·66	5·8	1·6
Consumption *per capita*	5·8	4·8	3·6

Sources: Rocznik dochodu narodowego 1960–5 (National Income Yearbook 1960–5), Warsaw, 1966, p. 2; K. Ryc, *Spozycie a wzrost gospodarczy Polski* (Consumption and Economic Growth of Poland), Warsaw, 1968, p. 316.

growth of national income, after a drastic drop in 1956–60, was barely maintained at the expense of a higher rate of investment. The 1·6 per cent annual real wage increase during 1961–5 is better than the (questionable) 0·66 per cent increase in 1950–5 but considerably worse than the 5·8 per cent achieved during 1956–60. A comparison of columns 3 and 4 of Table 9.1 reveals at a glance the failure of the Polish economic reforms: at the expense of an increase of 12 per cent in the average yearly rate of investment, a decrease of 2 per cent in the average yearly rate of

Table 9.2: Comparison of Planned and Actual Employment
Changes in the Socialized Sector in Subsequent Polish Mid-Term Plans
(in thousand persons)

	Plan	Fulfilment	Percentage deviation
1946–9	+ 1,059	+ 1,375	+ 29
1950–5	+ 6,258	+ 2,472*	−152
1956–60	+ 1,272	+ 605	−110
1961–5	+ 753	+ 1,263	+ 67

* This tremendous discrepancy is due to the fact that the 6-year plan envisaged increased employment of four million in collective farms. In fact, an increase of only 370 thousand was achieved. If we correct employment plan targets and fulfilment accordingly, then 103 per cent of plan fulfilment would be recorded.

Source: Official Polish data quoted in W. Krencik, *Dynamika wzrostu a zmiany w strukturze zatrudnienia i plac* (Dynamics of Growth and Changes in the Structure of Employment and Wages), Warsaw, 1967 (mimeographed), p. 16.

national income growth and of 362 per cent in the average yearly growth of real wages was achieved, taking the corresponding data of the previous FYP as 100. All these figures are from official statistics. If one takes into account that during the post-Stalinist period Polish agriculture (mostly private) increased its yearly average rate of growth from 1 per cent during 1951–5 to 2·7 per cent during the next ten years [18, p. 2], then the results of the economic reforms in the socialist sector look even worse.

The failure of the Polish economic reforms is also shown in the still very ineffective control of key economic variables by the Central Planning Board. The data presented in Tables 2.1, 9.2, 1.10, 9.3, and 9.4

Table 9.3: Comparison of Planned and Actual Wage Fund Changes in Socialist Sectors in Subsequent Polish Mid-Term Plans
(in milliard zlotys)

	Plan	Fulfilment	Percentage deviation
1955–60	+ 43·2	+ 58	+ 34
1961–5	+ 27·4	+ 59	+ 115

Source: Official Polish statistics quoted in Krencik, op. cit., pp. 15–16.

Table 9.4: Planned and Actual Stock Level in Polish Industry
(in milliard zlotys)

	Planned level	Actual level	Percentage deviation
1956	1·4	5·3	378·6
1957	3·5	12·1	345·7
1958	3·0	7·4	246·7
1959	4·2	5·0	119·0
1960	3·7	9·1	245·9
1961	4·8	12·1	252·1
1962	6·8	9·5	139·7
1963	6·3	10·0	158·7
1964	8·8	11·2	127·3

Source: Data of the Polish National Bank, quoted in *Ekonomika przemyslu* (Economics of Industry), Warsaw, 1966, p. 519.

indicate that the planners' control over relative shares of Sectors I and II, the level of employment, the volume of the wage fund, real wages, or stocks is extremely inadequate, and, where comparable data are available, they show hardly any improvement over the pre-reform period. The same may be said of short-term predictions of plan performance (three to four months beforehand), which are necessary to prepare the planning guidelines for the following year. These predictions also show a surprisingly high level of error (Table 9.5).

The continuing inability of the planners to achieve an equilibrium in the economy is witnessed not only by the constant partial shortages on the consumer goods market but also by the very high stock/output

Table 9.5: Expected and Actual Fulfilment of the
Wage Plan in Poland in 1965 (in milliard zlotys)

	Expected fulfilment	Actual fulfilment	Percentage
Total wage fund	169·0	201·8	119·4
Industry	77·3	90·9	117·5
Construction	21·1	24·4	116·1
Agriculture	6·4	9·5	148·4
Forestry	2·4	3·0	125·0
Transport and Communications	15·2	19·0	125·0
Domestic Trade	14·2	15·8	111·2
Municipal Services	5·2	5·9	113·4
Education, Science, Culture	11·9	14·2	119·3
Health, Welfare, Sports	6·6	7·3	110·6

Note: Sub-totals do not add up to total wage fund because minor sectors have been omitted for the sake of brevity.

Source: Reports of the Central Statistical Office on the fulfilment of the yearly national plan.

growth ratio (Table 1.4) and the equally high divergence between the planned level of stocks and fulfilment (Table 9.4). The latter ratio, like all plan/fulfilment ratios, does not of course measure performance alone, but also the planners' knowledge or ability to predict. When discussing problems of equilibrium, it is also instructive to note that the number of centrally rationed inputs in Poland, after a very drastic drop at the beginning of the reforms (from 1,575 in 1955 to 405 in 1958) and then a slow decrease until 1960 (325), rose again, and in 1965 was already 463 (Tables 2.6 and 2.7). The number of centrally allocated inputs does indicate, however imperfectly, the degree of disequilibrium, and it grew with the increase in the rate of investment in the 1961–5 plan.

B *Behavioural Evidence at the Central Planning Board Level*

This evidence falls into three basic groups. The first is the constant changes in the management mechanism. These are the best proof that the CPB considers the reform measures, some instituted quite recently, unsatisfactory and unable to do the job. The 'turnover' of reform measures in Poland is unbelievably high. For example, as a result of the IVth Plenum of the CC of the PUWP in July 1965, a broad group of changes were instituted on 1 January 1966, and on 1 January 1967. Less than three years later, the Vth Congress of the PUWP (November 1968) announced the need to change many of these new measures, including the success indicators (last reformed in 1967), the principles of ex-factory prices (1967), the system of investment financing (1966), etc. An examination of the number of changes in the *basic* elements of the management mechanism during the reform period (i.e. from 1956 on) reveals that hardly any lasted more than three years without basic changes or two years without substantial modification. For instance, the basic managerial bonus system underwent fundamental changes in 1957, 1960, 1964, 1970, and 1971 plus two modifications in 1961 and 1966, altogether seven changes in the course of twelve years. The same is true of success indicators, principles of the enterprise fund, etc. Obviously, this constant changing of the management mechanism has very negative effects on economic efficiency. It also indicates that the changes in the management mechanism are introduced without sufficient preparation and analysis of the problems involved, and/or that there is a deeper cause which makes these constant changes necessary. As we have already indicated, the latter is especially true (see also 9.2.2).

The second basic group of evidence is the CPB's inability to implement its own decisions, which is another interesting indicator of the deficiency of the reforms. Certain changes are enacted, made into law, etc., but in fact are not implemented. There are many examples of this phenomenon. The most glaring are even admitted publicly by the CPB or its spokesmen. For instance, in the theses of the Politbureau for the IInd CC Plenum of the PUWP (April 1969), we read, among other things: 'Between the IVth and Vth Congresses, our Party devoted much attention to improving investment. These problems were extensively discussed at the IVth Plenary Meeting of the Central Committee in 1965, and the VIth Plenum was exclusively devoted to ways and methods of improving investment. The resolution of the VIth Plenary Meeting of the Central Committee, despite the three years which had already elapsed, has not been implemented in many essential points' [20, p. 6]. Then follows a list of all the standard deficiencies of investment (too broad an investment front, much longer construction periods than planned, much higher investment costs than estimated, investment started without proper preparation, total investment higher than investment capacities, etc.). It is interesting to note that all these complaints were already voiced in 1956–7 during the critical examination of the 6-year plan experience [10, p. 104 and *passim*]. Another glaring example of the CPB's inability to implement its own decisions is the reform of industrial associations. First reformed in 1958, they were reformed again in 1965. Characteristically, in one Polish book on industrial management, the analysis of the 1965 reform of industrial associations is subtitled: 'Unfulfilled Objectives of the 1958 Reform' [6, p. 211]. Here is another official view: 'This properly conceived reform [of industrial associations] has not, however, been implemented' [15, p. 22].

The third basic group of behavioural evidence of the ineffectiveness of the reforms is the CPB's voiced dissatisfaction. This abounds in Poland where strong dissatisfaction with the workings of the basic elements of the system (usually accompanied by exhortation to work better and harder) is frequently voiced by the highest representatives of the party and the government.

The high-level criticism of the Polish economy was expressed as recently as September 1969 by B. Jaszczuk, former Member of the Politbureau of the PUWP and former Chairman of the newly created Economic Commission of the CC of PUWP.[1] Analysing the implementation of the recently announced (spring 1969) changes in planning procedures—towards granting enterprises greater say in plan construction—he pointed out that 'there are reasons for great anxiety ... The productivity of fixed capital does not increase; on the contrary, in the heavy, light, and building materials industries it is decreasing ... Labour intensity of a number of products is several times higher in Poland than abroad. Many of our enterprises are not specialized ... This leads to high costs of production, low economic effectiveness, and low quality of output' [9].

C Behavioural Evidence at the Enterprise Level

This evidence falls into two basic categories.

(1) *Enterprise Tactics at the Stage of Plan Formulation.* The behaviour of the socialist enterprise at the stage of plan building is influenced mainly by the principle of yearly plan targets coupled with the so-called 'ratchet principle'.

As one Polish expert on managerial economics aptly noted, supplying one-sided information is the most effective method of influencing administrative orders that the socialist enterprise has at its disposal [14, p. 157]. It is hardly surprising that it uses it rather frequently.

Information flow in the planning process is a two-way flow. It is worth noting that we encounter here a feedback interrelation between these information flows; since enterprises supply distorted information the higher authorities react by correcting them as unreliable but, not having detailed knowledge about the *real* possibilities of the enterprises, they frequently produced unrealistic and/or internally inconsistent plan directives; and the enterprises intensify information distortion in self-defence.

East European planners became aware of these distortions of information at a very early stage in the history of economic planning. Nevertheless, thus far, no effective remedy has been found. Two methods of tackling this problem have been tried. One is by establishing better control over data supplied by enterprises, especially by developing all kinds of technologically or statistically determined standards. This method has its obvious limitations, however. First of all, the higher authorities encounter the knowledge barrier: it is impossible to check effectively on enterprises when the ratio of white-collar workers in enterprises to those in industrial associations is of the order

---

[1] Mr. Jaszczuk has been relieved of both these posts after the Polish workers' unrest in December 1970.

of several dozen to one, and of those in enterprises to those in economic ministries of the order of several hundred to one. Secondly, since the causes for information distortion also apply to levels *above* enterprises (industrial associations and economic ministries also want to fulfil their plan targets), really effective control is not possible.

The other method is to develop an incentive system for optimal planning at all levels of industrial administration, from the enterprise up. (By optimal planning we mean here simply that reserves are kept at the technically necessary level.) These have been tried over a number of years in most socialist countries in two basic forms (or combinations thereof): incentives for plan overfulfilment and incentives for revealing reserves at the stage of plan construction. As we have discussed in 6.2.1, they failed because there are no effective incentive systems compatible with yearly planning tasks and ratchet principles.

Enterprise behaviour at the stage of plan construction is also influenced by the particular solutions used in the existing management mechanism, especially by the success indicator used. Depending on the type of success indicator, different input and output structures will create particularly favourable conditions for easy plan fulfilment in the future. For instance, with a gross output success indicator, it is advantageous to plan *cheaper* inputs than those the enterprise actually intends to use in the process of plan fulfilment, because turning later to more expensive raw materials facilitates meeting the gross output plan target. The wage fund limit makes it advantageous to plan more labour-intensive processes than actually intended, so as to have an extra reserve in the wage fund for meeting unforeseen emergencies, etc.

(2) *Enterprise Tactics at the Stage of Plan Fulfilment.* The tactics of the socialist enterprise at the stage of plan fulfilment is a broad and fascinating subject in what could be called 'economic pathology'. Because of the summary nature of our presentation, no more than a basic outline can be attempted here.

(a) *Shaping the Time Pattern of the Output Flow to the Enterprise's Advantage.* The optimal time pattern of output flow (always from the enterprise's viewpoint) is governed by the ratchet principle, the practice of plan revisions during the year, and the principles of the bonus system. These three factors make the enterprise vitally interested in an unequal distribution of the output flow, with as heavy a concentration of output in the fourth quarter as possible. There are at least three advantages in planning the planned output flow in such a manner. First, since the bonuses are paid quarterly in accordance with quarterly plan fulfilment data, and what is actually paid out cannot be revoked according to existing regulations, such a time pattern of output makes doubly sure that bonuses will be paid for a maximum number of months even if the *yearly* plan target is not met. Second, if, in spite of the enterprise's efforts to the contrary, its plan is nevertheless increased by the industrial association during the planning year, it will have ample reserves to meet it, or, depending on the situation, it can help its industrial association by agreeing to take on an extra burden above its original planning tasks (for an extra bonus of course—paid out of the industrial association's reserve bonus fund). In both cases it is beneficial to plan well below capacity for most of the year. Third, since the following year's plan is based on performance during the first seven to nine months plus the 'probable fulfilment' estimate (guesswork, in fact), to have a relatively low output figure for these months is very helpful in arguing with industrial associations that this year's plan target is the absolute maximum that an enterprise can possibly produce. The industrial association will not believe it, of course, but it can never be sure to what extent it is false. This uncertainty frequently has a beneficial effect on the following year's plan targets for the enterprise.

A good enterprise manager knows that in many cases (most of them much more subtle than the one described above) the 'proper' timing of decisions is essential to success. For example, it is advantageous to start producing new products in the second half of the year. The first phase of producing new output is, as a rule, characterized by high unit cost. To have this high-cost phase of output neatly concentrated in one year (by starting it appropriately late in the year) nicely inflates average yearly costs of production, discourages industrial associations from asking for a too big cost reduction in the following year, and in addition creates an automatic cost reduction reserve because, with growing experience in producing new output, production costs are bound to fall.

(b) *The Enterprise's Product-Mix Policy.* The discrepancy between the structure of supply and the structure of demand is a permanent, and one of the most serious, worries of East European countries. It shows itself in many ways, from a constant partial disequilibrium on many markets to a high ratio of stock increase to output growth, much higher than in market economies.

The causes of this discrepancy lie only partly in planning mistakes. To a great extent, they are the result of the enterprise's product-mix policy in violation, open or disguised, of the plan. Product-mix policy is the enterprise's most powerful method of meeting what can be called qualitative plan targets (value of output, productivity per worker, profitability, etc.), and one of the very few areas left where it still has room to manœuvre: if not always *de jure*, since it sometimes requires violating the product-mix plan, then at least *de facto*.

The whole problem of product-mix policy arises because two types of plan tasks are used simultaneously: one concerning the structure of input and output, the other requiring achievement of a certain number of qualitative targets. The trouble is that the former, as a rule, do not conform to the *easiest* way of achieving the latter. At the same time the existing management mechanism of socialist countries provides its enterprises with both incentives and plenty of opportunities to choose the easiest way of meeting qualitative plan targets.

First of all, these opportunities are provided by the existing price system, which is characterized by very large differences in profitability and/or accumulation (i.e. profit plus turnover tax) of different products or stages of production. Under such conditions, a relatively small product-mix manoeuvre towards more profitable products immediately improves most of the qualitative plan targets: profitability, productivity, and volume of output.

Sub-contracting provides another easy way of meeting or improving plan targets. By sub-contracting, an enterprise can, as a rule, increase its total production capacity, by switching workers and machines to later phases of output and hence improving its formal performance as measured by output plan indices (see 5.4.3).

(c) *The Attitude towards Risk and Innovation.* There is now abundant evidence that socialist enterprises have a very low propensity to innovate, that they try to avoid risk as much as possible. The reasons for this are twofold: first of all, there is the bureaucratic model of the socialist manager. A socialist manager knows from experience that he is practically never blamed for not doing something that was not explicitly required of him and innovation cannot, by its very nature, be explicitly required, except in non-operational terms. On the other hand, he also knows from bitter experience that, for taking risky action which turns sour, he can be made responsible and punished. Secondly, if he succeeds in his risky venture, his material and moral rewards will be very modest relative to the risk incurred. Restated in economic terms, the incentives to innovate are weak and the disincentives strong. There can be only one result: an insufficient rate of technical progress, which is the constant complaint of East European planners.

But cannot a socialist economy assure *strong* material incentives for its enterprises? It cannot as long as it is based on yearly planning and the ratchet principle. These principles reduce an enterprise's time horizon to one year and make it indifferent to long-term gains, since these will be appropriated by the state in the form of higher planning tasks. Without making an enterprise interested in *future* gains, it is impossible to make it interested in research and development.

Finally, the existing management mechanism makes a socialist enterprise not only indifferent but positively hostile to technical progress. This is due to the fact that the present set-up of the management mechanism frequently requires enterprises to suffer short-term losses for the sake of future gains for the state. The list of disincentives to R and D is a long one, and has been discussed in 7.6.

The CPB was quick to undertake a number of corrective measures. First of all, it made research and development part of the enterprise's yearly plan. Secondly, new products were made an important part of

the enterprise assortment plan, on which the fulfilment part of management bonuses depends. Thirdly, they created special funds at all levels
of the industrial hierarchy (from the enterprise up) from which R and D
is to be financed. These special funds, set apart from enterprise working
capital and its profit–loss statement, are to be used for financing especially risky and/or long-term research and development projects.
Finally, some countries (e.g. Poland) started to experiment with a
special, separate wage fund for technical progress, allocated to the
enterprise in addition to the wage fund for current production and
independent of current production results.

All these obviously helped to weaken the enterprise's unwillingness
to engage in research and development and to introduce new products
into their production schedules but, at the same time, must be considered
as half-measures only, many of them creating their own problems
(see 7.6).

To sum up, Polish economic reforms have not been able, thus far:
(1) to improve the overall performance of the national economy, either
quantitatively, as measured by the rate of growth of GNP, or, especially,
qualitatively, by lowering the cost of growth; (2) to increase the effectiveness of central planning as measured by an improved plan/performance
ratio or better control over key economic variables; (3) to eliminate the
basic negative aspects of enterprise behaviour which developed after the
introduction of the Soviet-type economic system and which still remain
one of the main causes of inefficiency at the micro-level.[1]

9.2 Reasons for the Failure of the Polish Economic Reforms

The effectiveness of economic reforms depends heavily on two factors:
(a) the quality of the blueprint for the reforms, (b) the policy of its
implementation. We shall discuss them in turn.

9.2.1 CONTRADICTION IN OBJECTIVES
The designing of reforms frequently encounters an interesting vicious
circle: without pressure, no extensive and far-reaching work on a new
system is carried out; under pressure, reforms must be initiated without
waiting for a detailed blueprint.

It is consistent with human frailty that, as a rule, no officially sponsored work is carried out on the design of a new system—technical,

[1] See [11, pp. 392–415] where it is persuasively argued that '... in a great many
instances the amount to be gained by increasing allocative efficiency is trivial while
the amount to be gained by increasing X-efficiency [i.e. efficiency at the enterprise
level] is frequently significant' [p. 413]. It seems to me that in Eastern Europe the
scope for improvement by increasing allocative efficiency is substantially greater than
in the West, but nevertheless the general conclusion of Professor Leibenstein also
holds true for centrally planned economies.

organizational, or economic—as long as the existing one is considered more or less satisfactory. This does not mean that no work on reforms is done during the 'no pressure period', but as a rule this work is not sufficiently far-reaching and comprehensive.

The decision to introduce an overall change arises, as a rule, abruptly —usually triggered off by a political crisis—and the crisis requires that the changes are introduced without delay. As a result there is insufficient time for preparing reasonable and detailed blueprints for the new system. This explains the many inconsistencies and initial setbacks during reform periods, as well as the reversion to old methods of economic management—inconsistent with the new model, but the easiest alternative available.

Advance preparation of a *workable* blueprint for the new economic system, on a theoretical level only, is impossible because: (a) it requires basic guidelines from policy makers as to what is politically and socially desirable and feasible; otherwise the elaboration of a new system would simply develop into one more 'postulational model'. Under favourable circumstances, there could be a feedback from theoretical works to official guidelines; there frequently is, but time lags involved differ considerably from period to period and from problem to problem, and the resulting guidelines may be inconsistent. (b) The complexity of the problems involved requires work of many teams— including many practical economists and managers who can be provided by the government only.

Can this vicious circle, which undoubtedly existed in Poland before 1956 and reappeared in the mid 1960s and again in 1969–70, be broken? This question is difficult to answer. Czechoslovak reforms also seemed to suffer from the fact that a sudden change in the political climate caught Czech reformers insufficiently advanced in the designing of the new system. On the other hand, the Hungarians prepared the basic outline of their comprehensive reforms at comparative leisure. The problem obviously requires further investigation on an interdisciplinary basis.

Whatever the answer to the above, there is no doubt that the basic feature of the Polish economic reforms is their eclectic character. This leads to numerous contradictions in the objectives of the reforms and in the reform measures introduced into the management mechanism. Some Polish economists [*15*, pp. 5–17] try to present this eclectic charac- ter of the Polish reforms as a virtue and as a proof of their pragmatic approach. I hope that they do so in their official rather than their pro- fessional capacity because there is abundant evidence that these assertions are profoundly mistaken.

As our study revealed, five basic groups of irreconcilable assumptions are mainly responsible for the failure of the Polish economic reforms, and they are summarized briefly below.

A *Simultaneous Use of Administrative Orders and Economic Parameters*

The Polish (and the Russian, GDR, and Bulgarian) reforms try to establish an economic model essentially controlled by administrative orders but 'combined with a wider use of economic instruments'. These efforts do not take into account that administrative orders inevitably clash with economic parameters and that, to protect the initial set of administrative orders, a new set of administrative orders has to be issued, and so on, until the point is reached where economic parameters are, in the main, reduced to the role of a residual force which nevertheless keeps pushing plan executants off the course determined by administrative orders (see 3.2.3.B).

The experience of the Polish economic reforms proves the above reasoning beyond any doubt. First, from 1956 on, we witnessed a number of efforts to broaden the use of economic parameters (but within the framework of the model essentially controlled by administrative orders), which proved futile. Twelve years after the Polish economic reforms started, the Vth Congress of the PUWP (November 1968) announced (probably for the hundredth time during that period): 'Rejecting the revisionist theories . . . we strive to strengthen the role of central planning . . . and, at the same time, to equip it to a greater extent with economic tools and economic incentives, at the expense of the number of administrative planned directives' [*17*, p. 16]. Again, however, there was no analysis of why the previous numerous similar efforts failed, and hence there is no reason to expect better results than before.

Secondly, while intentions to diminish the number of administrative orders were repeatedly voiced by the CPB, the actual number of administrative orders again reached an 'astronomical' figure. As we have pointed out, instead of the postulated decline, there was a rapid increase in administrative orders (see 3.2.3.C).

B *Preservation of the Basic Features of the Traditional Economic System with Changes in Enterprise Behaviour*

The Polish economic reforms retain the basic principles of the traditional system—yearly planning targets and the ratchet principle (their application implies that heterogeneous information carriers are used)[1]— but at the same time want to change economic behaviour. This is, however, impossible. (For this very reason, we call these principles the *basic*

---

[1] Out of the two broad types of economic reforms which have already emerged in Eastern Europe the 'state-parametric' reforms use heterogeneous types of information carriers (administrative orders and parameters), whereas the 'guided-market' model is based on homogeneous information carriers—of a parametric type only (state and market determined). This difference has profound repercussions on: (1) the character of planning; (2) the type of industrial organization; (3) the consistency of information transmitted; and (4) the quality of data for economic calculation. For discussion of these problems see [*22*, pp. 1–24].

determinants of economic behaviour, see 9.2.2). As we have tried to prove in Chs. 2, 3, and 5–7, the uneconomic behaviour of enterprises—summarized in 9.1.2.C above—is basically the product of those principles, with other elements of the existing management mechanism also playing a part.

The behaviour of socialist enterprise managers conforms by and large to the basic assumptions of economic theory. Socialist managers are essentially bonus maximizers and their behaviour can be explained, to the degree comparable to a profit-maximizing assumption of market economy, in terms of this goal (see Ch. 5, *passim*). If their behaviour is frequently 'strange' by market economy standards, this is because they are operating within 'strange' economic and legal environments. But, as we have tried to prove in this study, this behaviour is perfectly rational under the economic and legal conditions prevailing at present in most East European countries, and in most cases is the result of quite sophisticated economic calculations.

C *Simultaneous Use of Yearly Planning Targets and Long-Term Financial Norms*

The next inconsistency in the Polish economic reforms is the effort to combine yearly planning with long-term financial norms. The advantages of introducing stable financial norms have long been recognized by East European economists and planners. By extending the enterprise's time horizon, they hoped to create the basis for policy decisions beyond short-term manœuvres to which, under yearly fixed financial norms, the enterprise is forced to limit itself. Moreover, the stability of financial obligations is a necessary precondition for the effective functioning of economic incentives based on profit or profitability success indicators (see Ch. 5) and for broadening the enterprise's scope of decision-making, including a certain measure of self-financing, which is also advocated (see Ch. 7). Because of these advantages, long-term financial norms were always high on the list of reform measures.

All efforts to introduce a minimum financial stability into Polish enterprises proved, however, abortive. In practice, most financial norms are changed several times a year, and this practice is almost universal throughout Polish industry (see 2.2.2 and 3.2.2.C).

D *Simultaneous Decentralization at Enterprise and Branch Level*

The fourth basic inconsistency of the Polish economic reforms consists in the attempts to decentralize at the industrial association or branch level and at the enterprise level simultaneously (see Ch. 8).

As a result, the present 'dual character' of industrial associations emerged. On the one hand, they ceased to be pure government offices and became 'economic organizations' based on the 'economic accountability' principle, rewarded according to the performance of subordinate enterprises, etc. On the other hand, they did not become industrial corporations *sensu stricto*, at least formally, because of the belief that separate enterprises, rather than industrial associations, should remain 'the basic form of economic organization in socialist industry'.

Unfortunately, it is impossible to decentralize effectively at *both* the industrial association and the enterprise level. According to official pronouncements, the industrial associations' scope of authority should be broadened at the expense of the economic ministries with a simultaneous broadening of the enterprises' freedom of action. The Polish experience indicates, however, that expanding the *economic* functions of industrial associations inevitably leads to a diminishing of enterprise independence.

E *Preservation of Taut Planning with Simultaneous Changes in Management Mechanism*

The final fundamental inconsistency of Polish economic reforms consists of attempts to introduce changes into the management mechanism while retaining at the same time the policy of very taut planning. Effective economic reforms and very taut planning cannot be reconciled. This was pointed out by Polish economists at the very beginning of the economic reforms and has been only too well proven by subsequent experience (see 2.1.2).

9.2.2 THE FALSE POLICY OF TRANSITION

A *Two Approaches to the Problem of Reform Implementation*

The study of blueprints for economic reforms in the East European countries reveals an interesting correlation between their views on the character of the transition period and the scope of the changes intended. The countries which were planning ambitious reforms, such as Bulgaria,[1] Czechoslovakia, and Hungary, talked about a definite and relatively short (3–4 years) transition period and stressed that profound changes were needed, that the new economic system would represent a qualitatively new phenomenon. On the other hand, 'cautious reformers' (GDR, Poland, and Rumania) tend to present reforms as a slow, evolutionary process of constant improvements. This difference can well be seen by comparing the following statements: 'Dialectics indicate that a given social phenomenon may be improved only as long as it does not outlive itself ... Improvements do not change the qualitative characteristics of the phenomenon ... This pertained to our [Bulgarian] former system [of planning and management] as long as it was in the

---

[1] Initially it seemed as if Bulgaria was aiming for the 'guided market' model. After the invasion of Czechoslovakia she joined the ranks of 'cautious reformers' by switching towards the 'state-parametric' solution.

phase of improvements. The new system in its entirety, only as a whole
... represents qualitatively new phenomenon' [23, p. 428].

The same ideas as these were expressed by the CC of the Hungarian
Communist Party the very same year: 'The new mechanism consists of
a number of elements which are interrelated and which can have a
beneficial influence on the economy only if applied together. Therefore
particular elements cannot be introduced separately, in different periods.
Basic elements of the new economic mechanism should be put into
practice from 1 January 1968, after careful time-consuming preparations. Hence the years 1966 and 1967 are a period of preparation and
the next two years (1968 and 1969) will be devoted to the development
of the new mechanism' [16, p. 312].

And here is the Polish semi-official view: 'Poland bases her reforms'
implementation on the principle of *evolutionary* changes consisting of
experiments, of introducing new solutions of limited scope ... The
reforms' implementation is considered as a *constant* process ... The
reforms being carried out in Poland are not based on any new theoretical
or ideological orientation but mainly on *practical observations ...* '
[15, pp. 13, 6, 5; italics in the original].

It is not difficult to explain why the same 'dialectics' led Bulgaria and
Hungary to completely different conclusions from Poland's or the
GDR's. Only countries embarking on *fundamental* reforms can afford
politically (a) to criticize the previous system severely, and (b) to talk of
a *definite* transition period. The others have to try to convince their
populations that in spite of the fact that the reforms are hardly noticeable they are, nevertheless, profound: 'The changes which were implemented [in 1959–65] were not as radical as those of 1956–8 and hence
were perhaps not as noticeable', writes one Polish economist, 'nevertheless they were no less important than this first wave of reforms'
[19, p. 25]. Nothing could be further from the truth.

B *Transition Problems of Overall, Comprehensive Reforms*

Even assuming that a comprehensive reform is intended, its implementation must take several years and so the problem of the *optimal
sequence of change* arises.

The problem of the optimal sequence in implementing different parts
of the new system is *terra incognita* to a large extent. The discussion thus
far has hardly gone beyond the thesis that 'price reform is a necessary
prerequisite of successful economic reforms'. It is a very partial truth,
however.

It may be difficult to implement effective price reform at the initial
stage of general economic reforms. It is almost impossible to predict the
new scarcity relations which will develop *after* introducing the new
system. The thesis must be understood that the *first stage* of price reform

should be implemented at the beginning of the new system. The subsequent rounds will have to follow later on.

There is no optimal price system *per se*, irrespective of the management formula used, and especially irrespective of success indicator used [*21*, pp. 48–70]. It is now generally recognized that under the gross output success indicator the equilibrium price cannot be found in practice (the higher the price, the bigger the demand). The same, however, may be true under a profit-based success indicator, if other elements of management formula counterbalance its proper functioning. (These other elements may consist of internal cost-plus pricing combined with the use of profit as a planned target which is corrected according to actual cost-level). From this can be seen that we have here a two-way interrelationship: price reform is a necessary prerequisite of economic reforms, but, at the same time, there cannot be a successful price reform if the management formula is not changed simultaneously in such a way as to make an effective price reform possible.

The thesis that price reform is a necessary prerequisite of successful economic reform does not at all exhaust the required knowledge about the optimal sequence of change. To determine it, the interrelationships between different parts of the management mechanism and within the management rules have to be studied.

It seems that the theoretical rules one should adhere to are the following:

(1) First of all, one should look for—and change—those elements of the system which we shall call *basic determinants* of enterprise behaviour. The characteristic feature of basic determinants is that they induce a certain pattern of behaviour, almost irrespective of how other elements of the management formula are shaped. For example, the principle of yearly plan targets as a success indicator and a basis for the managerial bonus system gives rise to hiding reserves, bargaining for a low output–high input plan etc., irrespective of the construction of the management rules. Whatever the success indicator used—gross output, total profit, cost-revenue ratio, value added, etc.—and whatever the managerial bonus system—the negative consequences of a yearly plan target cannot be eliminated. The same is true of pure internal pricing, which virtually eliminates the pressure to economize, unless there is a reasonably well-functioning sellers' market, including intra-branch flow of capital. At this moment, however, it is enough to stress that one should start reforming the system by changing basic determinants of enterprise behaviour. The reasons are twofold: (a) changing basic determinants creates conditions for the effective introduction of new management rules; (b) it unleashes spontaneous forces of economic behaviour even before formal changes in management rules are introduced. It is easy to see that the very abolition of yearly plan targets—even with the gross output success indicator—would give rise to a change in behaviour

in, generally speaking, economically desirable directions (within the limits of the given management formula).

(2) If the new management mechanism and/or management formula cannot—for these or other reasons—be introduced as a whole, changes have to be instituted in 'blocks', which should include all of the most directly interrelated elements. The more interrelated a given block of changes with other parts of the system, the sooner the next block of changes should follow, to prevent 'rejecting the transplant' or making it ineffectual. An example may be in order here. If the reform of a basic managerial bonus system is under consideration, the minimum block of changes should include: (a) All incentive schemes within the enterprise; under Polish conditions these include: the managerial bonus system itself; the bonus system based on the factory fund; supplementary managerial bonus systems, e.g. for export effectiveness. (b) Other parts of management rules, which have pronounced incentive effects; under Polish conditions these include: rules determining the volume of the wage fund; rules determining the volume of the enterprise development fund (from which increase in working capital and decentralized investments are financed). (c) The incentive system of industrial associations.

What is and what is not a part of a block cannot be determined purely *in abstracto*, without reference to those elements of management mechanism which are still functioning. It, for example, depends to a great extent on the actual role of yearly plan targets. To illustrate: when the role of yearly plan targets is predominant, the incentive system of industrial associations is undoubtedly part of a 'managerial bonus block', but the rules determining the volume of the enterprise development fund, since they have little incentive effects under present system of *yearly* targets, could be omitted from this block with practically no adverse effects. Under a system, however, when yearly plan targets, if any, are mainly of informational character the contrary would be the case.

The determination of what the next block of changes should consist of and how urgent it is should be based on considerations of what are the other elements in the managerial rules and management mechanism which would most likely interfere with the working of the managerial bonus system. These can be found by asking, what are the conditions for the effective functioning of the bonus system? Two directions of investigation will lead to the proper answer to this question: (a) inter-relations within the management rules especially of all problems concerned with the proper functioning of the success indicator which is the basis of the bonus system; (b) interactions from the management mechanism, especially the type and quality of information carriers used (quality of price signals, contradictions between price signals and administrative orders, etc.), and the character of the macro-input system (rationing of the means of production, the sellers' market in general, formal and actual decentralized investment possibilities, etc.).

12

The practical difficulties of following the above rule—of choosing the proper block of changes and supporting it on time by the next move —are many, because our knowledge of the interrelationships within the management mechanism is far from perfect. More sophisticated models of management mechanism and model testing of reforms envisaged, as well as practical experimentation, could lead to substantial improvements in the optimal change sequence.

The most important conditions for the successful implementation of comprehensive economic reforms are, probably, political in nature. It seems that no serious economic reform may ever be implemented (and hardly properly formulated) under conditions of intra-party struggle or even rivalry among important sections of the party elite. Formulation of far-reaching economic reforms requires, first, considerable unity of views on basic economic and social questions, and then complete consolidation of power in the hands of one group. Such a situation appears to have been achieved in Hungary in the mid 1960s, but it did not exist in Poland after 1956 or in Czechoslovakia in 1967–8. As Polish experience seems to indicate, the rival party factions are quite capable of producing a prolonged 'reform stalemate' and/or making any reform effort ineffective, first by destroying its consistency by imposing 'compromise solutions' and then by effectively sabotaging its implementation (see 1.3.2.D).

C The Transition Problems of Piecemeal Reforms

As we have pointed out in section A above, Poland has chosen the way of evolutionary, partial changes in her management mechanism.

The attractiveness of a gradual, partial approach to economic reforms is multiple: it seems easier than the immensely complex task of overall change; it seems less risky because only part of the economy and/or of the management mechanism is involved; it seems wholly plausible, because the sum of good elements should result in a good whole.[1]

On a closer examination, however, the gradual, partial approach to economic reforms is full of serious difficulties which cast doubt on its very feasibility.

The gradual, partial approach to economic reforms is usually characterized by the lack of an overall, master plan, detailed enough to guide partial solutions and assure their consistency. The method used is to attack basic weaknesses of the existing system and to substitute for them 'better' solutions. This approach is understandable because of the complexity of the task involved. It leaves, however, something to be desired on two counts: inconsistency in the measures implemented, because of the lack of a sufficiently detailed overall, master plan; increased tendency of the system to reject and/or make ineffectual the

[1] After all, how many party leaders and even planners ever heard that the sum of partial optima does not necessarily produce overall optimum?

changes introduced, because of longer time lags between blocks of changes. Let us discuss them in turn.

The overall, master plan should serve two purposes:

(1) It should answer the question, 'how far do we go?', i.e. how radical should be the changes in the existing system. To provide this answer it should determine: the scope of the central plan; the relative authority spheres between the CPB, industrial associations, and enterprises; the basic instruments which should be used to equilibrate the plan during its construction and to institute necessary changes during its implementation.

This is essential in order that partial, detailed solutions may have approximately the same scope. Otherwise, some partial solutions are more far-reaching than others and inconsistencies flourish. For instance in 1969 a number of Polish enterprises were still testing certain changes in the management formula which were less radical than the changes introduced during the 1966–7 overall reforms. (Experimenting enterprises are exempt from generally binding economic regulations and are governed by the principles of their experiment.)

(2) The overall, master plan serving as a reference point and a check list of partial changes should help to assure that: the proper blocks of changes are selected without neglecting the basic interrelationships of the management mechanism and management formula; and that the optimal sequence of change is followed.

The lack of such a master plan must inevitably lead to multiple contradictions between different elements of the management mechanism. Using the analytical framework, presented in Part II, we can distinguish: (a) interrelationships within any of the composite parts of the management formula; (b) between composite parts of the management formula; (c) between management formulae on different levels of the plan executants; (d) within the management mechanism of a given branch of the economy.[1]

It is easy to provide examples of contradictions at all levels of the mechanism of plan implementation. For the purpose of illustration, let us choose the enterprise stimulation system.

Ad (a): Contradictions within the incentive system: between the specialized bonus conditions and the success indicators (existing); between the basic bonus system and the bonus for export effectiveness (existing); and between the basic bonus system and incentives based on the enterprise fund (eliminated by the 1966 reforms).

Ad (b): Contradictions between the stimulation system and the financial system: between three (out of four) obligatory success

---

[1] Let me stress that this list does not exhaust the basic interrelationships within the mechanism for steering the national economy. By assumption, however, we have limited the scope of our analysis to the management mechanism of socialist industry only.

Table 9.6: *The Basic Negative Side-Effects* (*Misincentives*)
of the Stimulation System Existing during 1956–63

Years	Type of incentive	Bonus conditions	Side-effects*
1	2	3	4
1956–63	Wage fund	Meeting plan target of commodity production	1, 2, 3, 4, 5, 6, 8, 9, 10, 11, 12, 15, 16, 19, 20
	Bonuses		
1957–60	Bonuses of white-collar workers	Meeting plan target of commodity production	1, 2, 3, 4, 5, 6, 8, 9, 10, 11, 12, 15, 16, 19, 20
1960–4	The bonus fund of white-collar workers	**Basic conditions**	
	—basic	Achieving financial results at least equal to the preceding year's level	1, 2, 3, 4, 7, 8, 9, 10, 11, 12, 13, 14, 18, 20
		Meeting plan target of commodity production in transfer prices	1, 2, 3, 4, 5, 6, 8, 9, 10, 11, 12, 15, 16, 19, 20
		Meeting wage fund plan	1, 2, 3, 4, 5, 6, 9, 12, 16, 19, 20
		Meeting cost of production plan	1, 3, 7, 11, 13, 15, 12, 9, 14
		Meeting the ratio of cost of production to value of commodity production	1, 3, 7, 9, 11, 12, 13, 14, 15, 20
		Meeting the export plan on time	6, 8, 10, 15, 19, 20
	—additional	Meeting the improvement of profitability target	1, 2, 3, 4, 7, 8, 10, 11, 12, 13, 14, 15, 16, 20
1957–8	Factory fund	Meeting plan target of financial accumulation	1, 2, 3, 4, 5, 7, 8, 9, 11, 12, 13, 14, 20,
		Meeting plan target of commodity production in transfer prices	1, 2, 3, 4, 5, 8, 9, 10, 11, 12, 14, 15, 19
1958–64		The same as in the case of white-collar workers bonus fund in 1960–4	The same as in the case of white-collar workers bonus fund in 1960–4

* The meaning of numbers in column 4: 1. falsification of planning data; 2. tendency to produce expensive (input-intensive) products; 3. fictitious introduction of new products; 4. economically unjustified subcontracting and expansion of services for other enterprises; 5. manipulating the volume of production still in process; 6. not revealing the existing possibilities of cost reduction; 7. reducing the cost of production by postponing capital repairs, forgoing expenditure for labour safety and hygiene, etc.; 8. lack of interest on behalf of workers and technical staff in revision of labour norms; 9. lack of interest in technical progress; 10. unjustified increase of employment and wages; 11. lack of interest in high quality output; 12. classification of finished products to higher quality grades than justified by their

indicators, either of which is simultaneously a general condition of bonus payment and total profit, the basis for determining the so-called development fund (existing); and between all success indicators and production indices (net or gross) determining the volume of the enterprise wage fund (existing).

Ad (c): Contradictions between the stimulation system at the enterprise and industrial association levels: between the principles of the managerial bonus systems at enterprise and industrial association levels (eliminated by the 1966 reform); and between the success indicators and the authority of the industrial association to compel the enterprise to undertake unprofitable courses of action (existing).

Ad (d): Contradictions between the stimulation system and the macro-input system (of means of production): between success indicators and the rationing of a number of means of production (still existing); between success indicators and the sellers' market in general (existing); and between profitability maximization and the limited scope of decentralized investment (expanded by the 1966 reforms, but still negligible).

To convey more vividly what such contradictions mean in practice, Table 9.6 presents, in a summary fashion, the negative side-effects of Polish incentive systems operating in 1956-63.[1]

The lack of consistency is, however, not the only problem which plagues the piecemeal implementation of economic reforms. The other, possibly even more important, is the phenomenon which we shall call 'rejection of transplants'. By this we mean that the economic system has a tendency to make partial changes wholly or partly ineffectual. This problem may be best explained with the help of an example, and for

---

[1] A similar picture is available for the 1945-55 period [2, Ch. 2 and especially pp. 58-9; and 3, Ch. 2] and for the years 1964-70 [2, Ch. 4; and 3, Ch. 7]. Compare also [4, *passim*] for an analysis of the malfunctioning of the factory fund and repeated efforts to improve it, and [5, Ch. 5] on the new incentive system, introduction of which on 1 January 1971 was 'postponed' after workers' unrest in December 1970. (The fact that the books referred to for the period 1964-70 were published respectively in 1965 and 1969 is not a contradiction, because the system introduced in 1964 is still functioning with only minor modifications. Moreover, there were no changes in other parts of the management mechanism substantial enough to affect the functioning of the basically unchanged stimulation system.)

---

technical parameters; 13. production of profitable products in violation of product-mix plan; 14. unjustified differentiation of bonuses among enterprises; 15. lack of interest in lowering input norms; 16. too wide application of piece-work; 17. charging part of production cost of so-called comparable to so-called uncomparable output; 18. lowering the stocks of finished output below obligatory level; 19. lack of interest in enterprise financial results; 20. maladjustment of output to market requirements.

Source: adapted from Borkowska S.: *Wspoldzialanie nakazow i materialnych bodzcow zespolowych w przemysle lekkim* (The Interrelationship between Directives and Collective Material Incentives in Light Industry), Warsaw, 1969, pp. 114 and 58-9.

this purpose we shall analyse the economic consequences of introducing in Poland interest payments for fixed capital in 1966 (interest payments for variable capital already existed). At the same time, we have to remember that in Polish enterprises the success indicator was then profit/cost ratio, so theoretically speaking, enterprises should have been sensitive to capital charges.

From 1 January 1966 interest payments on fixed capital were introduced in most branches of Polish industry (see 7.3). Its purpose at that time was limited to the incentive aspect only. Accordingly, interest payments were not charged into costs but deducted directly from profit, and interest rates were fixed at the 2·5 per cent and 5 per cent level, depending on the ratio of gross profit to the value of fixed capital. At the same time certain changes in interest payments on working capital were also introduced, including the right of enterprises to interest payments on their bank deposits.

As a result of introducing interest payments, the following changes in enterprise behaviour were expected: the sale and/or reporting to higher authorities of excessive machinery and equipment; diminished enterprise demand for investments financed from the budget and/or industrial associations' funds; better economic calculation of the enterprise's own investment; increased sensitivity to excessive accumulation of stocks both of inputs and outputs.

It is already evident that these expectations did not materialize. The question is, why? There are two ways of looking at this problem. One is to point out the number of deficiencies in the then existing solution of interest payments (always from the viewpoint of their limited objectives). Here we can list:

(1) The construction of the success indicator in the form of profit/cost ratio. Consequently up to a certain point, diminished profit resulting from increased interest payments for excessive stock of output may be counterbalanced by the cost reduction produced by a lower share of fixed cost per unit of output (under the assumption of constant prices).

(2) Low interest rates charged. If, according to a number of sources, marginal productivity of investment in US industry is around 10 per cent, it is probably higher in Poland where capital is much scarcer. It is especially true for enterprises' own investments which are characterized by very high productivity. For instance, according to an official decree, bank credits for enterprise investments should be extended, as a rule, for investments showing at least a 33·33 per cent rate of return.

(3) The net basis of interest payments also weakens the incentive impact of interest.

The real reasons for the weak impact of interest payments on enterprise behaviour are, however, much deeper and more fundamental. They consist of: (a) use of a success indicator in a form of yearly plan target; (b) widespread individual cost-plus pricing; (c) low resistance of buyers to price demands owing to a, b, and the so-called profit verification rule and the existence of a sellers' market: (d) the important role still played in enterprise management formula by output indices, which are independent of profitability.

Given these basic facts (which have been discussed in detail in Part II) there exists no effective formula for interest payments and no effective interest rate. Discussion of these problems—very interesting as they are for economists—will have practical meaning only after these basic determinants of enterprise behaviour have been changed.

In the preceding discussion we analysed a situation in which a change in the right direction, long advocated by the economists, was introduced into the management mechanism but did not produce any significant results. This was because other parts of the existing management mechanism interfered. These other parts are numerous, not always easy to identify and—most of all—not easy to change. Moreover, their very enumeration indicates that, in practice, fundamental and simultaneous changes on a broad front would be necessary to make even such a relatively small change as introducing payments on fixed and variable capital really effective. The same can be said of many other changes in management mechanism and/or management rules. The Hungarian Central Committee was therefore right in insisting that different elements of the new management mechanism '. . . cannot be introduced separately in different periods' [16].

9.3 The Communist System and the Limits of 'Social Engineering'

The study in depth of communist economic and social experiments can be of major importance for the advancement of the social sciences.

Despite theoretical difficulties involved, it may be useful to distinguish broadly between 'man-invented' and historically developed social and economic relations. By the former I mean relations introduced as an effort to implement certain economic or social (deductive) theories, which had no former historical predecessor. The *kolkhoz*, the labour accounting day, or the principles of price fixing of producer goods are a few examples.

What makes East European societies a unique subject of social research is the fact that they are—to an extent unparalleled in history—artificially created or 'man-invented' societies. In these societies, historically developed economic and social relations were replaced by 'man-invented' mechanisms, to an extent and with a speed unknown in the history of mankind.

The analysis of the emergence and functioning of these artificially created societies enables us to gain a better insight into a number of fundamental phenomena:

(1) The problems (and dangers) of tampering with a historically developed economic and social environment. These problems are similar in nature to the problems of destroying the equilibrium of the natural (physical and biological) environment. As we did not fully recognize the inherent dangers in the latter, so we did not take account of them in the former. Because East European societies represent the most extensive application of social and economic engineering, their experience is not only an important early warning signal, but also enables us to study a number of new factors: the qualitative change in the character of the problems involved when 'man-invented' relations become a predominant, rather than a partial, form of social relations; for example, the qualitative difference between the problems arising as a result of government interference in the market and the problems resulting from the abolition of the market, between price distortions and an arbitrary price system as a whole; the consequences of the replacement of historically developed institutions by man-invented mechanisms in many spheres of economic and social life (for example, new rules governing the services of veterinary surgeons or patent agents in Poland, which replaced existing contractual relations between interested parties with government-determined 'incentive schemes', with disastrous results).

(2) The analysis of artificially created societies enables us to gain a better insight into the inherent features of historically developed social and economic relations and/or mechanisms. It seems to me that these mechanisms possess two features of fundamental importance: they have built-in provisions for inherent weaknesses of human nature, from laziness to egocentrism to the superiority complex; they also possess built-in countervailing mechanisms which, by acting on our self-interest, induce us, by and large, to behave in socially acceptable (beneficial) ways.

The analysis of 'man-invented' mechanisms reveals that their failure may—in most instances—be ultimately traced to lack of one or both of these built-in features.

(3) The analysis of artificially created societies poses a fundamental question: Have we, the human race, already reached the stage of intellectual, social, and *ethical* development which would enable us to *invent* and then to *run* (to operate) a better *total* economic and social system than that which developed historically? Nobody questions our ability—empirically proved—to introduce successful *partial* improvements into historically developed economic and social mechanisms. To my mind the success of these partial improvements can be explained by the equally partial changes in human nature (for example, the limitation of the controlling role of the market mechanism in such spheres as health and education reflects the new level of social awareness of the human race today as compared with fifty or a hundred years ago). At the same

time, this limited character of change in human nature seems to indicate that we are still far away from the stage when *comprehensive* replacement of historically developed social and economic mechanisms would be desirable. Experience of the artificially created societies of Eastern Europe seems to support this thesis: first of all one can point to the difficulties these countries are encountering in economic, social, and political spheres; secondly, the essence of the reform movements is to reintroduce or to simulate—in one form or another—historically developed economic and social mechanisms. The guided market model, profit incentives, etc., all point in this direction.

References to Chapter Nine

1. Bergson A.: *Planning and Productivity under Soviet Socialism*, New York-London, 1968.
2. Borkowska S.: *Wspoldzialanie nakazow i materialnych bodzcow zespolowych w przemysle lekkim* (The Interrelationship between Directives and Collective Material Incentives in Light Industry), Warsaw, 1969.
3. Fick B.: *Bodzce ekonomiczne w przemysle* (Economic Incentives in Industry), Warsaw, 1965.
4. —— *Fundusz zakladowy* (The Factory Fund), Warsaw, 1967.
5. —— *Polityka zatrudnienia a place i bodzce* (Employment Policy and Wages and Incentives), Warsaw, 1970.
6. Glinski B.: *Teorie i praktyka zarzadzania przedsiebiorstwami przemyslowymi* (Theories and Practice of Management of Industrial Enterprises), Warsaw, 1966.
7. Goldmann J. and Fleck J.: 'Economic Growth in Czechoslovakia', *EP*, 2, 1966.
8. Hanson P.: 'East-West Comparisons and Comparative Economic Systems', *SS*, 3, 1971.
9. Jaszczuk B.: 'Conditions and Needs of Social Planning', *ZG*, 38, 1969.
10. Karpinski A.: *Zagadnienia socjalistycznej industrializacji Polski* (Problems of Socialist Industrialization in Poland), Warsaw, 1958.
11. Leibenstein H.: 'Allocative Efficiency vs "X-Efficiency"', *AER*, 3, 1966.
12. Lewandowicz Z. and Misiak M., eds.: *Reformy gospodarcze w krajach socjalistycznych* (Economic Reforms in Socialist Countries), Warsaw, 1967.
13. Misiak M., ed.: *Bodzce ekonomiczne w przedsiebiorstwie przemyslowym* (Economic Incentives in the Industrial Enterprise), Warsaw, 1963.
14. —— 'The Interrelationship of Directives and Incentives in the Management of Industrial Enterprises', in [*13*, pp. 135–68].
15. Pajestka J. and Secomski K.: *Doskonalenie planowania i funkcjonowania gospodarki w Polsce Ludowej* (Improvements in the Planning and Functioning of the Economy in People's Poland), Warsaw, 1968.
16. Resolution of the Central Committee of the Hungarian Communist Party on the Reform of the Economic Mechanism, in [*12*, pp. 310–28].
17. Resolution of the Vth Congress of the Polish United Workers' Party, Warsaw, 1968.
18. *Rocznik dochodu narodowego 1960-5* (National Income Yearbook 1960–5), Warsaw, 1966.
19. Szeliga Z.: *Kierunki i zalozenia reformy* (Directions and Assumptions of Reform), Warsaw, 1965.

20. Theses of the Politbureau for the IInd (April 1969) Plenum of the Central Committee of PUWP, *ND*, 5, 1969.
21. Zielinski J. G.: *Lectures on the Theory of Socialist Planning*, Ibadan-London, 1968.
22. —— 'Economics and Politics of the Two Types of Economic Reforms', *EP*, 3, 1969.
23. Zivkov T.: 'The New System of Management of the National Economy', in [*12*, pp. 424–35].

INDEX

Only names of persons mentioned in the text are listed, i.e. references are excluded.